FINDING LOST
SEASON 6

NIKKI STAFFORD

ECW Press

For Sydney and Liam

Copyright © Nikki Stafford, 2010

Published by ECW PRESS
2120 Queen Street East, Suite 200, Toronto, Ontario, Canada M4E 1E2
416-694-3348 / info@ecwpress.com

All rights reserved. No part of this publication may be reproduced, stored in a retrieval system, or transmitted in any form by any process — electronic, mechanical, photocopying, recording, or otherwise — without the prior written permission of the copyright owners and ECW Press. The scanning, uploading, and distribution of this book via the Internet or via any other means without the permission of the publisher is illegal and punishable by law. Please purchase only authorized electronic editions, and do not participate in or encourage electronic piracy of copyrighted materials. Your support of the author's rights is appreciated.

LIBRARY AND ARCHIVES CANADA CATALOGUING IN PUBLICATION

Stafford, Nikki, 1973-
Finding Lost, season 6 : the unofficial guide / Nikki Stafford.

ISBN 978-1-55022-951-6

1. Lost (Television program).
I. Title. II. Title: Finding Lost, season six.

PN1992.77.L67S736 2010   791.45'72   C2010-901403-0

Cover design: Barry Johnson
Back cover and text design: Tania Craan
Typesetting: Gail Nina
Front cover photo: Joseph Gareri/iStockphoto
Printing: Transcontinental   1 2 3 4 5

The publication of *Finding Lost, Season 6* has been generously supported by the Government of Ontario through the Ontario Book Publishing Tax Credit, by the OMDC Book Fund, an initiative of the Ontario Media Development Corporation, and by the Government of Canada through the Canada Book Fund.

Canada

PRINTED AND BOUND IN CANADA

ECW PRESS
ecwpress.com

Table of Contents

How Not to Get Lost v
"The End" ix

SEASON 6
February–May 2010

LA X (Everyone) 1
  Spot the Differences! 6
  Haroun and the Sea of Stories 22

What Kate Does (Kate/Claire) 28
  Hugh Everett III's Many-Worlds Theory 34

The Substitute (Locke) 38
  The Cave Ceiling 47

Lighthouse (Jack) 50
  The Lighthouse Dial 57

Sundown (Sayid) 62
  Deep River 69

Dr. Linus (Ben) 72

Recon (Sawyer) 82
  The *Lost* Locations Tour in Oahu 90

Ab Aeterno (Richard) 93
  Nestor Carbonell 104

The Package (Jin/Sun) 107

Happily Ever After (Desmond) 116

Everybody Loves Hugo (Hurley)   **128**
   Notes from Underground   **140**

The Last Recruit (Everyone)   **150**

The Candidate (Jack/Locke)   **160**
   Lost Haiku!   **169**

Across the Sea (Man in Black/Jacob)   **171**
   The Game of Senet   **182**

What They Died For (Everyone)   **184**
   Sawyer's Nicknames   **186**
   The Letter from Lucas   **196**
   Fear and Trembling   **197**
      Genesis 22: 1–18   **200**

The End (Everyone)   **205**
   Through the Looking Glass: The Mirrors   **224**
   "There Is No *Now*, Here": The Sideways Timeline   **256**
   The Stand   **258**
   Paradise Lost   **275**
   That's It?!: The Unanswered Questions   **289**
      "The New Man in Charge"   **292**

Lost Episodes   305
Sources   313
Acknowledgments   317

How Not to Get Lost — Season 6

The final season of *Lost* was one of the most talked-about television events of 2010. Any other show in its sixth season might be thought of as past its prime — perhaps there's a core group of fans, but rarely are the writers doing anything exciting half a decade into its run. But *Lost* changed direction with every season, and season 6 held so much promise for its fans that even people who hadn't watched it since the first couple of seasons were jumping back in to see how it would all wrap up. *Lost* had been riding a wave of critical acclaim for the previous two years, ever since a guaranteed finale date at the end of the show's third season had given the writers the yardstick to know how many episodes they had left to write.

Season 1 had been about trying to get off the island, season 2 was about learning to live on the island with a group of people who had become family, season 3 was about dealing with the original inhabitants — the Others — of the island, season 4 was about the outside world invading the island, and season 5 was about returning to the island. In season 6 the Losties asked a much loftier question: what was their purpose on the island? And why had they been brought there in the first place? The writers had explored various kinds of flashbacks and at the end of the third season they introduced the flashforward, but in the sixth season they gave us the flashsideways, creating an entirely new narrative line that had fans speculating about the characters as if they were strangers to us and we'd somehow been transported back to season 1 again. The mythology of the island and many answers to the fans' burning questions were finally revealed in season 6, and the show's finale sparked even more fervent discussion that will no doubt last for several years.

As with my previous *Finding Lost* books, this guide is intended to be read alongside the episodes. You can watch the entire season and then read through the book, or you could watch an episode and read the corresponding guide to it. These guides are meant to be more than simple plot summaries. Instead, what I strive for is an analytical, detailed, in-depth reading of each episode that will help you sort out the clues, work through the mysteries, and figure out the real meaning of season 6.

Besides writing these books, I also keep a blog called Nik at Nite (nikkistafford.blogspot.com) where, during the season, I analyzed each episode the night it aired and my readers and I discussed the episodes at length for the next week. In season 6 there was a *lot* to discuss, and many of the blog entries had upwards of 400 comments. I owe a lot to the regular commentators on that blog who show up day after day to discuss their favorite TV show.

Finding Lost is *not*, however, a substitute for watching the show. You will not understand what I'm writing about each episode if you haven't watched (or are in the middle of watching) it. This companion will provide a deeper understanding of the characters, the events, and the mysteries, but it will not be a replacement for *Lost* itself. No book could ever hope to do that.

The book is formatted episode by episode. Almost every guide is followed by some tidbit of information, either a small sidebar of interest, or a larger chapter on the historical significance of something. Just as life on the island is interrupted by flashes, so too will the episode guide be broken up by these asides. You can come back to them later and just focus on the guide in the beginning, or read through them to get a better understanding of the writers' references or of the actors playing the characters.

My summaries of the novels and other books referred to on the show provide a context-based analysis and ask the questions: why was this book featured in that episode, and how does it relate to the show and the characters? In each of the book summaries, I will give a brief rundown of the plot and point out the deeper meaning in each book, and then offer some suggestions of the importance the book has on the show and why it may have been chosen by the writers (these chapters will not spoil future episodes). Two of the books analyzed weren't referenced directly on the show, but are still immensely important to it: *Paradise Lost* paved the way for the classic story of good and evil, God and Satan, and black and white, while Stephen King's *The Stand* was hugely influential on all of the *Lost* writers, so much so that they make several allusions to it.

Some of the chapters will look at specific historical references on the show and explain them further, such as how one plays the ancient Egyptian game of senet. Others will look at themes running through the season, like the mirror imagery or the "rules." Some of the sidebars will provide a close-up of particular moments in an episode that you may have missed on screen.

Each guide will contain some spoilers for that particular episode, so I urge you to watch the episodes before reading on. Because I am a severe spoilerphobe, I've been careful not to spoil anything ahead of time, so if you watch an episode and then read the corresponding guide to it, you will be safe from having any surprises ruined. Each guide will feature a one-line summary of the episode, followed by an analysis. Following each analysis, you'll find special notes of interest, and they require some explanation:

Highlight: A moment in the show that was either really funny or made an impression on me.

Did You Notice?: A list of details in the episode that you might have missed, but are either important clues to later mysteries, or were just really cool.

Interesting Facts: Tidbits of information, outside the show's canon, that explain allusions and references or that offer behind-the-scenes material.

Nitpicks: Little things in the episode that bugged me. I've put these things in nitpicks because I couldn't come up with a rational explanation myself — but maybe you have an explanation, and if so, I'd love to hear it. Please read these knowing that I nitpick only to point things out, but not to suggest the writers aren't on their game. These are meant to be fun.

Oops: These are mistakes that I think can't be explained away and must be due to a production or continuity error.

4 8 15 16 23 42: In the late season 1 episode, "Numbers," Hurley reveals a set of numbers that have had an impact in his life, and it turns out those numbers have popped up everywhere, on the island and in the characters' lives before the crash. In this section I will try to catalog them.

It's Just a Flesh Wound: This is a list of all of the wounds incurred by the characters on the show.

Lost in Translation: Whenever a character speaks in a language other than English that is not translated for us or we see something written that's not immediately decipherable, this section will provide a translation wherever I could find one. Thanks to all of the fans who have provided these translations for me.

Any Questions?: At the end of each episode, I've provided a list of questions that I think viewers should be asking themselves at that point. Some questions will be answered in later episodes, but because these guides are meant to be read as one goes through the season episode-by-episode, these are questions you *should* be asking yourself at the end of each hour.

Ashes to Ashes: Whenever a character on the show dies, this section will provide their very brief obituary.

Music/Bands: This is a list of the popular music we hear on the show. In most cases I've provided in italics the name of the album where you can find the song, but if I haven't, it's because the song is featured on several compilations.

And there you have it, a guide to the guide. I hope you enjoy the book, and I welcome any corrections, nitpicks, praise (please? just a little?), and discussion at my email address, nikki_stafford@yahoo.com, or come on over to my blog. I cannot stress this strongly enough, however: the opinions in the following pages are completely my own, and if anyone out there has contrary opinions, I respect those. I don't expect everyone to have the same views as I do. What makes *Lost* so much fun to watch and discuss is how many possibilities this show presents to us. Ten fans can come away from any episode with 10 different interpretations of what they just saw, and that's what makes the show great, in my opinion.

Nikki Stafford
July 2010

nikki_stafford@yahoo.com
nikkistafford.blogspot.com
twitter.com/nikki_stafford
facebook.com/nikkistafford108

"The End": Season 6

Bang! "Come on!" Bang! Bang! The rock hit the hydrogen bomb repeatedly to no effect as Juliet, her face bloody and tear-streaked, screamed at it to just detonate already. "Come on, you son of a bitch!" Bang! And then . . . the screen went white. The letters of LOST appeared, only this time they were black, a negative version of the white letters over black screen that viewers were used to. And everywhere, fans screamed, "Noooooooo!"

It was going to be a *very* long eight months.

Once ABC confirmed at the end of *Lost*'s third season that the show would run for three more years, with 16 episodes per year, the wait between seasons became almost unbearable for the diehard fans who were always left with cliffhangers to keep them guessing throughout the summer, fall, and part of winter before the new season would start up again. The wait before the series' final season was excruciating, and even before it began, fans were already lamenting that this was *it*, that *Lost* was coming to an end and soon it would all be over. By June, collective rewatches of seasons 1 to 5 began popping up all over the Internet, with groups of fans going back to the beginning and watching everything in light of what they knew to be true at the end of season 5, and preparing themselves for the epic season 6 that was to come.

In June 2009, *Lost* was up for a Television Critics Association award for Program of the Year, but was beat out by *Battlestar Galactica*. At the end of the month, it was announced that *Lost* had been nominated for five Emmy Awards, including Outstanding Drama Series, Best Supporting Actor (Michael Emerson), Best Writing (showrunners Damon Lindelof and Carlton Cuse for "The Incident"), and editing and sound mixing. Michael Emerson took home the award in the fall.

Not all of the news coming out in June was good, though; one of the fan favorites on the writing staff was Brian K. Vaughan, who'd authored the graphic novel *Y: The Last Man*, which was alluded to in season 5 (see *Finding Lost — Season Five*, pp. 116–120). He'd cowritten two of the best episodes of *Lost* — "The Shape of Things to Come" and "Dead Is Dead" — among several others. But in a July 2009 interview Carlton Cuse simply mentioned that he'd moved on "to greener pastures."

After taking their usual month off with radio silence after the season 5 finale, "Darlton," as the fans called them, began to reappear in the media to talk about their show. Carlton brought up one of the major themes of the series that had been explored in season 5: "I think as writers we use the show to explore personal issues, spiritual or otherwise. We're mainly concerned by [the question of] how much faith and how much control do you have over your own destiny, something which is very fascinating to us, and obviously season 5 was an exploration of that with the time travel leading to an event at the end of the season, so that is going to be something we're going to explore a lot on the final season of the show. The writer's room is diverse and that diversity gets worked out in the characters."

But of course, what all of the fans were looking forward to was the big unveiling of the hints of season 6 at the 2009 San Diego Comic-Con. And Darlton didn't disappoint. In an event that was jam-packed with fans, with thousands of people lining up as early as the night before to try to get in, Darlton opened the panel "with a word from our sponsors." The first video they showed was a commercial for Mr. Cluck's, where Hugo Reyes, the owner of the company, appears wearing a Crocodile Dundee–type hat and with a didgeridoo slung over one shoulder, speaking in a terrible Australian accent — "G'day, mate!" — and saying that ever since he'd won the lottery, he'd had nothing but good luck.

Wait . . . what?!

He announces his new Mr. Cluck's Roasters, a new chicken meal (for $4.42!) that he dreamed up on a recent trip to Australia. What did the commercial mean? If Hugo had good luck, then maybe the numbers weren't cursing him anymore? And did his plane arrive home from Sydney in one piece? The next commercial was a quick one for Oceanic Airlines, boasting a perfect safety record since 1979. Um . . . is it possible the Jughead bomb really *did* reset time at the end of season 5?

The third mysterious clip they showed was from *America's Most Wanted*, where the host talked about a murderer-at-large, Kate Austen, who was on the run after she'd attempted to kill her "stepfather," Wayne Janssen. She'd rigged the building where he owned a plumbing company, cutting a gas line and allowing the toxic fumes to flow through the building, knowing exactly when he'd be there and when it would blow up. But on that particular day, he'd sent his apprentice to the building, and that man perished in the fire instead of Wayne. Kate had been charged with the murder of the man, but she evaded authorities and was now considered armed and dangerous. As the video ended, Damon turned to Carlton

Carlton Cuse, Terry O'Quinn, Damon Lindelof, Michael Emerson, Zuleikha Robinson, Elizabeth Sarnoff, Nestor Carbonell, Edward Kitsis, Jack Bender, and Adam Horowitz all smile for the cameras at the annual PaleyFest in February 2010. (Sue Schneider/MGP)

and said, "Funny . . . I always thought she'd killed her stepfather." (Well, technically she killed her biological father, but she'd been raised knowing him as her stepfather.) What was going on? Were they really going to attempt a do-over?

But just as fans were starting to feel a little uneasy about what Darlton were hinting at with these videos, Jorge Garcia stepped up to the audience microphone (to the delight of the fans nearby) and, looking a little shell-shocked, asked if Jack's bomb worked, and if so did it reset everything and therefore wipe away everything from the past five years? "Because we all hope that isn't the case," he laughed nervously, "because that would be like, you know, a *real big cheat*." And suddenly the smile wasn't on his face anymore. The audience roared with laughter, Darlton stuttered through an answer explaining that everything they'd shown us actually mattered, and it was clear Jorge's question had been set up ahead of time by Darlton. If Jorge was voicing the biggest concern among the fans, it probably meant that Darlton weren't going to attempt the do-over that Jorge was upset about.

Soon an audience member began heckling Jorge, saying he was hogging the mike. The heckler was none other than Michael Emerson, who oozed sarcasm as he mocked Jorge's acting abilities. The panel continued with more jokes than real questions being answered. At one point the camera cut backstage, where a diva-esque Nestor Carbonell was applying eyeliner (an inside joke on the fact that people always think he's wearing it because of his naturally dark lashes) and he was freaking out on an assistant that they'd given him cobalt when he always used onyx. Carbonell joined the rest of them onstage, and the next special guest was Josh Holloway, who got the crowd on their feet cheering with delight.

At the beginning of the panel Darlton addressed the question of whether or not they knew where the show was going, and they produced from inside their pockets (or, in Carlton's case, from an ankle holster) one page each of the final two pages of the finale script, then stapled them together and put them in a double-lock box, putting the keys around their necks. When Josh Holloway came out, he pretended to taser Damon and threatened Carlton — who he called "Lurch" and "Frankenstein" — demanding that they open the box up so he could look at the script. Carlton complied, but Holloway simply stared at the pages, apparently confused by what he saw. Snatching them away from Holloway with a snide, "Oh my god, you don't know how to *read*, do you?" Michael Emerson sat back down and began reading them out loud . . . and it was a fake ending to *Heroes*. The audience laughed, and the panel came to a close, but only after an "In Memoriam" video showed us all the characters we'd lost on the show over the years. The video ended and Dominic Monaghan came out on stage and waved to the fans without saying a word. Could it be? Would Charlie be appearing in season 6?

After the Comic-Con panel, fans had some fun with the ARG (alternate reality game) that was sparked by L.A. comedian Paul Scheer, who showed up at the panel and presented Darlton with his painting on black velvet that he called, "Damon, Carlton, and a Polar Bear." And it was about as classy as it sounds. Fans followed him to his website — www.damoncarltonandapolarbear.com — to watch him over the remainder of the summer as he began to stalk Darlton, finding out that they'd thrown his painting in the garbage, then rifling through said garbage, and discovering the script to the season 6 premiere in it. The website turned out to be part of the promotional machine for *Lost*, and it had been set up as a wacky storyline to keep fans occupied while waiting for their show. Along the way it showcased the work of various artists who had created limited edition *Lost* posters that fans could buy.

In November, it was announced that February 2 would be the show's premiere date (and that the premiere would be two hours), but that date soon hit a snag ... of presidential proportions. In January, news started circulating that the office of President Barack Obama was considering setting the date of the State of the Union address for either January 25 or February 2. If they chose the latter, the premiere of *Lost* would have to be pushed back another week, starting on February 9. Fans began an angry Twitter campaign, trying to get the President's office to reconsider. Finally, bemused White House Press Secretary Robert Gibbs said to the media that they would not put the SOTU on February 2, adding, "I don't foresee a scenario in which millions of people that hope to finally get some conclusion in *Lost* are pre-empted by the President." Damon and Carlton immediately rejoiced, jumping on Twitter and tweeting their happiness in 140 characters or less. Carlton confirmed the news, while Damon was more excited: "OBAMA BACKED DOWN!!!! Groundhog Day is OURS!!!!!!! (God Bless America)," he wrote. Before adding in his next post, "Okay. So Obama didn't technically 'back down.' He leveraged Carlton and I to do something on the show. Two words. MORE FROGURT."

In the month leading up to the finale, fan anticipation was running high. ABC released a publicity photo in which the cast was posed in a version of *The Last Supper*. Various alternate shots put characters in different positions, and fans went nuts trying to analyze why the characters were sitting in specific spots, in particular poses. Who was Christ? Who would be Judas?

Online, fans were madly uploading tribute videos to *Lost*, and some of them were quite extraordinary (to see my favorite, go here: www.youtube.com/watch?v=8nqmekTJTk0), much better than the lame non-commercials that ABC was showing. Because the rework didn't want to release a single frame of season 6, the commercials just said the final season was beginning and showed scenes of Jack dropping the bomb. The fan videos, on the other hand, took clips from the previous five seasons and began to weave them together to show some of the show's overarching themes.

The actors on the show, who were about two-thirds of the way through filming the season by the time it premiered, were already waxing nostalgic about the series in interviews. "It feels like high school's going to end, and we're getting wistful," said Terry O'Quinn. "There's a sweetness to these days." Michael Emerson was also feeling that the end was near. "Everyone has a sense of last moments," he said. "Maybe this will be the last scene we shoot at this old location ... or maybe this is the last time I'll talk to this particular character."

Matthew Fox announced that *Lost* would be the last television series he'd do. "I've done almost three hundred hours of [TV]," he said. "It's been two really great experiences between *Party of Five* and *Lost*. I'm ready to take it to the next step and see what I can do in that [film] world."

Rumors were rampant about which deceased characters might appear in season 6 (I won't elaborate here, so you can watch the season spoiler-free), and there were hints starting to creep out that something new was going to happen in the final season that would be unlike anything we'd seen yet on *Lost*. "We feel [that] tonally, it's most similar to the first season of the show," said Cuse. "We're employing a different narrative device, which we feel is creating some emotional and heartfelt stories, and we want the audience to have a chance in the final season to remember the entire history of the show. . . . We're hoping to achieve a circularity of the entire journey so the ending is reminiscent of the beginning."

Matthew Fox said he'd known what the final image of the series was going to be from the very beginning. When the finale was still in the works, Damon and Carlton tried to speak diplomatically about it, but admitted there was a lot of pressure on them to make their series finale distinctive. In light of the recent *Sopranos* finale, they knew that if they wanted to end the show on a note that would get people talking, they had to be creative. "With *Lost*, nobody can even guess what the ending is going to be," Damon said. "If you were to have a contest right now saying, 'In one paragraph, summarize what you think the last episode of *Lost* might be' — if you say it to one hundred people, you will get one hundred paragraphs that have nothing to do with each other. If you say that to somebody about *The Sopranos*, fifty people will say, 'I think Tony's going to get whacked,' maybe 10 people will say, 'Carmela is going to kill him, but he's going to get whacked.' But no one would have said, 'They're going to be eating in a friggin' restaurant — onion rings.' That's what was so brilliant about it — how do you do the unexpected?"

On a beach in Oahu on January 30, 2010, three days before the season 6 premiere, an estimated 15,000 fans attended the Sunset on the Beach premiere party to watch a screening of the first half of "LA X." Introduced by Darlton, the event was attended by almost the entire cast, as well as several of the writers and directors, which allowed fans to hobnob with their favorite TV actors and see the first hour of season 6 before anyone else did, including media.

Lindelof hoped people would like season 6, and that fans would debate what their favorite season was the way he remembered doing as a fan of *Buffy the*

Vampire Slayer. "There probably aren't that many people out there saying season 3 was their favorite, but they'll say season 3 was their favorite finale," he said. "And some people love season 4 because of all the freighter stuff. Some people love season 5 because of the time-travel stuff. The purists just love season 1. . . ."

Cuse agreed, and told fans to get ready for season 6, because a lot of it was going to be unexpected: "The mantra of the final season in a certain way is 'Anything can happen, be prepared.' We are nearing the end, so if there are any constraints that govern a series, they really go away in the final season. We always felt like *Lost* was at its best when it was really surprising. We did things that were unexpected. We do have a few surprises up our sleeves for this season, which we think are really exciting."

The fans had rewatched the series, made their tribute videos, boned up on their Dharma Initiative history, made lists of the questions they wanted to see answered, and turned their televisions over to ABC at 8:59 p.m. on the night of February 2, 2010. Now it was time to see how it was all going to end.

SEASON 6 – February–May 2010

Cast: Matthew Fox (Jack Shephard), Evangeline Lilly (Kate Austen), Terry O'Quinn (John Locke), Josh Holloway (James "Sawyer" Ford), Jorge Garcia (Hugo "Hurley" Reyes), Naveen Andrews (Sayid Jarrah), Yunjin Kim (Sun Kwon), Daniel Dae Kim (Jin Kwon), Henry Ian Cusick (Desmond Hume), Michael Emerson (Benjamin Linus), Emilie de Ravin (Claire), Ken Leung (Miles Straume), Jeff Fahey (Frank Lapidus), Nestor Carbonell (Richard Alpert), Zuleikha Robinson (Ilana)

Recurring characters: Hiroyuki Sanada (Dogen), John Hawkes (Lennon), Mark Pellegrino (Jacob), Sam Anderson (Bernard), L. Scott Caldwell (Rose), Kimberley Joseph (Cindy), Fredric Lehne (Marshal Edward Mars), Daniel Roebuck (Leslie Arzt), Dylan Minnette (David Shephard), Alan Dale (Charles Widmore), Mickey Graue (Zach), Kiersten Havelock (Emma), Sheila Kelley (Zoe), Fred Koehler (Seamus), Steve Boatright (Mike, Widmore's Goon)

6.1, 6.2 LA X

Original air date: February 2, 2010
Written by: Damon Lindelof, Carlton Cuse
Directed by: Jack Bender
Guest cast: Brad William Henke (Bram), Elizabeth Mitchell (Juliet), Dominic Monaghan (Charlie), Ian Somerhalder (Boone), Sean Whalen (Frogurt), Mark Ahsing (Customs Officer), David Coennen (Agent Smalley), Kesha Diodato (Agent Anne), Greg Grunberg (Pilot Seth Norris), Kelly Kraynek (Woman in Bathroom), Shawn Lathrop (Flight Attendant), David H. Lawrence XVII (Cab Driver), Percival Scott III (Security Officer), Troy Vincent (Oceanic Rep)

Focus: Everyone

As the 1977 Dharma recruits are returned to 2007 and deal with losing Juliet, the people on the beach struggle to find out what is happening inside Jacob's statue. Meanwhile, in a new, mysterious timeline, time seems to have been reset.

Contrary to season premieres of the past, "LA X" does not open with someone we've never met playing music from another decade from some remote location on the island. Instead, it seems oddly familiar, a repetition of the opening of the first flashback in *Lost*'s pilot episode, with Jack staring out the window of the airplane and talking to a flight attendant about his drink. But when we immediately notice that small details are different — such as the number of liquor bottles Cindy hands Jack — it's clear this isn't a flashback. No, once again, the writers on *Lost* have changed the game. We've experienced the flashback and the flashforward . . . welcome to the flashsideways. For in this world, the characters we've come to know and love are once again strangers, with different lives, different pasts, and different baggage.

Oh, and that island? It's at the bottom of the ocean.

As soon as the sideways world was introduced in this episode, fans began speculating about what it could represent. Just before Juliet dies, she struggles to tell Sawyer, "It worked." She had tried to detonate the old hydrogen bomb in order to create a world where Sawyer never came to the island and she never felt feel the pain of losing him. Her final unspoken words suggest that she's seen the sideways world where, as we've seen, her wish comes true. So what is this world? Is it a parallel world like the one Hugh Everett III had described in his groundbreaking quantum mechanics theory? (See page 34.) Was it caused by the detonation in 1977? Was it caused by something that preceded the events of 1977? Is it Heaven? Is it Hell? Why is Oceanic Flight 815 landing safely in Los Angeles, and what are the implications for everyone on board? Is everyone getting a do-over?

A do-over was exactly what Jack wanted, and it's why he decided to drop the bomb in the first place. When season 5 ended, we left everyone in different places, more separated than they'd ever been before. In 1977, Jack had just dropped a bomb down the shaft where Radzinsky was drilling the entry to what would become the Swan station, but when the bomb failed to detonate, the newly drilled hole instead set off enormous electromagnetic energy, causing Juliet to be yanked down the shaft where she lay broken at the bottom. Sawyer was emotionally shattered, Kate had tried in vain to save Juliet, Miles and Jin were nearby, and Hurley was tending to Sayid, who had been shot in the stomach and was slowly bleeding to death. Juliet regained consciousness at the bottom of the shaft, only to see the bomb next to her. She hit the bomb eight times with a rock, and on the final knock, the screen went white.

Meanwhile, in 2007, John Locke returned to the island after Ben killed him (as one can do only on *Lost*), and he led an expedition of the Others along with Richard Alpert and Ben Linus to the remains of the ancient statue where Richard had told him Jacob lived. Locke and Ben entered the statue, where the exchange between Jacob and Locke revealed that the man who looked like Locke was actually the mysterious Man in Black, who we saw briefly at the beginning of that episode. We don't know much about this man other than that he's been Jacob's nemesis for many years, and he's been unable to kill Jacob. So he convinced Ben to do it, and Ben did.

Jacob is now dead at Ben's hand. Meanwhile, on the beach outside the statue, Richard Alpert, who is also with Frank Lapidus and Sun, has just been shown the corpse of John Locke, and this revelation begs the question: what has just walked into Jacob's sanctuary, and with what intent? Jacob's dying words were, "They're coming," and it's unclear who he meant.

Many of the characters went through immense personal growth in season 5. This is in part due to the fact that more time passed in that season than in any other — season 1 showed us the first 45 days on the island; season 2 took place over about three weeks; season 3 covered another three weeks; season 4 took place over about 10 days . . . and season 5 covered the next three years. John Locke's quest to bring everyone back to the island failed while he was alive, but he succeeded in death. Jack had gone from being the rational man of science to the guy standing above a giant hole about to drop a bomb so he could destroy the island, change time, and erase everything that had happened to him over the previous three years. Kate had discovered the stabilizing force of motherhood. Sawyer and Juliet had fallen in love. Jin learned English. Sun became a mother, but that joy was tarnished by an overriding vengefulness because she believed that her husband was dead. Hurley was happy to be reunited with his parents, but when he began talking to the dead, he checked himself in to a mental institution. Sayid had married, buried his wife, become a hitman, turned to humanitarian work, resumed his hitman duties, and returned to the island against his will. While the thought of Ben Linus experiencing any sort of personal growth would make most *Lost* fans snicker, he did go off the island in a vengeful rage, vowing to kill Widmore's daughter, and while he was there he managed to murder John Locke. But he returned to the island believing that he may have been culpable in the death of his own daughter. His personal growth was limited, but it was there. When they all returned to the island, they were different people from the ones who had left.

And now, at the beginning of season 6, they have a lot of fallout to deal with as a result of what happened at the end of "The Incident."

Lost has often been seen as the journey of John Locke, but as of the end of season 5, it looks like Jack Shephard is the one who has undergone the most dramatic personal change. When we first met Jack, he was struggling with his father issues, but immediately stepped up as the terrified group's leader. He's struggled with feelings for Kate that have both made him happy and broken his heart; he's had to defend his very belief system against John Locke's; he's felt the pressures of leadership and rarely received any praise for the good things he's done, rather he gets blamed when something goes wrong; and he's lost both Kate and Juliet to Sawyer. The moments when Jack has smiled have been fleeting, instead his brow is in a perpetual furrow as he lies awake at night worrying about the next day while everyone around him sleeps. Some fans have come down hard on Jack over the years, mostly because of his occasional holier-than-thou attitude, refusing to consider an alternative perspective and bullishly deciding for others what is best for them.

Jack has been defined by his obsessive need to fix things, from healing a paralyzed woman who later became his able-bodied wife, to transfusing a badly injured Boone with his own blood in an impossible situation where death was actually the more merciful thing to give him. Jack's refusal to accept anything that cannot be empirically known has been his major flaw, and is often the very thing keeping him from being able to fix all those things that he believes need fixing. And he refuses to delegate responsibility, taking it all upon himself. But in season 5 we saw Jack's resolve begin to crack, and he was finally on a more meaningful journey.

In the sideways world, Jack is sitting in the same seat on the plane as he was in the pilot episode, and he's still talking to Rose. She looks over at him as the turbulence ends and tells him to "let go." While he still takes charge at the back of the plane, saving Charlie's life (against Charlie's will), he also steps aside uncharacteristically when Sayid offers to help. He turns to the flight attendants, asking for their assistance, and never loses his cool. And once it's over, he calmly returns to his seat and lets the authorities take over. This version of Jack is much calmer than the one we're used to, and a little less in love with responsibility.

On the island, however, Jack is dealing with an immense amount of guilt thanks to his actions. He deliberately dropped a hydrogen bomb into a shaft because he had faith in a higher power, a hard-won faith that even he was still struggling with. If he hadn't taken off to the station with the bomb, Kate wouldn't have enlisted Sawyer and Juliet to help her stop him. While Juliet chose to return to the island, and Sawyer decided to join her, it was Jack's actions that prompted their decision. No matter how many times people tried to talk him out of it, no matter how many times Sawyer punched him in the head, nothing was going to stop Jack from acting on his conviction.

He now believes he was wrong — in much the same way that John Locke admits he had made a mistake at the end of season 2 — and he follows Hurley to the Temple to try to save Sayid's life. Jack briefly steps up and takes charge once inside, telling the Japanese leader at the Temple, who we will find out in the next episode is named Dogen, to "do what you need to do," thus inadvertently giving the man permission to drown Sayid. As soon as Sayid's body is brought out of the water, Jack rushes over and immediately begins CPR, desperately trying to save Sayid's life in much the same way he pounded on Charlie's chest in "All the Best Cowboys Have Daddy Issues" after he found him unconscious, hanging in a tree. Similarly, in that season 1 scene, Kate begged Jack to give up his efforts to revive Charlie and accept that Charlie was dead, but Jack refused . . . and he managed to save the rock star's life. But this time, with Kate by his side and once again begging him to stop, he stops. He sits back, and finally realizes he simply can't fix everything. He will have to live with the consequences of his actions, and maybe it's time for other people to accept responsibility.

Throughout season 5 we watched Kate's joy as she became a mother to Aaron, but she also had to come to terms with the fact that Aaron wasn't really her son, and that his real mother was still trapped on an island on the other side of the world. Consumed by guilt and determined to right the wrong, Kate returned to the island, unintentionally got in the way of Juliet's happy family, and realized with horror that Jack was willing to obliterate everyone just so he wouldn't have to deal with the emotional pain of their failed relationship. In the sideways world, Kate is still a fugitive, still as wily as ever, and once again on the run. She seems very much the same person as she was in the pre-island world; is she doomed to simply repeat her actions in every parallel universe?

While Hurley has experienced tremendous changes around him, his character remains consistent — he's spent time in mental institutions, he's still the comic foil, he still pretends to be more in control of things than he really is (in this episode, fumbling with a gun's safety switch while yelling that he knows how to use it). But now the very thing that he thought proved he was crazy — his ability

Spot the Differences!

Original Flight 815	Sideways World Flight 815
Cindy offers Jack two liquor bottles, and he responds that this goes against all FAA regulations.	Cindy offers Jack one liquor bottle, and he tells her it'll be their little secret (he also appears to be less drunk).
The seat beside Jack is empty and Desmond is not on the plane.	Desmond sits in the seat . . . and he's wearing a wedding band!
Rose is wearing Bernard's ring on her necklace because his finger swells when he flies, he's in the bathroom, and Jack calms her down while the plane experiences turbulence.	Bernard is wearing his ring on his finger when he returns from the bathroom and Rose ends up calming Jack during the turbulence.
The turbulence becomes so fierce the plane crashes.	The plane gets past the turbulence and lands safely.
Charlie snorts heroin in the bathroom at the front of the plane, is thrown up into the air, and the plane crashes.	Charlie goes into the bathroom at the back of the plane and swallows a bag of heroin to avoid being caught with it.
Walt and Michael are sitting in the seats across from Hurley.	Walt and Michael aren't on the plane.
Hurley believes that he's cursed by the numbers.	Hurley believes he's the luckiest guy in the world, and he's famous because of his Mr. Cluck's chicken commercials.
Sawyer's sitting further back on the plane.	Sawyer's only one row behind Hurley.
Claire was sitting across from Jack and forward a couple of rows.	We don't see Claire on the plane.
Shannon and Boone were traveling together in first class.	Shannon doesn't get on the plane, and Boone is sitting in the same row as John Locke.
John Locke didn't go on the walkabout and is carried onto the plane, humiliated.	They have a wheelchair for John, and he makes up a story about going on the walkabout.
Jin and Sun are married, he's hopeful that after he delivers the second watch (he'd delivered the first one in Sydney) they'll be able to take off on a life together.	Jin and Sun aren't married — he's not wearing a wedding band at customs, and they refer to her as "Ms. Paik," which is her maiden name. She's wearing a small ring, so it's not clear if it's an engagement ring or just a ring. It's also not clear if she can speak English.

Sayid is sitting closer to Shannon and Boone near the front of the plane, and keeps to himself.	Sayid is sitting further back in the plane, and helps out Jack with Charlie.
Kate and the marshal are on the plane and he treats her like dirt.	Kate and the marshal are on the plane and he treats her like dirt. However, there seems to be the tiniest bit of compassion for her this time around.
Christian Shephard's body was on the plane in a coffin.	Christian's coffin never made it onto the plane.

to talk to dead people — is the thing that makes him the leader. For the first time, he gives the orders, and other people follow him. Hurley has always been the heart of the show, and he's established himself as someone other people can trust (maybe not with their deepest secrets, which he will inevitably blurt out, but Hurley is there for people when they need him). For that reason, he's always been a fan favorite.

In the sideways world, then, a cheer goes up from the audience when the biggest character change of all is represented by Hurley's declaration: "I'm the luckiest guy alive." No longer cursed by the numbers, Hurley's life has become a treasure trove of happiness since he won the lottery. Arzt, who only began talking to Hurley at the end of season 1 (and even then only did so to lecture him), now hangs off his every word like a drooling fan. When Sawyer speaks to him to tell him what he should do for his own good, Hurley just shrugs off the advice with confidence. This self-assurance is something that Hurley has deserved his entire life, and we are happy to see him get it.

Jin and Sun seem to be back to their season 1 selves on the plane, with Sun watching Bernard and Rose with a smile on her face, and Jin telling her to button up her sweater. However, the severity in Jin's voice seems to be absent, and when the two of them get to customs, Sun is referred to as "Ms. Paik" and there are no wedding rings on their fingers. In this parallel universe, they are not married. If the sideways world represents a place that has been subtly altered by events on the island, this detail could be referring to the fact that in the original timeline Sun is very unhappily widowed, and has returned to the island hoping to find the husband that she's been told is still alive.

At the beginning of season 1, Sawyer was a wise-talking con man, a monster of self-interest who only ever "helped" if he got something from the effort. Now, at the beginning of the final season, James Ford has tasted leadership (and surprisingly, he was an effective leader), he'd found love and security, and he'd grown enough to become a team player. But with Juliet gone, he's disappeared back inside the original Sawyer, declaring that he won't follow anyone anymore. He is a broken man. However, in the sideways world, James Ford seems to be a happier version of the Sawyer who took the original Flight 815. He's still a wiseass, but he's less angry. Is it possible that in this world, his life has not been devoted to finding the man who killed his parents? Is it possible his parents are alive?

The biggest surprise in the sideways world is the appearance of Desmond on the plane. He wasn't on the original Oceanic flight to L.A., so when he appears sitting beside Jack, reading a Salman Rushdie book and sporting a wedding band, it's clear something is vastly different about this particular world. It shouldn't come as a surprise that he would represent drastic change — at the beginning of season 5, Daniel declared that Desmond was different from everyone else, telling him "the rules don't apply to you. You're special. You're uniquely and miraculously special." Perhaps that specialness allowed him to somehow grow from the paranoid, empty man who was trapped in the Swan station for three years to the confident, serene man sitting on a plane and chatting casually to Jack.

Some fans speculated that Desmond wasn't actually there, that he appeared as a flash of sorts to Jack alone, to help lead him on a particular path (which is why Jack doesn't see him later when his eyes scan the passengers seated behind him). Others wondered if Desmond was proof that the island had never existed in the sideways world — therefore Desmond wouldn't have gone there in 2001 and caused the plane crash in 2004, so he could easily have been on the flight with everyone else. But why this particular flight? How did he just happen to be on the very same flight as the one that, in another world, he managed to pull out of the sky by forgetting to push a button? Perhaps Desmond's catchphrase, "See you in another life, bruthah," has become literal when it comes to the sideways world.

Desmond doesn't appear on the island timeline in this episode because, by the end of season 5, it would appear his story has been fulfilled. He spent his life searching for Penny, and he found her. Unlike almost everyone else on the show, Desmond got the one thing he wanted, and he found true happiness with her. He's been told by Eloise Hawking, however, that the island isn't done with him yet, so the menace of the island hangs over his life like the sword of Damocles, one that he can ignore for only so long before it falls on him.

The character who has not had a good life, however, is Sayid. He has always been, at heart, a lover, but circumstances have pushed him to become a killer and a torturer. He hates what he does, but it's been useful for him. He spent a lifetime searching for Nadia, but soon after he found her, he lost her forever. He has been used by many people who keep pulling him back into a life of violence, and he reluctantly agrees every time, because he's come to believe that that's who he really is. Sayid ended season 5 filled with self-loathing, but willing to help Jack accomplish his goal. A bullet in the stomach has stopped him in his tracks, and now he lies on the ground, bleeding to death.

His words to Hurley are heartbreaking: "When I die, what do you think will happen to me? I've tortured more people than I can remember. I've murdered. Wherever I'm going, it can't be very pleasant. I deserve it." With his life passing before his eyes, Sayid knows the bad things he's done far outweigh the good. He might have loved Nadia, but that love didn't stop him from committing atrocities in the name of revenge or duty. We've seen that Sayid is a devout Muslim, and now he's facing an eternity in Hell. In the sideways world, we don't see much of Sayid, but what we do see suggests that he hasn't changed much. There's still a quiet sadness about Sayid — and he still carries with him a photograph of Nadia. Only time will tell if his life is any better in the sideways world.

Then again, it pretty much has to be better. In one of the most baffling scenes of the episode, the Others in the Temple take an unconscious Sayid into the water and appear to drown him, only to have Sayid come back to life two hours later. What has returned? Is that really Sayid, or is he alive in the same sense that Locke is alive? Does he only appear to be Sayid? Could another entity be controlling him? Some fans speculated that if the Man in Black has taken Locke's body, perhaps Jacob now inhabits Sayid's. Or is Sayid dead, and this is the horrific afterlife he's been expecting? Considering the way the Others carried him out of the water in a Jesus Christ pose, are we to think he resurrected the same way Christ did? Or is it possible that the island can not only heal bullet wounds, but death as well? Is Sayid being given a do-over on the island?

While Ben Linus didn't have much personal growth throughout his time off the island, he was changed entirely from the moment he returned to the island. Ben spent his life beholden to Jacob, believing that he was one of "the good guys," doing everything in the name of the island. It's unclear if he actually knew Jacob had a nemesis on the island; after all, seeing as the Man in Black is really the smoke monster, then Ben has been working with Smokey. Jacob seemed to sneer

The production crew builds the base of Jacob's statue on the beach. (Courtesy KOS Tours)

at him with utter dismissal, and his final words to Ben — "What *about* you" — are shocking. Once Ben kills Jacob, everything he ever had faith in is gone.

If Jacob was the good guy, then Ben just killed him and is officially aligned with the island's evil. But if Jacob was the bad guy, then Ben devoted his life to the wrong side. In either case, Ben realizes in this moment that his whole life was nothing more than a colossal joke. The Man in Black appears to have manipulated him from childhood, using Jacob's cabin to pretend to be Jacob, getting Ben to go off the island and kill John Locke, bring the body back, and give the Man in Black a vessel convincing enough to get Ben to kill Jacob once and for all. Ben has given his life to a cause that was not real, and as he watches Smokey annihilate Bram and the other Jacobites who have come to the island, he realizes with a creeping terror that he really is one of the bad guys. If Jacob was the deity of the island, Ben has just destroyed him and thereby allowed Smokey to kill everyone who protects him. But most horrifically, Ben killed John Locke in cold blood, and despite what Ben Linus thought, John did not resurrect.

Ah, John Locke: the lone wolf who embarked on a spiritual journey of self-discovery in season 1, the only one who "looked into the eye of this island" and saw something pure and beautiful, not dark and soul-crushing. From the beginning of season 1, when audiences discovered with a mixture of shock and elation that he had experienced a miracle on the island, regaining his ability to walk, it has seemed that *Lost* might be about John Locke, and that his faith in destiny and in the island was the very key to understanding the series. But then . . . he died at Ben's hand in a cold, dirty motel room. Alone. At the time, audiences thought it was sad, but since we knew he was on the island, we all assumed he had simply resurrected, Christ-like, with a new resolve and confidence. Until it was revealed that the man who looked like Locke was a supernatural being who was borrowing his physical form, and John himself was gone forever.

So what was the point of building up such a rich character only to kill him a season before the series actually ended? That will become clearer in the episodes to come, but for now, it's important that the Man in Black looks like Locke. Locke and Jack have always been pitted against one another, and now that we see Jack is in the Temple, with other people who follow Jacob, and Jacob's nemesis looks exactly like Jack's, we can see the makings of a showdown between the two.

The revelation in this episode — in an awesome scene of brutality and violence — is that the Man in Black, as suspected, is actually the smoke monster.

In his human form he's impervious to harm, with bullets passing right through him (and seemingly not even puncturing his T-shirt). He disappears and reappears as the smoke monster, unleashing a torrent of fury and devastation. His wry comment to Ben — "I'm sorry you had to see me like that" — suggests that he doesn't like turning into a pillar of smoke.

It's also clear in some of the things that Smokey says that he's not only taken on John's corporeal form, but his thoughts and personality as well. In the central moment of the episode, Smokey refuses to let Ben call him a "what," insisting that he's a who. He has feelings, he has memories of his past, and most horrific of all, when he puts on a new body he takes in all of that person's memories as well. In one of the most devastating lines of the series, he explains to Ben that as Ben was choking Locke to death, Locke's final thought was "I don't understand." Smokey chuckles and says, "Isn't that just the saddest thing you've ever heard?" And audiences can't help but nod. It *is* one of the saddest things we've ever heard, because even in Locke's most obsessive or maniacal moments we knew he truly believed he was doing the right thing, and despite separating himself from everyone else on the island, he believed his actions would be for the greater good. Sure, time and time again, he was wrong; but more often than not he was *right*.

He came to the island a sad and broken man, filled with anger and resentment because his legs no longer worked, bogged down by his own personal woes, not least some whopping daddy issues that made Jack's look insignificant. The island gave John Locke his legs back, and in doing so earned his absolute devotion. Locke didn't want to leave the island, going so far as to thwart other people's attempts to do so. Smokey points out the irony that he has assumed the form of the only person who never wanted to leave the island, when doing so seems to be Smokey's primary objective. But Locke is a fitting body for him to be in. Despite his repeated failures, Locke had aligned himself with the island. And, just as the Man in Black forced Ben to kill Jacob because he couldn't, Locke had manipulated Sawyer into killing Cooper, and got Ben to move the island so he wouldn't have to. Locke "shout[ed] at the world for being told what he couldn't do," and the Man in Black is just as determined to do things in his own way, regardless of what it does to anyone around him.

In the sideways world, Locke is still paralyzed, but he's different. On the original Oceanic Flight 815, Locke was sad and angry, and was carried onto the plane because a wheelchair was unavailable. On this flight, there was a chair so he didn't have to endure that humiliation, but he also engages Boone in conversation, telling him about a walkabout he did in Australia as if it actually happened. We know it couldn't have happened because there's no way they would have allowed a paraplegic to go on a walkabout (and besides, had he gone on it he would have been on a different flight a week or so later than this one), and yet Locke tells the story as if it actually happened, as if he's not shattered by being turned away. There's an air of acceptance about him, as if he's stopped railing against life and against those who try to stop him, and has decided that maybe there *are* things he can't do, and if someone is going to tell him he can't, he might agree with them.

If the scene between Ben and Smokey is the centerpiece of the island story, then the one between Locke and Jack at the airport is the center of the sideways-world story in this episode. How fitting that the two men who carry the most emotional baggage to the island in the original timeline have lost their baggage in this one. Jack has lost his father's corpse, the very thing that dogged him while on the island and made him constantly doubt himself, and Locke has lost his "400 knives," as Charlie once put it, the very knives that not only were denied usage on the walkabout, but were the things that set him apart from everyone else on the island and turned him into the solitary hunter. Maybe without those things these two men will find the peace that they couldn't find on the island.

Locke tells Jack that he hasn't actually lost his father, he's just lost his body, suggesting a belief in a soul outside of the corporeal body. It's a commentary on the fact that while the Man in Black appears to be in Locke's body, Locke's soul is not in there, and that he has died a flawed but good man. He is not to be held responsible for the Man in Black's actions. In this scene, too, we see Jack and Locke behaving in a mutually respectful way — they don't seem to push each others' buttons, which might suggest those buttons just aren't there. And as they part ways, Jack offers a consult to Locke about his spine, which opens up so many possibilities for a different ending for these two: just imagine the idea of Jack being Locke's savior. The mind boggles . . . mostly with joy.

In this key scene, Jack tells John, "Nothing is irreversible." If he's correct, then perhaps the sideways world is where the characters are given a second chance of sorts. In this world we saw people looking just a little bit happier than we usually see them look, and we're thrilled to see Boone, Charlie, Arzt, Claire, Rose, Bernard, and even the marshal and Frogurt. Regardless of what this sideways world represents, it will be interesting to watch our Losties start over. This episode reminds us of everything these characters have lost, and how many people we've lost along the way. Now that the writers have put us back at the beginning, we can watch a new reality unfold. Will it be better than the one we've already seen?

Could it possibly be worse?

Highlight: Seeing Charlie again, even if it's the angry, broken Charlie.
Did You Notice?:
- When we first see Jack, not only is he looking out the window the same way he was in the first flashback of the pilot episode, he's also in the same position as the man on the cover of the *Mystery Tales* comic is (see *Finding Lost — Season Four*, p. 155).
- Rose is reading a *Weekly Woodsman* magazine. It's like she's getting ready for life on the island should the plane in fact crash.
- Though you don't see him, you can hear Greg Grunberg's voice as Captain Seth Norris.
- When we used to move to flashbacks and flashforwards, there was a familiar "whoosh" sound that accompanied the shift, but when we switch from the island timeline to the sideways world, we instead hear that sound from season 5 that always preceded a time jump.
- While it's not clear when the island ended up at the bottom of the ocean, it's obvious that the Dharma Initiative did inhabit it at one time, as you can see the sonar fence they built, their village, and the Dharma symbol on the tail of the shark.
- This episode did not endear the writers to the "Skate" fans (those who want Kate and Sawyer to end up together): when Kate sees Sawyer lying unconscious on the ground she immediately looks for Jack, and then runs to him, as if Sawyer wasn't even there.
- Miles saying, "Guess we're not in 1977, huh?" was another *Wizard of Oz* reference, recalling Dorothy's famous line, "Toto, I've a feeling we're not in Kansas anymore."
- Hurley doing the "commercial" for Mr. Cluck's refers to the Mr. Cluck's commercial shown at Comic-Con (see page x).
- Arzt is holding a field guide to insects, which is funny because in the other timeline he kept jars of insects on the island. He named each new species, and Nikki stole the Medusa spider from him in order to poison Paulo.
- Hurley shows the same wooziness around Sayid coughing up blood that he

The set for the Temple was built just off a soundstage, and the "jungle" was then added around it. (Courtesy KOS Tours)

did at the beginning of the series when he had to help Jack take care of the marshal. Luckily, he doesn't pass out this time.
- Death gave Jacob a haircut!
- Boone says to Locke, "If this plane goes down, I'm sticking with you." Sadly, in the other timeline the Beechcraft plane goes down and he's with Locke at the time. And . . . it kills him.
- Boone asks Locke if he's pulling his leg. This is not only a reference to the fact that Locke's legs don't work, but could also be referring to the fact that in the other timeline, Boone's leg is so badly damaged that it killed him — and right before he died Jack made one last-ditch effort to save him by pulling Boone's leg into a doorway where he was going to slam the door and amputate it.
- Richard Alpert is usually the perfect picture of calm, but for the first time we see him completely lose control. It's like the death of Jacob has opened him up to specific dangers, and we wonder what history he has with the Man in Black.
- When Jack is trying to revive Charlie he says he needs a pen. This time, he actually needs one, yet in the other timeline where he landed on the island, he only got Boone to go and look for pens as a way to get Boone out of his hair.
- When Jack tells Charlie he's alive (which was, in itself, a heartbreaking line, since we all know Charlie's dead), he responds, "Terrific," which is the same thing he said when he first saw the smoke monster.
- There were several references to slavery in this episode: the Man in Black suggests that he's somehow trapped on this island, and just wants to leave; when Bram and the others walk into the statue he tells them they're free and can go now; and when he sees Richard he says, "Nice to see you out of those chains," as if Richard was once a prisoner, too.
- Frogurt, sitting in between Locke and Boone, is wearing a red shirt. He's the annoying guy from the beginning of season 5 who was killed by a flaming arrow. (On *Star Trek*, it became a joke that extras in the cast who were destined to be killed on a mission were always wearing red shirts.)
- On the original Flight 815, Sayid was carrying a photo of Nadia wearing a traditional headscarf. In the sideways world he carries the bare-headed photo of her that we saw in the season 1 episode, "The Greater Good," which the CIA had shown him to prove that she was alive and well and

living in California. Either he was in Sydney doing the same thing he was doing in the other timeline — setting up his friend Essam to take down a terrorist network — or he's still in touch with Nadia and carries a more recent photo of her.
- The scene where everyone disembarks from the plane in slow motion is a counterpoint to the scene in "Exodus, Part 2," where we see all of them boarding the plane in slow motion.
- The corpse that Hurley and everyone come upon in the wall of the Temple is that of Montand, the first member of Rousseau's expedition who went down into the hole in 1988 and had his arm severed by Smokey in "This Place Is Death." The corpse sitting there is proof that the voice that yelled up for the others to come down was simply Smokey mimicking Montand's voice, since he was already dead.
- Kate knocks the marshal's head in the same spot as the briefcase had hit him in the original timeline when it flew out of the overhead compartment.
- Kate doesn't seem as keen to retrieve whatever's in the marshal's briefcase this time around.
- Cindy refers to the "first plane," which is Oceanic Flight 815, as opposed to Ajira Flight 316, which presumably they also know about.
- Dogen flips over the hourglass and refuses to let Sayid out of the water until the sand has run out. In a sense, Sayid was killed by time itself, which is significant on a show that uses time as a major theme.
- Another theme of *Lost* is the dichotomy between black and white, or light and dark, and the grains of sand in the hourglass are black and white.
- When the passengers are all standing around the baggage carousel, you can hear an announcement about a flight from Sao Paulo, Brazil, which could be a reference to Nikki and Paulo from season 3 (Paulo was from Brazil). Here's hoping that's the *only* reference to them in season 6.
- Zach and Emma, the children with Cindy, are the ones from the tail section whom Ana Lucia promised would see their parents again someday. It is rather upsetting that these little kids who just wanted to see their parents have not only been denied a happy childhood with their family, but they're being treated like servants by Cindy and the Others.
- Watch how disconcerted Miles looks as he's sitting next to Sayid's "corpse"; you can tell by the look on his face that he's unable to hear anything from Sayid, meaning Sayid isn't actually dead. When Hurley asks him what's

wrong, he simply says, "Nothing," meaning he can hear nothing from Sayid's "corpse."

Interesting Facts: Fans wondered why there was a space between LA and X in the title of this episode. The likeliest explanation is that the writers are using the X as a traditional marker for an alternate world. In a lot of science fiction, "X" is used to designate a universe parallel to the one we live in — *Earth X*, for example, is a Marvel comic about a parallel Earth. So the X is possibly referring to the fact that this L.A. is an alternate universe, and not the L.A. in our world.

Audiences shouldn't read too much into Shannon's absence on the plane; Maggie Grace was unavailable to film the scenes because she was working on a movie at the time, so the writers improvised by changing things so she would simply stay behind in Australia and Boone would return alone. The cab driver who Kate holds at gunpoint is played by the actor David H. Lawrence XVII. When he went to register his name on IMDb.com, he was the seventeenth David Lawrence in the list, so he added the numeral to distinguish himself from the ones already registered. The character that looks a little like John Lennon (and is only ever referred to in scripts as "Lennon" even though his name is never spoken on the show) is played by John Hawkes, who played Sol Star on *Deadwood*. He's the fourth *Deadwood* alumnus to appear on *Lost*, along with Robin Weigert, Titus Welliver, and William Sanderson. This casting call described Lennon as a "scruffy, edgy and charismatic spokesperson and translator for the president of a foreign corporation."

Terry O'Quinn says that he's intrigued by the idea that there may be some of John Locke still in Smokey. "The question that I've heard — even discussed a little bit on the set — is how much of Locke is in Smokey. Is there any Locke there? And honestly, on occasion [there is], because no one has instructed me otherwise. When I started talking about Locke and wondering what Locke's last thought was, well, I decided that Smokey would be surprisingly moved by that — that there would be some residual emotion that was contained that was John Locke's. So little bits of Locke keep popping up in Smokey. But that's just my choice, it's not anything anybody told me to do. I decided it would give a little flavor to the performance, so I'm going to go with that until somebody tells me to quit it."

Nitpicks: While I think the sound effect of Kate having tinnitus was very well done, the CGI on the underwater island was, once again, terrible. It looked like graphics from a bad video game, circa 1992. Also, Jack's mother asks him why he scheduled the funeral for only two hours after he expected the plane to land, and

I have to agree with her. Considering how unpredictable flight times can be, it seems utterly ludicrous that he would have made that decision. And having Dogen snipping Bonzai trees in his sanctuary seemed a little too clichéd.

Oops: The marshal takes away a silver knife and fork from Kate on the plane, but after the events of 9/11, silverware is no longer used on planes (a fact reinforced later when Cindy says she can't find any sharp objects to help Jack). Later, in the bathroom at the airport, it seems strange that a stall door would open outwards, the way Kate's does, but when the camera pans back, you'll see all the other stalls have opened inwards, meaning the production team altered the one stall door so that Kate could clock the marshal with it.

4 8 15 16 23 42: When the Shadow Seekers enter the statue, there are **4** of them. Sawyer overhears a police transmission calling out code 341 (3+4+1 = **8**). When the Others attack Miles and Sawyer in the jungle, Sawyer manages to take out **4** of them before being knocked unconscious.

It's Just a Flesh Wound: Everyone has tinnitus after the time jump. Sawyer punches Jack. Juliet dies of internal wounds. Smokey kills Bram's team by picking them up one by one and bashing them against the walls and knocking their heads together, and he impales Bram on Jacob's loom. The marshal loses consciousness after Kate hits him with the bathroom stall door and he cracks his head on the counter. The Temple Others hold Sayid's head under the water until he drowns. Off screen, Sawyer punches out four Others before they knock him unconscious with a rock. Miles has clearly been roughed up by the Others. The Man in Black karate chops Richard in the throat, knees him in the stomach, and carries the unconscious man away over his shoulder.

Any Questions?:
- What exactly is the sideways world? Has something caused it, or has it existed as long as the other timeline has, just running alongside it? Is it real, or illusory, or supernatural?
- How did Jack get that cut on his neck? It's too far down his neck to have been something that happened when he was shaving. Could it be some indication of what is happening on the island?
- Jack wonders if he knows Desmond from somewhere. Is he remembering the island, or the stadium in L.A.? When Des first sees Jack in the hatch in the original timeline, he instantly remembers him from the stadium, and yet here, he doesn't have a clue who Jack is.
- Did the hydrogen bomb actually go off? Fans are divided on the answer to

the question. Some believe that it couldn't have gone off, or they'd have all been obliterated. The tinnitus and shock to everyone was caused when the island time jumped at the exact moment that Juliet hit the bomb for the eighth time, and that's what caused the white flash. Some fans have suggested that if the electromagnetic surge happened at exactly the same time that Juliet set the bomb off, it might cause the bomb to implode rather than explode, sucking all of the atomic energy back down underneath the site. Thus, the Swan hatch was built on top of this reserve of energy, cementing it in, and this inspired Sayid's Chernobyl comment in season 2. Further, the button was put in place so that the energy from the bomb could be released one tiny bit at a time, every 108 minutes, thus defusing the very bomb that the gang set off in 1977. Therefore, everything that Desmond had to do for three years was as a result of Jack setting the bomb off. However, if he hadn't done it, the Incident (the electromagnetic surge caused by Radzinsky's drill cutting into the pocket) could have been catastrophic. Both worked against each other, in many ways canceling each other out but containing the effects of it underneath the area. Not only does this argument explain why Desmond was pushing that button, it also means Juliet didn't die for nothing: by detonating the bomb she contained the electromagnetic energy. It also explains the failsafe key: its original intention was to release the bomb's energy all at once. But when Desmond turned it, the electromagnetism partially contained it and caused the Swan to simultaneously implode and explode, sucking a lot of stuff into the hole while spewing other things out, like the hatch door that landed far away on the beach.

- Why is the island sitting at the bottom of the ocean in the sideways world? If the bomb *did* go off, could it have split off the universe in an Everett-esque way (see page 34) and created a new timeline where it went off, and a separate one where it didn't? And could the one where it went off and sunk the island be the one we're seeing in the sideways world?
- I asked this way back in season 1, and I ask it again: why *is* Hurley sitting back in coach when he could probably buy his own jet?
- Ben asks why Jacob didn't fight back. Good question. Could it be because he actually wanted to die for some reason? And did Jacob deliberately provoke Ben?
- Why can't the Man in Black cross the line of ash? What kind of ash is it?

- Didn't the people standing outside the statue see Smokey enter it when he came in to kill all of the Shadow Seekers? Why does Richard act like he doesn't know what's going on? Why doesn't he rush inside?
- Juliet says to Sawyer, "We could get coffee some time . . . we could go Dutch." Was that a line from early in their relationship? Or was she getting a glimpse of herself saying these words in another life?
- Why doesn't Miles tell Sawyer what Juliet meant by "It worked"? We saw in "Some Like It Hoth" that when he was looking at the corpse of Alvarez, he not only knew how he died, but what he was thinking in the moments before he did. Why didn't he know what Juliet was thinking, too?
- So . . . were the people at the Temple just the other Others that Richard sent on ahead back in season 3? Or are they always at the Temple? Why are they dressed so differently than they were in New Otherton? Cindy just had her regular clothes on in season 3, but now she's as drab as the rest of them.
- Who is the Japanese man in charge of the Temple? Why haven't we seen him before now?
- Can sideways-world Sun speak or understand English?
- What was wrong with the water in the Temple? Lennon and Dogen act like it's only recently started looking like iced tea. Why did it change? Jacob's death? Were the island's healing properties inextricably linked to Jacob?
- When Sayid is submerged in the water, is this the same procedure that young Ben went through when he was taken to the Temple to recover from the gunshot wound? Before Richard took him he told Sawyer and Kate that he would be never be the same, and his innocence would be lost. Was he drowned and brought back to life? Or was the procedure very different because Jacob was alive? Was he simply dipped in the water?
- Why is Hugo waiting for a cab? Doesn't he have a stretch limo that could pick him up? Perhaps the suggestion is simply that wealth didn't change him at all, and he'll still ride in coach and line up for taxis like everyone else.
- The Man in Black says he wants to go home. Where is home? More importantly, *when* is it?!
- What did the Man in Black when he said it was nice to see Richard "out of those chains"?
- What did Smokey mean when he said he was disappointed in everyone?

Ashes to Ashes: Juliet Burke was a fertility doctor who developed a treatment that allowed her sister, Rachel, who had been rendered infertile due to an aggressive chemo for her cancer, to conceive a baby. Juliet agreed to come to the island at Richard Alpert's request (when he was posing as a recruiter for Mittelos Bioscience) but when she got to the island, she discovered it was a one-way ticket. She fell in love with the late Goodwin, Ben was obsessed with her, and she yearned to go home. She found happiness first in the knowledge that her sister had given birth to a healthy son, Julian, and then in her love for James Ford. She died in his arms after a fall down a long mine shaft in an electromagnetic accident.

In *Finding Lost — Season Five*, I couldn't bring myself to write an obit for John Locke, but now that it's clear he really is dead . . . John Locke was a man who believed in miracles because one happened to him. Having suffered through a difficult life, he was never very good at making friends, and thus became a loner on the island, preferring solitude to the comfort of strangers. He occasionally gave sage advice but for the most part kept to himself, bagging a boar while everyone else nibbled on in-flight food. He became so single-minded in his determination to stay on the island and to protect it that he alienated himself from the rest of the group. But when Richard Alpert told him that he'd have to die in order to save the island, he agreed without hesitation, willing to sacrifice himself in the name of a place he believed was important. After a lifetime of failure, Locke reached his low point, and was about to commit suicide, but was talked out of it by Ben Linus. Linus strangled Locke to death with a cord and brought his body back to the island. Despite John Locke's final confused thoughts, he really was remarkable.

✍ Haroun and the Sea of Stories by Salman Rushdie (1990)

While the name Salman Rushdie might be familiar to many people for the sensational fatwa against him, issued by Iran's Ayatollah Ruholla Khomeini in the wake of what some Muslims considered to be blasphemous references to the prophet Muhammad in his novel *The Satanic Verses*, he is known by millions of readers as one of the greatest writers of the twentieth century. His magic realist style has won him the Booker of Bookers Prize for *Midnight's Children* (i.e. the best of the books that have won the Booker Prize) and he boasts both a popular and literary audience.

Soon after the fatwa had been issued, Rushdie and his family went into hiding. The Ayatollah Khomeini had ordered all good Muslims to kill both Rushdie and his publishers — in fact, the Japanese translator was indeed stabbed to death, and there have been attempted assassinations on his other translators and publishers. While in hiding, he decided to write a children's book for his then nine-year-old son Zafar. The result was *Haroun and the Sea of Stories*.

Haroun Khalifa lives with his father Rashid and his mother Soraya in "a sad city, the saddest of cities, a city so ruinously sad that it had forgotten its name." The city is located in Alifbay (which comes from the Hindustani word for "alphabet"), and the Khalifa family are the only cheerful people in the city. Soraya is a singer. Rashid is a storyteller, renowned for his wild imagination, and he's referred to as the Ocean of Notions and the Shah of Blah. One day Soraya stops singing. Mr. Sengupta, who lives upstairs with his wife, has no time for storytelling, and he says to young Haroun one day, "What's the use of stories that aren't even true?" Haroun is haunted by this idea and wonders if it means his father is a liar. One day Soraya runs off with Mr. Sengupta, and in a rage Rashid smashes all of the clocks, permanently stopping them at 11 o'clock. From that point on, Haroun can only concentrate on things for 11 minutes before he cannot focus any longer. Rashid finds a note that Soraya left behind, saying that she wants to be with Mr. Sengupta because his mind isn't filled with stories like Rashid's is, and that Rashid's mind has no room for facts. Haroun turns Sengupta's words against his father, asking him what the point is of stories that aren't true. The next day when Rashid gets up in front of a group of people to tell a story, he realizes he doesn't have any left to tell.

Rashid finds some hope when he's invited to speak in the Town of G (all of the places in Alifbay are simply letters of the alphabet), but when he does, he opens his mouth and all that comes out is the sound "Ark," like a crow. He has to speak in the Valley of K the following day, and he and Haroun are forced to take a bus there. The driver of the bus, Butt, looks like a parrot and he drives maniacally, zooming past rhyming roadsides with such dire warnings as "IF FROM SPEED YOU GET YOUR THRILL/ TAKE PRECAUTION — MAKE YOUR WILL." They arrive before sunset, as Haroun had requested, and Rashid reminds Haroun of a story he used to tell of "Khattam-Shud," which is a synonym for "The End":

"Khattam-Shud . . . is the Arch-Enemy of all Stories, even of Language itself. He is the Prince of Silence and the Foe of Speech. And because everything ends, because dreams end, stories end, life ends, at the finish of everything we use his name. 'It's finished,' we tell one another, 'it's over. Khattam-Shud: The End.'"

They are met at the bus depot by Buttoo, a candidate in an upcoming election. It is Buttoo who has brought Rashid to the Valley to tell stories to the people. They cross over Dull Lake and the weather keeps changing to match their moods, and Haroun realizes they must be in Moody Land, which was the subject of one of his father's most famous stories. Rashid reassures him that the Moody Land is just a story, but Haroun doesn't buy it. Buttoo puts them up on a houseboat called *Arabian Nights Plus One* (incidentally, the hero of many of the stories told in *One Thousand and One Arabian Nights* is Harun al-Rashid). Haroun finds he can't sleep, so he switches beds with his father. In the middle of the night, he's awakened by a Water Genie named Iff, from the Ocean of the Streams of Story, who had sneaked into the room mistaking Haroun for his father. The genie had been planning to disconnect Rashid from the stories. He explains that storytellers all subscribe to the Ocean of the Streams of Story. The Grand Comptroller of Processes Too Complicated To Explain (P2C2E) has ordered that Rashid be disconnected. Haroun, upon waking, immediately snatches Iff's Disconnecting Tool, knowing that Iff will be in big trouble if anyone finds out it's been taken. Haroun demands that Iff take him to Gup City in Kahani, where the Comptroller is, so he can stop them from disconnecting his father from the Story Supply.

He and Iff travel to Kahani on Butt the Hoopoe, a bird that Haroun brought into being by naming it (showing once again the power of imagination) and with whom he communicates telepathically. As they fly, Iff scoops up some Wishwater from a well and gives it to Haroun to drink, telling him he needs to concentrate on his heart's desire and it will come true. Haroun does what he's told, but can only focus on his mother leaving his father, and can't concentrate for longer than 11 minutes, and is unable to make the Wishwater work. So Iff tries again, this time in the Ocean of the Streams of Story, scooping up a storyline and telling Haroun to drink it. When the story goes berserk, Iff realizes the water has become polluted somehow. He says filth is entering the stories, and if they become polluted, they'll come out all wrong. They rush on to Kahani, and Iff says they might have to go to war with the leader of the Chupwalas: Khattam-Shud.

As they get closer to Gup City Haroun sees a Floating Gardener named Mali, who is literally made of vegetation that rears up out of the water and moves around. His job is to maintain the story streams by unwrapping the twisted story streams and weeding them. He tells them the pollution has gotten very bad: "Certain popular romances have become just long lists of shopping expeditions. Children's stories also. For instance, there is an outbreak of talking helicopter anecdotes."

When they arrive at Gup City they realize that Princess Batcheat has been kidnapped by the Chupwalas, and Prince Bolo is devastated. (The general murmur from the crowd is that Batcheat was less than stunning and had a screechy singing voice.) Bolo announces that they must save the princess, and then says they've caught a spy, which he reveals to be Rashid, who saw her when she was kidnapped. He gives them details of the Chupwala Army, while Haroun befriends a Page named Blabbermouth, whom he discovers is a girl disguised as a boy. The Guppee Army forms to fight against Khattam-Shud, and on their way there they see the ocean is even more polluted than it was before, and is freezing over in certain parts.

They meet the Shadow Warrior, a soldier with a shadow that moves of its own accord — "It was as though its life in a land of darkness, of being a shadow concealed in shadows, had given it powers undreamt of by the shadows of a conventionally lit world." The warrior is in constant battle with his own shadow, and when he speaks to everyone, it's in words that only Rashid can understand. He speaks only with his hands, in what Rashid calls "Gesture Language," and he tells them Khattam-Shud has become unstoppable: "He has plunged so deeply into the Dark Art of sorcery that he has become Shadowy himself — changeable, dark, more like a Shadow than a Person." Then he reveals that Khattam-Shud can be in two places at once, and therefore they will have to beat him twice.

As they enter Khattam-Shud's territory, they are engulfed in a Web of Night, and the strange darkness is being spread throughout the land by artificial means, which is the opposite of what a lightbulb does — when the mechanism is turned on, it sucks the light out of an area rather than illuminating it. They finally find Khattam-Shud on a dark ship with shimmery edges. He's a small man who speaks in a normal voice, which is rather anticlimactic for our heroes. Like the ship, he appears to be fuzzy around the edges, like he's not entirely real. He explains that they have been carefully ruining the stories in the ocean, because each kind of story needs to be destroyed in its own way.

The two armies begin attacking each other, and Haroun jumps into the water's dark depths. At the bottom he finds the Source of the Stories: "The Source of Stories was a hole or chasm or crater in the sea-bed, and through that hole, as Haroun watched, the glowing flow of pure, unpolluted stories came bubbling up from the very heart of Kahani . . . it looked like a huge underwater fountain of shining light." The boy realizes that if he can find a way to unplug the Source, the stories will begin to flow once again.

Haroun remembers an artificial light he has with him, resurfaces, and turns it on, illuminating the place in the midst of the battle. Suddenly in the light the unreality of the shadow warriors is unveiled, and they vanish. Khattam-Shud had tried to make the light and darkness two separate things in this world, but once blended, they function again. Khattam-Shud is defeated, Princess Batcheat is rescued, and the Guppee Army returns to Gup City in triumph. Haroun is called before the Walrus, where he is told he can have one wish. But when he thinks about it, he realizes that the only thing he wants is something no one can give him. The Walrus declares this nonsense, and says what he wants is a happy ending: "Happy endings are much rarer in stories, and also in life, than most people think. You could almost say they are the exceptions, not the rule." He says that Khattam-Shud had created an artificial anti-story, and at P2C2E House they can also synthesize happy endings. Haroun says if they can do that, then he wishes for a happy ending for his entire sad city.

Rashid and Haroun return home, and Rashid begins telling the stories of their adventures, becoming a master storyteller once again. And one night, Haroun's mother comes back and says her relationship with Mr. Sengupta is "khattam-shud." When Haroun wakes up the next morning, he sees the clocks have all started working again, and he declares, "time is definitely on the move again around these parts."

Haroun and the Sea of Stories is a book about the power of story, about the war between light and dark, and about revealing reality in order to find a happy ending. It's a perfect book with which to open season 6 of *Lost*, but unfortunately, if I talk about exactly why, I will give away too much of the season that is to follow. On a surface level, it's about how everything falls apart when the Ocean of Story becomes infected. Similarly, we see in "LA X" that the water in the Temple has turned brown, as if something has happened to take away its healing powers. Just as the Ocean of Stories can no longer produce happy endings if the water is polluted, so too is Sayid unable to be truly healed in the brown waters.

He first goes through a horrific process where he is tortured and drowned, and only then comes back to life — but what sort of life has he come back to?

There are several moments in Rushdie's book that are reminiscent of themes on *Lost*. Haroun speaks to the Eggheads at P2C2E House and they discuss the merits of science versus faith. The question that haunts both Haroun and Rashid throughout the book is "what's the use of stories that aren't even true?" Haroun wonders if Rashid is nothing more than a liar with social power, which is a good description of Ben Linus. As the Guppee Army enters the darkness of the Web of Night, Haroun can hear whispers all around him, much like the ones in the jungle on the island.

Haroun asks Mali the Gardener at one point how Bolo can be so sure of his target when everyone else in the army was so disorganized and unable to make up their minds. Mali replies, "It is Love . . . it is all for Love. Which is a wonderful and dashing matter. But which can also be a very foolish thing." Similarly, Desmond, who we see reading this book in the episode, has acted out of love in just about everything he's done on the show.

Some elements in the book could be seen as commentary on *Lost* itself. In order to travel to Gup City, Haroun has to ride on a bird that only came alive through his imagination, which shows how powerful imagination can be. *Lost* has demanded more from its audience than simple willing suspension of disbelief; it calls upon each of its viewers to use their imagination to interpret the show just as much as the writers have used theirs to create it. *Lost* itself is filled with "processes too complicated to explain," but like the Eggheads in P2C2E House, the writers attempt to give the viewers the tools to figure out the processes, stories, and mysteries in much the same way that Haroun figures out things by the end.

On their journey, Butt the Hoopoe splashes the water and Haroun can see the story streams being mixed up and blended. When he asks if that would ruin the stories, Butt counters, "Any story worth its salt can handle a little shaking up!" Just as Rushdie's writing often blends more than one genre, so too does *Lost* combine the genres of drama, comedy, romance, action-adventure, science fiction, and fantasy.

Much of season 6 is about the struggle between dark and light on the island, and how the world will plunge into darkness if the light on the island — and within each one of the characters — somehow goes out. The sideways world already looks like a place of happy endings, at least for most of the characters. But, as Haroun asks at the end of the book, is it real?

6.3 What Kate Does

Original air date: February 9, 2010
Written by: Edward Kitsis, Adam Horowitz
Directed by: Paul Edwards
Guest cast: William Mapother (Ethan Goodspeed), Rob McElhenney (Aldo), Dayo Ade (Justin), Jenni Blong (Lindsey), Traci Lee Burgard (Officer Rasmussen), Yasmin Dar (OB Nurse), Tania Kahale (Admitting Nurse), David H. Lawrence XVII (Cab Driver)

Focus: Kate and Claire

While Sawyer separates himself from the others to grieve for Juliet, Jack must decide whether or not to tell Sayid to take a pill that Dogen claims will save him. In the sideways world, we see what happens after Kate hijacks Claire's cab.

"What Kate Does" is probably the least satisfying of all of the sideways world stories in season 6, but there's still a lot to like about this episode. The title of the episode is meant to conjure up the title of the season 2 episode "What Kate Did." But interestingly, it's in the present tense here, suggesting that this is about what Kate does now, has always done, and always will do.

Kate's life has been marked by the fact that she tries to show her love and caring for others, but inadvertently hurts them instead. She killed her abusive alcoholic stepfather when she discovered he was her biological father, but she convinced herself she was doing it to protect her mother from further beatings from him ("What Kate Does"). She left her childhood sweetheart, Tom, and when she reunited with him, he was killed ("Born to Run"). She married Kevin and was deeply in love with him, but left him when she acknowledged within herself the deep-seated need to keep running ("I Do"). The only person she ever ran back to was her mother, the one woman in her life who actually pushed Kate away and told her never to come back ("Left Behind"). Aaron was the one person who made her stop running for three years, until she left him again. But this time, she's doing something so she can return to him and give him a better life, not abandon him like she did everyone else.

Kate's fear that she will hurt those closest to her forces her to keep everyone at a distance, always running from them so she won't get too close to anyone. On the island, she's the same way. She avoided all talk about what had happened to her before the crash, mentally running away from her problems and hoping to sweep them away in her new island life. And yet, she desperately wanted to get off the island, despite what awaited her in the outside world. Kate hates the thought of being corralled, and the island was one big prison to her. She ran from Jack and she ran from Sawyer. Aaron was the only person who eventually got her to stay still, but that didn't last long before she was running back to the island, then running away from Dharmaville, and now she leaves again.

Sawyer, too, is running away from everyone else, turning back into the solitary man he was in season 1. He's angry about and shattered by Juliet's death. Although that same day he was looking in Kate's direction as Rose was talking about being with the one that you love, he really did love Juliet in his own way. We discover in this episode that he was intending to marry her and settle down, but now that she's gone, he doesn't want to be with anyone . . . not even Kate. Just as Sawyer pined for Kate in her absence, it's not until he loses Juliet that he realizes how much he loved her.

The beautiful Emilie de Ravin, who proves how different Claire looks when she has access to hair care products. (Sue Schneider/Shooting Star)

Kate leaves the Temple, and brilliantly escapes Aldo and Justin, the two Others who have been assigned to watch her. But instead of running away from the Temple, she is running *to* something — Sawyer. When she gets to him, she realizes he doesn't want her anymore. As he pushes her away from him, she breaks down; she knows exactly how he feels, because, like him, she's always run away from everyone she cares about.

Sayid has spent a lifetime facing up to what he's done, and yet he just keeps coming back to the same violent behavior. Now, Dogen straps him to a table and forces Sayid to undergo the same tortures that he put other people through. Sayid asked Hurley in the previous episode what sort of place he was going to after he died. After what Dogen does to him, he couldn't be faulted for thinking he's in

Hell. Jack, who feels responsible for the death of Juliet and partially responsible for what happened to Sayid, stands before Dogen and ultimately throws a poison-filled pill (meant for Sayid) into his own mouth, willing to accept whatever might happen. Jack is ready to face his responsibilities, and will risk his own life to save those of the people he cares about.

Dogen refers to Sayid as being "infected," and says it's the same thing that happened to Claire. It's not clear exactly what he means, but it sounds a lot like what Danielle Rousseau referred to as the "sickness" on the island. In season 1 she explained that once her team had been in contact with the smoke monster, they became infected, and she was forced to kill all of them. The sickness, in essence, turned them into people very much unlike themselves, and made them dangerous. We saw Robert, Rousseau's husband, try to kill her, and the rest of her team go mad. Desmond was seen inoculating himself against a unnamed contagion every morning, but that was more likely due to the perceived radiation in the atmosphere (or that Inman was just screwing with him). As well, Claire had been inoculated against a sickness by Ethan, because he feared her baby might not survive on the island. But what happened to Rousseau's team is the closest thing to what has happened to Sayid. Perhaps the water, which used to be the healing water of Jacob, has now turned into something else, infected by Smokey. Does this mean Sayid will lose the caring side of him, and just become an even more dangerous man with no conscience?

In this episode, the island story feeds our curiosity and multiplies our questions about what happened to Sayid. Unfortunately, the sideways-world story lacks the same intensity, simply because it feels too familiar. Kate seems to be an only slightly harsher version of the Kate Austen we know. We've seen how much she hates to hurt anyone around her, even though they often *do* get hurt, and here she refuses to let Claire leave the cab, terrorizing her by waving a gun in her face only to realize Claire is pregnant, and then we see the old Austen remorse return.

It's in this moment that the logic of the episode breaks down: a woman on the run from the law, driving a cab that was probably long ago called in as stolen, would hardly backtrack to a spot near the airport and then offer to become the taxi driver for the girl she left behind. (Not to mention that Claire has little sense of self-preservation if she just gets back into the car driven by a gun-wielding maniac who just stole everything she owned and clearly is wanted by police.) And then she walks that girl up to the door of a house, just so yet another person could later claim to have seen her when her face shows up on the evening news? *And*

Josh Holloway and Evangeline Lilly, in happier times. (Chris Pizzello/AP Photo)

then they both go to the hospital, which is no doubt crawling with police officers?! Claire has been seen with Kate by the taxi driver and Lindsey, so when the police come to question her in the hospital it's clear they know she was with Kate . . . and yet they leave after about two questions and never check out the room where Kate is hiding a couple of feet away.

The message that we're supposed to take from all of this, of course, is that Kate and Claire were always meant to be entwined in some way and that some mysterious force is bringing them together. In the original timeline, Kate helps Claire deliver Aaron, and later raises him when Claire is unable to. Now she plays the part of Claire's protector, and you can see a glimmer of recognition on her face when Claire first says Aaron's name, as if she knows that name is important to her, but she just doesn't know how. Kate sees Aaron's heart beating on the monitor and stares at it like she knows it intimately — and in the original timeline, she does.

But the problem with the story is that they didn't offer enough of a break from the other timeline to make it interesting. When Ethan appears as the ob/gyn in the hospital, for example, it warms the viewers' hearts. Without the island, Ethan wasn't taken by the Others; he stayed with his parents, Amy and Horace (and kept his father's name, "Goodspeed") and became a successful doctor. He's not trapped somewhere trying to keep pregnant women alive and failing miserably; he's actually a happy person with a wonderful bedside manner. The little boy who turned into a pawn for the Others and who was eventually gunned down by Charlie is a completely different person here, and we can't help but smile to see how one person's life was saved because the island wasn't a part of it. But in the case of Claire and Kate, we don't have that feeling yet.

What *is* interesting in the sideways world, however, is the fact that secrets in the original timeline have become common knowledge in this one. Jack tells Locke that his father died; Locke tells Jack that he was paralyzed. Claire tells Kate that she was going to give Aaron up for adoption; Kate tells Claire that she's a fugitive. Of course, the circumstances of the sideways world make it difficult for anyone to keep secrets from one another: it's clear that Locke is in a wheelchair, that Kate is on the run from the law, and Claire having to meet the adoptive parents gives that one away to Kate.

Kate will only find redemption if she stops running and faces her demons and responsibilities. With the surprise appearance of Claire on the island in the final moments of the episode, there's a suggestion that we'll see these two similar Kates come together, and perhaps stop running, with Claire as their constant.

Highlight: Miles bringing Sayid up to speed on things: "As you can see, Hugo here has assumed the leadership position, so . . . that's pretty great."
Did You Notice?:
- In the opening of season 1's "Raised by Another," we saw a nightmare that Claire had, where she was no longer pregnant and she couldn't find Aaron. When she discovered his crib, it was drenched in blood. A menacing John Locke sat nearby at a table looking at Tarot cards, and his eyes were the black and white stones from the Adam and Eve skeletons in the cave, and he said to her, "He was your responsibility but you gave him away, Claire. Everyone pays the price now." The dream was prophetic: the pure Locke (represented by the white stone) has given way to the evil one (represented by the black stone) and one could argue that everything fell apart after Claire let Aaron go.
- Sawyer makes a snide remark to Kate about how Iraqi torturers who kill children should be given a second chance. This is another reference to the

Josh Holloway and Evangeline Lilly wait between takes to shoot the scene at the end of the dock. (Courtesy KOS Tours)

fact that on the island, death often seems merciful, whereas "bad" characters are allowed to live.
- Kate pulls out a killer whale doll from Claire's bag. It's the same whale doll that Kate bought Aaron when she was raising him; we saw it in "Something Nice Back Home" when Jack was yelling at Kate, and Aaron wandered out into the hall. Not only is it a clear reminder of the black-and-white theme on the show, but it's a fun detail, suggesting that Aaron was always destined to have that little whale.
- Dogen's torture session was a lot like the one Rousseau inflicted on Sayid in "Solitary," complete with Sayid being strapped to a table and electrocuted.
- Ethan tells Claire, "I don't want to stick you with needles if I don't have to," which is a sly reference to "Maternity Leave," when we saw Ethan sticking Claire with many unnecessary needles.

Hugh Everett III's Many-Worlds Theory

It's long been a favorite of sci-fi writers and filmmakers, and in the 2009–2010 television season it turned up in three different series — *Fringe*, *FlashForward*, and *Lost*. Hugh Everett III's theory on parallel universes was laughed at in his time, but is now one of the most influential theories in quantum mechanics. And many fans wondered at the beginning of season 6 if it could be the answer to what the sideways world represented.

Niels Bohr, the father of quantum mechanics, said that large objects obey the classical laws of physics, but that small objects — atoms — follow a more unpredictable path: in fact, atoms are able to occupy many spaces simultaneously. Inside each atom there is a nucleus with several electrons buzzing around it. They don't move in an orderly fashion, but rather are many places at once, flying around the nucleus, never touching but always attracted to it. Bohr stated that the moment an atom is observed, it immediately ceases this crazy behavior and acts differently, taking on only one property. Hugh Everett didn't buy this theory, saying it didn't make sense that an atom would behave differently just because someone was observing it.

Erwin Schrödinger didn't buy it, either. He developed his now-infamous cat theory in response to Bohr's hypothesis. The idea is that a cat is trapped in a sealed box with a bowl of radioactive matter such as uranium. Beside that bowl is a Geiger counter, which is attached to a hammer. The hammer is poised over a bottle of a toxic gas. If the uranium breaks down and releases a single atom of gas, it will trigger the Geiger counter, which will cause the hammer to break the glass, killing the cat. Schrödinger claimed that, according to Bohr, until the box is opened and the cat is observed, either dead or alive, it will continue to be both at once, because, he said, atoms are in several places at once until observed. So until someone opens the box, the cat is both dead and not dead. Schrödinger said that's not possible. Everett agreed.

The observer plays no role in Everett's theory; instead he believes everything obeys the laws of quantum mechanics, not classical laws of physics, and he introduced the idea of splitting, which is how parallel universes occur. It solves the paradox of Schrödinger's cat, for according to Everett's theory, the cat isn't simultaneously alive and dead; it exists in two different universes, dead in one, alive in the other. In the BBC Four documentary, *Parallel Worlds, Parallel Lives*, Everett's son, rock musician Mark Oliver Everett, otherwise known as E of the rock band Eels, decides to embark on a journey to discover more about his famous father. In that documentary, Everett's theory is explained thusly: "According to [Hugh Everett], with every choice and decision we make, with every event in our life that could happen in more ways than one, universes branch off in different directions. Every time we make a decision, we divide into two different versions of ourselves. This is how parallel universes are born."

Think of the movie *Sliding Doors*, where in one universe Gwyneth Paltrow's character makes it through the doors of the subway and on to the next stop, and in the other world she doesn't make it through the doors and is left standing on the platform. This one seemingly insignificant moment in her life branches off into two chains of cause and effect, and causes her two parallel lives to become significantly different from one another. The same idea has been used in *Star Trek*, *Donnie Darko*, Philip Pullman's His Dark Materials series, and countless other science-fiction stories.

In the BBC documentary a physics professor shows E an experiment where he demonstrates how a photon, passing through two slits in a wall, will split into two to pass through it, and then recombine on the other side. "A single object is in two places at once," he says, and it begs the question, if atoms can be in two places at once, why can't we?

- When Dogen says that Sayid's bullet wound was Jack's fault, he cuts to the heart of Jack's misery the most. By telling Jack that this is his chance to redeem himself, Dogen puts Jack in a difficult position, since redemption is the one thing Jack needs right now.
- Claire having false contractions is a parallel with the false contractions she had the first moment we saw her in the pilot episode, and then again in the jungle with Charlie in season 1.
- Dogen is playing with a baseball when Jack walks in the room, a reminder of his dad's comment, "That's why the Red Sox will never win the World Series."
- Dogen says to Jack that he needs to remain separate from his people because it makes it easier when they don't like his decisions. In "Stranger in a Strange Land," one of the Others (Isabel, the "judge" character that we never see again) claims that Jack's tattoo translates to "He walks amongst us, but he is not one of us." That episode has always stood out as being unrelated to the rest of the series, but Dogen's comment here makes it relevant. He is suggesting that he lives by the very credo that Jack has inked on his arm. But clearly Jack can't live like that; while he claims to be separate, he made himself one of the group early on and seems too altruistic to truly separate himself from other people.
- In the season 1 episode, "Born to Run," Kate used the alias "Joan Hart," the same one she uses in the sideways world.

Interesting Facts: Rob McElhenney, who plays Aldo, now stars as Mac on *It's Always Sunny in Philadelphia*. While uncredited, the mechanic is played by character actor Jeff Kober, who has appeared on dozens of television shows including *The X-Files* and *Sons of Anarchy*, and is known to *Buffy the Vampire Slayer* fans as the vampire Kralik ("Helpless") and the magic "dealer" Rack. Dayo Ade, who plays Justin, may be familiar to fans of *Degrassi Junior High*, on which he played the character "BLT."

When Arzt says, "I'm walkin' here, *I'm walkin' here!*" he's quoting the famous line from *Midnight Cowboy*, where Ratso Rizzo (Dustin Hoffman) is crossing the street and almost gets hit by a taxi.

Hiroyuki Sanada, who plays Dogen, is a Japanese actor who is well known in his home country, and is recognizable to North American audiences for his roles in *Rush Hour 3*, *Speed Racer* (with Matthew Fox), and *The Last Samurai*. He explained that *Lost* is very popular in Japan, and he was surprised and excited when Carlton and Damon contacted him to be on the show. In the month and a half before he got his first script, he watched the entire series so he would know what was happening on the island, because he believed Dogen would have known everything, so he should, too.

Dogen's name comes from Dogen Zenji (1200–1253), who was a Zen Buddhist master of one of the three sects of Japanese Buddhism. He brought Soto Zen to Japan, where it still thrives today, and he was the Master of the Eihei Temple for over a decade. His desire was to bring the peaceful principles of Zen Buddhism to as many people as he could, and his writings on the subject, his Dharma essays, are still revered today.

Kate insists that she's innocent of the crime she's being charged with, and she's quite convincing. At the San Diego Comic-Con that preceded season 6 (see page x), Darlton showed a clip of *America's Most Wanted*, which reported that Kate was charged with killing an apprentice at her stepfather's company who just happened to be in the building on the day it had been rigged to blow. Is it possible that Wayne had rigged the gasline to blow up the building and he set her up to take the fall, and that's why he wasn't there that day?

When asked if he thought Kate would end up with Sawyer at the end of the series, Josh Holloway made the Jaters (those fans who want to see Jack and Kate end up together) very happy when he said, "I think she would have a happier life with Jack . . . more so than with Sawyer."

Nitpicks: Kate reassures Claire that she didn't take her money when she returns in the taxi. If she didn't take any of Claire's money, then how did she pay the mechanic $200 for removing her handcuffs? Dangerous criminals in handcuffs don't get to carry a wallet full of escape money. Also, in New Otherton Kate is getting water from a tap outside of one of the houses, but if there's been no plumbing on the island for three years, how could that water possibly be clean?

Oops: Claire's ultrasound readout says the date is 10/22/2004, which puts the flight in October, not September. Damon Lindelof and Carlton Cuse confirmed that that date was indeed a production error. (The picture also says it's 9:29 in the morning, and considering the plane landed in broad daylight and Claire and Kate have been running around for several hours, that time must be wrong.)

4 8 15 16 23 42: The license plate on the taxicab that Kate steals is 4DQS554. (There are two 4s in that, and D is the fourth letter of the alphabet.) The time of the ultrasound is 9:24:**42**.

It's Just a Flesh Wound: Sayid is electrocuted as well as burned with a hot poker. Kate hits Aldo in the head with her water canteen and unleashes a bag of rocks on Justin. Aldo knees Jin in the stomach. Jin gets his leg caught in a bear trap. Claire shoots Aldo twice and Justin once.

Lost in Translation: As the two men grab Sayid and march him away, Dogen says in Japanese, "I'll take Jarrah. Do whatever it takes to get Ford back here." After Dogen finishes torturing Sayid, he says to Lennon, "Tell him he passed the test." Everything else is pretty much exactly as Lennon translates it.

Any Questions?:
- What is Dogen typing on that ancient computer? Is he keeping a diary of sorts?
- In the previous episode Lennon and his thugs insisted that Jack *had* to come with them immediately, and he had to come alone. And yet, in this episode, that urgency has evaporated. Why did they need him so badly just a moment earlier?
- In "Raised by Another," Claire goes to see psychic Richard Malkin, and he tells her that it's very important for her to get on the flight. On the island, Claire realizes he knew there was no family waiting for Aaron on the other side, and that once she was cast away on the island, Claire would be forced to raise her baby, which is what he wanted. Does Malkin play a part in the sideways world? If there's an adoptive mom in L.A., does that suggest that Malkin really was telling the truth, or are the timelines completely separate?
- When Kate tells Lennon that she knows how to get Sawyer back, she adds, "I can be very convincing when I want to be." Is she suggesting that she's always just used Sawyer when she needed him? Could she have been lying to him in the past about her feelings?
- Why was Dogen torturing Sayid like that? What did those tests prove? Was he looking to see if the smoke monster had inhabited him in some way?
- What does Dogen mean when he says the infection will spread? Does he mean it'll spread within Sayid's body, or to other people?
- Is it true that Claire has the same "infection" that Sayid has?
- What does Justin mean when he says Jin may be "one of them"?

Ashes to Ashes: Aldo was an Other and we first saw him in season 3 as he was keeping guard outside Room 23, where Karl was being held. He had an interest in time travel and physics (he was reading Stephen Hawking's *A Brief History of Time* while keeping guard), but he was easily fooled. Kate, Sawyer, and Alex tricked him with the old Wookiee prisoner ploy. Also, as is evident in this episode, he was a jerk.

6.4   The Substitute

Original air date: February 16, 2010
Written by: Elizabeth Sarnoff, Melinda Hsu Taylor
Directed by: Tucker Gates
Guest cast: Suzanne Krull (Temp Agency Interviewer), Katey Sagal (Helen), Eddie L. Cavett (Courier), Kenton Duty (Teenage Boy), Billy Ray Gallion (Randy Nations), Joshua Smith (School Kid)

Focus: Locke

The smoke monster finally tells Sawyer why he's been brought to the island. In the sideways world, John Locke struggles to decide whether to ask Jack to help him walk again or to accept what has happened to him.

By this fourth hour of the season, fan speculation about what the sideways world represented was running rampant. There are definitely similarities between the two worlds, and the characters are essentially the same. It's not wrong to simply imagine that the sideways world is what their lives would have been like if Jacob had never touched them, if they'd never been predestined to get onto a plane that was going to crash into the island, if they'd been allowed to make their own choices in their lives. If so, they'd still be Jack, John, Kate, and James, but their lives would be different as a result of following different paths.

In the previous episode, "What Kate Does," the sideways world story fell a little flat simply because it was too similar to the one we already knew. By the time this episode aired, some fans were saying that the sideways-world stories were all boring, and if season 1 of the show had included *these* stories, everyone would have switched the channel. I agree. Watching everyone have a pat, happy ending and drop the damaging baggage that has dogged them over the past few years *is* a little boring. But the reason these particular stories in season 6 transcend that is *because* we've seen the other world. As viewers, we impose the stories we already know to be true from the original timeline onto these alternate-reality stories — one begins to inform and alter the other. And that is what makes the sideways world so fascinating, fun, and exciting to watch.

Compared to many other characters, we know a lot about what John Locke's life was like in the original timeline, and when you look back over it, one thing stands out: John Locke's death certainly wasn't the first time he "didn't understand"; life threw him one confusing curveball after another. Born several weeks premature, Locke spent his formative years being tossed from one foster family to another, unable to comprehend why no one loved him enough to adopt him. In 1961, when he was five, he was seen by Richard Alpert, who (in the usual sci-fi corkscrew logic of time travel) had been visited by an adult Locke seven years earlier on the island in 1954. Locke had insisted Richard come and find him when he would be born in 1956, that he would be special and would ultimately be chosen by Jacob. Richard believed him and spent 50 years keeping track of Locke's life as a result, first visiting him when he was an infant in an incubator. Five years later, John failed Richard's Dalai Lama–type of test that would have determined if Locke was in fact the island's Chosen One (see *Finding Lost — Season Four*, p. 145). Little John Locke watched Richard walk away from him, not understanding why he was being abandoned once again.

Years later, Locke's birth mother, who Locke later discovered was a mental patient, found him and told him he'd been born through immaculate conception ("Deus Ex Machina"). Through her he was reunited with his father, Anthony Cooper, who simply conned him out of a kidney. Angry and betrayed, Locke became obsessed with Cooper, simply wanting to know "why," because he didn't understand why his own father would have done this to him. Because of the anger management classes he was forced to take as a result of his obsession with his father, he met Helen, but it was through his continued obsession with Cooper that he ultimately lost her.

Once again alone and distraught, Locke sought refuge with a group of people living on a commune that turned out to be an enormous grow-op. Not knowing about the illegal activities, Locke inadvertently brought an undercover DEA detective onto the premises. After his new family shunned him, Locke tried to kill the detective, but couldn't pull the trigger; instead he just wanted to know why . . . once again, he didn't understand why he of all people had been chosen as the cop's dupe.

Alone and suffering from severe depression, Locke returned to his small apartment in Tustin, California, but was once again face-to-face with Anthony Cooper when he ordered Cooper to stop his con games and leave his new victim alone. The confrontation ended with John becoming a paraplegic after Cooper pushed him out of an eighth-storey window. One of the orderlies, Matthew Abaddon, suggested that Locke try a walkabout, and so he began training for one while working a boring office job at a box company. After he was refused — again left confused and angry, demanding to know why they wouldn't let him do it — he boarded Oceanic Flight 815.

On the island, Locke's ability to walk was restored, and so he saw the crash as a miracle. For the first time in his life, something good had happened to him, and he believed the island was special, and that he was special because he'd been chosen out of all of the crash survivors to have experienced something magical. He became important to the group, hunting and catching wild boar, providing them with the sustenance they needed. In the early days, he was somewhat of a mentor to Jack, actually helping him work through his issues with seeing his dead father walking on the island, or telling parables to Boone and Kate and Sawyer about things that had happened in his life. He was confident, he was sage, and people looked up to him. But when he found the hatch, he became as obsessed with opening it as he'd been with trying to understand his own father. And when Boone died trying to open it, Locke saw the island turning against him for the first time. He carried Boone to Jack, and then returned to the hatch door, having a complete breakdown, banging his fists on the door and asking repeatedly, "Why?" He didn't understand why the island had done this to him.

The hatch was opened, and inside they discovered not a mystical portal, but a mystical Scotsman, who was pushing a button every 108 minutes. Locke wanted so badly to believe that there was a purpose to him being on the island, and he thought maybe this was it. He didn't understand why he had to push the button, but he did it anyway. When he lost his faith momentarily and stopped pushing it, the Swan station simultaneously imploded and exploded, causing Locke more grief and confusion than ever before.

In the aftermath of the explosion, he found a new purpose. He began drifting from the other survivors and from their quest to reach the outside world and be rescued (blowing up the Flame station and then the sub), and became far more interested in the Others, setting his sights on being their leader. He became even more single-minded in his devotion to the island, convinced that the survivors had crashed there for a reason, and that it was a special place they shouldn't be taking for granted. But when the island became unstuck in time, he knew he had to leave the island in order to protect it, and had to bring back the people who had left. Once again he didn't understand, but he agreed to the demand, not realizing he was simply fulfilling the Man in Black's selfish desires. He tried to lure everyone back, but Sayid looked at him like he was pathetic, Kate barely gave him the time of day, Hurley ran away from him in fear, and Jack told him he was

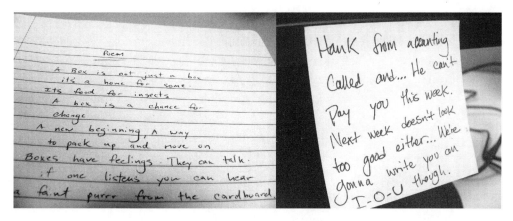

To film the box company scenes in "The Substitute," the production crew used the office of Dole Cannery. Up close you can see some of the hilarious notes that the production crew wrote up and left on desks. (Courtesy Ryan Ozawa)

crazy. He failed his mission. Life had thrown lemons at Locke, and the lemonade he tried to make turned out to be poisonous.

As Locke sat in a chair, scrawling his final words to Jack — "I just wish you'd believed me" — he was at his lowest point. Locke had had a lifetime of failure. He failed Alpert's test; he was the son no one wanted; he failed at his relationship with Helen; he brought the wolf into the marijuana-laden henhouse; he was wrong about not pushing the button; he believed he was following Jacob but he was the Man in Black's pawn; and he failed to bring back a single Lostie to the island. But he had also lived a life of confusion: he demanded to know why Anthony Cooper had taken his kidney; why the cop had chosen him as his dupe;

why the island had led him to the hatch; why the island had failed him after the hatch exploded . . . he simply didn't understand why these things happened to him. And in his final moments, he failed to take his own life; instead, Ben took it for him. As Smokey said in "LA X," his last thought was "I don't understand." There isn't a more fitting final thought for John Locke, and it's as sad as Smokey said it was.

This is the John Locke we've gotten to know for five years. Sad, kind, angry, courageous, willing, always abandoned, never loved, having a lot of love to give but unwilling to let go of his obsessions to give it. And that man's extraordinary life ended in a dirty hotel room, a cord wrapped around his neck. It is *that* life that provides the lens through which we now look at the other John Locke in the sideways world. The moment he tips out of the wheelchair and ends up face-down on his lawn with the sprinkler system going off around him, we immediately think, "Uh-oh" and brace ourselves for the tantrum that will no doubt be unleashed. But it doesn't come; instead, John begins laughing, and Helen — *Helen!* — comes running out of the house to help him. This is definitely not the same John Locke.

In the sideways world he's managed to hold onto Helen, he allows himself to be caught up in choosing fabric swatches for his upcoming wedding, he laughs at his own failures, and even after he's fired from his job and finds a gigantic Hummer blocking his entrance to his wheelchair-accessible car, he still finds a way to laugh about it. The other John Locke spent a lifetime asking why and longing for his life to be better; the sideways John Locke is content with his life the way it is and has accepted it. One of the key reasons for the difference is that in the original timeline, John believed in destiny . . . and, typical of the other destiny folks, he believed that life was doing things to him and he didn't understand why. The sideways Locke, on the other hand, doesn't believe in destiny, and instead takes responsibility for everything that has happened to him. Although Helen talks about destiny and miracles, you can tell John just isn't buying it. While we may wince as we watch Helen rip up Jack's business card, we realize that he's happy, and is sincerely okay with being in a wheelchair as long as he has Helen in his life. If this were the season 1 flashback, yes, it might seem sappy and boring. But we watch it within the context of the larger tragedy we know to be true, and it takes on a lot of resonance as a result.

When it was clear in season 5's "The Incident" that John Locke was actually dead, the revelation was shocking. After all of that character development, he didn't even make it to the final season. He was never going to be redeemed? He would never find happiness? Was this just karma's cruel joke? But perhaps the sideways world is another chance for him. Maybe over here, in this alternative reality (whatever it might represent) we'll get to see John find happiness at last.

But in the island timeline, why, then, did Smokey want John's body? It would seem that John's entire life really *was* destined to end in that hotel room simply so the Man in Black could assume his form. The island itself seems to be self-aware in ways, and if the time bloops at the beginning of season 5 were there to make certain pieces fall into place, then it purposely sent Locke to 1954 to inform Richard that he would be special . . . that way Richard ensured that Locke would eventually make it to the island, where the smoke monster appeared to Locke — and only Locke — as a flash of white, heavenly light that made him the island's disciple. He would be the one to see "Jacob" in the cabin, which would convince Ben that he was special, and then Ben would kill Locke to see if he would have a Christ-like resurrection (or so Ben says). When it appeared Locke did, Ben was ready to do whatever Locke asked him to do. And when Locke asked him to kill Jacob, he did it . . . not realizing the extent to which he and others had been manipulated.

So this, then, was Smokey's reason for choosing Locke. Just like the cop identified John as the one most "amenable to coercion" in "Further Instructions," Smokey knew that John would be the one who needed the island to be a place of miracles more than anyone else did. He would be the most gullible, the most open to doing whatever was asked of him . . . the one most "amenable to coercion." However, there's also a more immediate connection to John Locke, one that Smokey reveals in this episode. In the jungle, the Man in Black reveals to Sawyer that he feels trapped, and he just wants to be free. John Locke was similarly trapped — a paraplegic trapped in deeply frustrated life — and when he was miraculously able to walk again on the island, he tasted what it was like to be free after a long period of imprisonment. Being in Locke's body and sharing his memories, perhaps the smoke monster "remembers" how it felt for John when he stood up for the first time on the beach, and wants to experience his own version of it. His monologue in this episode, where he talks about his sad past, finally casts a tiny shaft of sympathetic light on him. Maybe Smokey isn't as bad as we thought he was.

The sideways world provides commentary on what has happened to John — just like a substitute teacher, John is only standing in for someone else. He wanted to be

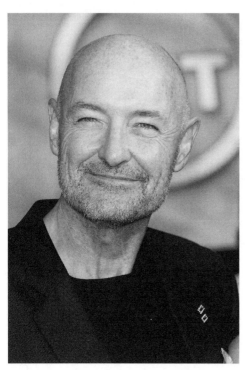

Only the brilliant Terry O'Quinn could have played John Locke, the Man in Black, and sideways John Locke with such subtle differences. (Sthanlee B. Mirador/Shooting Star)

the leader of the island, but he was never meant to be the leader . . . he was simply the stand-in until the teacher — Smokey — was able to resume his place at the front of the class. Just as a substitute teacher appears to be running the class but is actually following a lesson plan written by the regular teacher, so does John Locke appear to be walking around the island, but his body is being controlled by someone else.

This episode offers a huge revelation to viewers when Smokey takes Sawyer to Jacob's caves and finally reveals the answers to two big questions: why the people on the plane were brought to the island, and what the significance of Hurley's six numbers is. With a casual remark — "Jacob had a thing for numbers" — Smokey explains that the six numbers that have dominated everyone's life on the show correspond to numbers Jacob randomly assigned certain people on his list. Those six people — Shephard, Reyes, Ford, Locke, Kwon, and Jarrah — had been chosen by Jacob as possible "Candidates," people who qualify for the role of replacing him as the protector of the island. Smokey insists that the island doesn't need protecting from anything, and doesn't clarify what exactly Jacob is protecting. And because of what we know of him, we can't be sure he's telling the truth. (It's almost as if the writers introduced the character of Benjamin Linus to prepare us for the Man in Black.)

In a previous episode, we see Jacob touch each of the Candidates; his touch was probably to mark them and to lead them to the island, guiding them to make certain decisions in their lives that would lead them onto Flight 815. Sayid is one of the Candidates, and in "LA X" Jacob looks very sad when he realizes Sayid's been critically wounded as he lies next to the Dharma van. The urgency to save him was in part because he was a Candidate, and Jacob seems to have put the welfare of the island before Sayid's own well-being (since it would seem death might be preferable to what Sayid is about to go through if Dogen is to be believed). Was the test in the water some sort of experiment to see if Sayid really had what it took to be a Candidate? Similarly, Dogen pleads with Sawyer to stay in the Temple. Again, it's because he knows Sawyer is still a Candidate. But when Kate says she'll go and find him, he doesn't have the same concern. Now that we see her name crossed off the wall, it would appear she was once a Candidate but is no longer one. It's not clear why she was crossed off; was her name on the list that was inside the wooden ankh in the guitar case?

In this episode, we see more of what Smokey is all about (including an awesome Smokey-cam sequence where we see the island travels from his perspective), and despite him being juxtaposed as the dark counterpoint to Jacob — presumably the evil to Jacob's good — the writers go to lengths to humanize him. He tells Sawyer he was a man once, and pleads a case that he was actually wronged by someone else, and is the way he is because of what was done to him, not because he wants to be this way: "I know what it was like to feel joy, to feel pain, anger, fear. To experience betrayal. I know what it's like to lose someone you love." When he sees the image of a boy in the jungle, it unnerves him. The previously unflappable smoke monster is suddenly rattled, and John Locke's confusion and fury begins to seep through his cold exterior as he shouts John's signature line, "Don't tell me what I can't do!" Is Locke still in there somewhere? Who wronged him? Was it Jacob? Is it possible that Jacob is actually the bad guy and Smokey the good guy? Or is there no such thing as pure evil and pure good, and just like in the real world, the island offers only various shades of gray?

Highlight: A tie between Ben Linus's appearance as an anal-retentive European history teacher bitching about the coffee filters in the sideways world and the craziest eulogy ever: "John Locke was a . . . a believer. He was a man of faith. He was . . . a much better man than I will ever be. And I'm very sorry I murdered him."

Did You Notice?:
- Locke's neighborhood looked like the same one Nadia was in when he was doing her home inspection (which was also in Tustin, California).
- When Locke looks at the upholstery swatches, he at first chooses the one that's hunter green.
- When Locke is sitting in his cubicle, you can see a photograph of him and Cooper hunting on the day that Cooper told him he needed a new kidney

in "Deus Ex Machina." Beside that picture is one of John and Helen, and it looks a lot like the Desmond/Penny photo.
- John's boss, Randy, is the same Randy that we saw teasing him in "Walkabout" and was Hurley's awful boss at Mr. Cluck's Chicken Shack.
- Smokey says to Richard, "I'll be seeing you," which is an oft-used line in *The Prisoner* (see *Finding Lost — Season Three*, pp. 81–85).
- I hate to point this out, but it would appear Sawyer has thrown hygiene to the wind and has started using his shorts as a toilet. Ick.
- While everyone else, including Ben and Richard Alpert, were duped into believing that Smokey was John Locke, Sawyer instantly sees through the veil.
- Hugo refers to Randy Nations as a "huge douche" (ha!). In "Some Like It Hoth," he referred to Pierre Chang as a douche.
- Terry O'Quinn (or the stand-in, if that was a stand-in) deserves extra pay for having a tarantula scurry off his head like that. *Shudder*.
- In the original timeline, the loopy career counsellor who asks Locke what animal he would describe himself as was the fake fortune-teller that Papa Reyes hired to try to trick Hurley ("Tricia Tanaka Is Dead").
- Rose is the same no-nonsense person in this reality as she is in the other one.
- The last time Sawyer recounted the final scene in *Of Mice and Men*, Ben was walking him up the hill to show him the other island in "Every Man for Himself" (in that episode we saw that Sawyer read the book while he was in prison). Sawyer put himself in Lenny's place and was calling Ben "George." But in this instance, he sees himself as George, and Smokey is the Lenny he's out in the jungle to execute. (See *Finding Lost — Season Three*, pp. 35–39 for the synopsis of *Of Mice and Men*).
- Jack's cell number is the same in both realities.
- Helen is wearing a shirt that says "Peace & Karma, Joy and Tranquility," which is perhaps a comment on the karmic qualities of the sideways world.
- In the sideways world, John's alarm clock sounds exactly like the alarm in the Swan station when the numbers were counting down.
- In *Finding Lost — Season Four*, page 149, I talked about the biblical Jacob's ladder imagery that the writers have employed in the Locke flashbacks. In one he was lying at the bottom of the staircase, in the position of biblical Jacob looking up at Heaven ("Further Instructions"). In the other he's at

The Cave Ceiling

Aside from the six "Candidates" among the survivors (bolded here), you can see several other names all crossed out on the cave ceiling. The following is a list of the names I could make out, with suggestions of who they refer to in parentheses:

> 4 – **Locke**
> 8 – **Reyes**
> 10 – Mattingly (one of the names on the soldier uniforms the Others wore in 1954)
> 15 – **Ford**
> 16 – **Jarrah**
> 20 – Rousseau (Danielle or Alex)
> 23 – **Shephard**
> 37 – Rutherford (Shannon)
> 42 – **Kwon**
> 51 – Austen (Kate)
> 64 – Goldstein
> 71 – Straume (Miles)
> 77 – Franetzki
> 90 – Troup (Gary, the author of the terrible book *Bad Twin*; he was the guy who was sucked into the jet engine in the pilot episode)
> 115 – Bargas
> 117 – Linus (Ben or Roger)
> 119 – Almeida
> 195 – Pace (Charlie)
> 222 – O'Toole
> 233 – Jones (the soldier whose name was on the uniform Widmore wore in 1954?)
> 291 – Domingo
> 313 – Littleton (Claire or Aaron)
> 317 – Cunningham (one of the names on the soldier uniforms the Others wore in 1954)
> 346 – Grant

The remaining names had numbers that couldn't be made out:

> Chang (Pierre)
> Goodspeed (Horace, Amy, Olivia, or Ethan)
> Burke (Juliet)
> Lacombe
> Lewis (Charlotte)
> Faraday (Daniel)
> Aguila
> Costa
> Peterson

the top of the staircase looking down, like one of the angels or a God figure ("Cabin Fever"). In the end he seemed to have wrestled with the dark angel that is Ben, the way biblical Jacob did in the wilderness, but he lost the fight. Interestingly, in this episode, Sawyer and Smokey climb down island Jacob's wooden ladders, bringing the imagery full circle.

- Inside the cave is a scale with one white rock, one black one, which are reminiscent of the black and white stones in the pouch found with the bodies of Adam and Eve, the two skeletons that Jack found in "House of the Rising Sun." The stones presumably represent Jacob (white) and Smokey (black).

Interesting Facts: Jack's business card puts St. Sebastian Hospital at 8444 Wilshire Blvd.; in reality, there's a large art deco building at that address that houses an agency representing several Hollywood screenwriters and directors. In "Dead Is Dead," when Ben went to confront the smoke monster, you could see an ancient carving on the wall of the smoke monster being summoned by Anubis, the Egyptian god of the dead. In Egyptian mythology, when you died, there was a world between death and the afterlife where Anubis would guide you, and he would weigh your heart on a scale to see whether you had leaned more to good than evil. It's interesting that there is a similar set of scales in the cave.

Oops: On Jack's business card, the last dash in his phone number is missing.

4 8 15 16 23 42: Locke gets up at 6:15. St. Sebastian Hospital is located at 8444 Wilshire Blvd. Locke asks the class to open their books to Chapter 4. Many of the people Jacob touched all correspond to a number: 4–Locke 8–Reyes; 15–Ford; 16–Jarrah; 23–Shephard; 42–Kwon.

It's Just a Flesh Wound: Richard's face is beat up, and when Smokey cuts the rope holding him up in a tree, Richard drops to the ground heavily. When the moorings of Sawyer's ladder give way, Sawyer slams into the rock face.

Any Questions?:

- Considering how close John seems to be to his father in the sideways world, it would seem Locke didn't end up in the wheelchair because his father threw him out a window this time. Perhaps Cooper was still behind it somehow, but why else would Helen say they should invite his dad and her parents to a shotgun wedding? (Unless of course she meant that the shotgun was aimed at Cooper.)
- Why didn't Jacob tell Richard about the Candidates?
- Why is the usually calm and cool Richard Alpert completely unhinged and

running around the jungle with his Muppet arms flailing above his head? Is he in serious danger now that Jacob is dead? What is his relation to the Man in Black?
- What did Smokey mean when he said, "I'll be seeing you, Richard . . . sooner than you think"?
- Who is the little boy? Is it a younger Jacob? Could it be a younger Smokey? Does this mean that the dead people on the island aren't actually incarnations of Smokey, despite what fans have believed?
- How much does Ilana know? Does she know the Man in Black couldn't kill Jacob? Does she believe what Ben is saying? What does she mean when she says Smokey's recruiting?
- Why was she collecting Jacob's ashes? What does she plan to do with them?
- Why can Sawyer see the kid but Richard can't? Does that make Sawyer *the* Candidate?
- Why didn't Rose talk to Hurley at all when she was on the plane with him if he was in fact her boss?
- In the season 2 episode, "S.O.S.," we saw a Rose-and-Bernard flashback where Rose found out she had cancer and Bernard took her to see a faith healer named Isaac of Uluru, but he couldn't heal her. Nonetheless, she told Bernard that she was healed. If Rose has cancer in this reality, too, did she go to Isaac's place in Australia? Was Bernard so happy on the plane because he believed she'd been healed? Or have they both, like Locke, accepted the fact of her cancer, and they were just having a fun vacation in Australia?
- Who was Smokey when he was a real man? Did he look like the Man in Black we saw in "The Incident"? Or was that just another body that he'd taken on?
- Ilana says that Smokey is stuck this way and now can't change bodies again. Why? He was able to change them before, so why is he stuck in this body now? Is it because Jacob's dead?
- By "Kwon," was Jacob referring to both Sun and Jin? Or just one of them? We saw Jacob touch both of them at their wedding, so it's not clear which one is intended.
- Kate wasn't one of the numbers, but you can see she was a Candidate at one time and has now been crossed off. Why did Jacob reject her? Has she done something wrong?
- Why were the very people that Jacob thought were Candidates the same

ones who left the island (with the exception of Sawyer)? Is the fact that Sawyer is the only one who stayed behind significant?
- When Eloise sent them all back to the island, was she in cahoots with Jacob somehow?

Music/Bands: When Sawyer is sitting in New Otherton, he's listening to "Search and Destroy" by Iggy & the Stooges from the band's 1973 album, *Raw Power* (someone in Dharmaville had good taste!). In the song, Iggy Pop sings that someone has to save his soul, and he's feeling completely nihilistic. Eerily, he says his baby "detonates" for him. Sawyer must have been moving the needle back to listen to the same song over and over, because it's playing both when Smokey first peeks through the window, and again later when he returns.

6.5 Lighthouse

Original air date: February 23, 2010
Written by: Carlton Cuse, Damon Lindelof
Directed by: Jack Bender
Guest cast: Veronica Hamel (Jack's Mom), Dayo Ade (Justin), Sean Kinerney (Dogen's son)

Focus: Jack
Jack and Hurley find Jacob's lighthouse and are shocked to discover what's inside, while sideways-world Jack has a heart-to-heart with . . . his son.

Jack is a daddy?! The guy who has more father issues than Oedipus has become one himself? This had got to be the biggest surprise in the sideways world, and the most welcome; after all, there's no better way to come to terms with an unhappy childhood than to discover that you've foisted one onto your own offspring.

Jack has had more flashback episodes than any other character, and from the beginning of season 1, regardless of how interesting other characters have been, it has always been clear that Matthew Fox is considered the lead actor on the show, and Jack Shephard the main protagonist. From the first flashback, the problem that has plagued Jack the most has been his complicated relationship with his father. Christian Shephard was a prominent doctor who became the chief surgeon

Matthew Fox, looking like he could probably conjure up some poignant Jears at any moment. (Armando Gallo/Retna)

at St. Sebastian Hospital, and almost as if to ensure he would remain in his father's shadow, Jack followed him and became a surgeon himself. Christian always pushed Jack hard. When Jack was a child, he got into a fight with some bullies who had picked on his friend Marc ("White Rabbit"). When he had to appear before his father, brandishing a black eye, his father told him to stop playing the hero, because he'd fail, and added "you just don't have what it takes." Thus began a lifetime of Jack trying to prove his father wrong by attempting to do the impossible time and again.

As a med student, Jack operated on his first patient, and he did just fine until he accidentally cut her dural sac ("The Incident, Part 2"). Christian remained calm and told a panicked Jack to count to five, which Jack did before calmly finishing the procedure and saving the girl's life. In Jack's mind, Christian had humiliated him in front of the nurses in the room, and he became angry with his father for not believing in him. "Are you sure I'm the one who doesn't believe in you, Jack?" his father responded. After Jack became a surgeon, he performed emergency surgery on a woman and made her walk again. Sarah was so in awe of

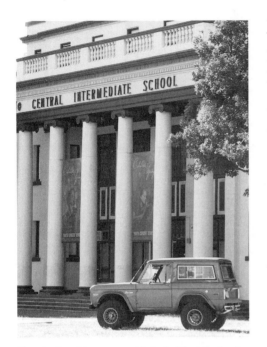

Even in the sideways world, Jack drives that ugly truck. Central Intermediate School near downtown Honolulu doubled as David's conservatory in "Lighthouse." (Courtesy Ryan Ozawa)

Jack performing this "miracle" that she fell in love with him and he asked her to marry him. In one of the most touching scenes between Jack and Christian (admittedly not in an episode but featured in the mobisode that preceded season 4), Christian gave his son a watch the morning of his wedding, and made him promise him that if he ever had a child, he'd treat him better than Christian had treated Jack ("The Watch").

Jack's long hours of being a miracle worker began to put a strain on his marriage, and Sarah eventually left him for another man. After the separation, Jack became obsessed with finding out who the other man was, and suspected it may be his father ("A Tale of Two Cities"). He confronted Christian at an AA meeting, where they got into a fight, and Christian began drinking again. Distraught by what had happened to him, Jack left for Thailand, where he met Achara in the most unfortunate episode of the series ("Stranger in a Strange Land"). She marked him with a tattoo that cast him as an outsider.

Back at the hospital, Jack realized Christian was performing surgery under the influence. He threatened to tell the hospital board of directors ("All the Best Cowboys Have Daddy Issues"). Christian pleaded with him to change his mind, explaining that the only reason he pushed Jack so hard was to make him the great man he turned out to be. He told Jack that it's not just his job that was on the line, but his life. A lifetime of father telling son he didn't measure up came down to this moment, and Jack finally came out on top, the one who *did* have what it took when his father didn't. But Jack didn't realize that his actions would come back to haunt him in a terrible way. Christian was let go from his job, and just as he warned, it was his life at stake as well as his job. Christian went to Australia to see his illegitimate daughter, Claire (a sister Jack didn't even know he had), and failing that, he went to a bar and drank himself to death, dying in an alley behind it ("Two for the Road"). Just before staggering out, however, he told Sawyer, who was sitting next to him in the bar, that he was incredibly proud of his son, but he simply had too much pride to pick up the phone and call him to tell him that.

After the plane carrying Jack and his father's body crashed onto the island, Jack's acumen as a doctor and his ability to problem-solve put him in the top position, and he became a de facto leader, even though he didn't want that responsibility.

For the lighthouse, the production crew only built a base, and then created the rest of the building using CGI. Watch when Jack and Hurley are standing next to the lighthouse; you can see the sun shining on their faces, which shouldn't have happened if the lighthouse had actually been 80 feet high. (Courtesy Ryan Ozawa)

He believed he was hallucinating when he saw Christian walking through the jungle, and smashed his father's empty coffin in a rage. At the end of the season, thinking he'd never see Jack again, Sawyer finally admitted to Jack what Christian had said in the bar, and Jack broke down. Jack's life had always been marked by pressure: time and again he came through, almost never getting praise for his actions. He doubted himself and lived in constant unhappiness. Life on the island would not offer him any respite.

The tension that arose between Jack and John Locke became central to the show; Locke was an older character who might have represented a type of father figure to Jack, but Jack sensed Locke's weakness and vulnerability and would argue with him, trying to break him down the way his own father had broken him down. Though Jack was the leader of the group, he was constantly questioned by everyone, regardless of how many times he saved their lives, and season after season, Jack looked more beleaguered. Jack insisted that he only believed in science, and could only believe in something that was in front of him that could be explained through reason. But Locke had faith in things he couldn't see, and pleaded with Jack to have the same. But the miracle that Jack had witnessed — Sarah walking again — had given him nothing but misery and Jack no longer had that kind of faith.

Throughout his time on the island, he'd been plagued by the insecurity his father had instilled within him. And life gave him plenty to be insecure about. He fell in love with Kate, only to find her sleeping with Sawyer, just as he'd lost Sarah to another man. As he always did before coming to the island, Jack buried his feelings deep and continued playing the hero. He returned to the people who were lost without his leadership, and helped lead them to a freighter that he thought would rescue them. But, just as Locke had warned him, he was wrong, and the people were actually there to harm them. He still managed to get off the island, and began a beautiful life with Kate, helping to raise Aaron and asking her to marry him ("Something Nice Back Home"). But, as always happens with Jack, happiness was fleeting, and he became obsessed once again with what Kate was sneaking off to do when he wasn't around, and he lost her. The guilt of leaving so many people behind began to build up, and he thought he was seeing his father around the hospital again. He began drinking and taking pills, and just like his father, was let go for working under the influence. He was not only haunted by his father; he had *become* him ("Through the Looking Glass").

With the rest of the Oceanic 6, Jack returned to the island ("316"), where, for the first time, he decided to take a back seat and let someone else lead for a change. Of course, we all knew how long *that* would last, and when Daniel Faraday returned and told him that he could reverse everything and make it so they had never even come to the island, never met one another, never hurt one another, Jack sat up and listened. When presented with something that defied reason, Jack Shephard believed it. His life had been one marked by constant disappointment before the plane crash, but since then, it had gotten even worse. The woman he loved had slipped through his fingers; people had died; there were no miracles for him on this island; he'd realized his father had really loved him but he'd never been able to talk to him . . . Jack had lost everything, and the idea of turning things around so none of it had ever happened to him appealed so much he was willing to let go of his constant pessimism and have faith. And so . . . he dropped the bomb. Literally. As a result, Juliet is dead, Sayid died and came back wrong, the Losties are scattered everywhere again, and he just doesn't know how to fix any of this anymore.

Just as references to *The Wizard of Oz* usually surround Ben, Jack is often identified with Lewis Carroll's *Alice's Adventures in Wonderland* and *Through the Looking-Glass* (see *Finding Lost — Seasons One & Two*, p. 33 and *Finding Lost —*

Season Three, pp. 204–206). The first Jack flashback was called "White Rabbit," and he followed the mythical white rabbit of his late father deeper and deeper into the jungle throughout that episode. Just as Alice entered a world of wonder and confusion and felt all alone throughout her journeys, so too has Jack entered the strange world of the island, and as a character he has always been very much alone. He mentions to his sideways-world son David in this episode that he always read *The Annotated Alice* to him as a child (which is editor Martin Gardner's annotated version of the two Lewis Carroll books), and in "Something Nice Back Home" we saw that he also read the books to Aaron at bedtime. In both of the books, when faced with the world of the nonsensical, Alice tries to impose the reason that she's learned from her Victorian education in order to make sense of what is happening around her, and she refuses to accept that things could exist without a logical explanation. Similarly, Jack looks for explanations for everything and won't accept that any phenomenon, no matter how weird, can't be explained away rationally. And if the book on David's bed wasn't a clear enough reference to Carroll's books, the fact that Jack sees his house through the looking glass made it a lot more obvious. It's as if his life exists on the other side of that mirror, and he's somehow stepped through it, like Alice did, into the looking-glass world.

The trek that Hurley and Jack take across the island brings back a lot of memories from the show's first season, not least being the trek that Jack took as he followed his ghostly father through the jungle. Hurley reminisces about their adventures in the jungle back then; they find the Adam and Eve skeletons from "House of the Rising Sun," and we finally find out where Shannon's asthma inhalers ended up, keeping in mind that Sawyer had been tortured in "Confidence Man" for them. These memories are painful for Jack, though, because they remind him how fresh his father's death had been in his mind in those early days after the crash, how confused and under pressure he'd been, and how the early days had led him to this point. In season 1, Jack had been suffering from an obsessive need to fix everything — including people and situations. Now, in season 6, he realizes that the one thing that needs fixing — himself — is irreparably broken, and even a supernatural island can't do the trick.

In the sideways world, the writers once again have come up with the perfect alternate reality for Jack. If this is a place where the characters work through their issues, Jack's world is tailor-made to help him understand his father — he becomes one. David is Jack's sullen teenage son, who is saddened by his grandfather's death, and who sees Jack as a distant, mostly absent father who pressures him into becoming even more than Jack was able to be. Jack is split from David's mother (who remains unseen in this episode, sparking the idea that it is someone other than Sarah), so unlike Jack, David doesn't even have the security of his parents being together. Although we see happy photographs of Christian around Jack's house, in this reality Jack seems to have the same tense relationship with his father that he had in the original timeline. His conversation with his mother, where he talks about how terrified he was of his father, is mirrored in the final scene Jack has with David, where the revelation that David is scared of Jack's disapproval hits him like a ton of bricks. Jack's response to his son is perfect: he acknowledges that his own father used to make him feel inadequate, and he adds, "I don't ever want you to feel that way. I will always love you no matter what you do; in my eyes you can never fail. I just want to be a part of your life." Not only do the words have an immediate positive impact on David, but we can see in Jack's eyes how much he longed to have heard those words himself. But deep down, he knows that his father really did feel that way; he simply didn't have the guts or the words to tell him.

Just as sideways-world Jack says, "I spent my whole life carrying that around with me," island-timeline Jack has been carrying that daddy baggage with him, and now Jacob enters the picture, someone Jack has only heard about the day before when Hurley mentioned him. When Jack sees the reflection of his childhood home in one of the mirrors in Jacob's lighthouse, his world comes crashing down. Christian had always used the phrase, "That's why the Red Sox will never win the Series" to suggest that fate overrides all other forces. The Red Sox had been one of the most successful teams in the Major League, but when they sold the team's most beloved player, Babe Ruth, to the New York Yankees, it sparked an 86-year-long losing streak known as "The Curse of the Bambino." People believed that no matter what they did, the Red Sox would lose because it was their destiny. And for much of the twentieth century, it seemed to be true. Christian subscribed to that idea, and as his alcoholism began to spiral, he clung to that phrase, suggesting that fate was making him fail. The phrase infuriated Jack, who, in "Outlaws," told Sawyer that his father went through life knowing that people hated him, and "instead of taking responsibility for it, he just put it on fate." Jack, on the other hand, has always taken the blame for his failures, and longed for praise for his successes, and has believed that he's where he is thanks to hard work and perseverance, and not thanks to destiny. In "The Glass

The Lighthouse Dial

If you look closely at screen captures of Jacob's lighthouse dial, you'll see many other names of people who were candidates at one time and have since been crossed off. Also, interestingly, Kate's name is *not* crossed off in this particular list despite having a line through it on the ceiling of the cave. Jacob asked Hurley to set the dial to 108, which lists "Wallace." The name has been crossed off, so the person indicated at that position is no longer a candidate . . . who could Wallace be a reference to?

The following is a list of the names I could read; all were crossed off except the six candidates and Kate. In parentheses I've made a few suggestions of who they could be referring to; a question mark indicates my best guess at what it said:

12 – Foster
13 – Bookett (?)
14 – Pryce (Ryan, the Other Hurley mowed down with the Dharma van)
15 – Ford
16 – Jarrah
17 – Barnes
18 – Kueffner
19 – Nguyen
20 – Rousseau (Danielle or Alex)
21 – McHenry
22 – Moorhead
23 – Shephard
24 – Kluxen
25 – Asher
26 – Bozarth
27 – Dorrie
28 – Holland
32 – Rutherford (Shannon)
33 – Novak
34 – Grimaldi
35 – Brennan (from Rousseau's team)
36 – Symanski
37 – Torres
38 – Lindstrom
39 – Mortoka (?)
40 – Dowsett/Dowsen (?)
42 – Kwon
43 – Barnes
44 – Martinez
48 – Stanhope (Harper)
51 – Austen (Kate)
58 – Burke (Juliet)

94 – Cohen
95 – Polletta (?)
96 – Greeson
97 – Pattison
98 – Horton
99 – Cookson/Goodson (?)
100 – Bardfield
101 – Faraday (Daniel)
102 – Montand (from Rousseau's team)
103 – Horsman
104 – Lewis (Charlotte)
106 – Sregzyaski (?)
107 – Thomson
108 – Wallace
109 – Friendly (Tom)
110 – Spots (?)
111 – Klein
112 – Horton
113 – Worden
114 – Yamada
115 – Bargas
116 – Lambert
117 – Linus (Ben or Roger)
118 – Chaver
119 – Almeida
120 – Rodriguez
121 – Neilson
122 – Freed
124 – Dawson (Michael)
125 – Owens
126 – Renti
127 – Mora
128 – Paddock

Ballerina," Ben showed Jack that while he'd been on the island, the Red Sox had miraculously won the World Series, and it strengthened Jack's resolve that there was no such thing as fate.

But now, standing in the lighthouse, that resolve falls apart. For he realizes that Jacob has been watching him his entire life, shaping events so the choices Jack thought he was making of his own free will were in fact guided by another's hand, and that he'd been pushed to move in certain directions merely to fulfill a destiny someone else had forced upon him. While he doesn't yet understand what that destiny is, the thought that his father might have been right tears him apart. Poor, beleaguered Jack gives way to an angry man who's at the end of his rope, tired of the smoke-and-mirror act perpetuated by the Man in Black and Jacob. And so he does the only thing he can in that moment: he smashes the mirrors.

Many fans expressed anger at Jack's impetuous destruction of the mirrors that might have provided some answers, in much the same way fans were angry when Locke blew up the Flame station in "Enter 77" moments after we'd seen the Dharma binders that could have helped explain a lot of what's going on. One could see Jack's actions as selfish, since his name wasn't the only familiar one on that dial, and he's got Hugo standing right there probably wanting to know if Jacob has also been watching him. But Jack's rage is understandable; just as he's starting to reconcile his feelings about his father, it turns out Dad wasn't the only person who had been shaping Jack's life to turn out a certain way.

Jungle Hair Claire has also been haunted by Christian, but where Jack has been influenced by Christian's presence, Claire was affected by his absence. And now her personal torment comes from the fact that, just as she was raised without a father, now Aaron will be raised without his mother. When Jin goes into her tent, we see the devastating effect of the separation. Claire's constructed the horrible squirrel baby of doom (the sight of which will probably haunt me for the rest of my days) out of what appears to be the skull of a baby boar with the tusks filed down, and *Coraline*-like button eyes and a pink-and-blue blanket. The "baby" is the stuff of horror films, and the thought that Claire has been rocking this thing to sleep night after night is heartbreaking. Dogen has said that she is infected the same way Sayid is, and the way she plants the ax in Justin's gut would suggest something has died inside of Claire. But the fact that she still cares about something — no matter how horrific it may look — suggests the old Claire is still in there somewhere.

Highlight: There are some great Hurley lines in this episode, including him complaining to Jacob that he just lied to a samurai, but the best line belongs to Jack, who, when they get to the lighthouse and the door won't open, says sarcastically to Hurley, "Does it say anything on your arm about the door being jammed?"

Did You Notice?:
- When Jack looks at his appendix in the mirror, there's another moment of recognition, the same one he had when he saw that wound on his neck in the airplane bathroom. Is it possible he's starting to remember the other timeline?
- Miles and Hurley have gone from the strategic game of *Risk* to the always-ends-in-a-draw game tic-tac-toe.
- In this reality, David is a big Red Sox fan, and the way Jack refers to them, it sounds like he likes them, too. Is it possible the Curse of the Bambino doesn't exist in this timeline?
- When Jack recalls that David always liked Kitty and Snowdrop, he's referring to Alice's two kittens at the beginning of *Through the Looking-Glass*, which are black (Kitty) and white (Snowdrop). Incidentally, *Alice's Adventures in Wonderland* famously ends with Alice realizing it had all been a dream — an ending that many fans feared would be repeated in the series finale of *Lost*.
- Claire tells Jin that she's been living like this since they all left, but Jin never left the island.
- Hurley wonders if the skeletons might be them if they'd time traveled. Since the skeletons first appeared in season 1, fans have speculated a lot on who they might be, and Hurley's suggestion is one of the more popular fan theories.
- Jack found the key to his wife's house under a stone rabbit, just like Miles reached under a rabbit in "Some Like It Hoth" to enter the dead man's apartment when he was a child.
- On the wall of David's bedroom, he had posters of Beethoven, The Who, and Meat Coat; in "The Moth," Charlie goes to Sydney to ask Liam to reunite the band Drive Shaft so they could go on tour opening for Meat Coat.
- At David's recital, there's a sign out front that says, "Welcome All Candidates!"

- David is playing the same piano piece that Daniel Faraday was playing in "The Variable" when Eloise told him to cease piano lessons and focus on science instead.
- Dogen's comment, that the kids are too young to have so much pressure on them, is a fitting comment on how much pressure Christian put on Jack.
- Hurley says Jack's going to have seven years of bad luck, but he smashed four mirrors, so that's more like 28 years.
- David says that playing the piano was something that meant a lot to Jack. In "The Man from Tallahassee," when Kate enters Jack's place in New Otherton, he's playing the piano.
- Jacob says that Jack is here because he has to do something, and that he needs to look at the ocean for a while . . . Locke looked at the ocean for a long time before he sensed his destiny on the island. We also saw the Man in Black staring at the ocean when he returned in Locke's body.
- Jin lies to Claire to deliberately lead her back to the Temple; this is perhaps the first time we've seen Jin be that deceptive, on the island at least.

Interesting Facts: In the scene where David is playing on stage, the actress playing the judge in the foreground is Damon Lindelof's mother, Susan Klausner.

Like many characters on *Lost*, Jack's son has a biblical name. In the Bible, David was a shepherd (get it? Shephard?) who was brought to King Saul's court as a musician. He gained notoriety when he single-handedly took down the giant, Goliath — something the king's soldiers had been unable to do — by hitting him between the eyes with a rock in a slingshot. He became a commander of the troops, and eventually became the King of Israel. Throughout his reign he united the country, expanded its territory, and made it possible for his son, Solomon, to build the Holy Temple. It is believed he wrote the poems in the Book of Psalms, which are songs in praise of God.

When Hurley walks down the corridor in the Temple, looking for one particular symbol, he stops at the Ancient Egyptian symbol of the shen ring and is about to push it when he's interrupted by Dogen. The shen ring is a circle with a line underneath it, usually represented in Egyptian drawings as a loop of rope with the ends protruding at the bottom. The word shen means "to encircle," and it's a symbol of eternity. When elongated into a longer oval, it becomes a cartouche, and the names of Ancient Egyptian royalty would be enclosed within the ring for protection. It's interesting that the timeline on the island appears to be circular, constantly coming back around with a cause-and-effect pattern, and the sideways-world timeline is like a straight parallel line running under it. Perhaps the shen ring represents the collision of the two worlds.

Nitpicks: That is such a badly photoshopped photo of Jack and his parents. Is the production person who does the photoshopping the same one who works on the CGI?

Oops: In "House of the Rising Sun," the Adam and Eve skeletons were not lying together, they were in separate spots in the cave. It's doubtful the survivors would have moved their rotting corpses to put them together.

4 8 15 16 23 42: "Lighthouse" is *Lost*'s **108**th episode (the sum of the numbers). David's mom lives at house **233** (the numbers add up to **8**). On David's answering machine, Dr. Sutherland says that the recital is on Friday the **24**th (a reverse **42**). On Hurley's arm, he's written that the lighthouse is "**88** feet, **4** levels." Hurley says he has to move the dial to **108**. Jack's house is at number **23** on the dial (which corresponds to his Candidate number in the previous episode). Jack smashes **4** mirrors.

It's Just a Flesh Wound: Claire buries an ax in Justin's stomach.

Lost in Translation: Just before Dogen walks away from Hurley, he mutters in Japanese, "You're lucky that I have to protect you. Otherwise I'd have to cut your head off."

Any Questions?:
- Dogen tells Jack that Jack always has the option to try to leave the Temple, but that Dogen would have to stop him. Yet he doesn't physically stop anyone else from leaving. Is Jack more important than the other Candidates?
- Who is coming to the island?
- What band is David listening to that he says Jack won't know? Is it Drive Shaft?
- Jack asks Hurley why they've never seen the lighthouse before in all their treks, and it's an excellent question, since it seems to be in the general area of where Sayid would have walked along the beach to find Rousseau's camp. Hurley says, "I guess we weren't looking for it." Could it be that Jacob didn't let them see it until he thought they were ready to?

Ashes to Ashes: Justin was an Other who was a low man on the totem pole, being bossed around by Aldo. Despite saying he wanted to kill Claire, he seemed to be an okay guy, but Claire ended up putting an ax through his stomach before he could snap her neck.

Music/Bands: When Jack is driving to pick up David from school, you can hear Mark Cook's "No Concern" playing on the radio, from his 2001 album, *An Evening with the Blues*. David is playing Chopin's "Fantaisie-Impromptu in C-Sharp Minor." Frédéric Chopin was one of the great classical masters of music of the Romantic period. Artists from this period in music looked to the technical proficiency of their predecessors while expanding the emotional depth of the music. Chopin was the natural heir to the legacy created by Ludwig van Beethoven in the Classical era, and he, in turn, became the progenitor to twentieth-century composers such as Sergei Rachmaninoff.

6.6 Sundown

Original air date: March 2, 2010
Written by: Paul Zbyszewski, Graham Roland
Directed by: Bobby Roth
Guest cast: Cas Anvar (Omer Jarrah), Anthony Azizi (Omar), Kevin Durand (Martin Keamy), Andrea Gabriel (Nadia), Salvatore Abbadessa (Cabbie), Addison Arquette (Lou), David P. Griffith (Screaming Other), Aramis Knight (Sam), Peter Stray (Doctor), Kailee Velasco (Eva)

Focus: Sayid

Dogen sends Sayid out to eliminate Smokey, but Sayid returns with a message that everyone who has not left the Temple by sundown will be killed. In the sideways world, Sayid's brother asks him to take care of a problem for him.

Sayid Jarrah has always been trapped between two extremes: he is a lover and he is a torturer. He lives with constant regret about the things he has done to other people, but no matter how many times he tries to leave that life behind and embrace a happier existence, he keeps getting pulled back in. He succumbs every time.

The first time these two extremes came together was when Sayid was a child, and he broke a chicken's neck with his hands so his brother wouldn't have to ("He's Our You"). He told himself he was doing it to save his brother, but deep down he knew that he had just done something his brother couldn't even find it within himself to do. And the sadness that pervades Sayid's life is this acknowledgment that he is not only capable, but willing to carry out violence.

Dogen dares Sayid to prove to him that he's still a good man. (Mario Perez/ABC via Getty Images)

As a soldier for the Republican Guard, Sayid was captured by the U.S. Army and forced to torture his own commanding officer for information ("One of Them"). He at first refused, until they showed him footage of the officer gassing a village that contained some of Sayid's relatives. After the Americans left, Sayid became a "communications officer" for the Republican Guard, torturing rebels who posed a threat to the state ("Solitary"). When one of those insurgents, Nadia, sat before him, he realized that he remembered her as a friend from his childhood, and his cold, steely resolve melted. In fact, he fell in love with her. In Nadia he could see his best and worst sides — the obedient soldier who could dutifully torture her for information was at odds with the man who simply wanted to love her.

After he helped her escape, Sayid was captured and abused by a man whose wife Sayid had tortured in Iraq ("Enter 77"). Sayid denied that he'd done anything to her, until the woman calmly told him about finding children torturing a cat, and how she could relate to the animal. She told him what it felt like to be entirely helpless and said that she has never felt safe since. Only then did Sayid admit what he'd done and beg her forgiveness. She forgave him and let him go. When he asked her why, she responded, "We are all capable of doing what those children did to this cat. But I will not do that. I will not be that."

Sayid attempted to stay on the straight and narrow after this while still searching for Nadia, a search that got a boost when the CIA offered to tell him where she was in exchange for helping take down a terrorist network in Sydney, one involving his friend, Essam ("The Greater Good"). Distraught by Sayid's betrayal, Essam's last words to him were "I hope she makes you whole again."

Sayid has been haunted by these words ever since, simply because he's never felt whole. He has always felt like two halves at war, because these two disparate personalities simply cannot coexist within him. He sees himself not as a killer but as a torturer, which is apt because he's spent his life torturing himself with his internal struggle.

The plane crash happened the day after Essam's suicide, and on the island Sayid became the willing leader to Jack's reluctant one, trying to get the people off the island, desperate to redeem himself in some way for what he'd done. But it wasn't long before he was called back into "service," torturing Sawyer and isolating himself from the group out of shame ("Solitary"). When he returned, he fell in love with Shannon, and stopped torturing others, and himself. Of course, that was short-lived when Shannon was gunned down by Ana Lucia, but Sayid made a major breakthrough by not exacting revenge. He got past it, and started back on that rocky road to redemption . . . until Henry Gale showed up and Sayid decided it was more satisfying to work through his grief by torturing Gale for information.

After Sayid left the island, he was finally reunited with his beloved Nadia. They got married, he started to put his other life behind him, and he saw a real chance at being the Sayid he always told himself and everyone else that he was. They lived happily ever after . . . for nine months, before she was killed by a hit-and-run driver the moment Sayid was distracted by Jacob. Whereas all of the other survivors who were touched by Jacob seemed to derive some hope or help from him, Sayid alone was deeply damaged by the encounter.

Once again, Sayid gave in to his dark side, allowing himself to be pulled in to the hitman business for Benjamin Linus, who had convinced him that Nadia had been killed by Charles Widmore ("The Economist"). One by one Sayid began killing off Ben's enemies, but it did nothing to assuage his feelings of loss. Even in the midst of a job for Ben, he simply couldn't keep his emotions in check and fell in love with his mark, who, it turned out, had been similarly double-crossing him. When Ben called off the vengeful rampage, Sayid turned his sights to humanitarian work, building homes for the less fortunate and trying to put his evil past behind him. *Again.* But the vicious cycle continued, and as usual the one to pull him back in was Ben Linus. Sayid returned to California and killed the man casing Hurley.

Of all the Losties, only Sayid was physically forced to return to the island, being taken in handcuffs by Ilana (a woman he had momentarily fallen for). Faced with a young Ben Linus after time-jumping to 1977, Sayid saw a clear choice: try to help the child and perhaps change him, or kill him and prevent what Ben Linus was going to do to him and everyone else ("He's Our You"). Ironically, it was Ben himself who had advised Sayid to face the fact that he is a killer. Finally embracing the killer within, he shot Ben before joining Jack on his nihilistic venture to set off the bomb, one that got him to the place he's in now.

Except . . . it's not clear exactly what that place is. Sayid died, and he's come back to life an empty, confused shell of what he once was. He doesn't seem able to show any emotions or to feel anything. Essam's final wish was that Sayid would ultimately become whole, but in order to do that, one of his extremes had to be sacrificed. Despite a lifetime of trying to rid himself of his dark side and prove he's a good person, he's tossed aside all goodness within him instead. Dogen says to him, "For every man there is a scale. On one side of the scale there is good, on the other side, evil. This machine tells us how the scale is balanced. And yours tipped the wrong way." In the amazing display of kung fu fighting that follows his statement, Dogen matches Sayid blow for blow, as if he, too, is capable of killing. But when he sees the baseball, Dogen immediately checks himself. He's able to use the memory of the biggest mistake of his past to stop himself from making mistakes in the present, and that baseball reminds him of what his mistakes have cost him before. Sayid, on the other hand, remembers the past, but has resigned himself to who he is. He is a killer, and he accepts that now.

For as much as we love Sayid, he is weak. In most cases, he has hurt people to help others — whether it was in the service of the Army, or to help Shannon or the other survivors, or out of his grief of losing Nadia, or to prevent a future Ben Linus, or, in the case of the sideways world, to help his brother. Every time he had hurt another person, he's had the option of saying no. And he never chooses that option. Nadia once told him that he was mistaken in thinking he was a killer, saying he was "pretending to be something I know you're not." But she said that a long time ago, and he clung to the idea that she was right for so long, only to keep disappointing himself. So now he's given up trying.

In the sideways world Sayid seems to have a richer understanding of who he is. He keeps loved ones at a distance so he can't hurt them. He refuses to answer Nadia's letters. He convinces his brother to marry her so she won't even be a temptation for him. He keeps her photograph to remind him of what he could have had, but we see he now has the sense to remain solitary. It's devastating to see that in a world where so many of the other characters have happy endings, Sayid's journey is so sad. Sayid's story has always been one of self-punishment, but in the sideways world he doesn't wait to be strapped to a table to have someone else inflict pain on him; he inflicts it on himself.

According to Dogen, Sayid is going to get worse, but for now, there's still some of the original Sayid in there. Dogen handing him a dagger and telling him to kill the smoke monster (which probably cannot be done) is a way of preying on Sayid's desire to prove himself. But Smokey's even more cunning: Sayid wants to prove himself to be a good man, but he will always put his own desire for Nadia above that, and will stop at nothing to get her back, as he proved in "The Greater Good." The Man in Black preys on vulnerability; Sayid has hit many low points in his life, but none have been lower than this. Lennon yells at Sayid at the end of the episode, "You just let it in!" and the line is significant not only because Sayid has let Smokey into the Temple, but because he has let him into his heart and turned it completely black.

Similarly, the Man in Black got to Claire at the moment when she'd been separated from her baby, and now the real Claire is hidden in an angry and vengeful heart . . . not to mention a mass of tangled, disgusting hair. When we saw her in "Cabin Fever," she was calmly sitting with Christian in the cabin, laughing and acting like she was okay with her separation from Aaron. It was like she wanted him off the island, away from her. But now we see she'd been under some sort of spell or delusion. Just as Dogen warns Sayid that the Man in Black will "come to you as someone you know, someone who has died," and in fact, he appeared to Claire as her father (someone she didn't know was dead) and she trusted him. It's unclear what happened next, but Claire soon realized that her friends had left her behind, and she was convinced the Others had her son. She became solely focused on getting Aaron back, and became the bane of the Others, setting Rousseau-like traps and basically turning into Danielle, another woman whose baby had been stolen by the Others. Claire knew what had happened to Rousseau, and she'd even met Alex, so she knew they were capable of kidnapping children. The knowledge has made her cold and calculating. Still

The *Lost* production crew sets up in front of a private home in Oahu, which will stand in as Nadia's house in the sideways world. (Courtesy Ryan Ozawa)

she hasn't thought through what her transformation has done to her, and how she can possibly reconcile this with motherhood if she ever does find Aaron.

The moment Kate finally finds Claire, she tries to explain what happened. But all Claire hears in that moment are the words "I took him" and "I raised him." She was told in "Raised by Another" that no one else could raise Aaron, and to allow that to happen would have catastrophic consequences. Claire glares back and tells Kate that she's not the one who needs rescuing, implying that it's Kate who'd better look out if Claire ever gets out of that hole. Sure, Kate deliberately lied to the outside world, saying that Aaron was hers, but given the circumstances, it seems clear Kate did the only thing she could. Without the lie, Aaron would have been made a ward of the state, so where's the advantage? She knew him, she loved him, she was there when he was born. She couldn't toss Aaron out of the helicopter in the hopes that a three-month-old baby would be able to fend for himself until his missing and possibly crazy mother would find him. She couldn't find her way back to the island before now to get Claire and bring her home. Similarly, Claire had been duped by Smokey, and it's not clear if she's still with him out of loyalty or fear. In this particular situation, there's no one to blame; there are only victims, including Aaron.

Apparently, Smokey doesn't lie. He makes promises to people, and claims that he keeps them, but he also chooses his words carefully. He could have promised Claire that she'd see Aaron again, but that could be fulfilled by simply showing her a photograph of him. Similarly, he has now promised Sayid something, but it's unclear what. One presumes he's told him he will see Nadia again. But it could be something entirely different. Given Sayid's psyche, that's an interesting question. Each one of his transgressions has eaten away at him. With every kill, it's harder and harder for him to find his way back to being a good man, but until now he's believed that there will be time to embrace the good side of him.

However, at the end of the episode, Ben Linus — the man who has repeatedly brought out the worst in Sayid, and the man who might have turned into a monster because of what Sayid did to him in the past — tells Sayid, "There's still time." But the dead look in Sayid's eyes terrifies Ben in a way we've rarely seen. Sayid responds, "Not for me." There's no more future for him. He has embraced the killer within, and let the darkness within him tip the scales. Sundown has come, and time has run out for Sayid.

Highlight: The incredibly creepy, slow-motion scene at the end where you can hear Claire singing "Catch a Falling Star" set to haunting music as she nonchalantly wanders through the path of dead bodies around the Temple.

Did You Notice?:
- Sayid arrives at Nadia's house with yellow roses. While red roses have long signified romantic love, yellow roses represent platonic friendship, making Sayid's intentions clear from the moment he arrives.
- Dogen talks about the scale of good and evil, immediately putting us in mind of the scales in Jacob's cave, which were perfectly balanced between good and evil. Smokey grabbing the white stone and throwing it into the ocean tipped the scales to the dark side, which is the same reading that Dogen is getting from Sayid.
- Sayid mentions that he's going to Toronto, which *must* mean that he's going to do something nefarious, since all Canadian references on *Lost* refer to something evil (see *Finding Lost — Season Three*, p. 105).
- Dogen warned Sayid not to let Smokey talk at all, and later Sayid says he didn't, but that's not true: Smokey says, "Hello Sayid" right before Sayid plunges the knife into him (to no effect), so technically it's already too late.
- Smokey asking Sayid, "What if I told you that you could have anything you want?" sounds a lot like Ben asking Locke what he would wish for if there was a box on the island that contained anything he wanted it to ("The Man from Tallahassee").

Deep River by Shusaku Endo (1993)

At the beginning of "Sundown," Sayid walks into Dogen's study and Dogen is reading *Deep River* by Shusaku Endo (1923–1996). I usually devote a full chapter to the books on *Lost*, and the reason this one is relegated to a sidebar is because its significance will only be clear once the viewer has watched the finale, and if I were to draw parallels between the book and *Lost*, I'd be spoiling some *big* things to come. So instead, I'll give a quick synopsis and urge you to read it for yourself.

Deep River is the story of four Japanese people who have lost something in their lives, and they travel to the Ganges River in India in search of it. Isobe is a man whose wife died, and her final words were to tell him to come and find her, because she would be reincarnated as someone else. Only after her death did he realize how much he loved her, and she him, and despite his doubts, he believes that the reincarnation of his wife may be in India. Mitsuko is a woman of reason, who met a man of faith named Otsu when she was in college, and she tempted him away from Jesus by telling him he could sleep with her if he renounced his belief in Him. She causes him to waver, but the momentary lapse begins a lifelong discussion between the two of them about what faith is, and he pursues his beliefs into the Catholic seminary while she continues to mock what he stands for. Yet as she mocks him, she's annoyed by his own serenity in the face of her own absence of feeling, hating that he seems to be content with life while she's still trying to find her way through it. She loses touch with him and later discovers he's in a church in India. Numada, a writer of children's stories about animals, contracted tuberculosis and suffered through several operations to save his life, all the while chatting with a myna bird that was in his hospital room. He almost died during one of the surgeries, but managed to pull through, only to find that the bird had died instead. He believes that the bird died so he wouldn't have to, and now wants to find a way to give something back to the bird. Kiguchi had been a soldier in the Burmese war and had marched along the Highway of Death, contracting malaria along the way. His best friend made a personal sacrifice in order to stay by Kiguchi's side, but the horror of what he did to save his friend's life haunted him until his death. Kiguchi is distraught by what happened to him, and travels to India to find peace.

Through their travels and discussions, the characters come to realize their true feelings of life, death, and rebirth, and whether they believe there really is a world after the one they're in. Endo's characters explore Catholicism, Buddhism, Hinduism, and beliefs of Heaven, purgatory, and limbo. Like the survivors of Oceanic Flight 815, these characters are all lost, and what they find in India surprises them; they were all in search of something, but many of them didn't even know what it was they were searching for. *Deep River* is a gorgeous novel that resonates deeply with the final season of *Lost*, and the series as a whole.

- Lennon and Dogen refer to everyone by their last names — Shephard, Reyes, Ford, and Kwon — the same way they're logged on the cave ceiling and in the lighthouse.
- When the van pulls up to Nadia's house, the goon who steps out is Omar,

one of Keamy's men from the island. Last time we saw him was in the big ambush near the helicopter at the end of season 4.
- Poor Keamy . . . in the original timeline, he was a Navy Seal and a killing machine mercenary. In this one, he's just a small-time gangster doing a bad *Goodfellas* impression and wearing a flashy pimp suit.
- Keamy frying the egg is reminiscent of Locke frying the egg for Ben's breakfast in "Eggtown."
- Keamy is wearing the watch that Jin was holding on the plane in "LA X." Presumably he's taken it from him before locking him in the fridge.
- In the sideways world Dogen's son is close to him and is a pianist, and Dogen is very involved in his life. In the island timeline Dogen is mourning him and blaming himself for his son's near death. It's nice to see Dogen enjoying being with his son in the sideways world, knowing as we do what Dogen lost in the island timeline.
- Smokey standing with his "followers" was reminiscent of the beginning of season 4, when Locke and Jack split forces and the people formed two camps. Interestingly, Claire was with Locke back then, too, but Kate and Sayid were with Jack.

Oops: When Sayid is confronted by Omar outside Nadia's house, you can see the license plate on Nadia's van, and it's the same as the one on Jack's vehicle.

It's Just a Flesh Wound: Sayid's brother suffered a punctured lung and internal bleeding when he was attacked off screen. Keamy's goon shoots Omar at the restaurant, and Sayid shoots the goon and Keamy. Sayid drowns Dogen and stabs Lennon, killing both of them. The smoke monster kills countless Others at the Temple.

Any Questions?:
- What has Smokey promised Claire if she helps him?
- The writers clearly don't want us to know what Smokey's real name is, so everyone avoids saying it, which becomes a little annoying in scenes such as the one where Dogen says, "Who?" and Claire responds, "You know who." They're making him sound like Voldemort. Does he have a name? Is it significant?
- As Dogen is recruiting Sayid to help him with the Man in Black, he says, "Things have changed." Is he referring to the immediate situation only, or is there a suggestion that the rules have changed now that Jacob is dead?
- Dogen tells Sayid that the smoke monster will not stop "until he has killed

every living thing on this island." This line is reminiscent of Ben's line in "The Beginning of the End," when he warns Jack that if he phones the freighter, "every single living person on this island will be killed" as if there was such a thing as non-living persons on the island. Is Dogen making the same distinction? Is this a suggestion that Sayid is, in fact, not living?

- Dogen explains that the smoke monster will appear to him as someone he knows who is dead. Is this confirmation that Ben's mother, Alex, Christian, and Yemi were all incarnations of the smoke monster? How does this explain the appearance of Walt, who is very much alive?
- Where did Dogen's dagger come from? Does it have special significance? Who made up the rule that you have to kill Smokey before he speaks? Was anything that Dogen said true or did he want the smoke monster to kill Sayid?
- We saw Sawyer in cahoots with the Man in Black in "The Substitute," and elsewhere Jin was with Claire. Now they're both gone. Where did they go?
- Why does Dogen want Shephard and Reyes in his office?
- Why is Jin tied up in the refrigerator at the restaurant? Where is Sun? Did she somehow ditch Jin at the airport?
- Did Jacob really save Dogen's son's life?
- When the smoke thundered past Kate's head, she was looking up at it, agog, probably because she'd never seen it so close before. Did she, like the others, actually see any images from her life reflected back at her in that moment?

Ashes to Ashes: Dogen was a businessman in Japan who had too much to drink one night before picking up his son from baseball practice. After surviving a car accident, his son was in critical condition, and Jacob came to the hospital, offering to save the child's life in exchange for Dogen coming to the island and becoming a Temple Master. Dogen did so, and has never seen his son again. He hated speaking English, and kept a distance from the people that he led.

Lennon died when he was stabbed by Sayid. He was a loyal follower of Dogen and spoke fluent Japanese, translating Dogen's words to the Temple people.

Many other Others died in the smoke monster's attack.

Music/Bands: Claire sings "Catch a Falling Star" when she's sitting in the hole in the Temple. This song has been referenced repeatedly on *Lost*: when Claire was going to put Aaron up for adoption, she asked the potential adoptive parents if they could sing the song to him, and says that her father used to sing it to her. In

"Maternity Leave," the mobile in the nursery plays that song. In "Whatever Happened, Happened," we see Kate singing the song to Aaron when she's walking up the driveway to Cassidy's house. The song was originally recorded by Perry Como, where he sings that if you catch a falling star and put it in your pocket, you'll have a bit of starlight with you all the time, so if bad things happen, you can cling to the light to forget all of your troubles.

6.7 Dr. Linus

Original air date: March 9, 2010
Written by: Edward Kitsis, Adam Horowitz
Directed by: Mario Van Peebles
Guest cast: William Atherton (Principal Reynolds), Jon Gries (Roger Linus), Tania Raymonde (Alex)

Focus: Ben
When Ilana finds out that Ben was the one who killed Jacob, Ben is forced to meet his fate. In the sideways world, we get an intriguing glimpse of what Ben might have been like if he hadn't become, well . . . evil.

Benjamin Linus. The villain we all love to hate. It's remarkable to think that Michael Emerson only joined the show midway through its second season, and yet fans cannot think of *Lost* without thinking of Ben. News of an upcoming Ben episode always brings a lot of anticipation among the fans, and this one was no exception: Emerson puts in his best performance of the season.

When we first saw Ben, he was Henry Gale from Minnesota, an unfortunate man who had been sailing around the world in a hot air balloon with his wife Jennifer. The balloon had crashed to the island, Jennifer died, and Henry had to bury her. Except . . . the guy telling the story wasn't *actually* Henry Gale, he was Benjamin Linus, and he'd borrowed someone else's life story for his own purposes. It was the perfect introduction to this truly nasty Machiavellian character.

There have only been three Ben-centric episodes, surprisingly (though many more episodes have felt Ben-centric). There are 29 episodes between our first introduction to "Benry" in "One of Them" and his first real flashback, and the silence worked well at keeping him a mystery. Viewers had no idea who he really was or where he'd come from, and could only piece together his backstory through what he'd told us — which, in true Ben fashion, mostly consisted of lies. In "The Man Behind the Curtain," after constructing an idea of what this person was all about, we finally saw who he was — and it was surprising. Ben Linus was once an innocent child, longing for a mother who died giving birth to him and cringing under the weight of his father's disdain and loathing. He developed a deep friendship with a little girl on the island named Annie, a character many fans thought we might see again, but who seems to have been there simply to show us that Ben was capable of loving, and of being loved. When Annie left the island, she took with her the only human connection Ben had ever had. Left alone with his alcoholic father, Ben disappeared into his own fantasy world, one where he could be together with his mother again. When he actually saw her standing outside, he chased her the same way Alice chased the White Rabbit, and that's how he met Richard Alpert and the Others. Richard promised Ben he could become one of them, but he had to go back to his father and be patient.

After Sayid tricked Ben into helping him escape, he shot Ben and left him for dead ("He's Our You"). Kate and Sawyer rushed Ben to the Others, and Richard Alpert told them that if he fixed him, Ben would lose his innocence and would never be the same. And then Alpert and Ben disappeared through the Temple wall.

Ben's life from that point on has been marked by his feeling that he was special, and that, like John Locke, he had been chosen by Jacob because he had a higher purpose. However, as he later discovered, he hadn't been chosen by Jacob at all; he was used for years as the Man in Black's pawn.

After his miraculous recovery, Ben seemed to turn into a double agent, working with the Others and staying in Dharmaville, pretending that everything was fine, but he was really helping the Others orchestrate an end to the Dharma Initiative's presence on the island. A tension arose between Ben and Charles Widmore — Widmore had believed that *he* was the rightful owner of the island, and he didn't like Ben thinking he was more important. When Ben took Alex from Rousseau, his job was to kill her, but in a rare moment of emotional strength — where he put another person before the island — he refused. He ultimately helped the Others Purge the DI, killing everyone (including his own father) and they took over the Dharmaville barracks and made Ben their leader. What Ben wasn't telling anyone, however, was that he couldn't actually see Jacob, and he wasn't really the Chosen One at all.

"Hey Ben, there's something on your shoe . . . ha! Tricked you. Again." "I totally strangled you." (Sue Schneider/MGP)

When the survivors of Flight 815 arrived on the island, Ben immediately rounded up the troops and began surveillance on them. Meanwhile he was dealing with the difficulties of being a father of a teenager (along with its requisite task of strapping the potential boyfriend to a chair and brainwashing him into not touching his daughter) and, more importantly, the knowledge that he had a cancerous tumor on his spine. If he was so special, how could he possibly have cancer? he thought. When he discovered that among the survivors was a man whom the island made walk again, he was faced with the notion that maybe he wasn't special after all . . . and that someone else on the island had been chosen by Jacob instead. Just as Charles had been suddenly faced with a man everyone believed was more special than he was, now Ben was faced with John Locke. Ben decided to prove to himself that John wasn't the special one, and took him to Jacob's cabin. When John saw "Jacob," Ben was shocked and jealous. He shot John, leaving him for dead. And when John lumbered out of the jungle, Lazarus-like, the very next day, Ben was convinced. He knew that he wasn't the leader, and everyone else knew it, too. Ben continued to play the part of the man in charge for a few more days — while trying to evade Widmore's forces — until one of the mercenaries killed Alex. At that moment, everything changed.

The island gave John a sign to leave, but Ben offered to do it himself, to revenge himself on Widmore for what had happened to Alex. He threatened to kill Widmore's daughter, but he couldn't pull the trigger when he had a chance. He tracked John Locke to a rundown motel, where he strangled him to death and then carefully brought the body back to the island. Did he do it out of revenge for the fact that John was special and he wasn't? Or did he really think he was doing the right thing? When he saw Locke alive again, he was obviously shocked; he claimed he'd had faith that John would come back to life, but it didn't diminish the shock of actually seeing it happen. He followed his new leader right into Jacob's inner sanctum, the statue, and was finally face-to-face with the man he'd devoted pretty much his entire life to.

The scene at the end of "The Incident" is beautiful in its sadness. Ben has sacrificed everything in his life to be the one who gets to run the island. He is the man behind the curtain, the huckster pretending to be the Wizard of Oz. He sends John Locke off to kill his father — in much the same way the wizard sent Dorothy on a fool's errand to bring back the witch's broomstick — never thinking that Locke would actually show up in camp with his dead father slung over his shoulder! Locke could hear the voice of "Jacob" when Ben never could, and he got real instructions from him when Ben only pretended he did. John rose up after Ben shot him, and then appeared to rise from the dead again after Ben strangled him and left him well and truly *dead*. Over the course of a few weeks, Ben has watched everything he worked for slip away — power; respect; and Alex, the one person he loved more than the island. And inside Jacob's sanctuary, he looks at Jacob, the deity for whom he's lost everything, and says, "What about *me*?" Jacob's dismissive response — "What *about* you?" — is the final straw: Ben kills him. He walks into that statue a broken man; he walks out of it completely destroyed. And when Richard Alpert grabs Ben by the back of the neck and shoves his face toward the corpse of John Locke, the horrific reality of what he's just done hits him: John *hadn't* been chosen by Jacob . . . he'd been chosen by the Man in Black. Ben had a chance to be Jacob's savior, but instead he became his murderer. The bad guy used Ben to kill the good guy. From that moment on, Ben goes silent, following Ilana and everyone else without comment. The old Ben seems to be gone.

The sideways-world story in this episode is a metaphor for everything that has happened to Ben in his life on the island, more so than with any of the other sideways-world stories. In this world, Ben is not the angry, ambitious, scheming weasel that he is on the island — he's nurturing, loving, attentive, and is willing to give up everything to help a student have a successful future. In other words, he's everything we always thought little Ben could have turned out to be, if life hadn't been stacked against him . . . and if he hadn't made such lousy choices along the way.

"*Doctor*" Linus is a European History teacher. In this world he hasn't devoted his life to a deity, but instead has spent a lifetime studying the past. The Ben we know is indifferent to his past, and seems to live very much in the present, always working toward Jacob's future. When we see him teaching a class on Napoleon's exile to Elba (see **Interesting Facts** below), we immediately see the link between the other Ben and the sideways one: like Napoleon, Ben might have lived on a glorious island and been called "Leader," but he never really had any power, and was never going to have any. In the sideways world, he's got a PhD, but just because people should probably call him "Doctor" doesn't mean he has any of the benefits or respect that go with that title. Dr. Linus wants to encourage the children who want to learn but is thwarted by the school's administration, a comment on the fact that Ben was always eager to know more about the island, but the island wouldn't give up its secrets to him.

The scene in the lunchroom is the key to the episode. As Dr. Linus complains about budget cutbacks and suggests reforms to improve the school, substitute teacher John Locke interjects, saying, "Maybe you should be the principal. It sounds like you care about this place, and if the man in charge doesn't, then maybe it's time for a change." When Linus says no one will listen to him, Locke kindly says, "I'm listening." Compare this scene to the later one, when Ben is being forced to dig his own grave while listening to Smokey try to tempt him to the dark side, promising him ownership of the island. In both timelines, John Locke is "substituting" for someone else and telling Ben what he wants to hear. Just as Linus paused and realized he could make his dreams come true, now Ben stops and thinks the same thing. But in both realities, when Ben decides to take the power he believes should be his, something gets in the way — Alex. In the island timeline, Ben stands before Ilana, telling her that he always thought the island was the thing he wanted, but now he realizes it was Alex. He threw away the only thing that meant something to him to control the thing that didn't mean anything, not without her on it. Ben didn't realize what really mattered to him until it was gone.

In the sideways world, Linus has a chance for real power again; he can rule the small island of the school, become a better leader to the teachers and students than the guy they are stuck with, and make it the place he always believed it could be. But when Principal Reynolds holds a metaphorical gun to Alex's future, saying he will "torch" her, Linus must make a quick decision — and this time, he chooses to sacrifice his power for Alex. He makes up for his past mistakes, and when he steps outside, knowing what he's lost, he sees the joy on Alex's face, and knows it was worth it. In this reality, he has done what any good parent does — put the child before himself — and it doesn't even matter that she doesn't know. *This* Ben makes *this* choice because he wants to.

Almost every character in this series has lost the one thing that mattered most to them. For Sun, it was Jin. Jack lost Kate. Kate and Claire both lost Aaron. Locke lost his faith and then the island. Sayid lost Nadia. Daniel lost Charlotte. Sawyer lost Juliet. Desmond lost Penny, but he stands apart because unlike everyone else, he got her back again.

"Dr. Linus" is not just about loss, but about giving up hope when you have nothing more to live for. Richard Alpert was cursed with immortality by Jacob's touch. He says to Jack, in a heartrending speech, that he'd given his entire life — "longer than you can possibly imagine" — to a man who promised him he was part of a larger plan, and so he's been loyal for years waiting for that time to come. And now, suddenly Jacob is dead. "So . . . why do I want to die?" he says. "Because I just found out my entire life had no purpose." Jacob is gone, and Richard has been left behind, faced with the wrathful Man in Black, who appears to be his enemy, and he has no plan now, no way forward. He has spent lifetimes following the bidding of one man, all for nothing. His hopelessness is one of the most touching moments in the episode (and one that will be even more important two episodes from now).

Similarly, we now know why Ilana always seems so glum. She says that Jacob was like a father to her, but we recall that when he visited her in the hospital when she appeared to be recovering from some severe burns, he wore gloves so he wouldn't touch her. She, too, has given her life to him, but he refused to touch her, either to give her immortality or to make her one of his Candidates. She's proven herself to him, but she's gotten nothing in return. Now he's gone, and she's continuing to carry out her important task of keeping the Candidates safe.

One must assume there have been several moments along the way when she's been exasperated with the people she's been protecting, thinking, "Why did he choose *them* over *me*?"

And that is why she looks at Ben and sees a kindred spirit. Just as John Locke reassured Linus that he was listening, she looks at Ben and tells him, "I'll have you." The scene on the beach ends with Jack, Richard, and Hurley rejoining the rest of the group (and Sun seeing Jack and Hurley for the first time since the Ajira flight). But while everyone else is smiling, Ben, Ilana, and Richard remain sullen. There's no joy in Jacob's disciples anymore: when he died, their futures died with him.

Highlight: Yet another patented Lapidus zinger flies at Ben after everyone's just found out that he killed Jacob: "You make friends easy, don'tcha?"

Did You Notice?:
- Arzt asks why he's dealing with lab equipment from the 1950s, which immediately makes one think of all of the outdated equipment on the island left behind from the Dharma Initiative.
- In the original timeline Ben killed his father with poison gas; now he gives his father gas (oxygen) to keep him healthy and alive.
- When Ben is being marched across the beach by Ilana, he walks with his arms flopping at his side like Pee-wee Herman.
- Alex asks Dr. Linus not to tell anyone what she told him about the principal, and he says, "A promise is a promise." That's the same thing Locke said to Jin when he promised not to let Sun come back to the island.
- Ben asks Miles if he still wants the $3.2 million; he's referring to the money that Miles tried to blackmail him for in "Eggtown." Miles has clearly found out about Nikki and Paulo's diamonds by talking to Hurley. (Or maybe he talked directly to Nikki and Paulo. How . . . unfortunate for him.)
- Nice one, Jack. You just go ahead and carry that kerosene lamp into the ship *filled with dynamite*.

Interesting Facts: Miles refers to Nikki and Paulo as "jabronies," which is the same thing Sawyer had called them (well, technically he messes up the line and calls them "jabonies" but let's not get nitpicky). A jabroni is slang for a wrestler who is scripted to take the fall.

This episode was directed by Mario Van Peebles, the actor and director whose father was the legendary director Melvin Van Peebles. Mario played his father in the docudrama *Baadasssss!* which was about his father's revolutionary film *Sweet*

Sweetback's Baadasssss Song. Mario has recently appeared on *Damages* and in Michael Mann's film *Ali* as Malcolm X. William Atherton, who plays Principal Reynolds, also played a high school principal in *Real Genius* with Val Kilmer; in fact, the role of Reynolds was written specifically for Atherton. Also, in a podcast, Jorge Garcia said that he came up with the line where Hurley asked Richard Alpert if he was a vampire (which had also been a fan joke for some time). He was surprised when the line wasn't taken out.

Ben's lesson on Napoleon at Elba wasn't arbitrary. After Napoleon had conquered much of Europe and had declared himself Emperor, other countries began joining forces against him. The Russians devastated his troops and sent him fleeing back to France, and as they followed him there, they began to get support from almost every other European nation, who rose up against France. Napoleon abdicated his throne which left Louis XVIII as the man in charge. The Allies drew up the Treaty of Fountainbleau and Napoleon signed it. In it they said he would be exiled to Elba, an island in Tuscany. Probably mockingly, they allowed him to keep the term "Emperor," and he would rule over the population of 12,000 people on the island. He spent almost a year there, and while there he made many positive reforms, including building hospitals and improving the local drinking water. But just as he had everyone convinced he was retiring for good, he managed to escape the island, make it past a patrolling British ship, and back to France. Upon his return, people rallied around him, and the police sent to capture him ended up kneeling before him. Louis XVIII fled the country, and Napoleon took his throne once again. His rule lasted 100 days before he was conquered in the Battle of Waterloo and was exiled, this time to Saint Helena. He died after living there for six years.

When Ben was rifling through Sawyer's things (including his copy of *Booty Babes*), he picked up a book called *Benjamin Disraeli: Justice Is Truth in Action*. It doesn't seem to be a real book, so it's probably just referencing Benjamin Disraeli (1804–1881) who was a British Prime Minister with the Conservative Party. He wrote many popular romance novels in his youth, but he was never seen as part of the literary movement in the Victorian period. His time in parliament was marked by his intense rivalry with William Ewart Gladstone, who was head of the Liberal Party. Of interest to *Lost* fans is the reference to Disraeli in Lewis Carroll's *Through the Looking-Glass*. In the chapter "The Lion and the Unicorn," Alice comes across a fight between a lion and a unicorn, which abruptly pauses for 10 minutes for tea time, during which Alice tells the Unicorn that she didn't realize unicorns were real. He tells her that he'll believe in her if she'll believe in him. Together, the lion and unicorn symbolize Great Britain and are on the royal coat of arms (Conservative). Carroll had been a big supporter of the Conservative Party, and in the book, illustrator John Tenniel drew the Unicorn to look like a caricature of Disraeli, and the Lion a caricature of Gladstone.

Ben also brushes over *The Chosen* by Chaim Potok (1967). *The Chosen* is a book that follows the lives of two boys: Reuven, an Orthodox Jew, and Denny, a Hasidic Jew. After Denny accidentally hits Reuven in the face with a baseball during a game, the two become friends, and the novel traces the six years of their friendship through high school and into college. The key piece that would link this book to Ben (besides Ben making people think he was the Chosen One) is through the relationship that Denny has with his father, Reb Saunders, an extremely pious Jew who has raised his sons in silence. He never speaks directly to them nor allows them to speak to him, and instead speaks to them through others. By the end of the book, he tells Denny (indirectly) that the reason he did this was to force Denny to explore his own soul and find his own way, and he apologizes for what he's done and gives him his blessing. What seemed at first like a distant and uncaring father-son relationship (like the one Roger and Ben have in the island timeline) is actually one that was founded upon some thought and caring (like the one Roger and Ben have in the sideways world).

Dr. Linus and Alex are reviewing her history notes and they talk about the East India Company. The company was a group of London businessmen who came together to import spices through South Asia. In 1813, the British government took away its monopoly.

Nitpicks: While this episode is one of my favorites of the season, you could drive a truck through the plot holes in the sideways world. Knowing that Alex needed to have her recommendation from the principal soon, Linus just needed to hold onto his evidence, wait for the year to end and for Alex to get her recommendation, and then hand over the evidence he has. Also, the island story in this episode exposes one of the biggest problems of season 6: with the focus of the series moving to the island's mythology — Jacob, Smokey, and the Candidates — the emphasis seems to have drifted away from the plot. Ilana had everyone on the beach, and told them to go to the Temple. They went to the Temple and she said, "I know! Let's go back to the beach!" Now they're back at the beach, where they will no doubt head back inland at some point when the story calls for them to be somewhere else. No wonder Sun looks so ticked off all the time. It's too bad the writers couldn't come up with a useful reason for everyone to be in certain places at once.

Also, there were several moments while Ben was digging that Ilana wasn't standing nearby. Why did he wait until she was close — and looking right at him — to start running away?

Oops: Watch the scene when Linus and Arzt are talking outside at the end of the episode; the second button of Arzt's shirt keeps mysteriously buttoning and unbuttoning itself.

4 8 15 16 23 42: The history club meets at 4.

It's Just a Flesh Wound: While it seems impossible that a Ben Linus episode wouldn't leave Ben with new broken bones or at least a facial laceration, other than Ilana throwing Ben down on the ground, there are no other moments of violence in the episode.

Lost in Translation: When Hurley is talking in his sleep, he says, "Cheese curds."

Any Questions?:

- Did Ilana take Jacob's ashes solely for Miles to listen to them? Does she have any other intended purpose for them?
- What does Ilana mean when she says Jacob was the closest thing she ever had to a father? What did he do for her that made her so loyal to him?
- The conversation that Ben and Roger have is the first time we've heard the island and the Dharma Initiative mentioned in the sideways world, and it raises several questions: when did the island sink to the bottom of the ocean? Jack's bomb probably doesn't exist in this timeline; does that mean someone else set off the Jughead bomb many years later? Was that, too, predestined? Did Roger and Ben have some time in the DI, decide it wasn't for them, and then leave? Did Jacob ever exist on that island? (We saw his statue's foot, which would suggest he did.) We could also see Dharmaville and the swing set at the bottom of the ocean, so we know the DI inhabited the island at some point. The question is, when?
- So how did Rousseau end up in L.A.? Does this mean she never went to the island in 1988? Were the numbers somehow stopped? When exactly did the rift happen in the timeline? Is Robert still Alex's father? Why is he not around?
- Miles says that Jacob cared about dying, telling Ben that right up to the moment that the knife went through his heart, he hoped he was wrong

about Ben. Jacob didn't appear to be someone who wanted to live — he didn't fight back or try to stop Ben, and it would have been easy for him to overpower him. Was Miles just trying to get Ben into more trouble? Is Miles correct that his thoughts about Ben meant that he cared about dying, or was he really only concerned about why Ben was doing what he was doing? And Jacob's final words were very dismissive of Ben, so what exactly did he mean by hoping he was wrong about Ben?

- Richard tells Jack, "Whatever you were looking for at the Temple, it's not there." So . . . why exactly did we spend so much of season 6 at the Temple?
- If Widmore was the one who was coming to the island, then why did Jacob have Hurley turn the lighthouse dial to the number next to the name "Wallace"? If every other name was the real name of a real person, shouldn't 108 have said Widmore? Again, the writers seem to have put in a purposely similar but wrong name just to throw us off the scent.
- What side is Widmore on? Who will he align with when he gets to the island? If Jacob is trying to lure him here, then it would seem he's on Jacob's side, but everything he's done in the past seems to have been in opposition to Jacob.
- How did Widmore find the island after Ben moved it?

6.8   Recon

Original air date: March 16, 2010
Written by: Elizabeth Sarnoff, Jim Galasso
Directed by: Jack Bender
Guest cast: Neil Hopkins (Liam Pace), Rebecca Mader (Charlotte), Jodi Lyn O'Keefe (Ava), Allen Cole (Sergeant), Christopher Johnson (Police Officer)

Focus: Sawyer

Smokey entrusts Sawyer with the task of finding out who has just come to the island. In the sideways world, we see that Sawyer's life is similar, but different in one significant way.

When we first saw Sawyer in season 1, he seemed like a bit of a cliché: The angry redneck who throws out caustic lines, has a racist streak, and prefers to keep to himself. But over the run of the series, Sawyer has become increasingly complicated, evolving from the lone wolf character to an invaluable team leader. His tendency to keep his emotions to himself has made him one of the toughest characters to read. Which is pretty fitting for a con man.

In season 1, Sawyer was hell-bent on revenge and lived by an "every man for himself" credo. We soon discovered that when he was eight years old, his mother had had an affair with a con man named Sawyer who bilked his father out of a lot of money and left his parents behind to clean up the mess . . . which his father did by shooting and killing his mother before turning the gun on himself ("Confidence Man"). Fittingly, Smokey tells James in this episode that he needed to focus Claire's anger on something she can hate, because that's what Ford himself had decided to do . . . and he focused it on himself. He changed his name to Sawyer and began playing out Sawyer's con: loving and leaving women and taking all their husbands' money, punishing himself as a substitute for the real Sawyer.

The always charming Josh Holloway at the season 6 premiere party, "Sunset on the Beach." (Marco Garcia/AP Photo)

The years of self-loathing began to take a toll, and he pushed everyone away from him. He met Cassidy and had to execute a longer con on her, but after taking all her money, he realized that as much as he thought he was conning her, he'd been conning himself, too ("The Long Con"). He actually cared about her, and hated himself for what he'd done to her. When he was in prison doing time for what he'd done to her, he found out he had a daughter with Cassidy who was named Clementine ("Every Man for Himself").

Out of prison, James followed a lead to the real Sawyer working at a shrimp truck in the Australian Outback ("Outlaws"). James traveled there and killed him, only to discover he'd been set up to murder some stranger who owed a massive debt. After getting drunk in a bar with Christian Shephard, he was deported from Australia via Oceanic Flight 815. On the island he retreated back into his Sawyer persona, pushing everyone away until Kate saw through his ruse and began to break through to him. He tried to make himself loathsome to her to continue punishing himself, but Kate was different from his other marks; he fell in love with her, and she with him. She began to bring out a softer side of Sawyer, unveiling his tough exterior to be nothing more than a shield. While he pilfered everything from the crash site and then charged people money to have some of "his stuff," he would always step up when the situation became serious and people needed help. While he conned the camp and took all their guns, declaring himself sheriff of the island ("The Long Con"), he remained in charge for about 30 seconds before he ended up in a polar bear cage. Of course, Kate helped make that experience a little more pleasurable for him, too.

Season 3 was the turning point for James, when John Locke tricked him into stepping into the brig of *The Black Rock*, face to face with the man whose con had changed his entire life: Anthony Cooper, a.k.a. Sawyer. In a rage, James choked him to death, but as he stared at the one thing he'd longed for his whole life — Sawyer's corpse — he realized how empty he felt. His entire adult existence had come down to this moment, and now he had nothing. James retreated from the others for a while but eventually emerged as a hero and a leader in season 4, saving Claire from an attack from Widmore's mercenaries and helping everyone through the jungle, keeping them safe from the freighter folk. In season 5 he time traveled to 1974, and as a member of the Dharma Initiative, became the head of security. His "every man for himself" creed now gone, Sawyer lived to protect everyone in the DI, and finally found success, happiness, and a purpose in life. Now that he was rid of the elusive Sawyer, James had no immediate motivation. But James didn't give up; unlike Ben and Richard, when he saw a future with nothing in it, he switched his focus to create a different future. His destructive personality was gone and he was now a protective leader. He fell in love with Juliet and they ended up together, but by 1977, when the others returned, and he saw Kate again, his world came crashing down.

Ben reminded Sayid that he was a killer, and in this episode, the smoke monster reminds James that he's still a con man, and a damn good one. Maybe Smokey sees his former self in James — in "The Substitute," he says to Sawyer, "I was a man once, *like you*" — someone who lost someone he cared about, as the Man in Black says he has, and who became vengeful as a result. Both of their lives

Ken Leung chats with his stunt double (left) before preparing for the outdoor scene where James finally tells him the truth, which was filmed on S. Beretania St. at Fort St. near Hawaii Pacific University. (Courtesy KOS Tours)

have been destroyed by anger, and both of them have used elements of trickery to make others (and themselves) suffer.

As we watch the scene between Sawyer and Zoe we remember all of the cons he's pulled before. He watches her intently as she talks, noticing how she looks away from him every time she tells part of her story that isn't true, and the moment she turns her entire body away from him to talk about her "boyfriend" in Guam, she discovers she can't con the con man. James pulls off a nifty double cross in this episode, telling Widmore he's going to lead Locke to his trap, and telling Smokey he's tricked Widmore, but he's conning both of them.

In the sideways world, James Ford is very similar to the guy we know, but he's definitely not called Sawyer, and he's a cop. He's channeled his desire to find Cooper — he still plans to kill him when he does, but he's calmer and more deliberate about his task. In this reality, Jacob didn't hand him a pen and encourage him to keep writing the letter that would consume him. However, there is still a sense of self-loathing. We've seen the other characters peering into mirrors throughout this season, but when he looks into one, he doesn't like what he sees, and he smashes the mirror the same way Jack destroyed the mirrors in the lighthouse. The image of James is now a fractured one, and we realize that, deep down, he's as broken in this timeline as in the other one . . . he's just a lot better at covering up that pain.

As in the island reality, James is still an avid reader, and surprisingly, he's chosen the same books in this timeline as he found in suitcases in the other one. He's reading *Watership Down* (see *Finding Lost — Seasons One & Two*, pp. 55–57), *A Wrinkle in Time* (ditto, pp. 142–144), and *Lancelot* (ditto, p. 263), which we saw him reading on the beach in the first two seasons. Perhaps the writers are suggesting that these books are critical to understanding that season. *Watership Down* is about rabbits who are forced out of their warren and must find a new home, but realize that any place is a home if they can make it together. Along the way they learn about themselves and the other rabbits around them, much like the survivors; in fact deception and the art of the con actually become ways to overcome evil. The protagonist of *Lancelot* is a vicious antihero (worse even than the one in *Notes from Underground*, see page 140), who presents, through a long monologue a view of the world that is so empty and nihilistic it forces the reader to judge him and to agree or disagree. Much like *Lost*, the book presents a series of possibilities and asks the viewer to use his/her experiences to determine which one they believe to be most correct.

Of the three books, *A Wrinkle in Time* probably has the most resonance for *Lost*. In it, two characters "tesser" through time (they time jump from one place to the next when time wrinkles together) because a larger, darker force is at work, called the "Dark Thing" or "IT," threatening to destroy all of society as they know it. (Incidentally, one of the characters is named Charles Wallace, and the name "Wallace" was marked as #108 on the dial of Jacob's lighthouse . . . the very number Jacob asked Hurley to turn it to.) By the end of the book, the characters realize what can actually conquer IT: love of other people, and connection to those around us. Those characters on *Lost* who have managed to move on from their biggest tragedies are the ones who have found other connections to cling to.

Smokey reveals more about himself to Kate in this episode, and the scene where he talks to her on the beach is probably the most important one for what is to come. He insists that he is not a dead man but is very much alive, and he just wants to leave the island. It turns out, just like every other person on the island, Smokey has been dealing with parent issues, only his are of the mom variety, which is refreshing, especially after the proliferation of daddy issues. He tells Kate that his mother was crazy, and reminds her that Aaron's mom is crazy, too. Did he turn Claire into a madwoman as some sort of experiment? Did his mother reject him in some way and he wants to see how far a mother must be pushed before she will reject her own? Or is there something larger at work? It's still not clear what exactly is going on with the smoke monster, but this scene

To film the scene between Kate and the Man in Black on the beach, the film crew had to set up a lot of shade to prevent the sun from shining directly in the actors' eyes. (Courtesy KOS Tours)

provokes sympathy for him. Maybe the line between good and evil isn't as easily drawn between Jacob and the Man in Black as we might think. Kate, however, looks like she isn't exactly buying his story.

At the end of the episode, Kate seems to be the only one Sawyer is comfortable enough to trust. From the beginning, Kate has represented a major attachment for Sawyer, but just like everything else in his life, she eludes him. The moment he thinks she's his, she seems to have turned her sights on Jack. He never knows where he stands with her, and that makes him uneasy; a con man doesn't like being conned. In the sideways world, his encounter with Kate at the end of the episode is fun. Not only do they seem to be destined to be brought together, but he seems bemused and intrigued by her. Now that we know he's a police officer, it makes the earlier scene with them together in the elevator even more astounding. He saw the handcuffs, he knew she was on the run from the law, he shared an elevator with the security guards who were looking for her . . . but he still let her go. Perhaps it was to protect himself; after all, if he turned her in and said he saw her on the plane with the marshal, he would have to explain why he'd been in Australia when he was supposed to be in Palm Springs at a conference. Or perhaps there was an innate feeling within himself that he needed to protect her. Maybe that connection with Kate — which might be a sense of love, a need to protect her, or just a mutual understanding that he doesn't have with anyone else — has crossed the barrier between the two worlds, and he just went with it. Regardless, we might actually get to see what his relationship with Kate would have been like had he not pushed her away like he did on the island.

While Sawyer kept everyone at a distance when he first arrived on the island, he was always a better person when he was with others. When he was helping his fellow survivors, he came alive and seemed truly happy. When he was with Juliet, he had found a security and contentment he hadn't experienced before. But alone again, as we saw in "What Kate Does," he retreated back into the angry, solitary man who can't find it within him to care about anyone, including himself. Just as before, James rejected the companionship of others, even though he needed it more than anything else in his life. He's spent a lifetime alone, simply because of the love and connection he had with his parents. Now, as he pulls Kate into his tiny circle of trust, he realizes that perhaps the only way to pull off a good con is to do it with someone else. We've seen how Sawyer's cons have backfired on him in the past, but in those situations he was working solo. By joining forces with the others, can he pull off the most important con of his life?

Highlight: Kate, after Smokey explains why Claire is upset: "Very insightful . . . coming from a dead man." Smokey: "Well, nobody's perfect."

Did You Notice?:

- Sawyer tells Jin that he's a man of his word, which is the same thing the smoke monster said to Sayid and Claire.
- In our introduction to sideways-world James, the writers manage to con the audience into thinking it's the same Sawyer.
- James's safe word is "Lafleur," which is the name he used in the Dharma Initiative, the one time in his life he felt safe and happy. It's a "safe word" in both realities.
- So . . . are we to assume that the other officers (or, at the very least, Miles), were listening to James having sex with the mark? *Awkward*. (Not to mention, James's actions were probably illegal.)
- Zach is still carrying the teddy bear he was holding in "The Other 48 Days," and now that we can see he carries it on a string, we know he was one of the Others that Jin and Eko saw in ". . . And Found."
- The smoke monster is always very formal in his speech. When Sawyer apologizes to him, he says, "I forgive you." It's interesting that the smoke monster doesn't seem to hold on to grievances with anyone around him for very long, and yet he's holding onto a parental grievance from many years ago.

- Sawyer got to a point in his life where he had to choose between becoming either a criminal or a cop. He chose cop. This idea supports the Many-Worlds Theory (see page 34), where, when Sawyer chose to be a criminal, a second world appeared in which he chose the opposite path.
- The scene where Sawyer finds Kate's dress in the polar bear cage was touching — it's like a lifetime has passed since the flirtation in the cages, and he's lost everything since then.
- Liam Pace seems to be in good shape, as if he got himself clean in the sideways world, too (if he was ever on drugs in the first place, which isn't clear). It's nice to see that in this world, when Charlie needs him, Liam is there for him, which is more than he ever did for Charlie in the other world.
- The Man in Black offers his hand to Kate to help her up, but she gets up on her own without taking his hand. Watch how many times he will offer his hand to people this season and they won't take it.
- James eats frozen dinners and Ben was feeding them to his father. It's as if both of them are attached to overly processed food (like they ate for years in the DI) and need it to be cooked using electromagnetic waves.
- James is watching *Little House on the Prairie* in the sideways world and we know that he was a fan of the show in the other timeline, too. In "Tricia Tanaka Is Dead," Kate tells Sawyer that if he apologizes to her they could have a clean slate. He says a slate is what Laura used to write on in "*Little House*." When she laughs that he calls the show "*Little House*," he says, "I had mono when I was a kid — missed two months of school. We only got one channel in my trailer."
- James shows up at Charlotte's apartment with a sunflower, just like the one he was holding when he walked in to his Dharmaville house to greet Juliet in "Lafleur."
- Charlotte is wearing a red shirt when she comes to the door (a subtle hint that she's dead in the other timeline).
- Sawyer tells Widmore that he needs his word that the people he returns with won't get hurt, "not even a hair on their head." In "The Shape of Things to Come," after Locke insists that Hurley come with him and Ben, Sawyer warns him, "You harm so much as one curly hair on his head, I'll kill you."
- When Widmore asks how he knows he can trust Sawyer, Sawyer replies, "Same way I know I can trust you." Which is another way of saying, "You can't."

The *Lost* Locations Tour in Oahu

For six seasons, *Lost* fans have watched scenes on the mysterious island, as well as flashback scenes in Los Angeles, London, Sydney, Seoul, Nigeria, Portland, Tallahassee, Canary Islands, New York, and others. Yet every one of those scenes was shot somewhere in Oahu, Hawaii, with the island dressed up to look like one of many other locations around the world.

When Ed Kos began operating KOS Tours seven years ago, taking tourists on trips around Oahu to show them the natural beauty of the island, he incorporated some movie locations from films such as *Jurassic Park* and *Godzilla*. After September 2004, he began including locations used on *Lost*. But as more diehard *Lost* fans began flocking to the island to see the locations used on their beloved show, Kos decided to focus some of his tours specifically on *Lost* locations. Now he offers combined *Lost* and movie tours that last two or five hours, and two very special *Lost*-only tours that last eight or ten hours!

According to Kos, his Hummer tours visit close to 75 different locations "depending on what tour you take." Some of the locations offered are:

Matthew Morici, one of the tour guides with KOS, has met most of the cast of *Lost*. (Courtesy KOS Tours)

- The submarine pier
- The Hydra Island sub pier
- The Tempest Station
- Hurley's golf course
- Dharmaville/New Otherton
- The hill where Hurley jumpstarts the VW van in "Tricia Tanaka Is Dead"
- The Iraqi prison where Sayid was a torturer
- The Losties' beach camp
- The site of the Oceanic 815 crash
- Anthony Cooper's house
- Nigerian cantina/ Jin's dad's house/ the school Sayid was rebuilding in the Dominican Republic (all the same building)

- The tower where Jughead was hanging in the 1950s
- The waterfall and pond where Kate and Sawyer swim and find a briefcase full of guns
- The temple where Sun and Jin were married in Korea

When the show was still in production, there was always a chance that tourists could actually see the filming as it was happening and catch a glimpse of the cast, and Kos has met Matthew Fox and Jorge Garcia along the way. He plans to continue running the *Lost* tours, certain that *Lost* fans will be around for years to come. (He and his associate, Matthew Morici, sent me some of their photos of the tourists goofing around in the various locations — acting out scenes and pretending to run from the smoke monster — and it looked like a *Lost* fan's dream.) If you're planning on heading to Hawaii soon, you can book your tour at www.hummertourshawaii.com. Just keep an eye out for those Hostiles. . . .

- When Sawyer comes back and tells Smokey that all of the people in the Ajira plane were dead, Smokey says, "What, that's terrible. What happened," in the flattest and most unconvincing way, as if he already knew.
- Sawyer reminds Smokey that he promised him a way off the island, and adds, "Deal's a deal." That phrase was used in a deleted scene in "Outlaws," when Kate reminds Sawyer that he said he'd give her whatever she wanted if she helped him hunt the boar, adding, "A deal's a deal." It was used again in "Born to Run," when Kate asks for a spot on the raft and Michael tells her he already promised it to Sawyer, and says, "A deal's a deal." And finally, in "Live Together, Die Alone," a surprised Michael looks at Ben and asks if he's really going to allow him to leave the island with Walt. Ben says, "A deal's a deal."
- James immediately telling Miles the truth and even showing him the Sawyer file proves once again that people in the sideways world are more communicative and open with one another than they were on the island.
- In the last line of the episode, Sawyer refers to Kate as "Freckles," an indication that the old Sawyer is back.

Interesting Facts: Zoe is played by Sheila Kelley, who starred on *L.A. Law* and *Sisters*, and who has found success with S Factor, a fitness course in L.A. that she developed specifically for women, which combines yoga, dance, and erotic moves such as pole dancing and striptease. She's married to Richard Schiff, best known as Toby Ziegler on *The West Wing*. Seamus, the chubby-faced guy with the gun, is played by former child star Fred Koehler, who starred as Chip on *Kate & Allie* for five seasons. After that stint he focused on school and got a university degree, and continued acting, with a prominent role on HBO's *Oz* (several other *Lost* alumni).

James first tells Charlotte that he wanted to become a cop after he saw *Bullitt*, the Steve McQueen movie. *Bullitt* is a 1968 film that is now considered a classic and years ahead of its time. McQueen plays Bullitt, a cop who doesn't play by the same rules as everyone else. When he's asked to guard a mobster's brother for protection, and the brother is killed, he covers up the murder in order to buy himself time to find out not only what really happened but also whether the police were even tailing the right guy. The movie's centerpiece is a fast-paced car chase through the streets of San Francisco, where Bullitt is being chased by the hitmen.

The episode of *Little House on the Prairie* that James is watching is from the show's second season, which first aired in 1975. In the episode, "Remember Me, Part 1," a widow finds out she has terminal cancer, and is worried about who will take care of her children. Mrs. Oleson's aunt decides to take the girl, and someone else offers to take the two boys and make them farmhands. Pa's friend Mr. Edwards suddenly decides to ask his girlfriend Grace to marry him, and he adopts all three of the children, keeping them together. The scene that James is watching is where Pa talks to Laura about her feelings about the widow dying.

Nitpicks: Are we really to believe that somehow Charles Widmore had all of those sonic fence pylons on the sub? Do they all fold down into special travel-sized squares?

Oops: During the scene in the hotel room at the beginning, the clock has the same time on it throughout.

4 8 15 16 23 42: The clock in the hotel room says it's **8:42**.

It's Just a Flesh Wound: Claire grabs Kate from behind, throws her to the ground, and is about to cut her throat. Smokey pulls Claire off her and throws her through the air, where Claire falls heavily to the ground. James cuts his hand when he punches a mirror. Charlotte shuts the door on James's mojo. Miles and James are jolted when their car is run into by someone else. James slams Kate into a fence when he captures her.

Any Questions?:
- If Widmore has spent 20 years trying to find this island again, why isn't he walking through the jungle and enjoying it for a few minutes rather than staying locked up in the sub?
- Why does Smokey need to gather up everyone? Why doesn't he just leave the island?

- Miles mentions that his father works at the museum. Is he referring to Pierre Chang? Was he raised by Chang in this timeline, too?
- Charlotte plays innocent when James comes to see her and acts like she was the person who was wronged, but it's clear she was looking for more than a T-shirt when she was rifling through his drawer. Was she looking for something in particular? Does she know the Sawyer story? Or did her inner archaeologist notice something in the drawer and she couldn't help herself, and just had to dig further? Either way, she can hardly play the innocent victim after what she did.
- Who killed all of the people from the Ajira flight? Widmore wouldn't have had a reason to. Was it Smokey?
- How did Liam get to the police station so quickly to bail out Charlie if he lives in Sydney?
- Smokey tells Kate that he had problems "that could have been avoided, had things been different." Is this a comment on how things are slightly different in the sideways world, and problems are being resolved over there?
- Is Smokey telling the truth about his mother? Why does he sound like a child when he talks about her?
- Was Smokey drawn to John Locke because John's mother was crazy, too?
- What's behind the locked door in Widmore's sub?
- Why did Claire have the sudden change of heart with Kate? Was she being sincere when she said she understood why Kate took him? Or is this another deception so she can finally get her revenge on Kate?
- What happened to sideways-world Kate between being with Claire and crashing into James's car?
- So . . . is the Man in Black feeding people one of Ben's rabbits?

Ashes to Ashes: Farewell to everyone else who was on the Ajira flight.

6.9   Ab Aeterno

Original air date: March 23, 2010
Written by: Melinda Hsu Taylor, Greggory Nations
Directed by: Tucker Gates
Guest cast: Steven Elder (Mr. Whitfield), Mirelly Taylor (Isabella), Titus Welliver

(Man in Black), Juan Carlos Cantu (Father Suarez), Davo Coria (Servant), Izzy Diaz (Ignacio), Santiago Montone (Prisoner), Jose Yenque (Doctor)

Focus: Richard

We finally see Richard Alpert's backstory, how he came to the island, and what Jacob's purpose is. In other words . . . ANSWERS!!

This was the episode the hardcore fans have been waiting for — those fans whose faith in the show has been unwavering, who believed the show was great but had the potential to be sublime, who didn't leave during season 3 and even managed to lure back some of those who did, who argued that while the show *could* be baffling at times it was still an example of how satisfying television storytelling can be. "Ab Aeterno" is one of those rare hours that makes television worth watching.

For six seasons *Lost* has engaged viewers' minds, and week after week the diehard fans have rushed to encyclopedias, bibles, physics textbooks, and philosophy treatises. We've translated Egyptian hieroglyphics, distinguished between the belief systems of Jean-Jacques Rousseau and John Locke, learned about the psychology experiments of B.F. Skinner, and discussed Stephen Hawking's theories about wormholes and time travel. We've read Lewis Carroll, William Butler Yeats, Flann O'Brien, Stephen King, and a graphic novel by Brian K. Vaughan. We've searched out all of the clues in the episodes and tried to piece together the increasingly intricate puzzle the writers have created for us. *Lost* has expanded our minds in ways a television show has never accomplished before.

But what "Ab Aeterno" reminds us of is that *Lost* is a show about people. The reason we became hooked on this show in its first season wasn't because of the literature Sawyer was reading or the references to Enlightenment philosophers; it was because the writers made the characters three-dimensional, showed us their backstories, and made us sympathize with and truly understand them. None of the science, philosophy, history, psychology, and literature would matter if the show didn't engage our hearts as well. We want the characters to be happy, we cheer for them as they work through their problems, we cry when they're in pain, and we long to know if they're going to be okay in the future.

"Ab Aeterno" is the epic story of Richard Alpert, a man who has been an enigma on the island since we first saw him in "Not in Portland" acting as a recruit for Mittelos Bioscience (a.k.a. Ben Linus) as he brought Juliet to the island under false pretenses. He seemed to be a right-hand man to Ben in a way, until a couple of episodes later, in "The Brig," when he handed John Locke a file that helped him convince Sawyer to kill Anthony Cooper. In this moment, Alpert seemed a little more important than your average, everyday Other. He knew more about the island than the rest of the Others, but still acceded to Ben. In "The Man Behind the Curtain," we saw Richard appear to Ben 30 years earlier, and mysteriously, he looked exactly the same, save for longer hair and tattered clothing. He had appeared to be Ben's inferior, but in their past association, we saw him talking to Young Ben and making the rules for him. How could Richard look the same? At the beginning of that episode, Ben had said to Richard, "You *do* remember birthdays, don't you, Richard?" Fans wondered, is it possible he doesn't age and birthdays are no longer relevant to him?

After that, due to an outside circumstance, Richard disappeared (actor Nestor Carbonell had been cast as a lead in the series *Cane*, and CBS refused to allow him to come back to *Lost* for guest appearances, until *Cane* was canceled due to poor ratings). His mysterious return was in "Cabin Fever," where we saw him watching John Locke from an early age, running an early psychology test on him, and trying to determine if he was the island's next leader. And slowly, through his appearances in the past throughout the time jumping in season 5, and from Ben's asides about who he was, we came to understand that Alpert had been on the island for a very long time, and was the advisor to the leader of the Others, working as Jacob's mouthpiece. So where did he come from?

In this episode, we find out exactly where. Richard's backstory is tied inextricably to his deep love for his late wife and his belief in a higher power. Apart from the stunning production, the movie-like feel of the episode, and the beautiful storytelling, Nestor Carbonell's acting stands out like a shining beacon. Who'd have thought the actor who played the quiet, ever-calm presence on the island was capable of such passion? Carbonell puts in a jaw-dropping performance, conveying heartbreak, agony, anger, confusion, and calm. The only thing they didn't ask him to do was smile. Poor Richard. . . .

The episode gave us a few of the answers we'd been seeking for several years: we find out once and for all why *The Black Rock* was in the middle of the island, and how the four-toed statue was destroyed — both happened at the same time when a tsunami caused the ocean to temporarily engulf the island, sending the ship straight through the statue. We see the natures of the Man in Black and Jacob as they are pitted against each other, and much of our sympathy for the Man in Black disappears when we realize he's the silver-tongued Satan on the

Nestor Carbonell puts in the performance of the season in "Ab Aeterno." (ML Agency)

island, trying to convince Richard that Jacob is, in fact, the devil he needs to kill. But the major revelation of the episode came in Jacob's monologue about what the island is. And while his metaphor left some eyebrows arched (Really? A wine cork?) it was a fitting one that helped make sense of what is going on in this place. On *Buffy the Vampire Slayer*, the town of Sunnydale was built over a "hellmouth," which was a doorway through which all of the creatures of Hell could enter the world. Buffy was the Slayer who was chosen to protect the world against the things that could emerge from the hellmouth, and was charged with the task of keeping it closed. Similarly, the island is the "cork" that keeps the wine bottle of evil safely stopped: "Think of this wine as what you keep calling Hell. There's many other names for it, too: malevolence, evil, darkness. And here it is, swirling around in the bottle unable to get out, because if it did, it would spread. The cork is this island. And it's the only thing keeping the darkness where it belongs."

A less bizarro explanation would be to look at the myth of Pandora's Box. In the Greek myth, Zeus gives Pandora — the first woman, designed to be sent into the world to punish men — a box that she is ordered not to open under any circumstances. Her curiosity gets the better of her and she opens it, unleashing all of the evil out into the world (of course . . . I mean, what origin story would be complete without a woman being blamed for all of mankind's evil?). Realizing what she's done, she quickly closes the box, trapping only Hope inside. So in this instance, one can think of the island as being the lid of Pandora's box, trapping all of the inherent evil underneath it, and Jacob is the one sitting on the lid, keeping it closed and not allowing the worst evils of the world out into it. The world does contain bad things, but Jacob is suggesting that he's keeping the absolute worst things from escaping. Perhaps instead of keeping Hope in the box, he has let it out, giving the people on the island the one thing they need to get through their troubles.

Jacob admits that it was he who brought everyone to the island, an extension of what we already knew from his beach chat with the Man in Black at the beginning of "The Incident." He's been calling boats (and later planes) to the island for centuries, trying to find the person who will replace him as the guardian of this hellmouth. He's also bringing them to the island to prove that the Man in Black's fundamental beliefs are wrong. He explains to Richard, "That man who sent you to kill me believes that everyone is corruptible because it's in their very nature to sin. I bring people here to prove him wrong, and when they get here, their past doesn't matter."

Jacob's explanation brings back the philosophical state-of-nature argument that was first hinted at in season 1 (see *Finding Lost — Seasons One & Two*, p. 147). Enlightenment philosophers often argued about what man's inherent behavior would be in a state of nature, without any laws or other authority. John Locke (1632–1704) argued that man was essentially good, and that experience was the thing that changed him. He believed that given a choice, man would choose the morally correct thing to do, and when they faced tyranny, they would rally for a government to protect them. Jean-Jacques Rousseau (1712–1778) believed that man was neither good nor evil, but that within society, he was easily corrupted. He believed sovereignty was the way to go, because people needed to be told what to do; however, he believed that people should have the right to overthrow that sovereignty if it wasn't protecting their rights. Thomas Hobbes (1588–1679) believed that man was essentially evil, and if left in a state of nature, individuals would be at war with one another and would eventually destroy themselves (think of the Man in Black summing up mankind in eight words: "They come. They fight. They corrupt. They destroy."). Hobbes believed in an absolute sovereignty under which man should be forced to give up all free will and be told what to do, for their own protection.

Jacob seems to have faith in man, and he believes that people should be allowed to make their own decisions. He brings people to the island, but he doesn't tell them what to do; instead he wants them to use free will to help themselves. While in "The Incident" he seems to concede that the Man in Black's eight-word summation may have been true so far, Jacob believes that people evolve and make "progress" with every group he brings to the island. The Man in Black, on the other hand, is clearly Hobbesian — he believes it's in man's nature to sin. He doesn't understand why Jacob keeps bringing people to the island if they simply turn into the same angry mob they do every time, destroying each other and the world around them. Jacob has clearly cursed him in a way that makes him unable to interfere and make the choices for them, but the Man in Black is still able to help lead them to certain decisions. He uses his powers of persuasion on Richard, convincing him that Jacob is the devil and needs to be destroyed. He offers to help get Richard out of the chains, but only if Richard will help him first. Richard wants to see his wife again, and he believes the Man in Black has promised him that he will, but what the Man in Black actually says to him is "The question is, Do you want to see your wife again?" He simply asks him a question, implying that he will let Richard see her again but never actually making the promise. The verbal cunning of the Man in Black is a key to his character, one that suggests he's not to be trusted no matter how much sympathy he conjures within us.

Richard Alpert is not inherently evil; he has made some mistakes, but they weren't exactly willing choices. He killed a doctor by accident, motivated by love for his wife and a desperate need for the man to help her. But the doctor let him down, and abandoned him in his hour of need. Alpert appeals to him, handing him the cross that represents his belief in God and his connection to Isabella (whose name means "my God is a vow"). The doctor tosses the cross aside as if it's worthless, showing his utter disdain for Richard and everything he believes in. After Isabella's death, as Richard visits with the priest in the prison, he asks for absolution, something the priest refuses to give him. Both science and faith have failed Richard. Richard's God hasn't turned his back on Richard, but the man who presumes to speak for God has. Richard still keeps his faith, and it's fitting that ultimately he becomes the man who speaks for the island's deity; unlike the horrible priest, Richard never presumes to know Jacob's intentions, he only conveys exactly what Jacob has told him to, nothing more or less.

The scene as *The Black Rock* approaches the island is awesome, dark, and terrifying, and the fact that Richard is the last person to see the looming Taweret statue before it is destroyed is appropriate, for he believes the statue to be the devil himself, and that first impression drives itself deep within his psyche. One hundred and forty years later, he is still unable to shake the feeling that the island is, in fact, Hell, and he has died on it. When he first meets Jacob, Jacob grabs Richard and dunks his head under the water, in effect baptizing him into a new way of thinking, in the process becoming Richard's new God. When he joins

To create the outside of Richard's home in 1867, the production crew built a thatched-roof cottage. (Courtesy KOS Tours)

Jacob, now with the added gift/curse of immortality, Richard buries Isabella's cross in the ground, and with it he buries his hope and his old faith.

At the end of the episode, the conversation between Jacob and the Man in Black offers us some more insight into the relationship between the two of them. No longer do we hear each one talk about the other, we see them together, which probably gives us the clearest perspective on who they are. The Man in Black declares his intention not only to kill Jacob but to kill anyone who might take his place; in other words, the Candidates. This scene coupled with the scene where Jacob talks to Richard allows us to start making pretty educated guesses about the Others. Are they people from various ships and planes that have been drawn to the island by Jacob but weren't killed by the Man in Black because they weren't Candidates? We saw Montand, Brennan, and Rousseau all listed on the lighthouse dial, so we can probably assume Smokey killed them when they arrived in 1988 in order to prevent them from fulfilling their potential Candidacy. ("Rousseau" could have referred to Robert, Danielle, or Alex, all of whom eventually died on the island.) Would this also suggest that the numbers Rousseau's party heard being transmitted were in fact read by Jacob in order to lure them to the island to become Candidates?

Despite the numerous answers we got in this episode, and the explanation of the way the island works (and why everything happened the way it did), what many fans will remember is the final scene between Isabella and Richard. It's heartbreakingly beautiful, and I dare you to watch it with a dry eye. Richard has spent many lifetimes pining for his wife, damning himself to immortality to avoid the hellfire he believes awaits him if he dies. Despite giving 140 years of service to the island, his "God" has abandoned him once more, and left him bereft and without purpose. But in this one gorgeous moment, Isabella reaches across the divide between life and death (via Hurley) to tell him that he's not alone, and that they've always been together. At the beginning of the episode, she tells him to close his eyes, and he does, and when he opens them his life changes utterly. He closes them again when Smokey tears into *The Black Rock* and kills everyone around him, and when he opens them he's alone. But this time, when she tells him to close his eyes, the act allows him to shut out the rest of the world, and see only her. He can't actually see her physically standing in front of him — only Hurley can do that — but instead he sees her with his heart, and knows that she's never left him alone. For a century and a half, she has been by his side, and though he feels he's been abandoned by Jacob, he'll never be abandoned by her. Carbonell is magnificent in this scene, and it is beautifully directed and shot. Again, this episode reminds us that only when the characters realize they're not alone and strive to work together can they find hope and success in their lives.

And now those efforts will have to be redoubled to stop Smokey, for Hurley has revealed that if they don't stop him, they will all go to Hell. He plans to uncork the island, so to speak, and allow the worst elements of Hell to seep into the rest of the world, which will turn the world into Hell on earth. Jacob believes that the way to keep him from doing that is to protect the doorway to Hell, to keep it covered so the darkness cannot invade the world. But when the Man in Black smashes the bottle against the log, he gives us a chilling illustration of how uncorking the bottle isn't the only way he can unleash the horrors of Hell into the world.

Highlight: Ben's reaction when Jack doesn't know who Richard was referring to when he was talking about the Man in Black: "Oh, *this* should be interesting."

Did You Notice?:
- When Richard tells everyone that they're all dead and are actually in Hell, it's a nod to the fan theory that had been discussed since the show's first season.
- It's interesting that Jack would tell Ilana that Richard, being suicidal, has lost his mind. Usually suicide would indicate that someone is mentally unstable, but considering what Richard's been through for over a century, it almost seems sensible. And anyway, only one day earlier Jack was

dropping a bomb down a shaft to change the course of time and erase everything that had happened to him for the past *three* years . . . that's the pot calling the kettle greasy.
- Richard and his wife wanted to move to the New World. Instead, he ended up on the island, which appears to be an even older world than the one he was in.
- Whitfield, the man who purchases Richard from the prison, declares that Richard is now the property of Magnus Hanso. Fans have long speculated that Hanso was the captain of *The Black Rock*. The Dharma Initiative was funded by the Hanso Foundation, run by Alvar Hanso, who was the great-grandson of Magnus. On the blast door map that Locke first sees in "Lockdown," there's a spot near *The Black Rock*'s location on the map marked, "Known final resting place of Magnus Hanso / Black Rock."
- When the smoke monster first encounters Richard, it moves in and assesses him the same way it did Juliet and Kate in "Left Behind," by moving close and appearing to take photos of him (you can see flashes going off).
- The Man in Black says to Richard, "It's good to see you out of those chains." It's the same thing that Smokey said to Richard in "LA X," just before punching him in the throat.
- Jacob tells Richard that when people get to the island, the past doesn't matter. But as we've seen for at least the first three seasons of the show, the past mattered a *lot* to the survivors.
- Jacob cannot bring Richard's wife back or absolve him, but he can give him immortality. It's like he can play God on the island, but he can't reverse what Richard's God has already done.
- Back in "Dr. Linus," Hurley asked Richard if he was a cyborg or a vampire, and Richard denies both but won't go into further detail, saying it's too hard to explain. Saying, "Jacob gave me eternal life" makes for a simple explanation. Perhaps he assumed Hurley would ask too many follow-up questions.

Interesting Facts: Richard's backstory begins on Tenerife, the largest of the Canary Islands, a group of Spanish islands off the coast of Africa. Beginning in the 16th century, many inhabitants on the island succumbed to disease or were sold into slavery thanks to immigration from the Spanish Empire. Richard and his wife were probably descendents of the original immigrants who came during that wave, so it's a sad irony that they succumbed to both of those things 300 years later. It's also interesting to think that Richard went from one island that he wanted to escape to another, where he would be trapped forever. Incidentally, the date the backstory begins is 1867, which is the year that Canada became a nation (and therefore, in the *Lost*verse, evil entered the world!).

When the priest visits Richard in prison, Richard is reading the Gospel of Luke, chapter 4. In the passage he is reading, Jesus visits Nazareth, which is the place where he grew up, and goes to a synagogue to do a reading from the Book of Isaiah. After he reads it, he sits down to begin teaching them, but everyone is staring at him strangely. They look at each other, having heard he was the Messiah, and say, "Isn't he the son of Joseph?" Because they'd seen him grow up from infancy, they were reluctant to accept him as anything other than the kid down the street (which is where the passage the priest reads aloud to Richard — "no prophet is accepted in his own country" — comes from). Jesus says to them that he realizes they want him to demonstrate some miracles, but he doesn't do that. He reminds them of the story of the prophets Elijah and Elisha, who, when they went back to their hometowns, did not heal all of the Jews, but instead they each healed one Gentile. Upon hearing the story, the people of Nazareth are infuriated (in the story they believe they are God's chosen people and that God would not heal a Gentile) and they take Jesus to a cliff with the intention of throwing him off, but he simply walks through the middle of the crowd and leaves them. Similarly, Jacob won't perform miracles or prove himself to the survivors, instead he wants them to find their own way without any prodding from him. In a way, both John Locke and Ben were rejected by their own people, who refused to believe they were special in any way. The Oceanic survivors rejected Locke, and the Others ultimately stopped following Ben.

Nestor Carbonell was as surprised to see Richard's backstory as the fans were. "I certainly never imagined that it was love or a crime of passion that would bring him to the island," he said. "I certainly didn't expect him to come from the Canary Islands. There were all these signs that perhaps he is of Egyptian origin. And I was thinking I'm going to have to adopt a different language. But I was really floored by how they addressed his whereabouts." He added, "A lot of the crew felt really sorry for me when Mark Pellegrino was slamming me in the water. But I have to tell you after being in *The Black Rock* for five days straight, I really welcomed that bath in the ocean tremendously."

Nitpicks: Even if the hull of *The Black Rock* was made of metal, I find it hard to believe that in a collision between a wooden ship and a giant stone statue, the ship is the one that would remain largely intact and the statue would crumble to pieces. When Richard dropped the nail, he couldn't reach it with his hands, but he could have stuck out his foot and gotten it easily.

4 8 15 16 23 42: Richard is reading chapter 4 of the Gospel of Luke. Jacob dunks Richard's head under the water 4 times.

It's Just a Flesh Wound: I usually don't recount injuries from flashbacks, but I will include anything that happened on the island: several prisoners on *The Black Rock* are impaled on Whitfield's sword. Richard's wrists and fingers are bloody from being in the chains. Jacob punches Richard several times. Jacob dunks Richard's head in the ocean repeatedly.

Lost in Translation: The literal translation of the Latin title of the episode is "from eternity," and is usually translated as "from the beginning of time" (though in the official podcast, Damon claimed the title translated to "eternal abs"). When Hurley is first talking to Isabella in Spanish on the beach at the beginning of the episode, he says to her, "Why? I don't know. Yes, I can help you, but I don't know how to find him."

Any Questions?:
- At the beginning of "The Incident, Part 1," we can see a ship that looks a lot like *The Black Rock* coming toward the island, and Jacob acknowledges that he brought it here. However, it's a bright sunny morning when he's talking to the Man in Black, and yet when *The Black Rock* finally does come to the island, it's during a nighttime storm. Damon joked in a podcast that Jacob must have whipped up a heck of a storm to bring the ship inland, but how did it switch from day to night? Perhaps Jacob has Prospero-like abilities to change the weather and the sky, which is why *The Tempest* was alluded to a couple of seasons ago (see *Finding Lost — Season Four*, pp. 82–85).
- Why was Ilana's head bandaged in her flashback with Jacob? How did he find her in the first place? Did she spend time on the island? Was she the child of someone he'd brought to the island? Was she hurt trying to protect one of his previous Candidates? Did he heal her face? After all, the extent of her burns would have left her disfigured in a way she is not.
- Why does Sun assume she's the Kwon Candidate? Does Ilana know this for sure or is this just an assumption at this point?
- Ilana reveals once and for all that she's on the island to protect the Candidates. In "LA X," Smokey presumed that she and the others were

there to protect Jacob. Did he really not know why they were on the island, or was he playing dumb so Ben wouldn't figure it out?
- At this point, most viewers assume that the dead people we've seen on the island are manifestations of Smokey — Alex, Yemi, and Christian have all been associated with him. But what about Isabella? Is it possible she was a ghost? I think the Isabella we saw in the bottom of the ship was actually Smokey, trying to break down the last bit of Richard's resolve. But I'd like to think the Isabella we saw standing with Richard and Hurley was in fact her ghost, since it's unlikely the Man in Black would have given Richard such a nice message. Also, the warning she gives to him about stopping the Man in Black is very unlikely to have come from him.
- If the smoke monster was impersonating Isabella, how was he able to play both her and the smoke monster at the same time? In "Dead Is Dead," Locke/Smokey hung back while Ben went looking for the smoke monster, because he couldn't be both things at once. Is he able to look like her but also make the smoke monster sound at the same time? (We don't see the smoke monster when Isabella runs up the stairs; we only hear it. Maybe he throws his voice.)
- When the Man in Black tells Richard to kill Jacob, he pulls out the same dagger Dogen gave to Sayid in order to kill Smokey. How did Dogen know to say exactly the same thing to Sayid that the Man in Black says to Richard? Both warn that if you let the victim speak first, it'll already be too late.

Nestor Carbonell

With his quiet, stoic manner and those impeccably rolled sleeves, Richard Alpert quickly became a fan favorite after his first appearance in season 3 of *Lost*. But no matter how many different sides of Richard we see — or how tremendous a performance the actor puts in — Nestor Carbonell can never escape one inevitable question in interviews . . . and the answer is no, he does *not* wear eyeliner.

"I actually read about it online, and the funny thing was the nicknames: Maybelline Man, Guyliner. Names I'd never heard before," he laughs. "The flipside of it is that I do watch the show and you can't argue with the fans — in many cases, it does look like there's eyeliner there! Sometimes it's the way I'm lit, and the makeup department made a point, so it wouldn't be a distraction, to put a base under my lower eyelashes to diminish the impression that I was wearing eyeliner." But he hasn't always been able to laugh at his trademark dark eyes. "It's not the first time I had to deal with it — I actually dealt with it as a kid quite a bit with my mom's friends. I would hear about it quite a bit, to the point where I actually cut my eyelashes off."

Nestor was born in New York City on December 1, 1967, and is of Cuban and Spanish descent. "My parents, grandparents, and great-grandparents were born in Cuba. But my roots are Spanish."

Nestor attended boarding school in Massachusetts with none other than Matthew Fox ("He was a year ahead of me but I certainly knew who he was") before he went on to an English literature degree at Harvard. While there, he decided to take a drama class, and that's when he found his true passion. He starred in an Off-Broadway play, *A Silent Thunder*, before finding roles in television and films, including starring on *Suddenly Susan* as Spanish photographer Luis Rivera from 1996 to 2000.

In 1999, he met his future wife, actress Shannon Kenny, when they were both working on the film *Attention Shoppers*. They were married in 2000 and now have two sons who were born in 2002 and 2005. (Kenny is a big *Lost* fan, but such a spoilerphobe that she wouldn't look at scripts when Nestor brought them home.)

After *Suddenly Susan*, Nestor got parts on *Ally McBeal* and *House, M.D.*, and starred as the hilarious Batmanuel in the short-lived superhero parody *The Tick*. In 2006 he met up with Matthew Fox again when they both appeared in the film *Smokin' Aces*. Later that same year he was asked to come to Hawaii to play a guest character on *Lost* named Richard Alpert, who would recruit Juliet Burke into the Dharma Initiative before being revealed to be one of the Others. Little did he know how important that role would eventually become.

"I figured it was another flashback," he says, "but when I got the script, I was pleasantly surprised that it was in the present day and that it didn't seem like that was the last you'd see of the character. They didn't tell me much, but I think they knew at that point that Richard was going somewhere. Usually in these roles, they bill them as 'guest star, potentially recurring,' but you never really know if they're going to recur that far and to what extent. In fact, my wife said, 'This is potentially recurring, but we're all going to come with you just in case, because it's a free trip to Hawaii.'"

Alpert appeared later in the season and was poised to become an important character in the series' arc (especially once a flashback to 30 years earlier showed him looking exactly the same as he did in the present) . . . when suddenly, he was cast in *Cane* on CBS, which meant he was now contracted to CBS and couldn't switch networks to play Richard Alpert over on ABC, a rival network. Because Damon and Carlton couldn't guarantee him a recurring role, he took the part in *Cane*, where he played Jimmy Smits' brother-in-law Frank Duque, part of a Cuban-American family that runs a rum business. The show got good reviews when it debuted, but the ratings dropped and it was canceled after 13 episodes. Bad news for Nestor . . . but good news for *Lost* fans.

After the 2007–2008 Writers Guild Strike, *Lost* returned to the second half of its fourth season with Nestor back on board. Richard Alpert appeared as a major character in "Cabin Fever," watching John Locke throughout his life and creepily not aging at all. By the show's fifth season, Alpert was so entangled in John Locke's story that fans wanted to know what *his* was. Who was this guy? Where had he come from? Was he really immortal? How had he become an advisor to Jacob?

As Nestor's star power grew with a role in *The Dark Knight*, in which he played the mayor of Gotham City, fans started demanding to know more about Alpert. In the months leading up to the show's sixth season, it was announced that Nestor was officially becoming a cast member of *Lost*, and Damon and Carlton promised that we'd finally see Richard's backstory. To his wife's delight, Nestor and his family rented a place in Oahu for the duration of the final season.

"Nestor is the kind of actor who attacks his role with such confidence, you come away with the feeling that he has the answer to every secret of the island," said Lindelof. "But beneath that confidence is an incredible vulnerability, one Nestor is finally getting to show off in episodes like 'Ab Aeterno.'" And show off he did. In a performance that left fans astounded at his dramatic range, Nestor showed there was a *lot* more to Richard than the calm, helpful advisor to the Others.

The writers set the backstory on the Canary Islands to make use of Nestor's fluency in Spanish. And when he looked into the history of the place, Nestor realized he'd be able to make Richard's accent authentic simply by using the one that comes most naturally to him. "I did a little research on the Canary Islands because I was concerned about the accent. And much to my surprise, I found that there are many similarities between the Cuban accent and the Canary Islands."

Nestor Carbonell has enjoyed the new places the writers have taken Richard's character this season and how he's finally allowed to be more human than he had been before: "I think one of the things that's always tugged away at him, and it was very frustrating to him last season, is that he always knew what was going on and then last season he had those moments where he was completely thrown by the time travel," says Nestor. "That's not something he knew anything about, when Locke comes to visit him in the 1950s and he goes to see him as a baby two years later. That sort of called into question how much knowledge and power he had; he keeps tapping leaders like a Panchen Lama, so he's really more of an advisor than a leader. I always felt like this guy's gonna have a bit of a complex, to have the power to tap a leader but not be a leader himself."

As *Lost* ended and it was announced he would be appearing on the USA comedy *Psych*, Nestor revealed that not every new aspect of Richard's character in season 6 thrilled him, however: "Terry [O'Quinn] takes me down with two little punches? Come on!" he laughs. "I'll go along with the smoke monster and everything else, but that to me is the most implausible moment in the whole show."

6.10   The Package

Original air date: March 30, 2010
Written by: Paul Zbyszewski, Graham Roland
Directed by: Paul Edwards
Guest cast: Anthony Azizi (Omar), Andrew Divoff (Mikhail), Kevin Durand (Keamy), Natalie Garcia Fryman (Ms. Kendall), Larry Joshua (LAX Customs Official)

Focus: Jin/Sun

Sun loses her ability to speak English when she runs from Smokey, who offers to take her to Jin. Meanwhile, Widmore tells Jin he's going to show him the package he's brought to the island.

"The Package" is an episode about being trapped and breaking free, which is what has marked the story of Sun and Jin from the moment we first met them. At the beginning of season 1, Jin and Sun were a difficult couple for fans to accept. Jin was harsh and kept Sun in her place, and Sun was meek, buttoning her top button, not talking to the others, and doing whatever her husband told her to do. Fans worried that they were a stereotype of Asian men and women, and even Yunjin Kim expressed her reservations upon first hearing what the characters were going to be like. But as the season progressed, a new picture began to form: Jin wasn't exactly the person he seemed to be, rather, he was a kind, loving man who had been pushed, not least by Sun's father, to behave in a way that was against his nature. And because he couldn't speak English, he was trapped by his very inability to communicate with the others and was separated from the rest of the group as a result.

The story of Sun and Jin began by portraying Sun as the subservient wife to the powerful Jin, and evolved into the story of a strong woman who has quietly controlled her husband's life without him knowing it, even though she was doing it out of love for him. Their life together has been one of silence, with each one keeping secrets from the other and not communicating . . . until they got to the island.

Sun's father, Mr. Paik, is the nasty CEO of a large company, but he also acts like a Korean mobster. As a child, Sun learned quickly to manipulate a situation for her own means: her childhood lies caused the firing of one of the servants and her adult deception caused the death of her lover, Jae Lee ("The Glass Ballerina"). As she got older, Sun was put under a lot of pressure to succeed and to marry a man of power, while her aspirations to go to college and make something of herself were dismissed as silly and unnecessary. After being rejected by Jae Lee, she bumped into Jin and it was love at first sight.

Jin was born to a prostitute mother, who abandoned him and left him with his father, a poor fisherman. Jin never discovered what his mother did for a living, and his father was a good and loving man, but Jin had a lot of ambition and longed to be something more ("D.O.C."). He moved to Seoul, told people his father was dead out of shame for the lowly position his father held in society, and worked for Mr. Paik at the hotel. When he and Sun fell in love, he asked Paik for her hand in marriage, and Paik agreed under the condition that Jin would come and work for him (". . . In Translation"). Jin eagerly agreed, unaware of the extent to which he would be beholden to Paik. Jin's employ began simply enough, with Paik having him run errands such as picking up a toy to give to an important ambassador ("Ji Yeon"). When Sun was blackmailed by Jin's mother, she paid him off with Paik's money so the woman wouldn't reveal herself to her son. Sun threatened to kill her if she ever came back, revealing a much darker Sun who was more like her father than we'd previously thought. Sun never told Jin what she'd done, and Jin wouldn't communicate to Sun the utter misery he endured working for her father.

Because she'd borrowed the money from her father to give to Jin's mother, she put Jin in her father's debt, who now turned him into one of his goons. Jin was asked to do things for Paik that became increasingly amoral and stressful to him,

Keamy says that some people were never meant to be together, but Sun and Jin's relationship is stronger than he realizes. (Yunjin Kim: Marco Garcia/AP Photo; Daniel Dae Kim: RD/Kirkland/Retna Digital)

and it began to break their marriage apart. Sun spent more days and nights alone, and Jin began to hate himself for the person he'd become. Neither one told the other how they felt. After an affair with Jae Lee that ended in his death (at the hands of Paik), Sun began plotting a way to leave Jin. With her new, secret grasp of English, she got an illegal passport. She planned to walk away from Jin at the airport when they were traveling to Sydney and then L.A. to deliver watches for her father ("House of the Rising Sun"). What she didn't know was that Jin was planning a similar escape, but one that involved both of them. He was going to deliver the package in L.A. and then disappear with her, finally out from under Paik's thumb. But just as Sun changed her mind at the airport and decided to stick with Jin after all, Jin was cornered by a man in the airport bathroom who revealed himself to be one of Paik's spies, and told Jin he'd never be free of Paik ("Exodus, Part 2"). Of course, Jin didn't tell Sun what happened in the bathroom, and instead boarded the plane in angry silence, leaving Sun puzzled.

And so it was with this hanging over Jin's head that they crashed to the island, and his hostility toward Sun was borne of his anger at Paik. Even though the island was technically a way of being free of Paik, he assumed they'd be rescued and Paik would know exactly where they'd been, since their plane crash would have been all over the news. Sun, meanwhile, was quiet and subservient to him because she carried the burden of knowing she'd been planning to leave him, and unlike Jin, could understand every word of English being spoken around her, yet she couldn't let him know that. Where Jin had been looking to escape with Sun, she'd been looking to get away from him. And yet once Jin discovered that Sun could speak English, they finally broke their silence and found their true feelings for one another.

Both Sun and Jin were trapped by who they'd become, and both had been thwarted in their plans to get out. In the sideways world, their plight is similar, but different. In this version of September 2004, Jin and Sun are not married because Jin never had the stones to ask her father for her hand. It seems he met Sun while already working as one of Paik's lackeys (in this reality, he wasn't forced into working for Paik, he chose to). Jin knew quite well what her father was capable of (in the island timeline, he didn't, or he probably wouldn't have had the nerve to ask for her hand in that world, either) and so he and Sun are having a secret affair, not unlike the one she was having with Jae Lee. Just as we were misled in season 1 into thinking that Jin was an overbearing tyrant, we're similarly tricked in the sideways world when he asked her to button up her sweater. But as revealed in the marvellous scene in the hotel room, Sun is as much in control of this relationship — if not more so — than she was in the other timeline. Her flirty unbuttoning of her sweater, rendering the heretofore bossy Jin a stuttering mess, is brilliant and shows that this relationship is only beginning, whereas their relationship in the other timeline was in a rocky spot by this same point.

On the island, Sun is now trapped in a similar way to Jin in season 1 — she can no longer speak English. Strangely, she can understand it, but cannot convey it to anyone else. She's feeling imprisoned by the group, and one can't exactly blame her at this point. She was lured back to the island by Ben Linus, who promised to take her to Jin. But since the return he's been completely ineffectual and doesn't know where Jin is. She turned to Richard Alpert, who was equally unhelpful (aside from telling her he watched Jin and everyone else on the island die). So she put her faith in Locke, only to find out he wasn't Locke. Now she's following Ilana, who seems as clueless as Sun is as to what to do next. When Sun completely loses it in this episode, it's a relief because she expresses the same frustrations many other viewers had at this point. It's disappointing that it's in Korean

— one wishes everyone standing there could have known exactly what she was saying to them so maybe they could find a clue — but at the same time, the subtitling lends a hint of comedy to the scene. The baffled look on Richard's face, coupled with the "don't ask me" shrug that Jack gives him, is hilarious.

Jin is also stuck where he is, taken by Zoe (who is quickly becoming the new Nikki on the island . . . will someone bury her alive in sand already?) and being asked a series of questions that don't matter to him. He had been trying to find his wife, was waylaid by Sayid's wound and going to the Temple, and is now slowed down by an injured leg (which seems to heal at the speed of light), and now just wants to get back to finding his wife again. But Zoe (a.k.a. the poor man's Liz Lemon) is too caught up in trying to find the pockets of electromagnetic energy on the island to let that happen. As Jin sits in Room 23 (a reminder of previous entrapments from past seasons), he refuses to answer any questions, until Widmore says that it's time that he show Jin "the package."

In the sideways world, when Sayid walks into the fridge and finds Jin there, Jin simply says, "Free." It's one of the few English words that he knows, because it's something he longs to be. Every character on the show wants to be free: free of the island, free of their hang-ups, free of their mommy or daddy issues, free of bad relationships, free of their past . . . free of the pain that seems to dog them at every turn. The island freed Locke from his wheelchair and Kate from her handcuffs, but it then put them in new positions of entrapment. The survivors tried desperately to get off the island in many ways, looking for the freedom that existed for them in the outside world, blind to the fact that many of them had felt as imprisoned out there as they do on the island. Even Smokey refers to himself as being in chains and being held captive on the island, trapped in a pillar of smoke that wasn't his doing. He wants to be free, but his freedom will only come at the price of everyone else's.

In one of the more peculiar scenes of the episode, Martin Keamy sits in the walk-in fridge with Jin, talking to him about his relationship with Sun. Keamy is a master manipulator, flashing those giant white teeth and pretending he doesn't know anything about their relationship while accepting thousands of dollars from Paik to put an end to it once and for all. But as he sits and talks to Jin, there's a strange sadness about him, and it's not clear if he's still playing the role of the cunning baddie or if he's speaking from some sort of knowledge. Remember, in the island timeline, it was Martin Keamy who caused Jin and Sun to be parted in the first place when he constructed the very bomb that blew up the freighter, leading

Sun to believe her husband was dead. Keamy says, "The heart wants what the heart wants," and apologizes to Jin, as if he understands how it feels to want something so badly you'd do anything to get it. But he quickly adds, "Some people just weren't meant to be together."

That line hangs over the Jin/Sun relationship. In the original timeline, soon after getting married they began to separate emotionally, and Sun longed to be free of Jin. On the island, they were separated when Jin abandoned her after finding out she was lying to him about how exactly she had come to understand English, but they came back together when she presented him with her handwritten dictionary of phonetic English (a gesture meant to un-silence him). They were immediately separated again when Jin left on the raft to try to find rescue, and he was stuck on the other side of the island for a few days while Sun worried about whether or not he was still alive. Soon after they were reunited, Sun realized she was pregnant, and was terrified that if the baby proved to be Jae Lee's, it would cause a rift between them that would break them apart once and for all. The baby was Jin's, but Juliet revealed to Jin that Sun had had an affair, causing him to leave her once again. He returned, because he realized that he still loved her and that he had given her reason to betray him. At the end of season 3, Sun began the trek across the island with everyone else while Jin stayed behind with Sayid and Bernard to stop the Others, and she once again had to worry that he'd been killed. After they managed to get to the freighter in the fourth season, Jin disappeared into the bowels of the ship with Desmond and Michael to try to dismantle a bomb (seriously, Jin . . . *stay with your pregnant wife*). She got onto the helicopter, which took off before Jin could join her, and she watched the freighter explode, believing once and for all that he really had been killed this time.

For three years she lived off-island believing she was a widow, even erecting a tombstone for Jin and visiting it with her new daughter, Ji Yeon. Through her daughter, Sun felt she still had a part of Jin with her, but it didn't erase the resentment and need for revenge that was building up inside her. She betrayed her father (who admittedly had it coming) through a savage company takeover, and then set her sights on killing Ben Linus. And once she returned to the island, she's been unable to find Jin, and her hope of ever being together again with him is receding.

So, perhaps Keamy is right, and no matter what Jin and Sun do, they are simply not meant to be together. But what he's missing is the tenacity of their relationship — seen from another perspective, life keeps trying to separate them, but it can't. Just like the tiny tomato that Jack finds in Sun's destroyed garden, some things simply refuse to die. No matter what happens, Sun and Jin keep finding each other, and maybe, some people just weren't meant to be apart.

Highlight: When Ben asks why they don't believe him, and Ilana responds, "Because you're speaking." Ha!

Did You Notice?:
- Sun's garden seems to flourish when things are going well, and falls apart when things on the island do, as if it reflects the events and temperaments on the island. In a sense it's her little Garden of Eden, one that died when everything went bad and when innocence turned into experience.
- Once again Smokey holds out his hand and someone (Sun, this time) refuses to take it.
- When we flash to the sideways world after Sun hits her head, Jin looks dead when he's sitting on the bed.
- For those who don't recall Room 23, we saw it in season 3's "Not in Portland" when Alex's boyfriend Karl was locked in it, strapped to a chair, *Clockwork Orange*–style, and forced to watch a bunch of subliminal messages flash by his eyes while being blasted with loud music. It was Ben's fatherly attempt to keep him away from Alex so she wouldn't end up pregnant . . . and dead, given what had happened to other pregnant women on the island. In the mobisode that preceded season 4, entitled "Room 23," it was revealed that Walt had been put into Room 23 so they could figure out what the extent of his specialness was, but he ended up scaring everyone and created a pile of dead birds outside his window in much the same way he'd killed the bird in "Special."
- When Jin first flips the switch in Room 23, we see the following series of images: Gerald DeGroot, the co-founder of the Dharma Initiative, with his goggles on looking through a microscope; the message "Think About" . . . "Your Life" with many Buddha statues around it; the phrase "We are the causes of our own suffering" laid over a graveyard that looks a lot like the one that has Jin's tombstone in it; a picture of the moon; doll's eyes; another Buddha; "Everything Changes" over an old stove and a drafting compass; three computer keyboards (interestingly, the top one has a number pad above it with nine keys on it . . . much like that one Charlie pushed in "Through the Looking Glass, Part 2" that had been programmed by a musician).

- Claire asks if her name was on the wall, and Smokey says no, but he's lying: "Littleton" was #313 on the cave ceiling, and there was a line through it. It's not clear why it was crossed out.
- Smokey tells Claire that once they get on the plane, "whatever happens happens," quoting Daniel's mantra from season 5.
- Keamy's portrayal as a lugnut in this episode is hilarious. First he shouts at Jin and Sun in English, as if they'll understand him better that way, and then he says listening to them speak Korean is like watching a Godzilla film (it's a *Japanese*, movie, Keams). Kevin Durand is great in this episode.
- Smokey says to Widmore, "A wise man once said that war was coming to this island." He's referring to Widmore warning Locke that a war was coming when he talked to him at his hospital bedside in "The Life and Times of Jeremy Bentham." Once again he's displaying that he has taken on John Locke's memories, along with his body.
- Paik has taken all of Sun's money and left her with nothing. It's similar to what she did to him in the island timeline.
- In the touching scene where Jin finally sees the pictures of Ji Yeon, you can see she's with Bpo Bpo, the dog that Jin gave to Sun in "House of the Rising Sun." (It's too bad Sun couldn't see Jin's face when he saw Ji Yeon for the first time.)
- When Mikhail walks back into the restaurant, he asks Keamy repeatedly who did this to him, as if the answer to that question was of the utmost importance. In the island timeline, Mikhail will be the one who creates the information files for each of the survivors, and again is focused on who each one of them is.
- It seems that Mikhail is destined to lose an eye in every reality.
- When Sayid emerges from the water at the end, it's reminiscent of *Apocalypse Now*, when Martin Sheen's character emerges from the water with a knife in his mouth.

Interesting Facts: Stephen King's *The Stand* was alluded to subtly in this episode (see page 258): first with the flash of an image of the moon in Room 23, and then when Sun begins to write down everything she's thinking, like Nick Andros is forced to in the book.

Many fans thought that in the scene where Keamy is taping up Jin's wrists, he says, "Just in case you figure out what's gonna happen to the island, I can't have you freakin' out." The closed captioning revealed he said, "what's gonna happen to ya," but many fans were unconvinced until Jorge Garcia, after reading the question numerous times on his blog, actually contacted Kevin Durand, who reassured everyone that he in fact said "ya" and not "the island."

Nitpicks: While I understand the storyline potential of Sun not being able to speak English, and how it not only links us with Jin in season 1 but also with Sun in the sideways world (see Any Questions below), it's a bit of a lame, soap-opera plot device. Miles seems to speak for the fans when he says, "She hits her head and forgets English? We're supposed to buy that?" You'd think Sun would have considered writing out what happened a little sooner than when Jack handed her a notepad. Also, on an island with limited paper, maybe Sun could have been a little thriftier with her notes, and not wasted some of that precious paper and space making little sad-face emoticons? I'm also annoyed by Zoe. This late in the game, no fan wanted a new character introduced, especially one as whiny and ineffectual as she is. Again, she's being used to advance the plot, but the less we see of her, the better. And do we really believe that Widmore's collapsible sonic fence (new travel-sized edition!) can really keep out Smokey? There's no way he's enveloped the entire perimeter of the island with it. And I really dislike it when the writers create these contrived and misleading terms to keep us from knowing the big reveal. Widmore refers to Desmond as "the package" throughout the episode, and I'll guarantee that after this, he'll never refer to him that way again. It was like the characters referring to John Locke as Jeremy Bentham to each other when they were off the island, when afterwards they *never* referred to him that way again. (Besides, Widmore telling Jin that he's going to show him his package just made him sound . . . pervy.)

Oops: If Ji Yeon is being raised with the help of Sun's mother in Korea (we saw in "This Place Is Death" that she left Ji Yeon with her mother while she was in L.A.) then Ji Yeon's birthday sign wouldn't have been in English in the photo. One could suggest that Sun was teaching Ji Yeon English at the time, but she spoke to her only in Korean on the phone, and Ji Yeon wouldn't have been able to read the sign when she was only two years old.

4 8 15 16 23 42: Jin and Sun stay on the **8**th floor of the hotel, and Sun is in room **842**. (Interestingly, on Jacob's list "Kwon" is number **42**.) Ben says that he's told them **4** times that he wasn't the one who hurt Sun.

It's Just a Flesh Wound: The people in Smokey's camp are shot with poison darts. We discover Keamy survived Sayid's attack but he's finished off by Jin. Mikhail is shot in the eye and killed. A pregnant Sun is shot in the upper abdomen.

Any Questions?:
- At the beginning of the episode, Sawyer offers Kate cocoa. Considering the Others would have been using the beach supplies for the past three years, how could there still be any cocoa? Did the Dharma pallet drops continue after the Swan station imploded/exploded?
- Smokey tells Sayid that it's a good thing he feels nothing, because it'll help him get through what's coming. What is coming?
- When Sun loses the ability to speak English, is that a suggestion that the sideways world is somehow bleeding into the island timeline? In the sideways world she cannot speak English, and the aphasia that Sun is experiencing on the island could be an indication of her connecting with that other person.
- Why is Widmore looking for the pockets of electromagnetism on the island?
- Why is Smokey so attached to Claire? Why won't he let her stay behind when she says she doesn't want to go on the plane?
- Why can't Smokey fly over the water? (Other than it being a convenient way to plug up a plot hole.)
- Widmore says to Smokey, "Obviously you're not John Locke. Everything else I know is a combination of myth, ghost stories, and jungle noises in the night." Does he actually know a lot more about the Man in Black than he's letting on? He seems to know he can shape-shift and that he can't cross the pylons, and he knows about the two sides of the war and about Jacob.
- Why is Keamy so sad when he talks to Jin? Is it all acting and he's just playing the calm-before-the-storm part, or is there something more genuine happening?

6.11 Happily Ever After

Original air date: April 6, 2010
Written by: Damon Lindelof, Carlton Cuse
Directed by: Jack Bender
Guest cast: Jeremy Davies (Daniel), Fionnula Flanagan (Eloise Widmore), Fisher Stevens (George Minkowski), Sonya Walger (Penny), Jonathan Arthur

(Simmons), Hannah Bell (Nurse), Kayren Butler (Doctor), Ben Cain (MRI Tech), Gerard Elmore (Clipboard Guy), Christopher McGahan (Techie), Sundra Oakley (Lawyer), Grisel Toledo (Nurse Tyra), Haley Williams (Widmore Assistant)

Focus: Desmond

Widmore puts Desmond through a test to see how resilient he really is. In the sideways world, Charlie tries to convince Desmond that there's something he needs to "see."

Desmond Hume has always stood out as being different from every other character on the show; even his flashbacks are presented non-traditionally — "The Constant" was unlike any other episode of *Lost*, and fans are still arguing about what exactly happened in "Flashes Before Your Eyes." In "Because You Left," a time-traveling Daniel tells Desmond, "The rules don't apply to you. You're special. You're uniquely and miraculously special." Daniel had just been explaining to Sawyer in that episode that a person could not go back in time to change something that would happen in the future, until he suddenly realized that maybe one person could: Desmond.

Desmond has been associated with certain big themes on *Lost* — destiny versus free will, time travel, love conquering all, and sacrifice. He believes that love, and Penny specifically, is his destiny, but he also believes that his choices can help shape his destiny. Desmond was pulled away from his first engagement to a woman named Ruth when he believed that destiny had called to him and apparently wanted him to become a monk ("Catch-22"). He had a strong feeling that he was meant to "leave everything behind, sacrifice all of it, for a greater calling." When that didn't work out, he ran into Penny, and fell in love with her the moment he saw her. Despite moving in with her, what he wanted more than anything was the approval of her father, Charles Widmore, and when instead her father told him he was worthless, he left Penny and joined the Royal Scots Regiment of the British Army. He was dishonorably discharged and believed he couldn't be with Penny until he got his honor back. So he entered a yacht race around the world. Just as Widmore had pushed Desmond away in the first place, then intercepted his letters to Penny, it seems he had a hand in controlling Desmond's destiny and perhaps got him to the very island he'd been trying to find for years.

Now on the island, Desmond was dragged into the Swan station by Kelvin Inman (whose first words to Desmond — "Are you him?" — were strongly prophetic). Trapped on the island with Inman, Desmond was forced to push a button every 108 minutes. He was told that doing so would save the world, and while he didn't want the task he was given, he wouldn't risk the chance of not fulfilling it. After Inman's death, Desmond accidentally caused the crash of Oceanic Flight 815, and tried to escape the island when he thought the world was going to end. He didn't get far before he was back on the island, and when Locke's faith wavered and he decided not to push the button, Desmond's faith in Penny and saving the world remained steadfast. This is the first time we see Desmond stand between people and disaster, even at the risk of his life — he turned the failsafe key, diffusing the electromagnetic energy once and for all. But in the blast that should have killed him, his consciousness traveled back to a time where he was still with Penny, and he believed he had a second chance ("Flashes Before Your Eyes"). He was met by Eloise Hawking, who told him he could not change the past, because the universe would simply course correct to set things back on their regular paths to meet their destinies, which is what always seems to happen to Desmond. Desmond's time travel was the first we'd seen, and it immediately marked him as special — it also kicked fans' speculation into high gear: *what* was Desmond?

What he encountered during the electromagnetic blast changed him. At first it showed him flashes of Charlie's future. In "The Constant," however, when Desmond's consciousness became unstuck in time like the protagonist of Kurt Vonnegut's *Slaughterhouse-Five*, it was clear that Daniel Faraday was right. Desmond was miraculously different, and the two of them communicated across time in a strange ping-pong game of mutual salvation. Desmond left the island, but now, against his will, he's back. And *boy* is he angry.

At each point in Desmond's life, no matter how many times he tries to exercise his free will, fate intervenes. When he chose to join the brotherhood, he believed it was destiny pushing him to do such a thing, but it ended up pushing him toward Penny. He chose to go on a race around the world, and fate put him on the same island his father-in-law believed he owned. When he decided to turn the key, knowing the act would kill him but possibly save others, fate intervened once more and let him live. He chose to leave the island once and for all several times, but fate always pulled him back to the island. Again.

The one thing that has spurred on each of Desmond's choices is Penny. His choice to leave Ruth at the altar kept him a single man; unbeknownst to him, fate was intervening to keep him for Penny. He chose to join the Army so Penny's father would see he was a good man. The race around the world was to regain

When Widmore hugs Desmond and tells him how blessed he is to have Des in his life, viewers know they're not in Kansas anymore. (Mario Perez/ABC via Getty Images)

honor in her eyes. He turned the failsafe key, assuming it would kill him, so that it would save the world for her. As I said a few episodes ago, every character on this show seems to be searching for something, and they're not sure what. Desmond is the only person who knows exactly what he's searching for, and "miraculously," he found her.

Inextricably tied to Penny is her father, Charles Widmore, and a driving force in Desmond's life, as Eloise acknowledges in the sideways world, is to get Widmore's approval. Without it, he knows he won't ever completely have Penny. In the original timeline, we can't think of the Desmond/Widmore tension without thinking of the scene in "Flashes Before Your Eyes," where a nervous Desmond goes to Widmore's office to ask for Penny's hand. He looks around the office at the artwork, notably a painting of a polar bear, one of a Buddha, and the word "Namaste" spelled backwards (suggesting a mirror image). After telling Desmond he's made a noble gesture, Widmore pulls out a bottle of MacCutcheon whiskey, and tells him about the great MacCutcheon and how the whiskey was his crowning achievement. He then pours only one glass and says, "This swallow is worth more than you could make in a month. To share it with you would be a waste, and a disgrace to the great man who made it. Because you, Hume, will never be a great man." The scene is shocking in its emotional brutality.

Contrast that scene to the one in the sideways world where Desmond strides into the office without sitting outside first or waiting to be allowed in. The artwork is warmer, and Desmond refers to his boss as "Charles." Widmore hugs — *hugs* — Desmond and pours a glass of MacCutcheon whiskey for him, telling him he is "blessed" to have Desmond working for him, and adds, "Nothing's too good for you." And watching at home . . . our heads explode.

In Desmond's case, the sideways world almost seems like a place of wish fulfillment. We feel that if Desmond so much as looked in Penny's direction Widmore would marry her off to him in this scene. Where other characters' lives have been more or less subtly altered, Desmond's sideways life is the complete opposite of the cold, harsh scene in "Flashes Before Your Eyes." Once again, the writers are counting on us to remember that scene and mentally contrast and compare it to this one to make the scene in the sideways world more effective.

The scene between Desmond and Eloise, however, is very similar to their original meeting in "Flashes Before Your Eyes." In both instances, Eloise comes off as kind and sincere, and then when Desmond makes any sort of comment about changing things, she turns nasty, offering grand statements about his decisions wreaking untold havoc on the universe. In "Flashes," she explains course correction to him, and tells him that though he believes he can change his future, he can't, and that "pushing that button is the only truly great thing that you will ever do." In this episode, she's similarly sweet to him, until she hears him asking one too many questions about Penny. It seems as if Eloise, too, can see the other timeline, and knows that in the island timeline he will marry Penny. She storms over and tells him in no uncertain terms that he needs to stop looking. "This is a serious problem. It is, in fact, a violation. What you're doing, whatever it is you *think* you're looking for, you need to stop looking for it." He asks her if she knows what he should be looking for, but she refuses to answer, simply telling him he's not ready.

Why would Eloise care if Desmond met Penny? How does Eloise know things? She's obviously aware of the other timeline, because it is only over there where Desmond longs for Widmore's approval. In both timelines she seems able to see back and forth in time, as if she has some of the same unique properties Desmond has, and yet the writers have never really explained who she is. She's inserted into important moments in the series to offer long explanations of fairly kooky things, but we never really know who *she* is. Damon Lindelof referred to

Dominic Monaghan and Henry Ian Cusick walk along the streets of downtown Honolulu between takes. (Courtesy Ryan Ozawa)

The *Lost* production crew sets up the scene where Desmond's car drives into the water (at the "Bowls" marina behind the Ilikai Hotel in Honolulu), while Cusick's and Monaghan's stunt doubles (center) wait nearby. (Courtesy Ryan Ozawa)

her as a "Johnny the Explainer" character, one who helps the viewers understand what is happening by summing up a lot of information for the viewers. In this particular scene, Eloise says that a "certain predictability comes with the territory." She says it in the context of planning events that involve rock musicians, but it could certainly be used in the larger context of who she is. What "territory" does Eloise inhabit? Is she all-seeing and all-knowing? Or is she basically like everyone else, except that she, like Desmond, has a special gift?

The scene in the bar with Charlie is another important one. In the island timeline, Desmond felt a responsibility to keep Charlie alive, constantly besting fate to see if he could beat it. In the sideways world, he's simply responsible for getting Charlie to a gig in one piece. In both realities, he tells Charlie the truth about his purpose, and gives Charlie the choice in the matter. On the island, he tells Charlie he's "gonna die," and in this one, he offers Charlie two options: to stay at the bar, keep drinking, and destroy his career (the decision Charlie originally made before the Oceanic flight in the island timeline) or to come with Des. But where the island Desmond was getting flashes of the future, in the sideways world, Charlie is the one getting the flashes, and he knows he cannot convey what they mean to him by telling Desmond, so he decides he's going to show him. He has seen a woman — who sounds remarkably like Claire — and has felt feelings that have told him another world exists that is more real than the one he's in. In a terrific choice of words, he asks Desmond whether he has ever experienced "spectacular, consciousness-altering love." In the other timeline, Desmond is the *only* one who has literally experienced a love that altered his consciousness, but in this one, he's happy to be single. That is . . . until Charlie gives him a glimpse of what he had in the original timeline.

While it was a thrill to see Charlie again, it was even more exciting to see Daniel. The director teased us leading up to Daniel's first line, showing us a figure wearing a fedora, who was clearly Daniel, but who looked like he'd be nothing more than a stand-in who wouldn't have any lines. Like Charlie, Daniel saw Charlotte and in that moment he got a very brief flash of feeling, a sense that he already knew her and loved her. He then scribbled a bunch of notes that only a physics genius could have managed, and where Charlie just talks about this other trippy world that's really cool, Daniel believes there's been a fundamental shift somewhere that has caused the world to change. Despite becoming a musician (a choice he was denied in the other timeline), Daniel is still the same person, with the same mind that thinks outside of the box. Where Desmond acts as a catalyst for change, Daniel acts as a *reason* for change. For most of season 5, Daniel insisted that "whatever happened, happened" (something Eloise repeats in this episode), but when he returned to the island after three years of study, he'd changed his mind. He believed that the variables in the equation — the characters themselves — *could* change time, and he came up with the idea of dropping the hydrogen bomb to reset time. It didn't exactly reset time, but it restored them all to 2007, where they could finally find the answers they'd been seeking. If the sideways world has been borne of Juliet detonating that bomb, then maybe they did get their wish; the plane didn't crash, and none of the island story happened, which is what Jack had been hoping for. But with cracks starting to show in the sideways world, how much longer will the Losties be able to maintain their blissful ignorance of the island timeline?

In season 2, Desmond was a guy living underground who'd been pushing a button to save the world. In season 3, he had time traveled back to a point where he met a woman who explained course correction and the futility of trying to change things. In season 4 his consciousness actually split off and entered a time eight years previous. In season 5 Daniel recognized that Desmond could *change* time when Daniel spoke to 2003 Desmond and inserted a memory into the mind of 2007 Desmond. And now, in season 6, it seems that Desmond alone can bridge the sideways and island timelines one to the other. It's still not clear what the sideways world is, but Desmond is the only one on the island who appears to have seen it and who knows it's there.

So many of the characters on this show are emotionally lost. But Desmond — uniquely, miraculously special Desmond — is the one character who knows what is most important to him in this world. As such, it keeps him grounded in this and every other world. Yes, he survived an electromagnetic explosion that has made him impervious to electromagnetic radiation, and apparently this will be important for some as-yet-unexplained reason. Widmore is going to ask him to make a sacrifice, and while we don't know what that is, there's a serenity about him now, as if he's caught a glimpse of a world where everything is going to be okay. Desmond isn't important because he's impervious to electromagnetism: he's important because he believes in love. And because he lives for someone else as much as he lives for himself, he's the only person on the show who *isn't* lost.

Highlight: The return of Daniel. I've never been so happy to see a dead character alive again.

Did You Notice?:
- I really wish the writers would stop teasing us by putting all of the favorite characters in red shirts. Desmond wears one in this episode.
- Watch Cusick's face when Widmore tells him he's brought him back to the island. There's a twitch in his cheek that travels to his eye and then turns into full-on rage. It's a brilliant piece of acting.
- Widmore tells Desmond that the island isn't done with him yet, which is what Eloise had said to him in "316."
- The electromagnetic tests are done inside a giant box, which brings to mind Ben's "magic box" parable in "The Man from Tallahassee."
- George Minkowski, who is driving the limo for Desmond in this episode, was the communications officer on the freighter sent by Widmore in season 4. In "The Constant," he's the other person suffering from the effects of consciousness-traveling, but he's not as lucky as Desmond and dies of a brain hemmorhage. He's the one who ultimately helps Desmond survive, leading him to Penny, the one who will save him; in this reality, he literally drives him there.
- In Widmore's office there is a scale on the wall with a white rock on one balance and a black rock on the other (which we saw in Jacob's cave when Smokey took Sawyer there in "The Substitute"), and a model of a boat, which could be *The Black Rock* but actually looks more like Desmond's boat, *The Elizabeth*.
- Charlie's not allowed to leave the state, which was also a limit put on Kate when she was settling her case in "Eggtown."
- Charlie and Desmond go to a bar called JAX, which sounds like "Jack's."
- The marina where Charlie drives the car into the water is the same place where Ben shot Desmond, almost shot Penny, and where Desmond beat him to a pulp.
- When Desmond is about to undergo the MRI, the technician asks him if he has any coins or metal objects in his pockets, which is the same thing they ask him on the island before they chuck him into the electromagnetic blaster.
- The technician gives Desmond a button, and tells him to try *not* pushing it, or "we'll have to start over again from the beginning." Desmond pushes the button anyway, as if it's in his nature to do so. In the other reality, he was forced to push a button, and the whole point was to make the count-

down start over "from the beginning" . . . every 108 minutes.
- The nurse that Desmond speaks to at the desk when he's looking for Charlie worked at the Santa Rosa Mental Hospital in the other timeline, and her name was Susie (she's Tyra here).
- When Desmond chases Charlie down the staircase in the hospital, it's like he's following the White Rabbit down the hole.
- When Eloise spoke to Desmond in "Flashes Before Your Eyes" she was wearing a shawl with a circular brooch on it. While some viewers thought it was an ourobouros (a snake eating its own tail) it's not quite that; the snake's head and tail are separate (see *Finding Lost — Season Three*, p. 66 for the photo). Still, it's in the shape of a circle, one showing the cyclical nature of life, but the fact that the head and tail aren't joined shows that the circle can easily be broken. In this episode Eloise wears a brooch of two straight lines parallel to each other, each with a star in the middle of it. It could be a hint that the sideways world is a parallel timeline, and that things are now running more linearly than circularly; also, the stars in the middle of the brooch look a lot like the mark that Juliet was branded with in "Stranger in a Strange Land."
- Daniel tells Desmond that he saw Charlotte eating a chocolate bar. If that line brought a tear to your eye it's because you remembered that the last thing Charlotte said before she died in Daniel's arms was "I'm not allowed to have chocolate before dinner," recalling the first words she said to Daniel when she was a toddler.
- Daniel says to Desmond, "It happened to you, too, didn't it?" Those are the same words Minkowski says to Desmond in "The Constant" after he realizes that Desmond is having the same broken consciousness.
- The stadium is a key place for Desmond in both realities: in the first one, he tells Penny he needs to get his honor back and leaves her behind; and in this one, he meets her for the first time.

Interesting Facts: The rabbit's name is "Angstrom." An angstrom is a unit of length used to measure wavelengths of electromagnetic radiation. Also, Harold C. "Rabbit" Angstrom is the main character of John Updike's series of Rabbit novels (*Rabbit, Run*; *Rabbit Redux*; *Rabbit Is Rich*; *Rabbit at Rest*; *Rabbit Remembered*). Updike said in interviews that he chose the name Angstrom after reading Kierkegaard's work and its existentialist, *angst*-ridden themes. Updike had been suffering from a crisis of faith, and looked to Kierkegaard's work for answers. What he found there restored what he thought he'd lost, and he remained a Christian the rest of his life (see page 197 for more on Kierkegaard).

The scene where Desmond is between the poles of energy, with his arms out and his whole body glowing is reminiscent of the scene in Alan Moore's *Watchmen* when Jon Osterman is disintegrated. Osterman's consciousness manages to piece a physical body back together, and this new godlike body goes by the name Doctor Manhattan. Like Desmond, Manhattan doesn't see time in a linear way like everyone else, but instead can see the past and future simultaneously.

Penny tells Desmond to meet her at the coffee shop at the corner of Sweetzer and Melrose in L.A. There is no coffee shop on that corner, but it could be the writers giving a nod to Neil Gaiman. In his *Sandman* graphic novel series, in Part VII of *The Kindly Ones*, a character hands a cab driver a hundred-dollar bill and tells him to take her wounded friend to her apartment at the corner of Sweetzer and Melrose.

Nitpicks: Seriously, what sort of moron throws the switch the moment he thinks he has a major problem fixed without warning everyone else in the room first, and then restarting the countdown? And why does everyone rush into the room immediately after the guy disintegrates? Wouldn't there have been tons of radiation still hanging in the air? Widmore was really scraping the bottom of the barrel with these recruits.

Oops: Desmond is not wearing a wedding band in this episode (Minkowski even comments on the fact) but he was definitely wearing one in "LA X." Presumably Cusick forgot to take off his own wedding band when filming the scenes in the pilot.

4 8 15 16 23 42: The luggage of the people on the sideways Oceanic flight is coming in on Carousel 4. On the side of the MRI machine are the numbers 15 and 46 (23 x 2).

It's Just a Flesh Wound: Simmons dies from electromagnetic radiation. Desmond is zapped with untold amounts of radiation and loses consciousness. Desmond gets a gash on his forehead from the car accident. Desmond faints at the stadium. Sayid shoots and kills two of Widmore's men.

Any Questions?:
- Widmore reassures Desmond that Penny and Young Charlie are both safe. Where are they? Penny wouldn't have willingly let Widmore take Desmond with him no matter what he told her, because she doesn't trust him. Considering how tenacious she's been in the past, tracking Desmond down

in L.A. in 2001 and then finding the island in 2005, there's no way she'd let him out of her sight that easily.
- Zoe tells Widmore that the tests on Desmond weren't scheduled until the next day, but only a couple of minutes earlier Widmore had said they didn't need Jin to translate the maps for a few more days. Don't they need the electromagnetic pockets to fully conduct the tests on Desmond, or are they two separate things?
- What sacrifice does Widmore need Desmond to make?
- Why does Widmore think that watching him zap Desmond with electromagnetic energy is going to make Jin want to help them find the pockets of energy? He never actually shows Jin what good it will do, so why would Jin help him now?
- We now know that the reason Liam was at the police station so quickly in "Recon" is because Drive Shaft is in town for a gig, but if so, why didn't he return to bail Charlie out?
- Is the "Penny" on the invitation list the same Penny that Desmond is looking for? If so, other than it being a nod to John Milton, why is her name now Penny Milton? In the original timeline, Widmore got Eloise pregnant and she raised Daniel on her own while he went and started a family with Penny's mother. In this one it would seem he got Eloise pregnant, had an affair, and came back to Eloise. Perhaps Penny has her mother's maiden name, or the surname of Penny's stepfather. If that's the case, why does Penny have a British accent? Widmore lives in L.A. now, not in England, and Penny is there, too. Sonya Walger should have used the same accent she used in *FlashForward*.
- At the bottom of Daniel's graph, he's written "imaginary time." Could that be a clue to the nature of the sideways world?
- How does Desmond know what Widmore wants him to do?
- Why did Sayid let Zoe go, especially when many fans would have been so happy to have seen her dead?
- Is the coffee shop where Desmond is going to meet Penny the same one where he met Libby and got her boat in "Live Together, Die Alone"?
- Why isn't Penny weirded out when Desmond knows her name?
- Why does Desmond need the flight manifest? Who does he mean when he says he needs to show "them" something? And how could a limo driver possibly find a flight manifest for anyone?!

6.12   Everybody Loves Hugo

Original air date: April 13, 2010
Written by: Edward Kitsis, Adam Horowitz
Directed by: Daniel Attias
Guest cast: Bruce Davison (Dr. Brooks), Lillian Hurst (Carmen Reyes), Harold Perrineau (Michael), Cynthia Watros (Libby), Archie Ahuna (Grandpa Tito), Kenton Duty (Teenage Boy), Jesse Smith (Waiter)

Focus: Hurley

As group leader, Hurley decides to reunite his gang with Smokey's; Sayid tells Smokey that Desmond is back on the island, and in the sideways world, everybody loves Hugo . . . especially one woman who remembers him from the other timeline.

For the first 17 episodes of *Lost*, Hurley was the happy, fun guy on the island. He was the one who found the last of the airplane's precooked food and handed out the little trays to everyone (giving an extra one to Claire). He was the one who tried talking to Jin when no one else did (and then asked him to pee on his sea urchin–stung foot). He endured Sawyer's cruel nicknames, cracked jokes with Charlie on the beach, and when he thought people were getting too down in the dumps, he constructed a golf course in a field. But Hurley was hiding a past that was as dark as anyone else's on that island. Happy, fun guy wasn't actually very happy at all.

Hurley's unhappiness started when he was a child, and his irresponsible father left town on a motorcycle, abandoning Hurley, his brother (who is only mentioned in season 1 and then never again), and his ma, Carmen ("Tricia Tanaka Is Dead"). As a teen, Hurley began overeating to mask the depression he felt with no father, and when he was in his 20s, he was at a party and walked onto a deck built for eight people that was already holding 23, and it collapsed, killing two. Blaming himself for the accident and unable to cope with the depression that followed, Hurley was put into a mental hospital by his mother ("Dave"). Already, Hugo Reyes' life was beginning to suffer from extremes.

Once he'd checked out of the institution, Hurley went to work at Mr. Cluck's Chicken Shack, and, on a whim, played the lottery using a set of numbers that another patient, Leonard, had repeated constantly. He was shocked when they won, and he took the entire pot: $114 million. Because of the instability he'd felt in his past, he was worried the lottery win would change everything — and

Everybody loves Jorge. (Marco Garcia/AP Photo)

Hurley was right: his friend Johnny stopped speaking to him and took off with Starla, a girl Hurley had asked out. Hurley began experiencing what he came to believe was the curse of the numbers — his grandfather died, his new house caught on fire, people became sick or hurt around him . . . and yet, amidst every disaster, he was physically untouched. His father returned and though Hurley suspected his motives, he chose to have hope instead and started to renew his relationship with him. But the curse of the numbers continued. In desperation Hurley boarded a flight to Australia to find out more information about the numbers, and discovered the man who'd originally heard them along with Leonard had been similarly cursed.

Hurley boarded Oceanic Flight 815 but never made it home. On the island, he acted like everything was fine, but he was dogged by one thing: fear. Fear of the numbers, and fear that people would find out he was crazy. He was very sensitive about the latter, becoming angry when someone would just say casually, "Aw, you're crazy." When he first saw the numbers etched into the hatch at the Swan station, he was thunderstruck. Instantly, he believed the curse had come back to haunt him, and that the bad luck that had followed him would befall everyone on the island. After that, every time anything bad happened on the

Both Mr. Cluck's chicken shack and the Santa Rosa Mental Health Institute play a role in Hugo's sideways world. (Photos courtesy Ryan Ozawa [left] and KOS Tours)

island Hurley believed it was his fault. He tried to find the silver lining in each situation, refusing to allow himself to stay sad for too long (as if the island was healing his depression as it had healed so many others) but things kept happening. When Libby died, Hurley saw his one chance at love on the island slip away. Finally, he decided he no longer wanted to be ruled by fate: he was going to make his own luck ("Tricia Tanaka Is Dead"). He conquered his fear by jumping into a van with Charlie and hurtling it down a hill, and both of them arrived safely at the bottom, hooting with joy as they drove the van around in circles. Hurley realized that, if he were truly cursed, Charlie would have died (since Hurley's bad luck always strikes at someone else, which is the curse of the compassionate). He didn't realize fate really did have something else in store for his best friend. Charlie would ultimately, inevitably, die. But in that brief, silly, free moment, they were both gloriously okay.

In the fourth season, he began to see things. The first, appropriately enough, was Jacob's cabin. Truly living a life of secret extremes, Hurley found himself in the middle of a war between Locke and Ben as to who spoke to Jacob, and therefore, who owned the island.

Hurley got off the island. Once home, things were okay at first, but he was guilt-ridden because he was lying to everyone around him and because he'd left so many people behind ("The Lie"). He began seeing the numbers again, and when he saw the most definitely dead Charlie in a convenience store, he re-admitted himself to the hospital where he'd been before ("The Beginning of the End"). There he quietly sat for the remainder of his time off the island, being visited by several of the people who had died on the island — but Libby was never one of them. He came back to the island because he believed people needed him to, and when he ended up in the 1977 timeline, Hurley made the most of it as he'd always done, becoming a cook in the Dharma Initiative cafeteria.

Keeping in mind the number of characters who have claimed, yearned, demanded to speak directly to Jacob, it was Hurley that Jacob came to . . . of course, after he was dead. There's nothing halfway about Hurley.

Now he's a leader, and he's as reluctant as Jack was. It's not that he doesn't want the responsibility (he got past that feeling in "Everybody Hates Hugo") rather it's because he doesn't think he's the best man for the job. Once again, Hurley is afraid.

While Hurley has always seemed like the comic relief, he's been through more than just about anyone on the island. Aside from the Shambala happiness in the Dharma van, two other moments on *Lost* stand out as truly happy moments for him: when he was about to go on the picnic with Libby, and when he did his cannonball after thinking they were all about to get rescued. With the Libby picnic, he forgot the blankets, and because of that Libby returned to the Swan station to get them . . . and was shot and killed by Michael. When Hurley jumped into the ocean to do the cannonball, he thought he was about to be rescued, he assumed his family would have spent all of his cursed money, and he believed he could enjoy the island water for the first time since they'd arrived there, because, as he said to Bernard, he was finally free. But the moment he emerged from the water, everything changed. Charlie was dead, the freighter folk were not there to rescue anyone, and Hurley felt more alone than he ever had on the island. Hurley's happiness is always followed by astounding tragedy. No wonder the guy is afraid.

But one thing remains consistent: Hurley is the heart of the show. He is a good person, so far from being one of the many con artists who always stab other characters in the back. Back in "LA X," we saw him vainly trying to turn the safety off the gun, warning Jacob that he knew how to use it. Hurley doesn't know how to use a gun any more than Aaron would. Whenever any character feels let down or alone, Hurley is the one person they can turn to. He was the one who broke the news to Claire about Charlie. He was the person Claire entrusted to take care of Aaron whenever she slept. Off the island, Hurley was the only person who flew all the way from the United States to see Ji Yeon and accompany Sun to her husband's grave. He's the one person Jacob visited to ask him directly to return to the island, letting everyone else make their own decision. This fact alone seems both amazing and totally logical — Hurley *can* bring people together. He was the one Isabella used as a translator to cross time and space to talk to her long-lost husband, Richard. Hurley might have seemed like a comic foil at the beginning of the series, but he's vitally important now. He may be the person that everyone loves, but Hugo simply wishes he could be luckier.

And so, in the sideways world, he gets his wish. The cost? Losing everyone around him. Hugo is completely alone, save for his ever-loving, ever-nagging, head-smacking ma (what I would give for a spin-off show of these two in a house bickering all day long . . .). He's not dating anyone, he doesn't appear to have any close friends, there aren't any confidantes, and we don't see his father in the picture. His wish was to be lucky, but he has no one to share that luck with. It's as if all of the bad things that happened to everyone around him in the other world caused him to be alone in this one.

Hugo is confident, loving, giving (as we see from Pierre Chang's introduction to him in the opening), and outgoing. He's not afraid to branch out and try new

Hugo gets a second chance at that beach picnic with Libby . . . and this one goes *much* better. (Courtesy Ryan Ozawa)

things, to travel around the world, and to keep amassing an even greater fortune. What he *is* afraid of . . . is dating. He doesn't know why anyone would want to be with him, and he dreads the blind date that his mother sends him on. Libby intrigues him because his mother didn't set her up to meet him, nor does she seem to be interested in his money; she just believes they should be together. The fact that she's a resident of a mental hospital doesn't seem to faze Hugo. Fundamentally this is the same Hugo we've always known. He wants to believe Libby because he's always given people a chance. He lets go of his fear of dating and takes the step of asking her out, looking past the fact that she's probably crazy by saying, "We've all got something, right?" And this time when he invites her on a picnic . . . he remembers to bring the blankets.

The moment where Hugo remembers Libby and everything that happened on the island is a beautiful one, because where Charlie needed a near-death experience and Desmond had to be zapped with electromagnetic energy for them both to see the other side, Hurley just needs a kiss. Nothing more. His mind is more open than everyone else's. He usually accepts what people say at face value. The only time we've ever seen him adamantly argue a topic was when he insisted Miles was wrong about his theories on time travel (see *Finding Lost — Season Five*, pp. 169–172) but that's because the one thing Hurley will stand by is his love of popular culture knowledge (Ewoks notwithstanding). Now that Hugo has seen that the island world exists, what will this mean for him?

On the island, Hurley is still scared. After Ilana blows up in front of everyone in what has got to be one of the most shocking moments in the entire series, Hurley is utterly lost. Michael appears from the dead and tells him that everyone is looking to him to make decisions because he's the only person who's talked to Jacob (except for Richard, but Richard has dropped all of his Jacob talk now). Michael tells him he needs to prevent everyone from blowing up like Ilana did. Hurley is confused — does he follow Richard? Does he take everyone back to Smokey? Does he help them blow up the plane to stop the smoke monster? Does he stop them from doing it because it will hurt people?

Jack has relinquished his leadership and has let Hurley lead him ever since Hurley spoke to Jacob in "LA X." He's still metaphorically staring out at an ocean and trying to decide what to do, and he talks to Hurley and tells him that just as he tried to do in season 5 when he first visited Dharmaville in 1977, he's letting other people lead him. This is tough for Mr. Type A, the guy who's always been in control of everything, even his own fear. Where Hurley allows himself to be crippled by his fear, Jack explained to Kate in the pilot episode that he will let the fear in for only five seconds, and after that he shuts it out completely and refocuses on the task at hand. Now he admits to Hurley that since Juliet died, his initial reaction was to fix things the same way he's always longed to fix everything else. But he's suddenly come to the realization that he just can't. "You have no idea how hard it is to sit back and listen to other people tell me what I should do," he says. "But maybe that's the point. Maybe I'm supposed to let go." Jack has come to an important realization about himself — he might be more helpful to the group if he's part of it, not necessarily leading it — and Hurley needs to realize that maybe having a big heart and understanding people are exactly what make a great leader.

As Hurley leads his group over to the other camp, Smokey talks to Desmond, who looks exhausted but extremely calm. He asks Desmond if he knows who he is, and Desmond says, "Of course. You're John Locke." It's an odd thing for him to say. Sawyer took one look at Locke and knew it wasn't him. Does Desmond truly believe he's John Locke, or is he making a more insightful observation? Could part of John Locke still be alive? We know Smokey has Locke's memories, so is it possible that Locke is still in there somewhere? Or is Desmond simply making the same mistake that Ben and Richard both made? Notice at the end when Smokey strides back into the camp to tell Sayid they won't have to worry about Desmond anymore, you can hear the Locke music playing over the scene, as if to suggest this is Locke talking.

Smokey takes Desmond over to the well, and again fear becomes the topic at hand. Smokey explains some of the history of the well before asking why Desmond isn't afraid. The smoke monster has been this way for a long time, and he's used to people fearing him when he comes near. Desmond never looks afraid in his presence, and that reaction confuses Smokey. When Desmond responds, "What is the point in being afraid?" Smokey, for the first time, has no response. He actually opens his mouth for a moment, and then closes it. What *is* the point? Fear doesn't get us anywhere, it doesn't help us, it only paralyzes us, preventing us from doing what needs to be done in many cases. This response is unacceptable to the smoke monster, however. When he'd come face-to-face with Eko, who first stared him down and then later told him he had no reason to be scared or to repent, Smokey made mincemeat of him. But when he surrounded Ben and could feel the regret and fear in him, he let him live. Smokey doesn't tolerate people who aren't afraid, because fear is what keeps them in line, and it's what allows him to get inside their psyche. Without fear, we cannot be overcome by darkness.

Highlight: Hurley asking what to say to the Man in Black when they get to the other camp: "I mean, how do you break the ice with the smoke monster?"
Did You Notice?:
- Pierre Chang is still a speaker, but he's introducing philanthropists rather than trying to confuse the unknown viewers of Dharma videos.
- Chang says, "In a world of conflict and strife, there is but one fact we can all agree on: everybody loves Hugo," and the line not only sounds like it's from a movie trailer, but it also is a line that works in both timelines. No matter what side of the war you're on — Man in Black or Jacob, Widmore or Ben — no one seems to have a beef with Hurley.
- Hugo is called only "Hugo" in the sideways world, never Hurley. We never found out what caused him to get that nickname, but I'll bet it involved a bad burrito.
- Carmen is sending Hugo on a blind date with a woman named Rosalita, which is already a hint that the Santa Rosa hospital will come into play.
- It's fitting that it is Michael who comes to talk to Hurley. In all Hurley's time after the crash, the only person he ever hated was Michael, so having this final scene between them is touching, because it allows Hurley to finally forgive him for what he did, even if he doesn't say it.
- Hugo doesn't look in a mirror in this episode, unlike the people in all of the other sideways episodes. Instead he simply looks at the reflection of himself in Libby's eyes.
- In the sideways world Hugo doesn't appear to have ever been in the mental hospital, so he was lucky long before the lottery win.
- Sawyer complains to Smokey that they're just sitting there doing nothing, and Smokey responds that there's a difference between doing nothing and waiting. This is the same conversation that Sawyer had with Jack in "Namaste," but in that case, their roles were reversed, and Jack accused Sawyer of doing nothing.
- Richard Alpert is more distraught about *The Black Rock* blowing up than he is about Ilana, who suffered the same fate only an hour earlier. However, given what we know about what *The Black Rock* means to him, it's understandable.

- The island picture on the wall of Dr. Brooks' office is the same one that was there in the other timeline.
- In the mental hospital's rec room, the chalkboard has drawings of an island, several fish, a shark, an alligator, a big sun, and what looks like a baby pram in the corner with a butterfly coming out of it. In the other world, there were similar drawings of islands and sharks and butterflies.
- When Richard Alpert said that Jacob had told him what the island was, I really wished that Jack had jumped up and said, "What?! You *know* what the island is? Then WTF is it?" But alas, everyone just sat there acting as if Richard hadn't just said one of the most profound things in the series.
- Michael reveals in this episode that the whispers we've been hearing all series long are the dead people on the island who have done bad things and are trapped there. Which means . . . the island is actually a purgatory, but only for some (if you die on the island, you risk being trapped in the island's purgatory, but the people who crashed onto the island aren't all trapped in it). While some fans were unhappy with the explanation (either because they'd assumed it all along or because they just thought it was a lame answer and wanted something bigger), it works in the sense of giving those fans who believed the island was a purgatory their due, without suggesting that all of the other characters were actually dead.
- Just as people in the sideways world get flashes of recognition that cause their memories to come flooding back, you can see all of the memories of his discussions with John Locke come flooding back on his face the moment he sees him at the end of the episode.
- In the island timeline, Ben was the creepy guy who was watching the private lives of others. But in the sideways world, when he sees Desmond sitting near the school, he goes all *To Catch a Predator* on him, demanding to know why he's spying on everyone.
- At the end of the episode, we get that familiar image of John Locke on his back looking up that we've seen so many times — when he falls in the parking lot while chasing his mother ("Deus Ex Machina"); after his father pushes him out of the window ("The Man from Tallahassee"); after the plane crash ("Walkabout"); after the boar knocks him over ("Walkabout"); when he's in the pit of bodies after Ben shoots him ("The Man Behind the Curtain"); when he ends up in the desert in Tunisia ("The Life and Death of Jeremy Bentham"); and when Ben strangled him on the floor.

The beach camp where Ilana goes boom. (Courtesy KOS Tours)

- When the two camps are joined, Smokey has accomplished what John Locke couldn't: the Oceanic 6 (minus Aaron) back together in one place.

Interesting Facts: In the opening montage of pictures of Hugo and his philanthropic works, there's a picture of him holding a dark-haired Chihuahua. The dog, Nunu, belonged to Jorge Garcia and his girlfriend, and was the subject of many of Jorge's blog posts. Sadly, after filming wrapped on *Lost* and Garcia was heading to the airport to leave Hawaii, Nunu was hit by a passing motorist and died in Garcia's arms. Garcia and his girlfriend delayed their trip in order to bury the dog at the Pet Garden in the Valley of the Temples in Kaneohe, Hawaii, with a bronze plaque bearing only her name. He posted on his blog, "If you'd like to leave a flower or a toy, I'm sure she'd love it."

The names used in the Mexican restaurant are tributes to Bruce Springsteen's second album, *The Wild, the Innocent & the E Street Shuffle* (1973). In "Incident on 57th Street," Springsteen sings about Spanish Johnny, a guy who can't seem to find a girlfriend until he meets a girl named Puerto Rican Jane. "Rosalita (Come Out Tonight)" is considered one of the greatest rock songs of all time by many fans and critics, and is about a Romeo-and-Juliet type of love between the singer and a girl named Rosalita.

Samm Levine, who plays the clerk in Mr. Cluck's who takes Hurley's order, is a character actor who's appeared in dozens of sitcoms, and is best known to TV fans as Neal Schweiber on the excellent *Freaks and Geeks* (strangely, he was uncredited in the episode).

Henry Ian Cusick revealed in one of Jorge Garcia's *Geronimo Jack's Beard* podcasts that when he went in to record the ADR for this episode (this is when they record overdubs of lines of dialogue or noises that the actors made that weren't picked up properly by the microphones), as a joke, on the first take he recorded a gleeful "WHEEEEE!" when Desmond was pushed down the well.

Nitpicks: While Hurley's fear of meeting women works for the storyline in this episode, it seems unlikely that he didn't have hundreds of girls clamoring to meet him when he was suddenly worth millions of dollars. Do the writers seriously think there aren't people out there who will date other people just for their money? Also, considering the fact that all of the previous Candidates are dead and Ilana hasn't had a clue what to do now that she's on the island, one wonders what her "training" consisted of. Jacob hasn't told her anything she needs to know; she doesn't seem to understand how to use dynamite; she's not even sure which Kwon she's meant to protect. We've seen her covered in bandages in the hospital, so this isn't the first time something's gone "ka-blam" in her face. The character of Ilana is one of the great disappointments of the series. She was built up for almost two seasons, seemed to have an important purpose, but was completely ineffectual once she found herself in the midst of it. She amounted to as much as Caesar did in season 5. We don't have any backstory on her, we don't know why or how Jacob chose her. All we know is either he made a very bad choice or he's a terrible "trainer."

4 8 15 16 23 42: Ilana retrieves 4 sticks of dynamite from *The Black Rock*. Desmond's order at Mr. Cluck's is number 42. There is still someone playing Connect 4 at the hospital.

It's Just a Flesh Wound: Desmond deliberately rams his car into John Locke's wheelchair, sending John flying over the car.

Lost in Translation: When Widmore toasts Desmond, Desmond responds, "Sláinte," which is a toast used often in Scotland and Ireland meaning, "To your health."

Any Questions?:
- Considering Hurley can speak to dead people, is it possible that Dave in the mental hospital ("Dave") wasn't a figment of Hurley's imagination, but

rather someone who had died and appeared to Hurley to mock him for some reason?
- Now that we've seen that Pierre Chang is indeed the man at the museum (and therefore Miles's father) it raises the question: why is Miles's last name Straume in this reality?
- So far, the people who have seen the other world are Charlie, Daniel, Libby, Desmond, and Hurley. The first three are dead in the other timeline (as Hurley says, "dead people are more reliable than alive people"). Desmond could see it because of his exposure to electromagnetism. The odd man out seems to be Hurley, but the subject of many novels and poems is the idea that madness can bring with it a sort of clarity and a way to see into the heart of things. Could Hurley see the other world because he was mentally unstable in it, or is he special for another reason?
- Smokey says that getting everyone together is the only way he can leave the island. Why? He's never fully explained what he means by this, nor why he needs to get all of those people off the island in order for him to escape. We saw in "Ab Aeterno" that it's more likely he just wants to kill them all. Why doesn't someone ask why he needs them all together?
- What will Hurley use Jacob's ashes for?
- Why does the smoke monster see Desmond as a threat?
- Libby says that when she got her flash of the other timeline, it felt like Hugo had been at the hospital with her. Since the people having the flashes only seem to see their *own* lives, is this an indication that Libby did, in fact, know that Hurley was in the hospital with her before the plane crash?
- When we saw the boy in the woods previously, he had golden hair. Why is it dark brown now? Why can Desmond and Sawyer see him, but Richard Alpert can't?
- Back in the episode "The Other Woman," we heard the whispers and then Harper (the therapist for the Others who was also Goodwin's wife) was suddenly standing there. She disappears again immediately after. Now that we've seen Michael similarly appear when the whispers begin, does it mean Harper died? What terrible thing had she done in her life to trap her in the island purgatory? Was she, the jilted wife, the one who told Ben about Goodwin and Juliet and got Goodwin killed? It seems unlikely that she would have done that, since her biggest fear was Ben finding out.
- Is it possible Sayid is trapped in a living purgatory?

- Smokey says that Widmore is not interested in answers; he's only interested in power. Is that true?
- What is Desmond's purpose in the sideways world now? Is he the shepherd who has to lead the flock down a certain path? And if so, what is that path?
- Why does Desmond hit John Locke with a car? Does he think if he kills John Locke that Smokey cannot inhabit his body? Or does he think that by hitting him with a car he might cause the moment that will make Locke see the other side? If so, that seems a little harsh compared to the way Hurley had his revelation. Is it to push him to the hospital where he'll be forced to meet with Jack? Poor Locke . . . no matter what the timeline, the guy can never catch a break.

Ashes to Ashes: Ilana was chosen at a young age by Jacob to protect his Candidates, and she said he was like a father to her. She trained her entire life to get to where she is on the island, and the moment she had almost all of the Candidates together to protect, she died when she grossly mishandled some dynamite.

Music/Bands: Daniel is playing Chopin's "Fantaisie-Impromptu in C#-Minor," which apparently is the only piece of classical music the *Lost* writers have ever heard of.

Notes from Underground by Fyodor Dostoevsky (1864)

As Hurley is rifling through Ilana's possessions, he finds a copy of Fyodor Dostoevsky's *Notes from Underground* in her bag. Told from the perspective of an angry antihero who is entirely misanthropic, it's a look at a downtrodden person who feels society is to blame for why he is the way he is, but through his words we see that he is actually the one responsible for much of the unhappiness that has befallen him.

Notes from Underground opens with a note from the author, saying that the narrator of the following pages is not a real person, but people like him no doubt exist. He explains that the book will be divided into two parts: the first, "Underground," will be an introduction to the man and his opinions, and in the second section, we will look at one particular bad memory in this man's life.

"Underground" opens with a narrator who prides himself on how spiteful he is. He is filled with contradictions, one minute saying that he has a liver condition, the next saying he doesn't know what's wrong with him. He admits that he is filled with opposites, that "I felt them positively swarming in me, these opposite elements." He was in the civil service, in a low-paying job he hated, but he's left it because a relative died and left him 6,000 rubles. He is 40 years old, and at one point complains that only "fools and worthless fellows" live beyond the age of 40, even though he plans to live twice that long . . . out of spite. He seems to harbor a hatred for humanity and for himself. *Lost* fans would almost be best imagining Benjamin Linus as the narrator, although the speaker has a lot less confidence than Ben has.

After his initial introduction, the narrator distinguishes between two types of people: men of action and men of consciousness. The former group acts without thinking of the consequences, and they therefore can make decisions more easily. People in the latter group, in which he includes himself, overanalyze every situation until they always end up talking themselves out of performing any action at all. It was this section that caused Jean-Paul Sartre to call *Notes from Underground* the first existentialist novel (see page 197). If existentialism argues that man makes choices based on his own free will and is responsible for the decisions made, here the narrator suggests that sometimes the profound knowledge of just how far-reaching those choices can be might render a person inert.

The narrator talks about how the man of action tends to adhere to the laws of science, whereas the other man overthinks the sciences until they don't make sense anymore. He tosses aside the idea that two times two equals four, suggesting that such easy maths and sciences suggest an inevitability, or fate, or destiny. He disagrees with anyone who believes in fate; he believes in free will. He believes anyone who goes strictly along with blind faith is useless. But even as he upholds his consciousness as some sort of ideal, he doesn't have any respect for himself. He explains the plight of the conscious man by suggesting that the only pleasure a conscious man has is in a toothache, and that he moans and groans and gets his pleasure not only from the noises he's making, but from knowing he's annoying everyone around him. The base pain of the toothache is something the man doesn't have to overanalyze; he just feels it, and he derives pleasure from that.

In the next chapter the narrator reinforces everything he's said already, adding that he tried to fall in love, but found he was filled with suffering that extended from boredom, and it's this boredom that offers the worst pain in his life. Again he says that the only people who are able to act are those who have "no trace of doubt" in their minds. He says sometimes we feel hate or love simply to escape the boredom, and then wonders, "perhaps I consider myself an intelligent man, only because all my life I have been able neither to begin nor to finish anything." He is drawn to the idea of romantic love, but at the same time repulsed by it because of what he knows of society. He then differentiates between inertia brought on by too much consciousness (i.e., not doing anything because the enlightened man has thought through all consequences and talked himself out of it) and mere laziness.

In *Lost*'s season 5 episode "Namaste," Sawyer explains to a fairly high-strung Jack that he's going to sit and read a book and figure out what to do next. Jack wants to dive right in to doing things, but, somewhat cruelly, Sawyer says that's the attitude that got people killed, and he won't be that kind of leader. Dostoevsky's narrator distinguishes between the man of action and the man of consciousness; the man of action, like Jack, just jumps in without thinking too much about the consequences. Conversely, the man of consciousness's disadvantage is that once he's seen something from all sides, he overthinks the situation until he is no longer able to act. He explains that "to begin to act . . . you must first have your mind completely at ease and no trace of doubt left in it." This line reminds us of Desmond's determination to push the button, Locke's resolve that the button was useless, and Jack's conviction that he was right to drop the bomb.

The next section of the book is an integral chapter and probably key to why the writers chose to show it on *Lost*. First, the narrator comments on the notion that man will always act in his own best interests and, if given the choice, would always act for good. He says this idea is naïve, and that man often chooses things that lead to his own destruction, "desiring in certain cases what is harmful to himself and not advantageous." He says man often does things to achieve a certain unnamed "most advantageous advantage," one more important to man than anything, but he doesn't tell the reader what that advantage is right away. He says this advantage is what breaks down every system of logic, everything that the laws of nature and reason dictate to be in our best interests. He discusses the idea that when man creates civilizations, he is less apt to go to war, and counters with the statement: "it is the most civilized gentlemen who have been the subtlest slaughterers," and "civilization has made mankind if not more bloodthirsty, at least more vilely, more loathsomely bloodthirsty." He says some would argue that the laws of nature and reason show man that, ultimately, he has no choice, and things will play out a certain way because they simply have to, based on these laws. He wonders if boredom is what often leads mankind to do bad things. But he says if someone were to stand up and tell people to forget what the laws of nature demand, and instead live by their own foolish will, no matter what the consequences, that person would no doubt find himself many followers. And therein lies that most advantageous advantage: "What man wants is simply *independent* choice, whatever that independence may cost and wherever it may lead."

Like so much of the plot, and subplots, and undercurrents on *Lost*, this section is about free will versus fate, but while the narrator rails against the idea of destiny, he says that given free will, most men choose unwisely. (Incidentally, in this section he refers to building tables of logarithms up to **108**,000.) The Man in Black said to Jacob in "The Incident," "They come. They fight. They destroy. They corrupt. It always ends the same." He's suggesting that even when given a choice, men choose badly, and things go haywire. Like the narrator in the book, the Man in Black believes that a system of logic always leads people to the same end point, tricking them into thinking they actually had a choice along the way. Jacob counters, "But it only ends once. Anything before that is just progress." To him, free will is essential, and he believes man is actually evolving with every choice made along the way. He would agree that free will is the most advantageous advantage.

The narrator continues his point in the next chapter, where he anticipates the reader's objection that even free will can be explained away by the laws of nature. He says that man refuses to accept that his free will could be subject to the laws of nature: "You see, gentlemen, reason is an excellent thing, there's no disputing that, but reason is nothing but reason and satisfies only the rational side of man's nature, while will is a manifestation of the whole life, that is, of the whole human life including reason and all the impulses." He says that reason is limited to what a person learns, whereas human nature, and free will, make up the entirety of a person and encompass more of him. Sometimes reason and free will can co-exist: when it comes to a person's individuality and personality, many "maintain that this is really the most precious thing for mankind; choice can, of course, if it chooses, be in agreement with reason; and especially if this be not abused but kept within bounds." But he says ultimately, a man will do anything to maintain his sense of choice and free will and will make bad choices simply to show that he can, even purposely going mad to be rid of reason once and for all.

Again, this section provides a commentary on the season 2 discussions between Locke and Jack and the way the debates over science versus faith continue throughout the series. Locke argued that the survivors were all following an unknown destiny; Jack said there was no destiny and that they were responsible for the choices they made. But over time there was a suggestion that, through one's choices, one could reach his/her destiny, bringing the two ideas together. Both Locke and Jack have made bad choices, and in doing so, they demonstrated their free will and ability to choose, even if that choice led to disaster.

The next chapter opens with the narrator's assertion that he's actually been joking, but after making that proclamation he continues his narration along the same lines. He says that man is always building and following new roads just to find out where they'll lead, and keeps taking tangents because he fears that the main road may be the one he was predestined to take. Man likes to make those roads, but he similarly, in this way, likes to destroy them. And ultimately, that's because, while man spends his life trying to attain a certain object, he purposely creates roadblocks because he doesn't actually want to attain it, and if he does attain it, the desire will have been achieved and there's no more sense of anticipation: ". . . man is a frivolous and incongruous creature, and perhaps, like a chess player, loves the process of the game, not the end of it." While man may spend lifetimes trying to achieve certainty in life, sacrificing everything, even his own life, in that quest, "to succeed, really to find it, he dreads, I assure you. He feels that when he has found it there will be nothing for him to look for." He then says that while we strive to do things for our well-being, there's also a love of suffering, and sometimes man brings on his own suffering because there's a perverse pleasure in it. He says that while earlier he'd said consciousness could be a bad thing, he said it's actually a good thing, because despite the inertia that can be brought on by it, a conscious person can flog himself, "and that will, at any rate, liven you up. Reactionary as it is, corporal punishment is better than nothing."

While this section is an excellent comment on how fans felt leading up to the finale (we can't wait to see how it ends! but we don't want it to end!) it gives credence to Jacob's side of things, that everything leading up to the final end is just "progress." Rather than focusing on the end point, one must appreciate the process leading up to it. Once fans saw the series finale of *Lost*, they began discussing everything that had led up to it, and several fans jumped back to the beginning for a rewatch the next day. The end of a journey isn't nearly as interesting as the road leading there, and for the characters, the journeys they've taken throughout the series will take on greater resonance when they get to the end of it.

Next Dostoevsky's narrator talks about a crystal palace, referring to the building that was constructed for the Great Exhibition in London in 1851, which was constructed entirely out of crystal and iron to represent a utilitarian society. (Dostoevsky had seen it on a trip.) The narrator wants to stick his tongue out at the structure and reject it, but then immediately says that if he were to desire to live in a crystal palace, nothing would dissuade him from that goal. You could tell him a henhouse is as good as a crystal palace for getting out of the rain, and he would counter that man lives for more than just shelter from the rain. But then he wonders aloud why he would ever desire something unattainable like the crystal palace and not be content where he lives: "Can I have been constructed simply in order to come to the conclusion that all my construction is a cheat? Can this be my whole purpose?"

Finally, much like when he had claimed to be joking, the narrator now claims that he's been lying the whole time, and assures the reader "there is not one thing, not one word of what I have written that I really believe" (a statement he immediately contradicts in the next sentence). Then in a long section that could be imagined as a fan yelling at Ben Linus, he constructs a long damnation of himself as if it were uttered by his readers, calling himself a liar and a cheat and pointing out every contradiction he's made along the way. He says he's been listening to people for 40 years from the underground, and that what will follow are his confessions. He's not sure why he's even addressing his readers or imagining readers at all, considering that he never intends to publish these words: "Every man has memories which he would not tell to everyone, but only to his friends. He has other matters in his mind which he would not reveal even to his friends, but only to himself, and that in secret." He says it has been said that there's no such thing as a true autobiography, because nobody is going to reveal absolutely everything about themselves, especially his or her dark side. But then he explains the psychology of referring overtly to his readers, saying that all writers imagine an audience, even if it's just to raise up their writing and make it more "dignified." Writing out the memories he is about to share with us is his way of purging them from his mind.

He then begins with his story, and we read it in the context of the way he's set himself up in this opening half of the book. This section is crucial to understanding the flashbacks on *Lost*. The people on the island keep secrets from each other, and from everyone else, but we can see through the flashbacks how full their lives have been. Some fans have wondered if the flashbacks aren't history as it actually happened, but history as the characters *remembered* it (hence the visual trope of the eye, which indicates that what we're about to see is from that character's point of view only). Perhaps there is more to each character's story, but they're not letting us see it.

In Part II, the narrator tells a story of something that happened to him when he was 24, offering a practical application of the theories and philosophies he outlined in the opening section. Sixteen years ago he was an angry and antisocial young man, working in an office where he despised most of his colleagues. He read a lot of literature and was drawn to the Romantics. One day as he is walking by a tavern he sees a man thrown out of a front window, and realizes he would have loved for that to happen to him, just so people would notice him. He enters the tavern, where he is pushed aside by an officer walking past him. He's so angry about this offense that he begins to tail the officer, finding out where he lives and works and goes on the weekends, and he becomes so wrapped up in his obsession that he decides he is going to walk toward him on the boardwalk and force the officer to move out of *his* way. But every time he walks toward him he ends up moving out of the way at the last minute, as the officer barrels through the crowd of people like they don't exist. Eventually, the narrator buys a coat that's beyond his means (he even borrows money to do so) and some new gloves, thinking that if he looks the part, the officer might move out of his way because he sees him as his equal. When he eventually does pull it off, and bumps into the officer, he's victorious (even though the officer doesn't seem to have noticed him and continues on his way without saying anything). But soon after, he's suddenly overwhelmed with guilt and shame that he had become so obsessed with bringing another person down.

The narrator describes his escapist dreams, where he is always a noble hero. They are filled with romantic notions and language, and it gives some insight into the fact that even though the narrator seems like a misanthrope, he is certainly capable of understanding and feeling love. Giving in to an urge to connect with the world, he begins having tea once a week with a man and his two daughters, and even though he doesn't say much of anything, it makes him want to reconnect with more people, so he goes to meet his friend Simonov.

The next section takes the book to a level of awkwardness that rivals television's *The Office*. When he gets to Simonov's apartment, he is there with two other former schoolmates, Ferfichkin (whom the narrator describes as looking like a monkey, and seems to particularly detest) and Trudolyubov (whom the narrator doesn't mind as much, though he thinks he's too narrow-minded sometimes). They're all discussing their plans for the following day, which is to take their friend Zverkov out for a farewell dinner. Zverkov is a successful officer, another person the narrator detests. He used to mock the narrator when he was in school because the narrator was smarter than everyone else and had good grades. He would boast of his conquests of women, and when the narrator attempted to call him on it one day, the joke flew back in his own face. Zverkov has become more successful than all of them and has a lot of money, and now the three men are trying to pool their money together to take him out. The narrator interjects that he, too, will donate some money, and they are all horrified, but unable to say no to him. It's clear they don't want him there, and he doesn't want to be there, but now they're all stuck. The narrator goes home and wishes he hadn't said that, because he can't afford to go and doesn't have any clothes that aren't stained.

He shows up at the restaurant at 5, which had been the designated time, but everyone else arrives at 6, a fact that annoys the narrator. Zverkov arrives and is patronizing to the narrator, who eventually causes a scene, saying that he's paying his own way and is as entitled to be there as the rest of them. Throughout the scene the narrator begins drinking heavily (and he has almost no tolerance for alcohol), and everyone else is tense and tries to pretend he's not there. Eventually they move to a different part of the restaurant and the narrator paces up and down the restaurant for three hours, resenting that the men don't see him as the "literary man" that he believes he is, and alternately feeling bad about what he'd done and wanting to just sit and enjoy their company. They then get up to leave and go to a brothel, and the narrator asks Simonov for his money back. Simonov throws the money at him and leaves in disgust. The narrator, distraught, decides he will go to the brothel and slap Zverkov in the face.

He gets into a sledge, alternately telling the driver to go faster and then telling him to stop and let him off. Just as he explained earlier in the book that by thinking a situation through, a conscious person finds himself unable to act, now the narrator can't actually decide whether or not he should go to the brothel and slap Zverkov or just return home and send a letter the next day apologizing for his behavior. Eventually he decides he must go through with it, only to arrive at the brothel and find that the men are not there. After he despairs that he won't get to fulfill his destiny, a young prostitute appears, and he decides he will sleep with her.

After they have sex, the narrator realizes he hasn't spoken to the girl, Liza, at all, so he begins to regale her with a sad tale of woe about how her life is going to turn out if she continues her current line of work, suggesting her looks will go quickly, she'll be riddled with disease, and that the madam of the brothel won't take her to a hospital if she needs one as long as she can perform her sexual duties. He then describes the joy of marriage and children and why she needs to take up a more traditional life than the one she's got here. He tells the story in high romantic language. She suggests that her parents were the ones who sold her into this life, and then tells him that his story sounded like it was from a book. He's severely offended. She says that she was genuinely moved by what he told her, but he returns to his story of how terrible her life will be and makes the already dire future look worse. By the time he realizes Liza is in agony on the bed, wracked with sobs, he's fascinated that his story had this effect on her and he becomes more interested in her. At first he's horrified that he made her cry and jumps up to leave, but she sits up and has a "half insane smile" on her face. He tries to tell her he was wrong, and then gives her his address in case she ever wants to talk. Before he leaves, she retrieves a love letter to show him that she is loved, and he sees it as something she'll treasure, but he believes it represents a life that is unattainable to her now.

He returns home, and that day he vows to make things right with Simonov and his group, writes them a letter saying he didn't mean what he said or did, but was simply intoxicated, and returns Simonov's money with the letter. He gets his servant, Apollon, to deliver the money. He then begins to wonder if Liza will take him up on his offer to come to his place, and begins to fret that if she does she will see how shabby his apartment and clothes are. His thoughts turn to Apollon, who he believes is arrogant and puts on airs around him, and that he spitefully takes the seven rubles the narrator pays him every month and does nothing to earn it. He decides he'll be spiteful back, and he'll withhold Apollon's money for this month. When Apollon comes to his room, the narrator rails at him, yelling that he didn't call for him, but Apollon simply answers that he'd come because he wondered if his master had any orders to be carried out. The narrator finally foists the money on Apollon, calls him a "torturer," and when Apollon tells him he'll call the police for the narrator's insulting behavior, the narrator screams at him to do it . . . and that's when he notices Liza standing in the doorway.

At first both of them are surprised, and the narrator is upset that she saw him in such a terrible rage. Apollon leaves, and the narrator rushes after him to tell him to get their tea together, but Apollon ignores him until the narrator is in a frenzy. He rushes back to Liza, screaming that he's going to kill Apollon, and then he sits there seething. She quietly tells him that she wanted to get out of the place she was in. He sits in silence before she asks him if he'll answer. He erupts, yelling that perhaps she just wants him to save her, and that he can't, and just as he thinks he's going to bring her to tears again, it is he who crumples onto the sofa, sobbing, "I can't be good!" She sits next to him with her arm around him, comforting him, and he's disgusted that their roles have switched. He sends her away to the other room, where she sits quietly as he paces his room anxiously, hoping she'll leave. Finally she stands up and says goodbye, and he takes five rubles and stuffs them into her hand as she leaves. She storms out of the place and he immediately regrets what he's done, calling after her, but she doesn't stop. When he gets back up to his room, he sees the five-ruble note on his desk and realizes she must have thrown it back at him before leaving. He races down the stairs and out into the snow, but she's gone.

Here he ends the book, saying he never should have said this much already, and he talks about how, essentially, everyone is divorced from life. The book ends suddenly, with an outside author, in italics, saying there were several more pages of the manuscript but he decided not to include them there.

Notes from Underground is an enigmatic book, one that features one of the most well known antiheroes in literature, a man who is so loathsome yet who tries to conjure our sympathy for him, but we can see why others regard him with such disgust and we feel little sympathy for him at all.

The novel is appropriately tied to *Lost* because of its existentialist philosophy and its bleakness, and you can see which characters might identify with the narrator. It's found in Ilana's possessions after she dies, and considering how sad she was that Jacob had used her for much of her life, but never saw her as a Candidate, one can imagine her identifying with the novel's deeply thwarted and angry narrator. He cannot get past the memory that has afflicted him for most of his life, just as many of the characters on the show carry around baggage from their former lives and cannot overcome the hurts they have suffered or have inflicted on others. The narrator comments that as he paced the room after humiliating himself in front of Simonov and the others, he realizes that 40 years would go by and he would still "remember with loathing and humiliation those filthiest, most ridiculous, and most awful moments of my life."

The narrator often refers to things in black-and-white terms, just as many of the themes on *Lost* are presented as opposites. When he talks about the incident where the officer wouldn't move out of his way, he says, "Either to be a hero or to grovel in the mud — there was nothing between." Just as the Losties argue about fate and destiny or good and evil, the narrator sees things as being in clear opposition rather than blending together. When he decides to reach out to Simonov, it's like he realizes that despite separating himself from the world, what he really needs is human contact. But when he does reach out to make that connection, it goes terribly wrong. He eventually finds contact with Liza, but that goes badly, too. Similarly, the characters on *Lost* are always looking for connections with others, even when those connections often end badly or make them feel worse. Jack had a strong connection with Kate, but it ended so badly he was willing to erase every memory of it just to take the pain away.

As the narrator tells Liza about how terrible her life is and will be, he says his life isn't a walk in the park, either, but at least he's not a slave. She, on the other hand, is, and he tells her, "If you want to break your chains afterwards, you won't be able to: you will be more and more fast in the snares. . . . It's like selling your soul to the devil." Similarly, Richard Alpert was in chains once, was let out of them, but has been a prisoner ever since, metaphorically chained to Jacob. The Man in Black feels like he's chained to the island, and most of the survivors have felt imprisoned by the island, by their past, and by their own memories. Dostoevsky's narrator tells Liza that he is not a slave, but he clearly is, enslaved to his shame from the memory of what happened on that fateful day 16 years earlier. He'll never break free from his chains; will anyone on the island be able to break free of theirs?

6.13 The Last Recruit

Original air date: April 20, 2010
Written by: Paul Zbyszewski, Graham Roland
Directed by: Stephen Semel
Guest cast: Andrea Gabriel (Nadia), Christopher Amitrano (Burditt), Todd Coolidge (EMT #2), Teresa Huang (Surgeon), Yvonne Midkiff (Receptionist), Kasim Saul (Guard), Skyler Stone (EMT #1)

Focus: Everyone
Jack comes face-to-face with the smoke monster while Sawyer makes plans to escape the island without it. In the sideways world, all of the stories begin to come together.

Season 5's "Follow the Leader" was an episode about, well, leaders. Who is equipped to lead, what makes a good leader, and which of the characters were successful ones. "The Last Recruit" explores similar territory, but focuses as much on the followers.

From the beginning of the series, Jack has been the group's leader. With power comes responsibility, and the amount of responsibility that was heaped upon Jack was enormous. Not only was he charged with concocting all of the plans to find supplies and shelter and procure rescue, but he had to tend to every medical disaster that befell the survivors, from shrapnel wounds to slivers in their pinkie fingers. He was the decision maker and the tiebreaker, and people looked to him to fix things but often resented him for the decisions he made. He struggled with his own resistance to delegating; he needed to be in complete control. Jack was a beleaguered leader with feisty followers, but when Ana Lucia showed up in his camp with only four remaining survivors out of her initial 23, Jack knew he'd done a better job at keeping his people safe. His defining moment as a leader was in "White Rabbit," where he stood up and gave his infamous speech: "Every man for himself is not going to work. It's time to start organizing. We need to figure out how we're going to survive here . . . Last week most of us were strangers, but we're all here now. And god knows how long we're going to be here. But if we can't live together, we're going to die alone."

Sayid always seemed like another good choice for leader. A full two episodes *before* Jack's pivotal speech, it was Sayid who stepped up on the rock and tried to rally the troops. He explained to everyone exactly what had happened when they tried to get the radio signal working, and then suggested forming three separate groups, each with its own leader: one in charge of finding fresh water, another looking for food, and the last would search the plane for useful electronics. His speech and organization were both impeccable; he considered the immediate needs of the group, put together a workable concept in an orderly fashion, and aimed at a future in which he could do something to get them rescued. But few people were willing to follow someone who'd worked for the Republican Guard, and while his ideas seemed sound, in this situation people trusted the doctor over the military man. Sayid quietly moved to the background again. Two episodes later, he and Jack had the group's first big disagreement when Jack wanted to go to the caves and Sayid wanted to remain on the beach. He stayed behind with the people on the beach, but was never treated like their leader. By the time Jack called upon Sayid in "Confidence Man" to help him extract information from

Sawyer, their positions were solidified: Jack was the leader and decision-maker, and Sayid the follower whose actions, like those of the rest, would be guided by Jack Shephard.

When Jack and the others were kidnapped at the beginning of season 3, it seemed like the perfect opportunity for Sayid to step up, but instead, it was John Locke who did. While many of the survivors were distrustful of Locke, he gave a stirring speech in "Further Instructions," telling them he would find their missing people and bring them home, but in the meantime they had to attend to immediate concerns. This speech sounded much like the ones both Jack and Sayid had given. Even Hurley shook his head and joked that he had a moment of déjà vu. However, Locke quickly returned to his lone man routine, and never really emerged as a leader until the beginning of season 4, when the group split into two, half going with Jack and the other half with Locke. Once again Jack made decisions, but his leadership had evolved and he treated his group more democratically, bringing more people into the fold and looking for group decisions rather than letting them all fall to him. Locke, on the other hand, took his group to New Otherton and treated it more like a dictatorship, one where he provided everyone with food and safety, and they in turn didn't ask questions and accepted his decision-making. As one might imagine, his leadership didn't last long. Locke had a larger purpose and wasn't much interested in leading the survivors anyway, and instead turned his sights to leading the Others. But just when it looked like he was about to become their leader once and for all . . . bloop! The island began hiccupping through time.

Sawyer seemed like the least likely candidate to become leader (even Walt seemed like a better option), and his "every man for himself" motto was the very thing Jack had warned against in his speech. Sawyer pretended he didn't care about the others, but despite his hard exterior, he had moments of real caring, and he often stepped forward and quietly became part of the group when he believed they may be threatened in some way. But in "The Long Con," Sawyer declared himself the new sheriff in town, the man with the guns. Through Sawyer's character, the writers questioned the idea that a leader isn't the guy with the medical ability, the military know-how, or the hunting skills; he's just the guy who can instill the most fear and obedience in his people. His role as sheriff lasted about as long as his speech did, and it looked like Sawyer was nothing but a mockery of what a leader should be.

By season 4, however, that image had begun to change — and so had Sawyer. Locke was ineffectual and Jack was out of the picture, so Sawyer stepped up to keep his group safe. He was no longer just the guy who controlled the arsenal; he was the guy who would use the arsenal to protect his people. By season 5, with everyone blooping around in time, Sawyer was actually keeping his group together, urging them to continue on to the Orchid station to try to put a stop to everything. While he didn't always have it together, and while sometimes his decisions were trumped by Juliet or Locke, he was the guy people looked to. When Sawyer ended up in 1974, Locke was no longer with him at that point, and everyone began following his lead. He led them right into the Dharma Initiative, where he protected his people and kept their secret, and he became a de facto leader of the Dharminians, the head of security. After all his empty claims in "The Long Con," Sawyer really was the sheriff. And this time, he deserved it. Things were calm and predictable in Sawyerland . . . and then some people from his past — most notably Kate — returned, turning his world upside-down.

Sawyer and Jack had an interesting discussion about how a leader should lead, and Sawyer, surprisingly, told Jack that a good leader sits quietly and contemplates his next move, where a bad leader — namely Jack — reacts quickly and gets his people killed. In this moment, Jack has deferred to Sawyer as his leader, and calmly tells Sawyer that he's happy to do so. Until the day after, when Jack crazily ran through the jungle telling everyone to follow him so he could drop a bomb down a shaft. And, as his nature dictates, Sawyer followed him. In "The Last Recruit," Sawyer is only pretending to follow Smokey, all the while devising a plan to rally his compadres to follow him off the island, leaving everyone else behind.

Throughout the sixth season, characters no longer seem to be struggling with the question of which one of the alpha-males should be leader. Instead, they're trying to learn how to follow and listen to one another. Smokey has become the leader of one group (admittedly with most of his people following him reluctantly) and Hurley has become the leader of the other. Hurley's ability to talk to the dead — something that he once saw as a curse or proof that he was crazy — now makes him invaluable, for he's the only one who can listen to the island dead, who seem to know more about what's going on than anyone who's alive.

Sayid is in no position to lead anyone. At this point he is blindly following Smokey because he can't *feel* enough to make a decision on his own. In "Follow the Leader," he agreed to follow Jack to get the plutonium core of the bomb — he did it because he figured the worst thing that could happen was that the bomb would go off and if that happened, he said, it would "put us out of our misery." Turns out, that *wasn't* the worst-case scenario. Sayid isn't miserable — he isn't anything. He says he can no longer feel sadness or happiness. And yet, with his gun poised at Desmond in an attempt to fulfill Smokey's orders and get back the one thing he wants, Sayid is confronted with Desmond's piercing question: if he gets back the woman he loves, how will he explain to her what he's become, or what he did to get her back? For the first time in several episodes, viewers see a tiny glimmer of the old Sayid shining ever so dimly through that empty exterior. Sayid has done a lot of things in his life, and many of them were in aid of finding Nadia, or of avenging her death. And what would she think of those things?

Just as the two groups have finally combined on the island, we start to see the storylines in the sideways world come together. Desmond "Hit-and-Run" Hume (on the heels of mowing down John Locke in one of the craziest scenes of this series *ever*) has now tracked down Claire as she's about to visit an adoption clinic. And he just happens to know a lawyer she should use, who just happens to also be Jack Shephard's lawyer, who just happens to be on his way over for the reading of his father's will, in which document Claire also just happens to be mentioned.

In more believable storylines, Jin and Sun are told their baby is fine. There is a strange moment when Sun seems to recognize John Locke — and not as a guy who ever helped her, but as someone who scares her — and she begins yelling about him. It's not clear how she knows him; perhaps being shot in the stomach has provided her with one of those flash moments, but we aren't actually shown one of those clarifying moments of recognition that we got with Hurley or Desmond. At the end of the scene with Jin and Sun, they are together in her hospital room and it looks like everything is going to be fine. If this is where they end the Jin and Sun story in the sideways world, it's nice to see a happy ending. On the island, their lives catch up to the happiness of the sideways world as Jin and Sun *finally* get back together again, giving us the reunion we've longed to see for so long. But as usual on that island, their happiness is short-lived.

Sawyer recruits Kate to act as point on his expedition, a marked difference from Jack's leadership in the first two seasons, which always had one rule: never invite Kate along. Jack thought he was protecting her, while deep down, he knew Kate would just follow them anyway and probably get herself — and everyone else — in deep trouble. But maybe Jack liked the idea of Kate following after him, like it was a test of her desire to be with him. Regardless, Sawyer gives her the respect she's longed for on the island and asks her to accompany him.

Fans cheered when Sun and Jin finally landed in each other's arms once again (even if that sonic fence gave everyone a scare). (Mario Perez/ABC via Getty Images)

In the sideways world, the scenes between James and Kate are a "Skater's" dream (Skaters being the people who want Sawyer and Kate to end up together). The flirtiness between them in the police station is fun to watch. It's surprisingly similar to their relationship in season 1 — Sawyer pretended to be something he wasn't, Kate saw through his ruse, called him on it, and he relaxed around her. However, in season 1 Sawyer is angry that she's figured out his tragic past, whereas in the sideways world, James is merely bemused, saying, "Oh, I *like* you." And . . . the Skaters rejoice. (I've never subscribed to either of the Kate ships on the show, but even I was almost a Skate convert in that moment.)

Kate is involved in another important pairing in this episode, and that's with Claire. Sawyer makes a harsh decision, one Jack would likely not have made, announcing that Sayid and Claire aren't welcome on his boat. He tells Kate that Claire is crazy and has no right to raise Aaron. Considering Aaron was taken from Claire and her current mental state is the result, this isn't really Sawyer's decision to make. Besides, Kate came back to the island just to find Claire, and Sawyer is undermining Kate's entire reason for being there. One of the saddest moments in the episode is when Claire stands near the tree, watching as everyone abandons her a second time after she'd just told Jack that she'd felt abandoned by them three years earlier. When Kate reaches out to Claire at the boat, and declares that if Claire doesn't get on the boat then she's not going either, she becomes a hero. This is possibly Kate's finest moment in the series. In "Sundown" Kate faced Claire for the first time and told her things that inadvertently hurt Claire, but in this case she tells Claire exactly what she needs to hear.

Jack has come over to the Dark Side, but where everyone else is hell-bent on getting off the island, Jack is trying to understand Smokey's agenda. He's not with him — despite what Claire or Smokey say, Jack does not see himself as the last recruit — but he believes that if he can just figure out what Smokey wants, then he can protect everyone else. He tries to follow Sawyer, even making it as far as getting on his boat, but he realizes that if the smoke monster wants them to leave, maybe they should be asking why: "We were brought here because we were supposed to do something, and if that thing wants us to leave, maybe he's afraid of what happens if we stay." The tables have turned: Sawyer is reacting rashly to the situation, and he risks getting everyone killed, whereas Jack is the one who is staring out at the water, thinking things through, exactly the way Sawyer did back in "Namaste." Jack then decides he won't lead, and he won't follow: he will simply return to the island on his own, and see where it takes him.

In the sideways world, Jack walks into an operating room to see none other than John Locke on his table (fresh from the Desmond hit-and-run). When he sees the mirror reflection of John's face, he instantly says, "I think I know this guy." Jack knows Locke better than just about anyone, even if he battles with him constantly — and maybe because of it. Jack was Locke's nemesis, but you could see even on Jack's face throughout each season that regardless of what he was saying, his faith in his own convictions was wavering as Locke talked. Locke's theories and ideas stuck with Jack long after the two men were separated, and the irony of Jack facing off against Smokey is that Jack is more a resurrection of John Locke than Smokey is. He has John's faith and beliefs, and realized John was right about everything (it's not a coincidence that Jack's name is a diminutive of "John"). Jack jumps off a boat to stay on the island, something that John Locke would have done three years earlier, and Jack would have mocked. Locke was the first to forge the ideas that were important to the people on the island, but he was never accepted as a leader. Jack was the leader, but he didn't have the ideas that would help anyone. And now, Jack returns to Smokey — intent on being a follower until he can figure out how to become an even better leader.

Highlight: Sawyer referring to Lapidus as "that pilot who looks like he stepped off the set of a Burt Reynolds movie."

Did You Notice?:

- When Jack and Smokey are talking, Jack tries to ask him if he was actually Christian Shephard all of those times he saw him walking around. Smokey never comes out and offers the information, but instead prods Jack to tell him what he's really thinking about, and then admits to having done it. (It's difficult to take Smokey at his word, but since he confirms something most of the audience has long suspected, I think it's safe to say he's telling the truth. However, I don't believe that he was all of the dead characters all of the time.)
- In the ambulance, John says Helen's name and then adds, "I was gonna marry her," which could have been the John from either reality talking. He was intending to marry her in the other timeline but she didn't accept his proposal.
- When Claire talks to Jack on the island, we hear the Claire musical motif again, once again suggesting she's being genuine and this is the same Claire we once knew, despite how things may appear.
- When Hurley refers to Anakin, and Sawyer asks who the hell Anakin is, many fans thought that was disingenuous, because Sawyer is the guy who makes many of the *Star Wars* references. However, I find it plausible that he wouldn't have watched the prequels and would be an original trilogy fan only.
- Sawyer offers Kate an apple, as if he's Satan in the Garden of Eden.
- Sawyer refers to Zoe as Widmore's Number Two, which is another reference to *The Prisoner* (Number Two is the person who speaks for the boss, but Number Six, the main character, is never allowed to see the boss).
- I guess Smokey's stick told him what it was supposed to be used for.
- Ilana speaks with an American accent. This could suggest that in both timelines she was born in the U.S., but in the original one Jacob removed her to an Eastern European country when she was young so he could train her.
- We hear Ilana's surname for the first time — Verdansky — and she is a partner in the law firm Sweetzer & Verdansky. The first name is a reminder that Desmond and Penny met in a coffee shop at the corner of Sweetzer and Melrose.
- Sawyer asks Kate if she's ready to get wet. Skaters cheer loudly.
- Sawyer says that Claire has been drinking Smokey's Kool-Aid, which is the

second reference he's made to the Jonestown Massacre (see *Finding Lost — Season Five*, pp. 205–206).
- Ilana asks Jack if he believes in fate (we all know his answer to that one) and brings Claire into the room. Fate seems to exist more prevalently in the sideways world, as if there really is a greater power bringing everyone and everything together.
- Jack tells Sawyer, "The island's not done with us yet." Sawyer responds, "Yeah, well, I'm done with this island." This is the same exchange Desmond had with Eloise in "316" when she told him the island wasn't done with him yet. She was right.
- Sawyer also tells Jack that if he wants to take a leap of faith (off the boat and into the water), then take it. In "316," Eloise tells Jack that by taking Locke's body back in the coffin as a proxy for his own father, he's taking a leap of faith. In the season 2 episode, "Orientation," Helen tells Locke to stop obsessing over his father and take a leap of faith with her. In that same episode, Locke tells Jack that they need to keep pushing the button, and that it's a leap of faith they need to take together.
- After Jack jumps from the boat, Kate yells, "We have to go back!" echoing the Cry of the Jearded Jack at the end of season 3.
- When Jack first sees John in the operating room, he can only see a mirror reflection of his face, which, considering the many times people have looked into mirrors in the sideways world, could be a suggestion that when he saw him he could detect something from the original-timeline John in his appearance.

Nitpicks: Does Claire have absolutely no sense of self-preservation? First, she climbs into a taxi being driven by a woman who held a gun to her head only a few hours earlier. Then she has this creepy Scottish guy tailing her everywhere; he follows her into an elevator, bombarding her with suggestions that she really needs to change her mind about the adoption and come with him. Most women wouldn't have gotten into the elevator unless other people were also on it, but she rides along and then eventually agrees with him and goes to see his lawyer, which sidetracks her from the appointment she'd had scheduled with the adoption agency. It was a bit of a ridiculous scene, and felt forced in as a way of getting Jack and Claire together in the sideways world.

Lapidus's line when Sun and Jin were reunited — "Looks like someone got their voice back" — was pure *cheese*.

And finally, surely I was not alone in shrieking in terror when Jin and Sun ran toward each other on the beach. Zoe had only just given the call to turn off the sonic fence. In the past we've seen the deactivation take a few seconds, but Jin and Sun ran toward each other immediately and I, along with many other fans, was convinced they were going to be zapped into oblivion the moment they hit the force field around the fence. It's too bad the writers hadn't thought that one through, and simply had Zoe or someone walk through the fence first to make it clear it was turned off. The reunion we'd waited so long for would have been so much more rewarding if fear hadn't been a major part of it. Be sure to watch this scene twice; it's a beautiful moment the second time around.

Oops: Desmond's head has completely healed, even though he had a bandage on it just a couple of hours earlier when he was driving over John with his car. (And if you noticed the timeline discrepancy in this episode, see page 256 for an explanation. Warning: there are spoilers there for the rest of the season.)

4 8 15 16 23 42: The Western Pacific Adoption Agency is on the 15th floor.

It's Just a Flesh Wound: Sayid is tripped by James with a garden hose and falls headfirst onto the ground. An explosion from Widmore's camp sends Jack flying through the air, causing momentary hearing loss and cutting his neck.

Any Questions?:

- If Smokey was Christian Shephard on the island, then how did Jack see Christian sitting in the waiting room at the hospital in "Through the Looking Glass"? We know Smokey can't leave the island, so it couldn't have been him. Was it Christian's ghost?
- What does Sun mean when she says she knows John from somewhere else?
- When James caught Kate, was the marshal called?
- Why does everyone keep saying that once Smokey talks to you you're under his control? It hasn't been evidenced in many of the characters (he's talked to Alpert, Sawyer, Kate, and Jack extensively, and not one of them seems to buy a thing he says).
- How did Desmond survive falling headfirst down that deep well without a serious spinal injury?
- If Claire is genuine, does that mean Dogen was lying when he said she'd been infected the same way Sayid had been? Or did he genuinely mistake her loyalty to Smokey for infection?
- Smokey asks Jack, "Sawyer took my boat, didn't he?" Why did he call him Sawyer? Both Locke and Smokey have always called him James.

6.14 The Candidate

Original air date: May 4, 2010
Written by: Elizabeth Sarnoff, Jim Galasso
Directed by: Jack Bender
Guest cast: Katey Sagal (Helen), Kevin Tighe (Anthony Cooper), Casey Adams (Wheeler), Ken Elliott (Orderly), Noelle Maile Holck (Nurse), Christopher McGahan (Paul), Alan Seabock (Sub Commander)

Focus: Jack/Locke

In the sideways world, Jack tries to convince John to let him perform surgery so he can walk again. On the island, Jack helps Sawyer lead everyone to a sub, all the while insisting he is going to stay behind.

If you thought an underwater scene couldn't get any sadder than the one at the end of "Through the Looking Glass," think again.

"The Candidate" is an episode about trust. Trust has been a major theme on *Lost* from the beginning of the series, simply because it's one of the things we all live with every day. Trust brings peace of mind and allows us to be happy and comfortable. If you trust your friends, colleagues, and family, you can be content. The moment trust is broken with someone, the relationship crumbles. Without trust, we lose everything.

In season 1, the survivors trusted Jack, and he struggled to figure out who among the others he trusted. He proved that the only person he could rely on was himself, when he wore around his neck the key that opened the briefcase of guns and when he wouldn't let anyone in on his plans. In season 2, the survivors first wondered if they could trust the new people from the tail section of the plane (a trust that was marred by the fact that one of them had accidentally killed Shannon), and vice versa. Ben entered everyone's lives, and slowly built up Locke's confidence, only to betray it at the end of the season. Ben's very presence was the locus that caused so much mistrust among all of the survivors throughout all of season 2. Michael was ultimately the one who betrayed everyone's trust, making the newly comfortable survivors a lot more paranoid. In season 3, Jack decided to trust Juliet, but when he brought her back to the camp, no one else did. She tried to earn their confidence throughout the season, but because she was "one of them," even the fans wondered. In season 4, the freighter folk came to the island and trust or lack of it split the group in two. Locke refused to believe

To help keep Smokey at bay, Widmore sets up moveable sonic pylons (left). When filming the close-ups of the Ajira plane, the production crew simply used the front end of a plane prop only, since they didn't need it to fly. (Photos courtesy KOS Tours)

their motives were benevolent, and Jack believed rescue was at hand. Jack let down his guard for the first time since coming to the island — turns out, he was wrong. In season 5, Daniel told the time-jumpers that they had to trust his instincts on what they could and couldn't do in the past. When they were stuck in the 1970s, Sawyer, Miles, Jin, and Juliet had to learn to rely on the Dharma Initiative, and more importantly, earn the DI's trust back. They lost that stable situation when Hurley, Kate, Sayid, and Jack came to join them in 1977 and things went haywire. And then Jack got everyone on side to trust him when he said he could drop a bomb into a shaft and start their lives over again.

Now in season 6, Jack has lost that trust he had in himself because of what happened after the bomb. The hearty confidence in himself that Jack displayed throughout season 1 was gone, and he said to Dogen, "I don't trust myself; how can I trust you?"

Throughout the season, the Man in Black has urged everyone to trust him, from the survivors in the present to Richard Alpert in the past. He's painted himself as Jacob's victim, who he's told them is a devil trying to ruin their lives. But we've seen so many of his assurances turn out to be lies that he's about as trustworthy as Ben Linus at this point.

In this episode, Smokey says he needs Jack to help convince the others to trust him. Jack, of course, doesn't know how he can do this if, once again, he doesn't trust Smokey himself. Once on the sub, Jack has a moment of clarity and realizes what the Man in Black has been intending all along: he needed them all on the sub so he could box them in and destroy them. But Jack's also put together that Smokey's had plenty of opportunities to kill them himself, and he hasn't done it. Why not? Realizing that just like Richard Alpert can't kill himself, neither can Smokey kill any of the Candidates, Jack pleads with Sawyer to trust him. Sawyer looks in Jack's eyes, and though Kate has almost always been swayed by doing the same, Sawyer can't bring himself to trust him. Jack told everyone the freighter folk were well intentioned, and he almost got them all killed. Jack came back to the island and basically destroyed Sawyer's quiet, nice life. Jack's plan for reversing all the bad in their island lives got Juliet killed. It's hard to blame Sawyer for pulling out the wires in that moment.

But this time Sawyer was wrong. He'd told Jack only a few days earlier that a good leader needs to think through a problem to find the solution, and ever since Jack came face-to-face with Smokey, he's done nothing but watch him, talk to him, and try to figure out what his true motivation is. Jack did exactly what Sawyer told him to do. Just as he did in "Dr. Linus," when he closed his eyes and had faith that Richard's dynamite would not go off, Jack believes completely in his assessment of Smokey. But no one in this group trusts anyone else anymore. They've simply been through too much to be free from paranoia.

In the sideways world, Jack is having similar problems getting John Locke to trust him. Just as the old Jack would have done, the sideways Jack takes it upon himself to decide what is best for someone else, and he goes behind John's back to try to figure out exactly why John is refusing to have elective surgery. It's none of Jack's business, but at the same time, he's baffled that a man who cannot walk wouldn't want to at least try to. So he goes to see Anthony Cooper, and if that scene isn't giving fans exactly what they've wanted to see for six seasons, I don't know what is. Sorry, Cooper; karma's a bitch.

Understandably, John feels betrayed by Jack when he finds out Jack had gone behind his back to find Cooper. Jack wants John to put his faith in him, but Jack has already betrayed his trust. Out of anger, he tells Jack why he's in the wheelchair, and ironically, he was paralyzed in a plane crash. In the original timeline, a plane crash made him walk again; in the sideways world, it put him in the chair. He told Jack that he was a new pilot and he'd foolishly told his father to trust him. Now John lives with the guilt every day that he's responsible for his father's vegetative state, of course not knowing that in a parallel world, Cooper was the toss pot who threw him out a window, fully hoping he'd die. In a scene where Jack seems to use all of the show's favorite catchphrases at once, he tells John that what happened happened and that he needs to let it go. In "Orientation," Locke asked Jack why it was so hard for him to believe. Jack countered by asking Locke why it was so easy for him, and Locke told him that it had never been easy. Similarly, in this scene, when Jack tells Locke to let it go, Locke asks him how it's so easy for Jack to let it go, and Jack says it isn't, but he was hoping Locke could go first. The scene in the hospital hallway is effectively a mirror image of the one in "Orientation."

In the past, Jack dismissed Locke as being crazy, but now he realizes he was right. Like Locke, Jack now refuses to leave the island and puts his faith in things he can't see. Now that Locke is dead, he and his actions are being analyzed by many of the other characters. Smokey has John Locke's personality inside him, and while he can feel what Locke felt and knows everything Locke knew, he also stands apart from it like a spectator looking in, and judges Locke for the way he was. In "LA X" he explained to Ben Linus that Locke was "weak, pathetic, and irreparably broken." Sawyer likewise knows instantly that the Man in Black is not John Locke, saying, "Locke was scared, even when he was pretending he wasn't. But you . . . you ain't scared." In "The Last Recruit," Smokey told Jack that the reason he chose John Locke's body was because John "was stupid enough to believe he'd been brought here for a reason, because he pursued that belief until it got him killed, and because you were kind enough to bring him back here in a nice wooden box." For the Man in Black, walking around looking like John Locke is an ironic joke; Locke was the island's disciple, whereas the Man in Black is its worst enemy. Jack defends Locke in that scene, saying that John was the only person who believed in the island. Smokey replies, "John Locke was not a believer, Jack; he was a sucker." But Jack — who was Locke's bitter rival during their time on the island, who hated Locke for getting Boone killed and for not telling him about the hatch, who goaded Locke for believing in the button in the Swan station, who actually held a gun to Locke's head and pulled the trigger (it wasn't loaded, unbeknownst to Jack), who dismissed Locke as crazy, who told him he was wrong about moving the island and letting the others leave, and then who told Locke he was nothing but a crazy old man when they met off the island — has now come full circle, realizes his mistakes, knows that Locke was right, and he has become the newly christened (literally, by the end of this episode) disciple of the island. John Locke has, posthumously, won the acceptance of the one

The sub behind the pier was actually just a fake top of a sub that sat in some mud, but because the director only shot from the other side of the dock the audience was fooled into thinking it was the real thing. The sub-top came apart in two pieces for easy moving. To create the dock, the crew took an existing flat dock and built an intricate structure over it so the characters could run around on it during the gunfire sequence. To film the scenes inside the sub, the cast and crew (Josh Holloway seen here) went to Pearl Harbor and filmed inside the U.S.S. *Bowfin* Submarine Museum. (Photos courtesy KOS Tours; bottom right photo courtesy Ryan Ozawa)

person he wanted it from, and Jack is now probably wishing he'd never told Locke what he couldn't do.

Of course, all of the character development and thematic explorations of the episode pale in light of what happens at the end. In a devastating turn of events, the submarine carrying all of the Candidates (plus Kate, Lapidus, and an extra Kwon) blows up. The bomb isn't quite as destructive as it might have been thanks to Sayid. In an ultimate act of heroism, in a final moment of human emotion, Sayid grabs the bomb and runs, sacrificing himself in order to reduce the impact of the bomb, hoping to give the others enough time to leave. His death happens so quickly and the fallout is so awful that we barely have time to mourn him, but it's worth pausing for a moment to consider what a huge moment that was in the series. Many fans mourned Sayid in "LA X," thinking he'd died in that episode. We felt the loss, looked at the sadness of Sayid's life, the potential he had for good, and the way destiny always seemed to lead him to use his power for evil instead. Sayid cared about the other survivors, he rarely put himself before anyone else, and he loved with more depth and passion than he could bear at times. He loved Nadia and Shannon and spent his life wishing he was a better man. In his death, he once again put aside his own needs for the greater good. Eko often mentioned the Gospel of John, and many of the verses from that book were etched on his stick. In John 15:13, Jesus says to his disciples, "Greater love has no one than this, that he lay down his life for his friends." Sayid died and was cruelly resurrected into a life without feeling, but in his final moment, he acted out of love for the other people.

The long, emotional goodbye, however, was saved for the deaths of Jin and Sun. "Destiny is a fickle bitch," Ben Linus once said, and that could certainly be said in the case of Jin and Sun. From its first moments, their relationship seemed to hang on fate's whim. Jin first found a note in the Korean destiny books saying his true love would appear orange, and when Sun walked by wearing orange, he fell in love with her instantly. Their love was passionate, but her father's cruelty eroded their marriage, and Sun began to hate the man she was with. They drifted apart emotionally, landed on the island unable to tolerate each other, but in those four months on the island together they got to know each other better than they ever had before, and fell in love all over again. But nothing is easy for these two, and they were separated cruelly. Sun has spent three years mourning her husband, while Jin has spent three years assuming he'd never see his wife again, but content knowing she was safe off the island.

We've been waiting since the end of season 4 for these two to be reunited, and once that finally happened, they had about 12 hours together (with not, I might add, a single moment of privacy). The moment Jin declared in the previous episode, "We'll never be apart again. I promise you," we should have known they were doomed. More obvious famous last words have never been spoken. But the truth of his words is heartbreaking. Sun begs Jin to go and save himself, but he refuses. Just as Sayid sacrificed himself for everyone else, Jin holds Sun's hand tightly and refuses to let go. He's been apart from her for so long, but his heart has never stopped being connected to hers. In their final moments, they look into each other's eyes — a sight both of them had given up hope of ever seeing again — and say their silent goodbyes. As the piano music quietly plays and we watch the sub sink deeper and deeper into the vast ocean, they die, their entwined fingers slipping apart, but their bodies forever together inside their watery tomb.

Highlight: Jack wakes up in the boat and Sayid says, "At least you didn't have to paddle." Oh, Sayid. You and your wacky deadpan delivery.

Did You Notice?:
- Jack displays his impeccable bedside manner to Locke again when he tells Locke his dural sac ruptured and he thinks he put most of it back together. While Locke might not know what a dural sac is, we know that it's the same thing Jack accidentally cut open in the infamous surgery story he tells Kate where he counted to five and continued on.
- Bernard tells Jack, "I hope you find what you're looking for." This is the same thing Kate said to Jack in "Lighthouse" when she ran into him in the jungle.
- Sawyer gets the upper hand (in an amazing scene where he grabs the gun away from "Doughboy"), but gives it up for Kate, exactly the same way he did when they were breaking rocks and he dropped the gun because Juliet threatened to hurt Kate.
- Sawyer reminisces about the good old days he and Kate spent in the cages, and says, "except the last time, the gun was to my head." He's referring to when Danny Pickett, the Other who was eventually shot and killed by Juliet, was holding a gun to Sawyer's head in the rain.
- Watch the background when Jack walks into the nursing home where Cooper is staying; there's an elderly woman who flirts with Jack from a nearby table.

- When John is asleep in the sideways world, he mutters, "Push the button . . . I wish you had believed me. . . ." Both of these phrases are things he conveyed to Jack in the other timeline, the latter in his suicide note.
- Jack gets an Apollo bar out of the vending machine. In "The Incident," we see Jacob get an Apollo bar out of the same machine, but now the open hall has been closed off by a door.
- The music box that Claire brings to Jack is playing "Catch a Falling Star." (See pages 71–72.) She tells Jack she's never even met her father but maybe he had visited her when she was very young, and the music box was his way of letting her know the song he sang to her. In the other timeline, he visited her five years previous to the car crash in "Par Avion." Apparently he skipped that visit in this timeline (maybe Claire's mom wasn't in the car crash this time round).
- Claire tells Jack they're strangers, and he says, "No, we're family." This reiterates the speech he gave the whole group back in "White Rabbit," saying that a week earlier they had been strangers, and now they were together.
- Locke is wheeled out of the hospital room by an African American orderly, just like he was in "The Man from Tallahassee" and "Cabin Fever."
- When everyone washes up on shore, Kate rushes to Jack, telling him how worried she was about him, but she doesn't seem to notice Sawyer bleeding to death on the sand beside them.
- When Hurley and Kate both start crying on the beach (a moment that made many *Lost* fans cry harder than they already were), it seemed genuine, but considering this was one of the last episodes shot for the series, it was probably a pretty emotional moment for all of the actors in the scene.

Interesting Facts: I asked on my blog if anyone could explain why the sub took so much longer to surface than to dive, and the following explanation was given to me by a reader named Casey: "A submarine is filled with hollow tubes. When they are empty (filled with just air) the sub floats on the surface like a regular boat. To submerge, a submarine opens these tubes to the outside water and they flood. There is no active work, they just open up and let the water in, and the sub becomes less buoyant and dives. They merely steer the sub while it dives. When it reaches the designated depth, they close the tubes and the sub stays at that level underwater. For a sub to rise again, that water has to be expelled from the ballast tubes. You can't just open the tubes to let the water out the way you let it in. If you did that, it would sink further. Instead you have to actually pump the water out, which means you have to expend mechanical energy that is diverted from the main engines. The water being pumped out of the tubes is being pressed against the pressure of the entire ocean above the sub, so it takes quite a bit of power and a lot more time. It's a slow process to rise, whereas diving is pretty much automatic and fast once you open the tubes."

Nitpicks: It seems strange that Jin and Sun speak English to each other after their reunion. Regardless of the fact that Jin has spoken English for the past three years in the Dharma Initiative, he would still quite naturally fall back to his more comfortable Korean, especially considering Sun would have spoken Korean for the past three years. I was so relieved when they spoke Korean to each other before dying. Also, Emilie de Ravin was a lot better at playing pregnant in season 1. She would lean back one arm and slowly lower herself into a seat, the way pregnant women do. In the scene with Jack (where her basketball tummy is obviously fake) she just sits down in the chair without any difficulty. And if the hospital records indicated that John had had extensive oral surgery following the accident, why wouldn't they have indicated the nature of the accident itself? And finally, while I *hate* to nitpick that death scene, I can't help but think the poetry of Jin and Sun dying together is marred by the fact that the Paiks are now going to raise Ji Yeon. That poor little girl. . . .

Oops: When Jack breaks everyone out of the cages, it's the middle of the night, but when they're walking over to the runway it's daytime, yet the two areas are right next to each other. Then they get onto the sub in the day, and crawl onto the beach at night.

4 8 15 16 23 42: Widmore says he has a list with **4** names on it: Reyes, the Kwons, and Ford. At the nursing home, you can hear an announcement over the intercom for housekeeping to pick up line **23**.

It's Just a Flesh Wound: More like a bloodbath. Seamus is thrown against the cage and killed. At the Ajira crash site, Smokey is shot several times before he breaks one guy's neck and shoots the other one. Jack pushes Smokey with the butt of his rifle, knocking him into the water. Kate is shot in her left shoulder. Claire shoots two of Widmore's people; Smokey shoots and kills three of them. Sayid is killed when the bomb explodes. Frank is hit in the head with an iron door and loses consciousness. Sawyer is knocked unconscious when a beam hits him. Jin and Sun drown.

Any Questions?:

- If Smokey can't in fact kill a Candidate but, rather, must get them to kill

Lost Haiku!

Back at the end of season 3, I started a tradition of occasionally posting tributes to *Lost* episodes in haiku on my blog. I don't know what it is about haiku, but the fact that we're limited to five, seven, and five syllables just seems to make people work harder to make it even funnier. As my readership grew, people began to chime in with their own posts. Throughout season 6, my readers and I were able to find our way through a season that became particularly dark by recapping the episodes each week in haiku. Here are some of my favorites of the season:

"LA X"
Here at The Temple,
We have a nice Jacuzzi
Use at your own risk.
(humanebean)

"What Kate Does"
What is in the pill?
Herbs, roots, all natural things.
. . . and COUGH! poison COUGH!
(Batcabbage)

"Sundown"
Listen to Claire sing
"Catch a Falling Star," dream of
decayed skull bay-bees.
(Joan Crawford)

"Dr. Linus"
When Jack asked Richard
"Want to try another stick?"
Richard missed the hint.
(Joan Crawford)

"Recon"
Smokey tells Kate that
his mama was crazy. HA!
Look who's talkin', bud.
(humanebean)

Miles and Sawyer
sitting in a tree K-I-
S-S-I-N-G.
(Chuck Power)

"Why'd you become a
cop?" *"Bullitt."* "Tell the truth!" "'Kay.
Beverly Hills Cop."
(Batcabbage)

"The Package"
Run run run run run
run run run run run run run
run run run TREE! *Bonk!*
(Blam)

"Happily Ever After"
The embodiment
of love in all its glory:
Thy name is Desmond.
(Nikki)

Hawking, Faraday,
Widmore, Milton . . . Just what *is*
this family's name?
(Blam)

"Do you need a ride?"
"I'm pregnant." "And I'm Desmond.
Let's go get a room."
(Blam)

"The Candidate"
Even if Jack were a
DENTIST, he'd manage to cut
the damn dural sac.
(Nikki)

themselves, then how did he kill Montand in "This Place Is Death"? Montand didn't kill himself, and we saw earlier this season that Montand's name was among the names of the Candidates on the lighthouse dial.
- In the scene where Jack goes to visit Bernard (who seems an awful lot like the chiropractor/guardian angel character played by Danny Aiello in the film *Jacob's Ladder*), Bernard seems to know a lot about what's going on, and his memory for minor events that happened three years previous is impeccable. Is it possible that he's had a flash of the other world, like Desmond and Hurley, and is now acting like Desmond, helping shepherd people through to see the other side? If he is, does that mean Rose can see the other side, too, and she already knew who John Locke was in "The Substitute" when he came to her temp agency?
- Who built that really elaborate bamboo staircase that leads up to the Ajira flight?
- Why is Smokey allergic to water? Is he related to the Wicked Witch of the West?
- Just before blowing up, what did Sayid mean when he said, "It's going to be you, Jack"? Is this confirmation that Jack will, indeed, be the new Jacob?
- In "The Package," Sayid tells Smokey that he can't feel anything, and Smokey says, "Maybe that's best, Sayid. It'll help you get through what's coming." Did he know Sayid was going to kill himself?
- At the end of the episode, Smokey says he's off to finish what he started, and that not all of them are dead. Does he know the sub explosion didn't kill everyone? Or is he referring to Desmond?
- Is Lapidus still alive or was he killed when the iron door hit him in the head?

Ashes to Ashes: Seamus was one of Widmore's lackeys, and an annoying and constantly angry one at that. He will be remembered as "Doughboy."

Sayid Jarrah was born in Tikrit, and under the harsh thumb of his father, he learned how to suppress his feelings. He became a torturer in the Republican Guard, where he encountered Nadia, his childhood sweetheart. He helped her escape, and then spent the next eight years looking for her. After he got off the island as part of the Oceanic 6, he was reunited with her and was blissfully happy while married to her. She died, and he returned to the island a broken man. Like Lazarus, Sayid died twice, but the second time he died a hero, sacrificing himself for his friends and proving that, ultimately, the light that was in him won out over the darkness.

Sun and Jin Kwon have been married for six years, three of which have been spent apart from one another, with Sun believing Jin was dead. No matter how many times they've been separated, they've always managed to come back together, and they loved each other deeply and passionately. They are survived by one daughter, Ji Yeon.

6.15   Across the Sea

Original air date: May 11, 2010
Written by: Carlton Cuse, Damon Lindelof
Directed by: Tucker Gates
Guest cast: Kenton Duty (Young Jacob), Allison Janney (Mother), Lela Loren (Claudia), Titus Welliver (Man in Black)

Focus: Man in Black/Jacob
In the origin story of Jacob and the Man in Black, we see the nature of their relationship, Jacob's real purpose on the island, and the reason the Man in Black wants to leave.

When we saw Jacob for the first time in "The Incident," he was weaving a tapestry on a loom. Throughout "Across the Sea," we see him and the character the writers refer to as "Mother" weaving several tapestries, or simply adding to the same one. A tapestry consists of interweaving two lines of threads, one line running horizontally and bisected by the line running vertically. When hundreds or thousands of these threads are woven together, they tell a story, and by removing a section of the tapestry or inserting a different colored thread, one can alter the story and change it. In Greek mythology, the Three Fates were women who determined the course of the lives of every individual, with one Fate weaving the thread onto a spindle when a person was born, the second Fate measuring out the thread to decide the nature of a person's life, and the third Fate cutting that thread, determining the way a person would die and when. The suggestion was that a person could not change his or her life, because the Fates had already determined what it would be.

Jacob's tapestry tells the story of the island and civilization as he knows it. As he grows and becomes more confident in who he is, his tapestries become better

Titus Welliver gives a brilliant performance in "Across the Sea." (Sue Schneider/MGP)

and tell more elaborate stories. Similarly, Mother's tapestries are more complex than Jacob's, and she sits on the cave floor for hours weaving and dying the wool by laying it across her legs and rubbing various dyes into it. The colors that she puts into her threads are then literally written on her body, and she in turn writes them back into the stories on her tapestry. Her tapestries, however, take on a more sinister tone. She believes that she controls fate, and has written the destinies of both Jacob and his brother. When Jacob eagerly begins his own tapestry work, she looks at it wearily, as if his own version of the island story is unimportant in the greater scheme of things. Jacob, we now know, wants to tell his own story, because he believes that his own free will was sacrificed in the name of something greater. The tapestries are all he has.

What we know about Jacob and the Man in Black has been primarily learned through "The Incident" and "Ab Aeterno." We've gleaned most of that knowledge from the things the Man in Black has told us about himself and his past, and what Jacob and the Man in Black have said about each other. In "LA X," Jacob referred to the Man in Black as "an old friend who grew tired of my company," but in this episode we discover that he wasn't merely an old friend, he was his twin brother. There is a clear rivalry between them, established by the Man in Black's simple question, "Do you know how badly I want to kill you?" at the beginning of "The Incident" and made overt by the all-out war they wage against each other in "Ab Aeterno." The Man in Black, from his clothes to his demeanor to his very presence as the smoke monster, has been depicted as the island's evil, the bad guy, the devil, darkness. Jacob, dressed all in white and appearing like some guardian angel to the others on the island, is the good guy, the deity whom they worship, light. But when you put black and white together, you get gray. And this episode shows us exactly how gray this entire situation is.

The Man in Black, as the smoke monster, has killed mercilessly. He killed Rousseau's team in 1988, he killed hundreds or thousands before them, and we've seen him killing the survivors of Flight 815. He tore the pilot to shreds and tossed his corpse into the jungle canopy. He judged Eko and then killed him; he judged Ben and let him live. He has appeared to people on the island as their dead loved ones, leading them to places that are good for them and places that are bad. Smokey is manipulative, and he never gives people anything without asking for something in return. In "Ab Aeterno," he sat before a helpless Richard, and as he was about to undo his chains he first made sure Richard would do anything he asked. The devil doesn't give anything for free.

But if the Man in Black is the devil, Jacob is like an Old Testament God. He puts people through the same trials that God put Job through just to prove Satan wrong, and he won't (or can't) absolve them of their sins. He leads people to the island, knowing they'll be at Smokey's mercy, but then he expects them to help themselves, refusing to step in. He commands respect from them, using Richard as an intermediary. He's separate from the people, refusing to see them or let them enter his home, the statue, without an invitation, and never shows himself to them and never joins them. He's vengeful, as we see at the end of this episode, and we discover that the smoke monster exists because of Jacob's need for revenge. He killed his own brother and created a monster in his place.

As children, they were denied being raised by their own mother. The fear that was instilled in Claire back in "Raised by Another," that whatever she did, she could not let another person raise her son without serious consequences, is subtly raised in this episode. Because Jacob and his brother were raised by this woman, they were trapped on an island and refused the ability to exercise their own free will. They were loved — it's clear Mother cares about both of them deeply — but she lied to them about who they were, what existed (or didn't exist) across the sea, and about what happened to their real mother.

Jacob is portrayed as a boy with very little imagination, who is always clothed in white and is clearly the good one. He's obedient, doesn't know how to lie, and doesn't ask a lot of questions (in the beginning, anyway). His nameless brother is always dressed in black (kind of dooming the poor kid from the start), does know how to lie, is inquisitive with a wild imagination, and has an intuition that allows him to see to the heart of things and simply know how they work. Mother has a clear preference for the Boy in Black, and Jacob knows it. When Brother runs away from Jacob and Mother and tells them he's going to leave the island, Mother

In the moment where Jacob loses his free will, Mother forces the guardianship of the island onto him. (Mario Perez/ABC via Getty Images)

looks distraught and says, "Whatever you have been told, you will never be able to leave this island." And yet we've seen in "The Incident" that Jacob was able to leave the island, which is how he touched the Candidates. So clearly she made it so one son would always be by her side because of how connected she felt to him, and she didn't put the same restraint on Jacob. Mother tells her other son that he's "special," a term we've heard a lot on *Lost*, but as with most people on the show who have been deemed special, the Boy in Black never meets his potential. As someone who was special, could see what others couldn't, and could use his imagination to make the best of things, he seems to have been the best Candidate to protect the source of the island, and Mother clearly believes he will be. When Jacob turns out to be the one she forces the guardianship upon, she seems to be as surprised as he is.

Because the Boy in Black is capable of asking a lot of questions and is not necessarily satisfied with the responses, he's bound to become frustrated. In many ways, the exchanges between him and Mother in this episode almost reflected the unspoken dialogue between the writers of the show and the fans. At this stage in the season, some fans were becoming worried that the seeming billions of questions would go unanswered, because there simply wasn't enough time to answer all of them. When Mother says to Claudia at the beginning of the episode, "Every question I answer will simply lead to another question," it's almost like the writers are telling us exactly why they can't possibly answer everything. Near the end of the episode, the Man in Black becomes as frustrated as the viewers, saying to Mother that he's spent 30 years with people he despises, trying to find his way back to the Source, searching for ways to harness and use it. She's visibly upset, and says, "You have no idea . . ." to which he replies, "I have no idea because you wouldn't *tell* me, Mother!" In the absence of answers, the Man in Black is forced to use his own ingenuity, and in so doing he comes up with a way off the island through harnessing the energy of the Source. Similarly, fans have come up with various theories about *Lost* in place of answers, many of which are more ingenious than the answers ultimately provided by the show.

Jacob isn't all good, despite what Mother tells him. And similarly, the Man in Black isn't all bad (after all, in a podcast the writers confirmed that when the Medusa spider bit and paralyzed Nikki in "Exposé," it was actually the smoke monster in the form of a spider — we have *got* to give him some love for that). In "The Substitute," Smokey told Sawyer, "Before I was trapped, I was a man like you." In a way, he *was* a lot like Sawyer. He refused to follow charlatans, he struck out on his own, he kept his distance from people and followed his own rules. He felt harsh feelings of revenge, and killed the person responsible for the death of his mother. Also in that episode, he tells Sawyer, "I know what it's like to feel joy, to feel pain, anger, fear. To experience betrayal. I know what it's like to lose someone you love." Now we know the betrayal he felt was from his lying mother, who wasn't actually his mother . . . and yet *she* was also the person that he loved and lost. The betrayal also came from his brother, who killed him and turned him into Smokey. He later tells Kate in "Recon" that his mother was crazy, and now we know he was telling the truth: "Long time ago, before I looked like this, I had a mother just like everyone. She was a very disturbed woman, and as a result of that, I had some growing pains. Problems that I'm still trying to work my way through. Problems that could have been avoided, had things been different." He's right; Mother is clearly disturbed. His growing pains were brought on by having to leave his mother and brother and go to the other tribe, who he says were despicable people. If things had been different — if she hadn't murdered Claudia — he would have had a happier life, he wouldn't have killed anyone, and he wouldn't have been killed. And . . . he might have been able to leave the island.

But this episode doesn't explain what exactly Smokey *is*. We know the Brother in Black was thrown down into the cave where the Source was, and his body floated out of the back of it into the river. The smoke monster flew out, suggesting the two are separate, but that one was born of the other one's death. The smoke monster had all of Jacob's brother's personality, his memories, thoughts, and feelings, and even though he now looks like John Locke, he still seems to act like Jacob's brother. Despite us seeing Jacob's brother's dead body in the river, he tells Kate that she's wrong when she calls him a dead man. He says, "It's kill or be killed, and I don't want to be killed," as if he doesn't realize he's been killed already. It's still not clear what the exact connection (or disconnection) is between the two, but this might be all the information we get, and, like the Man in Black does with the Source, we have to piece the puzzle together for ourselves.

The Source is a new element introduced by the writers, a glowing light in a cave in the center of the island that Mother claims is the reason they're all there. Her job (and the duty she passes down to Jacob) is to protect that light from anyone else ever finding it. She says there's some of that light in every person, but they always want more. The light, in this sense, could be almost anything: love, hate, confidence, power. Or perhaps, bringing back the Pandora's Box analogy (see page 96), it's hope. Everyone has some hope in them, but they yearn to have the very thing they're hoping for. Hope is so important, but people want more than that. If hope were gone, people would be empty shells, like Sayid. Mother later tells Jacob that the light is "life, death, rebirth; it's the Source, the heart of the island." However, she asks him to never go down there, telling him that if he did, what would happen to him would be worse than death. Is she referring to what happened to Sayid? Is that what happened to the Man in Black? What is the Source? Could it be connected to the water in Dogen's Temple? If so, then when Jacob died in "The Incident," it would explain why the water in the Temple turned brown, and why the light went out. It would also explain why, when Sayid went into it, his resurrection was only partial, leaving him a shell of his former self. As we see at the end of the episode, when the Man in Black enters the cave, he turns into the smoke monster. (Or the already existing smoke monster, lying dormant inside the cave, used his body to rejuvenate itself and come forth once again.)

But perhaps the water is like the ring in J.R.R. Tolkien's *Lord of the Rings*. In that book, the ring was desired by many, because it would give a person absolute power. It could take even the kindest heart and corrupt it, so it is put around the neck of a hobbit to carry off to a place to destroy it, but even he begins to become corrupted by the end of journey. The ring on its own is harmless . . . it's what it promises to greedy men that makes it the corrupting thing it becomes. Similarly, the

The various construction stages of the cave entrance that houses the Source of the island. (Courtesy KOS Tours)

Source could be harmless to someone with a pure heart, but because both Sayid and the Man in Black were murderers when they went into the water, it destroyed them, and gave them a fate worse than death.

Like Kate, all the Man in Black has ever wanted to do was run away. Leave the island, find out what is across the sea, and broaden his horizons. He says in "Recon," "They think they're protecting the island from me, when in fact all I want to do is leave." And he's telling the truth. He has killed previous Candidates or found ways for them to kill each other, but that's because Jacob keeps bringing them to the island. Mother was the one who cursed him with the inability to actually leave the island, or he would have left long ago and none of this would have happened. In this episode, he becomes a sympathetic character, and we know that he really did have feelings and once loved other people. All of that was taken away from him by a destiny that had been written for him, and over which he had no control. He spent a lifetime trying to change his fate, and wiled away his hours playing a board game that allowed him some control over the outcome, using his cunning; a cunning that did him no good in a world where his destiny had been predetermined. The rules he could make were ones that only affected a few black and white stones on a checkerboard. The rules that Jacob and Mother made controlled his very existence.

Mother and Jacob weaved a tapestry that determined how the island's story would unfold, and what the outcome would be. But through his cunning, the Man in Black is trying to change the story and take it away from both of them. When Ilana and Bram last visited the cabin in "The Incident" before burning it down, they found a piece of Jacob's tapestry, held to the wall with a knife. It had been cut out of Jacob's picture by the Man in Black, changing the story that Jacob had told. Before he killed Mother, the Man in Black destroyed her loom and tapestry, and in "LA X," he did the same to Jacob's.

The Man in Black isn't interested in weaving any stories of the island; he's out to end them all.

Highlight: Titus Welliver's performance when he wakes up and realizes that Mother has destroyed everything around him. He is amazing in this scene.

Did You Notice?:
- Claudia is the third pregnant woman we've seen (after Claire and Rousseau) who has come to the island, given birth, and then had her child raised by someone else.

- We can assume that Mother spoke Latin throughout her time on the island, as did the Man in Black and Jacob (at least in the beginning). But when she's talking to Claudia there's a violin screech partway through the scene that indicates we are hearing English, even though they are continuing to speak Latin.
- Even at birth, Jacob is the quiet baby who doesn't even cry, and his brother makes his voice heard from the beginning.
- Mother says the men on the island are dangerous because "they come, they fight, they destroy, they corrupt. And it always ends the same," which is the same thing the Man in Black said to Jacob at the beginning of "The Incident."
- The Boy in Black says to Jacob, "One day you can make up your own game and then everybody will have to follow your rules." And now we know that Jacob did exactly that.
- Even as adults, the boys tend to use childish language when speaking (Smokey's talked like a child in some scenes, too) as if they were never exposed enough to adults and don't know what grown-up talk sounds like.
- In "The Substitute," Smokey threw the white rock out of the cave and muttered to Sawyer that it was an inside joke. Some fans were annoyed by the scene because they assumed it was just an inside joke between the writers and fans. But in fact, we see here that he was referring to the fact that he always played with the black game pieces and Jacob used the white, and the goal of the game was to remove all of one's opponent's pieces from the board. Smokey was simply removing Jacob's piece from the game once and for all.
- In "Everybody Loves Hugo," Smokey explains that when compass instruments went crazy, the inhabitants of the island began digging holes. However, compasses with magnets were only developed around the year 1000 A.D., and the events in this episode take place 2,000 years ago. So the explanation given in this episode — that they noticed places where "metal behaved strangely" — seems a lot more plausible.
- The Man in Black's dagger is the same one he later gives to Richard, and Dogen gives to Sayid.
- Jacob tells the Man in Black that Mother never asks about him, but when he returns to the cave, it's clear she always does, an indication that Jacob has learned to lie.
- Mother tells Jacob that he doesn't really have a choice, he must drink the water that will make him the new guardian of the Source. This is why he

believes so strongly in giving the people he brings to the island a choice in how they handle their lives, even if the very fact that he brought them to the island in the first place took a lot of their choices away from them.
- Just before the Man in Black stabs Mother, she picks up the black stone from his game and looks at it with affection, showing that he's still her favorite.
- Mother thanks the Man in Black right before she dies, as if she's been on the island a long time, is really tired, and just wants this very long life to end. In "LA X," Ben wonders why Jacob didn't fight back. Despite what Miles said, perhaps Jacob was simply tired, like she was, and death was a relief for him.
- When Jacob finds the Man in Black in the stream, his body is lying there looking a lot like Shannon's did when Boone found her in the stream in season 1's "Hearts and Minds."

Interesting Facts: Allison Janney, who plays Mother, is a brilliant character actress who's been in many television shows and movies, and is best known as White House Press Secretary C.J. Cregg on *The West Wing*.

The producers confirmed that the events we see on the island with Mother happened about 2,000 years ago (interestingly, around the time of the birth of Christ . . . and Brian). They've marked this time frame in the episode through the Roman dress of the man that Jacob and his brother see. We can probably assume that before the Romans came to the island, the Egyptians were there first, and that they built the statue on the beach. Perhaps Mother was originally an Egyptian.

Fans had a lot of fun with Mother's response to Claudia's questions. My favorite was a joke that popped up on Twitter: "Knock, knock." "Who's there?" "Every question I answer will simply lead to another question."

Back in season 2, there was a tie-in book related to *Lost* called *Bad Twin*. The PR bumpf announced that it had been written by Gary Troup, the guy who was sucked into the jet engine in the pilot episode. While the book is poorly written and has only a tenuous grasp on the true meaning of the show, the premise involves a guy who has a twin brother perceived as being "bad" (of course, the protagonist is good) and he spends the novel looking for him. (See *Finding Lost — Seasons One & Two*, pp. 302–304.)

While we never actually hear the name of the Man in Black, Kristin dos Santos of *E!* revealed after the *Lost* finale that in the script he had a name . . . Samuel. This is the same name the writers had used in the original casting call that brought Titus Welliver on board. Samuel is a Hebrew name meaning "name of God." In the Bible, Samuel is the last of the Old Testament prophets who speaks to God and passes his words on to the people. He traveled the land telling people they needed to repent, and basically took on the role of judge in biblical times. Eventually he anoints Saul as King of Israel, and anointed David as Saul's successor. Dos Santos didn't reveal who her source was, but perhaps she was simply going by the casting sheet, which named that character Samuel. Since the writers often make up fake names and descriptions of characters when casting them, it doesn't necessarily mean they really intended this name to stick to the character. Besides, it takes a lot of skill to have a character with no name, and it's clearly a deliberate choice not to name him in the episode.

Some of the ideas raised in this episode resemble the tenets of Gnosticism, which is the overriding philosophy of Philip K. Dick's *VALIS*, a book referenced on *Lost*. (For more on *Lost*'s relation to Gnosticism, see *Finding Lost — Season Four*, pp. 52–53.)

Nitpicks: I adore Allison Janney, but her Latin is terrible. Also, it seemed odd that the Boy in Black didn't know what "dead" was. They've killed fish to eat them, and they've kill wild boars (we see Jacob and his brother running through the jungle with spears) so it wasn't believable that he wouldn't understand that concept when he can understand so many more complicated things.

Oops: In "Lighthouse," when Hurley found the bodies of the Adam and Eve skeletons in the cave, it was unclear why they were lying together when they'd clearly been apart in "House of the Rising Sun." It was *possible* that the survivors moved them — although why? . . . and . . . ew! But now that we see they were originally together the way Jacob lays them out, it's clear that this is just a production inconsistency. When the writers were working on "Lighthouse," they'd probably formed a notion of the events of "Across the Sea," and so they put them together, hoping we'd forget they'd previously been apart.

It's Just a Flesh Wound: Mother bashes Claudia's head with a rock and kills her. Young Jacob pummels the Boy in Black. Mother knocks the Man in Black's head against a wall. The Man in Black stabs and kills Mother. Jacob beats his brother, then throws him down, grabs him by the neck, and throws him into the river, where the Man in Black hits his head on a rock and floats to his death. In other words, this is one big happy family.

Lost in Translation: The Latin incantation that Mother gives is "*Nam non accipimus hoc quasi vulgarem potionem, sed ut ille sit quasi unus mecum.*" It

The Game of Senet

In "Across the Sea," Jacob's brother finds a mysterious board game on the beach, and somehow knows intuitively how to play it. He doesn't know what the game is, but Mother claims that she left it there for him. The game is senet, and it's one of the oldest board games in history, originating in Ancient Egypt (the earliest reference to it is from 2650 B.C.).

Senet is believed to be the ancestor of backgammon and chess. It consists of 30 squares in 3 rows of 10, and each player has between 5 and 10 pawns. The player throws a handful of sticks, which act like dice, telling the player how many spaces to move the pawns. Surprisingly, despite the immense popularity of the game (it was found in numerous tombs of the Ancient Egyptians), there are no written rules explaining how one plays the game. Presumably it was so popular people simply passed the rules on from one generation to the next by word of mouth, and never saw the need to write them down.

In 1980, historian and Egyptian scholar Peter Piccione published the first extensive article on senet and how it was played; after having studied the game for years, he believed he'd uncovered the real meaning behind it. He explained that the Egyptians believed that after one died, one had to pass through a series of steps to get to the afterlife, and the squares on the board represented the various areas of the underworld that one passed through to get there and be reunited with Ra in the afterlife.

Since senet is a game of skill, there's a suggestion that Egyptians believed they could actually alter their own paths through the underworld. "At the most, the game indicates that ancient Egyptians believed they could join the god of the rising sun, Re-Horakhty, in a mystical union even before they died," writes Piccione. "At the least, senet shows that, while still living, Egyptians felt they could actively influence the inevitable afterlife judgment of their souls — a belief that was not widely recognized by Egyptologists."

In some forms of the game, players would begin on the 15th square, making that position one of the keys to the game. In others, where one began on the first square, the 15th square earned the player an extra turn, and the 16th lost one (interesting that both of these are Hurley's numbers!).

The players first had to jockey for position to get onto the first square, then try to force their opponent to move backward, much like in backgammon, says Piccione. By the end of the game, "The departure of the senet pieces from the board was tantamount to nothing less than the deceased's passage out of the netherworld, union with Ra, and eventual deification."

translates to, "Because we don't accept this as a simple drink, but so that he shall be as one with me," meaning that on its own the wine is just a normal drink, but the sanctity of the communion it represents joins them together, and therefore raises the drink to a loftier status.

Any Questions?:
- Did many of the objects on the island come from shipwrecks?

- Did the island call Claudia's boat to its shores so the babies would be born there? Or did Mother do it?
- So . . . because Claudia only chose one name, Mother couldn't come up with a second one? Does she lack that much imagination?
- How does Claudia appear to Jacob's brother? Is he like Hurley, and can see dead people when others can't? Is she trapped in the same island purgatory as Michael? What did she do wrong? Or is she a ghost like Isabella was at the end of "Ab Aeterno"?
- What did Mother mean when she said she made it so the boys couldn't hurt each other? Jacob not only pummels the Man in Black twice in this episode, but he eventually kills him. It doesn't look like her spell worked.
- Is Mother telling the truth when she says that Jacob's brother can never leave the island? Jacob says that he'd have to kill Jacob *and* all of the remaining Candidates before he can do that, but is that really the case? Or could the Man in Black kill everyone and *still* not be able to leave the island?
- How did the Man in Black figure out that he could leave the island via the Donkey Wheel Express? There are many things that he says he simply knows and doesn't have to figure out . . . is this one of them?
- How did Mother manage to drag her son's body out of the well after she knocked him out, and then fill in the wells, burn down the village, and kill all of the people single-handedly? It doesn't seem possible. Was she the smoke monster before the Man in Black was, and when she died, the smoke went back into the cave momentarily, only to be immediately released again by the death of the Man in Black?

Ashes to Ashes: Claudia was a Roman woman, pregnant with twins, who washed up on the beach of the island after a shipwreck. After giving birth to two sons, she was brutally murdered by Mother.

Mother is a woman of unknown origins who was already on the island when Claudia arrived, and she raised the boys. Clearly favoring the Man in Black, she nonetheless loved both of the boys but tried to push them to a future she believed they were destined for. She was stabbed by the Man in Black.

Jacob's unnamed brother lived a difficult life, mostly because he could see the truth of things when everyone else was blind to it, and no one would listen to him. He felt loved by his mother, but when it turned out that she had lied to him and had killed his birth mother, he never forgave her. Dressed in black from the moment he was born, he was somewhat cursed to be seen as the bad one. He was inquisitive and longed to expand his horizons, but these were unwelcome attributes in a place where everything, including the horizon, looks inward. He was killed by his brother, Jacob.

6.16 What They Died For

Original air date: May 18, 2010
Written by: Edward Kitsis, Adam Horowitz, Elizabeth Sarnoff
Directed by: Paul Edwards
Guest cast: Kenton Duty (Young Jacob), Mira Furlan (Danielle Rousseau), Tania Raymonde (Alex), Michelle Rodriguez (Ana Lucia), Ashlee Kyker (School Kid), Ernesto Lopez (Officer), Wendy Pearson (Nurse Kondracki)

Focus: Everyone

Jacob finally appears to the remaining Candidates and tells them why they were brought to the island while Ben joins with Smokey to confront Widmore. In the sideways world, John makes a life-changing decision and Desmond pulls more people together.

"We're very close to the end, Hugo."

The penultimate episode of a series always offers challenges to its writers. The series finale is the one that everyone will tune in to, that everyone will talk about, and that will wrap up most storylines and provide a fitting end. The episode that comes before that stands the risk of being too thin if the writers attempt to hold back all the best parts for the finale. In rare cases, it also runs the risk of overshadowing the finale by being too suspenseful and promising more than the finale can live up to. Luckily, "What They Died For" did exactly what a second-to-last episode should do: it brought all of the remaining stories together, setting them up nicely for what was sure to be an explosive finale.

Ben is finally back, and not just Ben, but *evil* Ben, the one that we've loved for years. In this final season, one of the themes that has come to the forefront has been that of rivalry; specifically the three key rivalries of the show: Jack versus Locke, Jacob versus the Man in Black, and Ben versus Widmore.

Charles Widmore has been shown to be sinister, opportunistic, and cruel, from the way he abandoned Eloise after she had Daniel, to the way he talked to

Desmond or made choices on Penny's behalf without her knowing it, and used all of his efforts to get the island back for only one purpose: so he could have it. He didn't care about island spirits and deities or Jacob and Smokey. He just wanted it to be his. He knew the island was special, and he wanted it for himself.

It's not clear how Widmore got to the island in the first place, nor how he made all his money, but when we first saw him in "Jughead" in 1954, he was already a cocky know-it-all who believed that no one knew the island better than he did. We saw him again in the 1970s, in a relationship with Eloise and the father of the unborn Daniel Faraday, and while Eloise was the leader of the Others at that time, it was clear Widmore had his eye on that title. When Young Ben was taken to the Temple and healed by the island, Widmore turned his evil eye in Ben's direction, knowing he wasn't going to let this upstart take something that he believed rightfully belonged to him. Ben became a member of the Others but remained a spy inside the Dharma Initiative, and when he finally had the nerve to bring down the DI in the devastating Purge, Widmore's days were numbered. Ben became the leader. Upon discovering that Widmore had been leading a double life off the island (with a wife and daughter), Ben had him ejected from the island ("Dead Is Dead"). Widmore became single-minded in his effort to return to the island, buying up antique ephemera at auctions that might help him locate the island, now that he no longer had the coordinates ("Flashes Before Your Eyes"). When he realized that Desmond had his sights set on his daughter, Widmore turned into the overbearing father, doing everything he could to keep this unworthy Scot from getting any closer to Penny. Some fans wondered if Widmore orchestrated the race around the world for the specific purpose of finding the island, through Desmond. Regardless, Desmond landed on the island in 2001 and Widmore still didn't know where it was. When Ben discovered that Widmore was trying to locate the island through radio frequencies, specifically the exact one that was contacting the Looking Glass Station, he jammed the frequencies. Only when Charlie unjammed the signal could Penny — using her father's equipment — locate the island. However, her transmission fell into Widmore's hands, and he immediately sent a freighter full of mercenaries to the elusive island with the sole purpose of finding Ben and getting him off the island, knowing that only then would he be able to have the island back once and for all.

The scene where Ben enters Widmore's bedroom in "The Shape of Things to Come" illuminated this age-old rivalry for viewers, and we finally saw that Widmore had nothing but loathing for Ben, calling him "boy" and telling him that

Sawyer's Nicknames

Jack: Doc
Juliet: Blondie, Babe
Cindy: Earhart
Jin: Buddy, Hoss
Ava: Sweetheart, Honey
Miles: Partner, Sunshine, Enos
Zoe: Sweetheart
Widmore: Chief
Kate: Freckles, Sweetheart
Lapidus: That pilot who looks like he stepped off the set of a Burt Reynolds movie, Chesty, Hoss
Seamus: Doughboy
Charlotte: That redheaded chick that hates me
Smoke monster: Smokey
Desmond: The Magic Leprechaun
Hurley: Bigfoot

he'd get the island back someday. Ben, similarly, had a sneering hatred for Charles Widmore, and threatened him and blamed him for Alex's death. There was no clear-cut good guy or bad guy in this scene: both Ben and Widmore have done terrible things, and in terms of the larger war on the island between Smokey and Jacob, it was unclear where their allegiances lay. The backstory shown in "Dead Is Dead" helped to further illustrate their rivalry and fill in the missing pieces, and made fans even more excited for the face-off that now seemed inevitable.

And thankfully, just as we were beginning to think Ben had forgiven Widmore and taken sole responsibility for Alex's death and Widmore might be working for the same side, it all falls apart the moment they see each other. Widmore says he's working for Jacob, and Ben immediately aligns himself with the opposite side, now resigned to the fact that, after all this time, the smoke monster had been "summoning" *him* rather than the other way around.

Despite its shocking conclusion, however, the confrontation between Widmore and Ben is ultimately a bit of a letdown. Widmore tells "Benjamin" why he'd come back to the island, explaining that Jacob had come to him, made him see the error of his ways, and told him what to do on the island to make everything right. In this scene we hear the Jacob music in the background, and often the music is used to let us know if someone is sincere. In this case, the presence of the Jacob theme confirms that Jacob had visited Widmore, since it only plays when Jacob is in a scene or when he's affected someone within the scene.

However, from the moment we first saw Widmore in "Live Together, Die Alone," we've been led to question what he says, and know that he's a selfish man so hell-bent on power he'd sacrifice anything and anyone to get it. Though he rushed to Penny's side in "The Incident" when he thought Ben was going to kill her, Widmore probably wouldn't have grieved for his daughter the same way Ben has grieved for Alex. There's a coldness to Widmore in every scene — even in the sideways world, he rolls his eyes when talking about his son and wife and talks about how good the single Desmond has got it. So the thought that one quick chat with Jacob would allow this guy to see the error of his ways and convert him to the good side isn't very believable at all.

And yet, unless he'd talked to Jacob, Widmore wouldn't have known Desmond's importance, or how to get back to the island, or what his mission was. Of all the people for Jacob to entrust with this most important task, Widmore seems like the least likely, considering how unfaithful he's been in the past. Also, Jacob would have told Widmore that the key thing in all of this is not to let Smokey off the island, and yet when Smokey starts telling him that when (not if) he *does* get off the island he'll kill Penny if Widmore doesn't talk, Widmore begins singing like a canary. Since it's clear that if Smokey gets off the island, Penny and everyone else will die anyway, it seems like a silly thing for Widmore to have done. The writers have spent five years building up Widmore as a man of extreme cunning, only to end his character abruptly, making a stupid move that had almost no thought behind it. It was uncharacteristic of the character and a disappointing end to him.

Lost has explored rivalries starting at their beginnings, through their development, their build-ups, and ultimately their ends. Jacob killed his brother, turned him into the smoke monster, and trapped him on the island against his will. Their hatred for one another runs deep, and the Man in Black eventually finds a loophole in Jacob's rules and slips right through it to kill him. Jack and Locke had an intense rivalry that began as a student/mentor relationship, quickly developed into animosity, and then bloomed into full-on loathing. By the time Locke died, Jack was starting to believe he'd been right, but couldn't admit it to himself, much less to anyone else. The continuation of their relationship, despite John's death, has been one of the key arcs explored throughout this season.

And now, the final rivalry comes down to a scene in Ben's hidden room. Unlike the scene in "The Shape of Things to Come," there is no long discussion or further audience enlightenment on the reasons for their enmity; instead,

Widmore tries to cut Ben out of his discussion, once again showing his disdain for him, and Ben reacts by shooting and killing Widmore, uttering the line, "He doesn't *get* to save his daughter." In this one line we realize that despite his admission to Ilana in "Dr. Linus" that losing Alex was his fault, he still blames Widmore. Like Sayid, he will never be able to suppress the killer inside him, and just as Sayid killed the man in "The Shape of Things to Come" and then agreed to be Ben's hitman, now Ben kills Widmore in cold blood and immediately offers to kill anyone else Smokey needs him to. Ben is a sympathetic character because of where he's come from and what he's been through. But it's interesting to note that in each of the rivalries listed above, it was Ben who ended the discussion by killing one of the feuding parties. Jacob, John Locke, and now Widmore all died at Ben's hand. Just as Jacob and the Man in Black were more similar than they'd like to think, and Jack has become the new John Locke on the island, Ben, too, is a lot like Widmore. Immediately preceding the scene where Ben kills Widmore, Smokey offers him the island. Ben can't get Alex back, so he decides he'll take the other thing he's always wanted: power.

In the sideways world, Ben becomes closer to Alex, and we're happy to see Danielle Rousseau again, alive and well — with her hair combed — and raising her daughter like she was always meant to do. Once again the sideways world seems like a place where people get what they had coming to them karmically. Danielle has a loving and supportive relationship with her daughter, and tells Ben how much she appreciates everything he's done for Alex (consider what he did for her in the *other* timeline), telling him he's like a father to Alex. Ben feels an affection for Alex that goes beyond the teacher/student relationship, as if he can almost detect that she's meant to be like a daughter to him, so the moment she says that to him, he becomes very emotional. Danielle's comment that she'll use fewer onions "next time" indicates that in the future, maybe Ben will become more of a personal presence in Alex's life. Maybe Danielle and Ben were meant to raise Alex *together*.

Desmond, meanwhile, is working on bringing everyone else together, and he deliberately gets himself thrown in jail in order to round up Sayid and Kate and get them to . . . a concert. When we see other characters mentioning the same thing, it looks like the writers are setting up the concert in the finale as the place where big things are going to happen. Will the two worlds somehow come back together? We know Jin and Sun won't be there, nor will John Locke or Sawyer (who won't go because the redhead who hates him will be there), so perhaps they have another setting for these characters, but it's exciting to see everyone preparing for it. It's also fun to see Ana Lucia briefly (and to see that, as in the other timeline, Hugo simply blurts out that he knows her without having any filter between his brain and his mouth). But Desmond's assertion that Ana Lucia's "not ready yet" would suggest that the characters are being led to something in particular, and not everyone we've seen on the show is going to be participating.

As Desmond rounds up everyone in the sideways world, Jacob finally gets the remaining Candidates together to confirm why these particular people had been brought to the island. From the beginning of season 1, it's been clear that the people who survived Oceanic Flight 815 were there for a reason. Their lives had crossed paths before they'd even stepped on the flight. Sawyer had a fling with the woman who called out Hurley's winning lottery numbers. Locke's mother stayed at the same mental institution as Hurley and Libby. Hurley owned the box company where

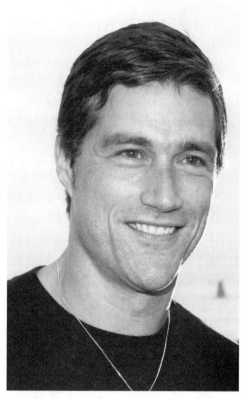

In "What They Died For," Jack steps up and becomes the true hero of the story. (Marco Garcia/AP Photo)

Locke worked. Ana Lucia had accompanied Christian Shephard on a road trip and later flirted with Jack in the airport. Claire and Jack were siblings and didn't know it. Shannon's father was killed in the car accident that had temporarily paralyzed Jack's future wife. Sayid had been detained by Kate's stepfather in Iraq. Desmond had talked to Jack at a sports stadium. Eko had investigated a miracle claim by a woman who was married to the psychic who put Claire on the plane. Libby gave Desmond his boat. Locke had done a home inspection for Nadia. Sun's father had worked with Widmore. Daniel was Penny's half-brother. Kate's friend Cassidy had a child by Sawyer. Many characters have told each other not to mistake coincidence for fate (see **Did You Notice?** below) but these links are far more than coincidental.

Many fans wondered why "Across the Sea" happened so close to the end of the season. They felt like the episode contained answers that could have been revealed much earlier in the season without spoiling much of anything, allowing the action from "The Candidate" and this one to follow each other without a break. However, it's more important that we have the backstory of Jacob and the Man in Black fresh in our minds when watching this episode. Jacob was not given a choice in the matter of his island guardianship. Mother held the wine out to him and told him to drink it or everything would go to Hell (literally). She actually said to him that he didn't have a choice. He drank it reluctantly, and has spent two millennia doing a job he never signed up for in the first place. But along the way, he's been calling one group of people after another to the island in an attempt to find someone who will replace him, while sitting back and watching the drama unfold as Smokey picks them off one by one.

Jacob's not quite as cruel as his backstory would make him out to be. In this scene he explains that despite what Jack saw in the lighthouse, Jacob didn't ruin their lives by bringing them to the island; he gave them an opportunity to work through their issues and realize that there are bigger, more important things to focus on. They needed to drop their petty grievances and see how important this community of people was to them. He says, "I didn't pluck any of you out of a happy existence: you were all flawed. I chose you because you were like me, you were all alone. You were all looking for something that you couldn't find out there. I chose you because you needed this place as much as it needed you." (Of course, he doesn't mention the over 250 casualties from the plane crash who died instantly or shortly after, or the dozens of people who have died since. But let's not focus on them. Ahem.)

One of the most touching things Jacob says is that he crossed out Kate's name because she became a mother, suggesting that motherhood is an even more important job than the island guardianship (making mothers everywhere beam with delight). That could explain why "Littleton" was also crossed out on the cave wall: Claire had become a mother on the island and was therefore no longer a Candidate. Perhaps he also crossed out Rousseau's name before her death, because he hoped she would one day get Alex back. This assertion suggests that the Kwon Candidate was, once and for all, Jin. Sun had become a mother, so he would likely have crossed off her name if it had been referring to her. This shows that Jacob doesn't seem to put the same sort of importance on fatherhood (not only is Jin a father, but Sawyer is one, too). Considering the terrible fathers many of these characters had, coupled with the fact that Jacob never actually had one, it's not surprising he would feel that way. It also means that all of the Candidates are men, though, which is a tad disappointing.

Jacob tells all of them that he wants to give them the one thing he was never given: a choice. In this ultimate decision, free will triumphs over fate. However, he follows that up by saying that one of them *must* choose it, thus removing the notion that they could all choose to say no.

And, not surprisingly, Jack steps up. As I've already stated, Jack was the person set up as the protagonist of the story from the beginning. The writers took a chance with this character by making him deeply flawed, often unlikable, and somewhat insular. He trusted no one but himself, he was a reluctant leader, and he wanted off the island as much as anyone else. He dismissed Locke's theories about the island, he refused to believe in fate, and he was one of the few people who left the island. But it was only when he was off the island that the true meaning of what he'd left behind hit him.

Locke went through an important journey, but he was a convert from the beginning. His faith wavered, but he got it back, and he continued on, trying to make Jack see his way of thinking. Locke's death in "The Life and Death of Jeremy Bentham" seemed like such a waste of a complex character, and it was surprising to think that his life had been meaningless. But it hadn't been. Everything that Locke believed in has been taken in by Jack, mulled over, and now Jack has come around to Locke's way of thinking. Locke once told him that his faith in the island had "never been easy." There was no easy conversion for Jack, either — his acceptance of faith was a hard-fought battle, one that he spent many years struggling with, but now that he has it, he will cling to it more strongly than John Locke ever did. Unlike Locke, who had several mistaken changes of heart, Jack does not waver in his convictions. In "The Last Recruit," Jack said that when he left the island, he felt like a part of himself was missing. When he was on Sawyer's boat, he was unable to stay there because something just felt wrong. He already knew then that he was destined to be the new Jacob. We know as he drinks Jacob's water that he will remain as loyal to the island as Locke ever was, probably more so. When Jack takes the job, he becomes the true hero of this story.

Highlight: When Miles says that he lived in the Dharma houses 30 years before Ben Linus did, "otherwise known as last week."

Ben decides to wait in New Otherton for Smokey, whose sudden appearance literally knocks the wind out of Richard. (Courtesy KOS Tours)

Did You Notice?:
- For anyone who ever thought Jack had something up his butt, the family size box of Super Bran cereal on his table is especially amusing.
- Jack stitching up the bullet wound in Kate's shoulder parallels the scene in "Pilot, Part 1" when Kate stitches up the wound in Jack's side.
- Jack is the one who urges everyone to keep moving, telling them that if Smokey needs Desmond, then they'll have to get to Des first. Again, he's carefully reading the situation, as he did earlier, and figuring out what they have to do next.
- If the nurse cleaning up Ben seemed a little hostile to him, it's because this is Nurse Kondracki, the woman who was having the affair with Principal Reynolds that Ben threatened to expose. Perhaps Reynolds has put the kibosh on the relationship. Interestingly, in the original timeline, she is the E.R. doctor who deals with Desmond after Ben shoots him, and she reassures Penny that Desmond will be okay. In one timeline she's patching up

Desmond after Ben shot him; in the other she's patching up Ben after Desmond beat him up.
- When Ben admits that he now knows the smoke monster was the one summoning him, and not the other way around, we know that he realizes he'd been used for years in a complex plot devised by the Man in Black in order to kill Jacob.
- In the sideways world, John and Alex both refer to Ben as "Dr. Linus," as if they're the only ones who respect him and the title.
- When Desmond asks Kate how she's doing, she says, "Terrific." That's what Charlie said when he first heard the smoke monster, and what Lapidus said when he looked inside Ilana's crate and realized Locke was actually dead.
- Alex saying in the sideways world, "Why would someone want to hurt you? You're like the nicest guy ever" is a great moment of juxtaposition with the Ben Linus from the other world, to whom she said, when Ben told her Widmore's men were dangerous, "More dangerous than you?"
- Danielle says to Ben that if he doesn't accept their dinner invitation, they'll have to kidnap him, which is another wink at what really happened in the other world.
- When Hurley finds Jacob, he asks where he's been, and Jacob says, "It doesn't matter, I'm here now." Back in "Lighthouse," when Hurley asks the same question, Jacob answers the same way. Someone should tell him it kinda *does* matter when people are dying in his absence.
- John says to Jack that it can't be a coincidence that of all the doctors in L.A. who could have operated on him after he was hit by the car, it turned out to be Jack. It's the same thing that James said to Kate when her car smashed into his (". . . of all the cars in Los Angeles, you smash into mine"). And when Locke saw Jack in the hospital in "The Life and Death of Jeremy Bentham," he says to him, "Of all the hospitals they could've brought me to, I end up here. You don't think that's fate?"
- The discussion between Jack and John in Jack's office touches on many of the same points that sparked many an argument between them in the Swan station in season 2. But here, Jack calmly listens to Locke, respectfully disagrees with John's sense of destiny, and John waves his hand as if he's not trying to be crazy. Yet back in season 2, Jack would have blown an artery in pure frustration at dealing with Locke, and Locke would have bullishly stuck to the hopeless task of trying to convert the man of science. The

conversation here is the same one, except in brilliant counterpoint to what happened in the earlier seasons.

- Jack tells Locke that he's "mistaking coincidence for fate." In "What Kate Did," Locke marveled at the fact that Eko had found the missing piece of orientation film he'd been looking for, and had somehow brought it across the island back to him. Eko replied, "Don't mistake coincidence for fate." Locke used the same line later on Desmond, when Desmond was surprised to hear about the Beechcraft plane crashing onto the door of the Pearl station.
- Ana Lucia's very funny and gruff line, "I'll have to say I shot all of you trying to escape," becomes sad when you remember she was shot so Henry Gale could escape.
- Smokey says he likes the feel of his feet on the ground because it reminds him that he was human. This is the first time he admits that he's no longer human.

Interesting Facts: In one of the *Geronimo Jack's Beard* podcasts with Jorge Garcia, Henry Ian Cusick talked about this episode, saying that when he made the call pretending to be the Oceanic employee, he considered doing it in an American accent but chickened out at the last minute. However, in the scene, he *is* speaking with an American accent.

When filming the scene where Desmond beats up Ben Linus, Cusick accidentally punched Michael Emerson in the eye and gave him a black eye. The shiner he sports in the rest of the episode (and in the finale) was not makeup.

Nitpicks: This is a minor nitpick for every mention of "Oceanic Flight 815" in the sideways world. I don't know about you, but when I have to fill out those customs forms on flights I *always* have to check my boarding pass for the flight number. I can never remember it before or during the flight, and I certainly don't retain the flight number in my head afterward. How is it that every character knows they were on Flight 815, like the number was etched onto their brain?

While I'm sure John was a good substitute teacher, I doubt that kids would be welcoming him back after his convalescence as if he were a long-term teacher at their school. Also, I checked with a police officer, who confirmed there's no way they would have held a woman in a jail cell, where the men could see her going to the bathroom. But it worked for the scene. And Alex's Napoleon reference would have been cleverer if they hadn't already beaten it to death in "Dr. Linus."

Oops: At the beginning of the episode, Jack pulls a thread from a shirt to patch up Kate's shoulder wound. We see him pull it out and lay the shirt on the ground, but when the camera pans back he's still trying to get the thread out of the shirt.

Also, when Desmond comes to the police station and asks them if they know about the hit and run and the subsequent beating of a teacher, Miles and James say yes. But Ben didn't report the beating incident, so there's no way they could have known about that. Also, Hurley sees Jacob in a clearing in broad daylight, and Jacob tells him to bring his friends to him. They're only a few feet away, so it would have taken Hurley about 10 minutes to grab them and bring them back to Jacob, but when he does, it's nighttime. There's no reason it would have taken Hurley that long, especially when he knows the clock is ticking and he only has until Jacob's fire burns out.

It's Just a Flesh Wound: Desmond beats up Ben. Smokey grabs Richard by the throat. Smokey slices Zoe's throat. Ben shoots and kills Widmore.

Any Questions?:
- What is the significance of the larger blood spot on Jack's neck? Is there a suggestion that one timeline is bleeding into the other?
- When Smokey steps up onto the dock, you can see that he's no longer wearing Christian Shephard's shoes that Jack had put on him in the coffin. What was the significance of those shoes back in season 5 on the island? It was clear that by putting them on Locke's corpse Jack had made him a proxy of his dead father, and on the island there were scenes where we saw Locke/Smokey carefully taking the shoes off to get into the boat, and then carefully putting them back on, as if there was something sacred about them. And now they're gone. Maybe they were just really uncomfortable.
- Ben gives Miles a walkie-talkie in case he needs him. Is he planning on doing some end-run around Smokey?
- Is Richard Alpert dead?! That was quite a tackle to the throat that Smokey gave him, but we know that the Man in Black can't kill Richard (or he would have done it long ago), and I also don't believe they would have shown us Richard's incredibly rich backstory in "Ab Aeterno," only for it to all end like this.
- The scene where Ben just calmly tells Smokey everything — that the outrigger belongs to Widmore, and that Widmore is hiding in his closet — is great, but is he telling him everything because he can't wait for Widmore to get his, or is there a sense that he's in the smoke monster's thrall in this moment?
- Right after Smokey slits Zoe's throat (YES!!), he says to Widmore, "You told her not to talk to me; that made her pointless." Other than the fact she was pointless *long* before he slit her throat, what does he mean? Many characters

The Letter from Lucas

Right before the series finale of *Lost* aired, Damon Lindelof and Carlton Cuse received a letter from a man they'd both been fans of for most of their lives: George Lucas. After years of dropping *Star Wars* references into various episodes — usually through the dialogue of characters like Hurley and Sawyer (see *Finding Lost — Season Five*, page 195) — they were shocked and honored to receive a letter from the man who'd created *Star Wars* telling them what an extraordinary job they'd done. At a special live event where Michael Giacchino showcased the music of *Lost*, Damon and Carlton came on stage and Damon read the letter aloud:

> Congratulations on pulling off an amazing show. Don't tell anyone . . . but when *Star Wars* first came out, I didn't know where it was going either. The trick is to pretend you've planned the whole thing out in advance. Throw in some father issues and references to other stories — let's call them homages — and you've got a series.
>
> In six seasons, you've managed to span both time and space, and I don't think I'm alone in saying that I never saw what was around the corner. Now that it's all coming to an end, it's impressive to see how much was planned out in advance and how neatly you've wrapped up everything. You've created something really special. I'm sad that the series is ending, but I look forward to seeing what you two are going to do next.

Damon Lindelof tweeted after the event that "George Lucas' letter to us made me feel like I was staring into the twin suns of Tatooine all over again. My life is complete." And after he read it at the event, he added, "I just want to apologize to Mr. George Lucas for everything I said about the prequels."

have been told not to talk to Smokey, including Sayid, but he didn't think *they* were pointless.

- In "The Shape of Things to Come," when Ben entered Widmore's bedroom, Widmore said, "Have you come here to kill me?" and Ben responded, "We both know I can't do that." Fans assumed that Ben and Widmore had a relationship similar to the one between Jacob and the Man in Black, and that they simply weren't able to kill one another. Yet in one movement in this episode, Ben destroys all of that by killing Widmore. Was he suddenly able to do so because Jacob was dead?

- What happens when a person drinks the potion after the incantation is spoken over it? Jack has a look of serenity on his face, as if he knows a lot more than he did previously. Does he take in all of Jacob's memories and knowledge when he drinks it and/or does it cause instant immortality? That could be why both Jacob and Mother say, "Now you're like me" when the water is drunk.

Ashes to Ashes: Zoe was a geophysicist and a bad liar who was part of Widmore's inept team of recruits that he brought to the island to try to save it from the smoke monster. She will be remembered as the most annoying character on the show since Nikki and Paulo.

Charles Widmore was a business magnate who has had a longer relationship with the island than just about anyone, but his lack of personal connection to the island has kept him separated from it. He's had very little personal connection to anything in his life, for that matter, and even his own daughter seemed more like a possession he kept to himself than a flesh-and-blood person. He is predeceased by his son, Daniel Faraday, and is survived by his daughter, Penelope Widmore.

Fear and Trembling by Søren Kierkegaard (1843)

In the early seasons of *Lost*, the writers referenced the works of various Enlightenment philosophers through the names of their characters. Locke, Rousseau, Hobbes, Hume, and Burke were not name-dropped by chance, but instead, worked to allude to their theories on man in a state of nature and his relationship to society. These philosophers all believed that man was shaped a certain way, and argued about men as creatures who all fell under the same umbrella, individualism be damned. But as the seasons went on, the writers began introducing more complex philosophies by overt references to concepts such as mirror imagery or the Self/Other dichotomy.

In season 6, the reigning philosophy on the show is existentialism, something explored intimately and referenced widely throughout the season. This chapter will only scratch the surface of the tenets of existentialism, which is a complicated and deep topic, and from there will enter into a discussion of Kierkegaard, widely considered the father of existentialism, and why his work was important to *Lost* as a series.

Existentialism looks at man's existence within the world (for ease of discussion I will use the masculine term here), and how man can only come to an understanding of himself as an individual, not as one of a collective (the Borg on *Star Trek*, for example, are not existentialists; Jean-Luc Picard, on the other hand, is). It argues that existence comes before essence; in other words, man shouldn't live within a strict framework of rules that is imposed on him by tradition, but instead should strive to find his unique individual existence through his own choices. Unlike the Enlightenment philosophers, existentialists don't believe there is one essence that is common to all people; instead, each individual has a unique existence. Man is fully responsible for the state of his life, whether it's good or bad; existentialism rejects the idea of destiny or fate, and instead focuses on how man finds his sense of self and his purpose in the world using his own free will. The angst and dread that man feels is a direct result of the pressure of having this responsibility heaped upon him, which creates anxiety within him. Often, to come to a better understanding of himself man must struggle against his own nature, overcome his despair, and achieve an awareness of who he really is. Then, by using his free will, he becomes part of society and finds his place in it; only then will he understand his reason for being and find contentment. Existentialism is often marked by a rejection of rationality and absolutism, a sense of alienation and anxiety, a feeling of nihilism, and a sense that while we are free to make our own choices, sometimes that freedom can be overwhelming and awful.

Jean-Paul Sartre (1905–1980) was the most prominent existentialist philosopher of the 20th century. Existentialism rose up after WWII because of the feelings of despair and angst that many people felt in the years after the war. A sense of "Who am I?" and questions about what exactly one's place was in the world began pervading literature, popular culture, and philosophy at the time. Sartre argued that the French underground during the war persisted despite the torture and hardships they endured because, when one's spirit reaches such depths, the self can still declare its existence with a defiant, "No!" Where René Descartes had argued, "I think, therefore I am," Sartre turned that declaration on its head, saying in the negative version that one can still find affirmation: as in "No!, therefore I am." When faced with a void of nothingness, Sartre argued that one must use one's will to fight back against it, making decisions for oneself as if he were making them for everyone.

It is generally agreed that Kierkegaard (1813–1855) was the father of existentialism, with his philosophies firmly based within Christian existentialism. He, too, talked about man using choice to fight against the darkness, but he talked about the existential choice — a catch-22 of sorts (see *Finding Lost — Season Three*, pp. 140–144) — that man was often faced with. Kierkegaard's philosophy was grounded in a rejection of the Hegelian absolutist notion that everything that was real could be explained rationally. Hegel's methodology was a dialectical one, stating that for every thesis there was an antithesis, or opposite notion.

Kierkegaard, on the other hand, believed things were more complicated than that, and that the uniqueness of the individual meant that not every action could be explained rationally. Faith and belief are not necessarily rational notions and cannot be explained, yet they are very real. He argued that Hegelian beliefs discounted the freedom of the individual to make his/her own choices. Hegel claimed that the realm of the ethical was universal; in other words, when one acted ethically or morally, it was with the greater good in mind. The only other way to act would be selfishly, thinking only of oneself. Kierkegaard argued that there was a third level that Hegel hadn't taken into consideration: that of faith.

One of Kierkegaard's best works is *Fear and Trembling*. On *Lost*, it's the book that falls out of the deceased Montand's backpack when Kate shakes its contents onto the ground in "LA X." *Fear and Trembling* focuses on the biblical story of God asking Abraham to sacrifice his son Isaac in Genesis 22:1–18 (see sidebar). Kierkegaard states that Abraham was the father of faith. He was a prophet to whom God promised a son, telling him that he would be heir to the greatest nation on the earth. Abraham's wife Sarah was barren, and Abraham was 99 years old, but he had faith in God, and suddenly Sarah was pregnant. After Isaac's birth Abraham loved his son more than anything and had great hopes for his future because of everything God had promised. But when God sent an angel to tell Abraham that he had to travel to Mount Moriah to sacrifice Isaac on an altar, Abraham didn't hesitate, and he made the three-day journey to the mountain, left the donkey and servant at the base, and had Isaac carry the kindling with which he would light the sacrificial pyre. He bound Isaac to the altar, lit the pyre, and held the knife aloft, when suddenly God told him he had passed the test, showed him a ram caught in some bushes, and Abraham sacrificed it instead. He returned to his home with his beloved son and God told him that because of his faith, he and his descendants would be truly blessed.

The story of Abraham's near-sacrifice of Isaac is one that children learn at a young age in Sunday school . . . but it's one of those stories that always makes listeners uneasy. Kierkegaard was one of those uncomfortable listeners, and he

Genesis 22: 1-18

¹And it came to pass after these things, that God did tempt Abraham, and said unto him, Abraham: and he said, Behold, here I am.

²And he said, Take now thy son, thine only son Isaac, whom thou lovest, and get thee into the land of Moriah; and offer him there for a burnt offering upon one of the mountains which I will tell thee of.

³And Abraham rose up early in the morning, and saddled his ass, and took two of his young men with him, and Isaac his son, and clave the wood for the burnt offering, and rose up, and went unto the place of which God had told him. ⁴Then on the third day Abraham lifted up his eyes, and saw the place afar off. ⁵And Abraham said unto his young men, Abide ye here with the ass; and I and the lad will go yonder and worship, and come again to you.

⁶And Abraham took the wood of the burnt offering, and laid it upon Isaac his son; and he took the fire in his hand, and a knife; and they went both of them together. ⁷And Isaac spake unto Abraham his father, and said, My father: and he said, Here am I, my son. And he said, Behold the fire and the wood: but where is the lamb for a burnt offering?

⁸And Abraham said, My son, God will provide himself a lamb for a burnt offering: so they went both of them together.

⁹And they came to the place which God had told him of; and Abraham built an altar there, and laid the wood in order, and bound Isaac his son, and laid him on the altar upon the wood. ¹⁰And Abraham stretched forth his hand, and took the knife to slay his son. ¹¹And the angel of the LORD called unto him out of heaven, and said, Abraham, Abraham:

and he said, Here am I.

¹²And he said, Lay not thine hand upon the lad, neither do thou any thing unto him: for now I know that thou fearest God, seeing thou hast not withheld thy son, thine only son from me.

¹³And Abraham lifted up his eyes, and looked, and behold behind him a ram caught in a thicket by his horns: and Abraham went and took the ram, and offered him up for a burnt offering in the stead of his son. ¹⁴And Abraham called the name of that place Jehovahjireh: as it is said to this day, in the mount of the LORD it shall be seen.

¹⁵And the angel of the LORD called unto Abraham out of heaven the second time, ¹⁶And said, By myself have I sworn, saith the LORD, for because thou hast done this thing, and hast not withheld thy son, thine only son: ¹⁷That in blessing I will bless thee, and in multiplying I will multiply thy seed as the stars of the heaven, and as the sand which is upon the sea shore; and thy seed shall possess the gate of his enemies; ¹⁸And in thy seed shall all the nations of the earth be blessed; because thou hast obeyed my voice.

wrote *Fear and Trembling* to ask the questions that many people have asked, chiefly, how could Abraham have done this? Was there ever a moment when he wavered in his faith and worried he couldn't go through with it?

Hegel believed faith was below reason because you either had it or you didn't, and it didn't require any particular effort to have it. He said people had to move beyond faith and use their reason to vanquish their doubt. Kierkegaard disagreed; he argued that faith is not something one moves beyond, and that Abraham's faith was so strong that he was willing to kill his own son to prove it. Reason is using your mind to know something; faith is using your heart. What Hegel left out of his argument, he said, was passion, and it is this passion that always accompanies faith and cannot be reasoned away.

Kierkegaard (who wrote this book under the pseudonym Johannes de Silentio) writes that he heard the Abraham story as a child and loved it, and every time he heard it, he loved it more, but it also confused him more. He began to wonder: how could Abraham have walked that long three-day journey to Mount Moriah and never once have doubts? How did he explain this to Isaac? Why didn't he tell anyone what he was doing? Was he ever filled with so much fear that he just wanted to turn around and not do it? "He knew that it was God the Almighty who was trying him," he writes, "he knew that it was the hardest sacrifice that could be required of him; but he knew also that no sacrifice was too hard when God required it — and he drew the knife." Kierkegaard imagines four different scenarios for Abraham.

In the first one, Abraham leaves with Isaac as his wife Sarah watches from the window. He arrives at the mountain and tells Isaac the truth about what he's going to do, and Isaac begs for his life. Abraham grabs him by the throat and says it's *not* actually God's will, but his own, believing that, in his last moments, it's more important for Isaac to have faith in God than in his father. Isaac's reprieve, then, would strengthen the boy's love of God but ruin his relationship with his father.

In the second scenario, Abraham kisses his wife goodbye, joylessly walks to the mountain, binds Isaac, says nothing, holds the knife up, and is halted by God. He sacrifices the ram instead, but his joy is gone. "From that time on Abraham became old, he could not forget that God had required this of him." Isaac is not brought closer to God, and Abraham has been destroyed by the experience.

In the third scenario, Abraham goes to the mountain and along the way realizes that God is simply testing his love for his son. He leaves Isaac at the base of the mountain and walks to the mountaintop alone, begging God's forgiveness and telling Him he can't possibly go through with it. His relationship with Isaac is intact, but Isaac will never understand the power of God or the extent of his father's faith, because Abraham hasn't gone through with the sacrifice required of him.

In the fourth scenario, Abraham pulls out the knife, but just before God stops him his hand trembles as he holds it aloft, showing his faith wavering. Isaac sees it, and it shakes Isaac's faith in God for life. In each of these four possible scenarios, Kierkegaard tries to use reason to understand exactly how Abraham could have gone through with it; in each case Abraham is not the father of faith, but someone who was filled with doubt.

Kierkegaard expresses great admiration for Abraham. He discusses how Abraham must have felt dread along the way (and he emphasizes the journey itself, imploring his readers to understand what it must have been like to travel for three days just to commit such an act). And in doing what he did, he was acting out of the absurd, which Kierkegaard argues is the only way to describe how faith could cause a person to do that:

> All that time he believed — he believed that God would not require Isaac of him, whereas he was willing nevertheless to sacrifice him if it was required. He believed by virtue of the absurd; for there could be no question of human calculation, and it was indeed the absurd that God who required it of him should the next instant recall the requirement.

He states that Abraham had a fear of God, which is why God tested him. He also loved Isaac completely, which is why God chose Isaac as the very thing he had to sacrifice. Then, he says on that long journey, Abraham had plenty of time to change his mind, turn around, and go back home, but he didn't.

Kierkegaard adds unequivocally that he himself couldn't have done the same thing. He says he believes that God is love, "but I do not believe, this courage I lack. For me the love of God is, both in a direct and in an inverse sense, incommensurable with the whole of reality." He adds that "the dialectic of faith is the finest and most remarkable of all; it possesses an elevation, of which indeed I can form a conception, but nothing more." Faith must be paired with passion, for it is through this religious fervor that Abraham was able to do what he needed to.

In Kierkegaard's argument, meant to show the fallacy of trying to use reason to explain passion or absurd acts, he focuses on the difference between the religious and the ethical. If someone heard this story in a church and then went home, bound his son, and sacrificed him, he would be considered a murderer. Why, then, do we not consider Abraham to have been a potential murderer? When a man acts with a focus on himself, he is being selfish, and a focus on the individual usually exists outside of what is generally socially acceptable. When one acts ethically, one is thinking of *everyone else* around oneself, not only of oneself. The ethical person obeys a set of rules that other people in society also obey, and their actions are for the greater good. In order to do this, argues Kierkegaard, they must have an "infinite resignation"; in other words, they resign themselves to the universal, to giving up thinking of themselves and instead focusing on the ethical side. What Abraham did, argues Kierkegaard, is that he made one more step. He didn't resign himself to God's will and to the universal, but instead he resigned himself to the faith that God wouldn't make him do something unethical. In order to have faith, one must have made that infinite resignation and then make that second movement, that leap of faith into the virtue of the absurd: "Faith therefore is not an aesthetic emotion but something far higher, precisely because it has resignation as its presupposition; it is not an immediate instinct of the heart, but is the paradox of life and existence."

He distinguishes between the tragic hero, who acts within the realm of the ethical (i.e., the figures in Greek mythology who sacrificed their children for the good of their country) and the knight of faith, who must make that extra leap of faith where he will get back what he's lost. He says that the tragic hero is admired; the knight of faith is misunderstood. Abraham must have felt anxiety about the circumstances, he reasons, because of the tension between the ethical and the religious.

Using Hegelian reasoning, Kierkegaard then presents three "problemata," and in each section he parodies the Hegelian desire to use reason to explain things, because in the case of Abraham, the story simply cannot be understood rationally for all of the reasons he'd already explored. He suggests that Abraham's actions were performed within a teleological suspension of the ethical, or the act of setting the ethical aside to achieve his ends (teleology refers to a purpose or endgame), which he believed would be a righteous one. Abraham acted entirely outside the ethical; his act was an individual one, with the difference that it was between him and God. Killing Isaac was for his own good because it would prove his unwavering faith in God, and it was for God because it proved that such a God-fearing follower existed. Kierkegaard says that bringing these two ideas together — working for the individual and for God — is expressed in the word "trial," or temptation. But he adds, "A temptation — but what does that mean? What ordinarily tempts a man is that which would keep him from doing his duty, but in this case the temptation is itself the ethical . . . which would keep him from doing God's will." And therein lies the paradox, and in it, he shows how difficult it is to understand how a knight of faith works.

Throughout Kierkegaard's philosophical writings, he distinguishes between belief and faith. When one believes in something, one knows it to be true; we believe that two plus two equals four because there's no question that it does. But when one has faith in something, there is always the possibility that one could be wrong. A faith in God risks there not being a God, but having faith in such a thing is a much more difficult thing to have than believing that the sky is blue or that grass is green. Faith involves a teleological suspension of the ethical, because there is a belief that what might appear to be an unethical action will actually result in the greater good. For example, think of Sayid telling Essam in "The Greater Good" that if he becomes a suicide bomber, it will be for a good reason. The discomfort in that scene is the same as the one Kierkegaard says Abraham would have had; he is trapped between what he believes is right from a religious standpoint and what is ethical.

One can have faith in God, but one cannot believe in God because He is not something that is seen or explained rationally. It's a much harder thing to have faith than to have belief, because the former involves uncertainty. Locke has faith in the rightness of pushing a button, but he doesn't *believe* in it because he knows that he might be wrong. Jack has faith that if he drops a hydrogen bomb, it will reverse time; he doesn't believe it will, because he knows he could be wrong. One can believe in science, but faith is a much more difficult thing to have, and it requires struggle, anxiety, and constant questioning of oneself.

Locke had faith in the island. He knew he might be wrong, but he had experienced a miracle that had given him faith. When Boone died, Locke told Jack that his death was a "sacrifice that the island demanded." Just as Isaac was a sacrifice that God demanded, Locke had resigned himself to Boone's death, making the leap of faith that his death would serve a higher purpose. Jack couldn't understand Locke's faith, because it couldn't be rationalized. Just as Kierkegaard often finds himself unable to explain in simple terms how Abraham could have done what he did, neither can anyone but Locke really understand what Locke was thinking.

Throughout the series, Jack has been forced to question himself. Just as Kierkegaard explores how Abraham could have done what he did, so too does Jack begin to question in his mind how Locke could have done what he did. And then when Jack suffers his own existential crisis once he is off the island, he must begin to ask what his purpose is. He suffers the angst and dread that, according to Kierkegaard, accompanies the exercise of free will. He continues to dismiss Locke, but ultimately chooses to return to the island. And once he makes that choice, as said above, he finds his purpose, discovers his role in society, and becomes content. He drinks Jacob's water. Jack has followed an incredible journey. Just as Abraham walked for three long days with his only child at his side, assuming that he was going to kill him (and probably running through all of the scenarios in his head and dealing with the apprehension and dread that accompanied his task), so has Jack been on a journey for three long years, wrestling with similar questions and difficulties and trying to make a decision. When he steps up to become the new Jacob, he does so with complete faith. Just as he sat next to Richard and had faith that the dynamite wouldn't go off (but you could tell by his face he knew there was a possibility he'd be wrong), now he drinks the water, taking a leap of faith by virtue of the absurd.

In "Catch-22," as Desmond is bottling the wine in the monastery, he comments to a fellow monk that it's strange the labels read "Moriah Vineyards," since Mount Moriah was the place where Abraham had been asked to sacrifice Isaac — not a very happy place to name your wine after. The monk counters that it was on that mountain where God spared Isaac, insinuating that it *was*, in fact, a happy place. Desmond says, "Well, one might argue then, God may not have asked Abraham to sacrifice his son in the first place."

"Well then," the monk replies, "it wouldn't have been much of a test, would it, Brother? Perhaps you underestimate the value of a sacrifice."

Just as Abraham had to go through everything to show the world what true faith was all about, so does Jack endure his long journey to find faith in the island and understand his importance to it. There's no rational explanation for why he drinks the water; he just has faith that in doing so, he is serving a greater purpose and finding his place in the world. He drinks the water with the same conviction that allowed Abraham to hold that knife aloft. There's no rationality in what either man does, but their faith makes them stronger men than anyone else around them.

6.17 The End

Original air date: May 23, 2010
Written by: Damon Lindelof, Carlton Cuse
Directed by: Jack Bender

Guest cast: François Chau (Pierre Chang), Jeremy Davies (Daniel Widmore), Fionnula Flanagan (Eloise Widmore), Maggie Grace (Shannon Rutherford), Rebecca Mader (Charlotte), Elizabeth Mitchell (Juliet Carlson), Ian Somerhalder (Boone), John Terry (Christian Shephard), Sonya Walger (Penny), Cynthia Watros (Libby), Neil Hopkins (Liam Pace), John Pyper-Ferguson (Bocklin), Alan Seabock (Sub Captain), Eric Nemoto (Oceanic Rep), Erin Little (Jane), Ross Woledge (Roger Cook), Christina Souza (Nurse)

Focus: Everyone

With Jack as the new Jacob, the remaining survivors try to vanquish the smoke monster once and for all to save the island, while in the sideways world, the characters finally realize where they are.

"I need you to go find my son . . . he has work to do."

And with those words at the end of "So It Begins," the mobisode that preceded season 4, Christian Shephard sent Vincent through the bamboo forest to wake up Jack so he could become a hero to the survivors of the crash of Oceanic Flight 815. The series began with Jack's eye opening to a new world, new people, and the beginning of the most important three years of his life. Three years later (six in "viewer years"), that eye closes, leaving behind a world that has been utterly changed because Jack was in it. Viewers at home were elated, bereft, confused, crying, overjoyed, cheering, screaming, furious . . . if the aim of this finale was to be polarizing, Darlton achieved their goal beautifully.

Many television series finales have gone down in history as being either groundbreaking, baffling, upsetting, or perfect (warning: spoilers ahead). *M*A*S*H*, the most-watched series finale of all time, tied up each character arc while delving into the psychological impact the war had had on each of the characters. It is a beloved finale, one that was beautifully written and acted, and satisfying in the way it concluded the story. Similarly, *Six Feet Under* has been lauded for having one of the best series finales of all time, featuring a long flashforward that shows us how each major character in the story will die in the future, intercut with scenes from their lives along the way.

But not every show has ended so conclusively, and that's where *Lost* comes in. *Newhart* ended with the revelation that the entire series had been a dream. *St. Elsewhere* concluded with the even more shocking (and less comedic) revelation that the characters and storylines had existed inside the mind of an autistic boy who had been staring into a snow globe with a hospital inside it. *Angel* ended with the main characters rushing headlong into a battle that they couldn't possibly win, but rather than showing us the outcome, viewers were left with the perpetual image of our heroes forever willing to fight à la *Butch Cassidy and the Sundance Kid.*

Some finales are remembered for being less-than-successful wrap-ups of the series. Patrick McGoohan's *The Prisoner* (which was a huge inspiration for *Lost*, see pp. 81–85 of *Finding Lost — Season Three*) ended with the main character, Number Six, being paraded through a cave and watching some bizarro psychedelic shenanigans before racing through a labyrinth in pursuit of the elusive Number One, who turned out to be . . . him. It didn't make a lot of sense (and the fact that the network gave an already exhausted McGoohan only two days to write it didn't help) and viewers were unhappy. Similarly, *Roseanne* ended with the revelation that Roseanne's husband, who had suffered a heart attack at the end of the previous season but had recovered in time for the show's uncharacteristic and confused final season, had actually died of the heart attack, and the ninth season had been nothing more than a series of Roseanne's fantasies, which she was using to work through her grief. Again, it was an unsatisfying conclusion to a show that hadn't been good in a long time. *Seinfeld* managed to maintain a high caliber of comedy throughout its nine years, but its ludicrous finale — where everyone who the four main characters had annoyed or offended over the years were paraded into a courtroom to make allegations against our heroes — was another big letdown. Fortunately, the terrible finale didn't overshadow the series that had preceded it.

In recent years, the most famous finale has belonged to *The Sopranos*. No fan of the show will forget his or her reaction when that series ended: the Soprano family meet in a small diner, with the suspense building as daughter Meadow tries repeatedly to parallel park her car but can't seem to get it into the spot, and various undesirable characters stare at Tony as if there's an assassination plan afoot. As Meadow finally parks the car and walks up to the door, Tony looks up . . . and the screen suddenly goes black and quiet. After 10 seconds of empty silence, the credits roll with no sound. For a moment many fans thought their cable service had faltered, and when the credits began rolling, viewers sat in shock. As the realization dawned on them that the black void had been intentional and that it was up to viewers to decide what actually transpired in that final 10 seconds, reactions moved either to praise or damnation. It's hard to even talk about *The Sopranos* with anyone now without the conversation centering on the finale.

Carlton Cuse, Damon Lindelof, and Jack Bender had a ton of pressure going into the finale, and what they produced was phenomenal. (Marco Garcia/AP Photo)

And so, in this storied history of television show enders, Damon Lindelof and Carlton Cuse had to come up with an ending that would convey the message of the show, that would offer up some answers to the myriad mysteries they'd weaved for six years, that wouldn't repeat the territory (or mistakes) of other series finales, and that would be remembered. In the minds of many viewers, they succeeded. However, within minutes of the episode's conclusion, social networking sites such as Twitter and Facebook lit up with angry and baffled responses from fans, demanding to get the last six years of their life back and saying they'd been let down. The main bone of contention was the fact that the writers hadn't provided enough answers to the show's many mysteries. Why was Walt special? What had happened to Young Ben when he was taken into the Temple by Richard? Who were the Others? *What was the island??!!* Critics of the finale suggested that in not answering these questions and leaving too much of the series wide open, the writers were being lazy, leaving it up to the viewer to answer the questions for themselves and not providing a satisfactory conclusion. For a show that had been so focused on mysteries, science, and knowledge, the writers seemed to have thrown too much of that fertile material out the window in the finale.

It was a valid argument. *Lost* demanded a lot of its viewers, sending us rushing to libraries, bookstores, and Wikipedia following every episode. They filled episodes with Easter eggs, encouraged fans to participate in online games that would enrich their understanding of the show's minutiae, gave us hints about which books to read, built up the mysteries with new questions every week, playfully avoided answering anything in interviews but watched as we speculated with our own theories, and then . . . left most of those questions unanswered in the end. Damon and Carlton put a lot of emphasis on the "questions" in their interviews and podcasts, and so it was only natural that fans would expect "answers" to follow.

But just as Jacob sparked the action on the island but preferred people to make their own decisions; just as Desmond couldn't tell the characters in the sideways world what to see and instead had to help lead them to their own answers; just as Sayid handed Jin a box cutter to cut his wrist restraints in "The Package" rather than doing it for him — it's up to viewers to find those answers for themselves. The *Lost* writers intricately wove together the threads of their story, and gave us the tools with which to come up with the answers ourselves. If you've read *The Third Policeman* (Flann O'Brien) or *Slaughterhouse-Five* (Kurt Vonnegut), to my mind, the two most important literary allusions made in the series for *Lost* fans to bring to the finale, you will have a very different interpretation of the show's many mysteries than someone who hasn't.

Lost was about sloughing off labels and categorization, about how the world couldn't be simplified into black-and-white concepts, that Locke wasn't an unwavering believer and Jack wasn't a staunch agnostic. There was no right or wrong, and similarly, there are no right or wrong interpretations of the finale or what the sideways world represented. Believe it or not, the answers to those questions you're still asking yourself are all right there in the show; it's up to you to find them. Fans who'd rewatched the first five seasons before season six began had an easier time with the finale than those who hadn't, because they could more easily piece together the mysteries from the seasons that were now fresh in their minds.

Lost has always been an intensely personal show — a Christian might interpret a given scene one way; an atheist another. A Muslim would bring his/her belief system to the show to inform the viewing; a Buddhist would focus on different aspects. Parents may watch the show with some sympathy for, say, Christian Shephard, while teenage viewers would identify with the children in the story, or with Kate's freedom, or Sawyer's independence. We brought our own personal memories, flashbacks, lives, and belief systems to *Lost* and it informed how we received it. Five minutes after the finale concluded, an angry fan tweeted at Damon Lindelof, "I hope your house burns down and you rot in hell." It seemed like a shockingly personal thing to say to him, but upon reflection, if you're going to write a show that's as intense and personal as *Lost*, you'll have to steel yourself for the personal reactions that are sure to follow.

Lost tackled the big questions, questions that in the real world have no definitive answers. In "The Substitute," the Man in Black says the most important question the characters are all asking is, "Why are you on this island?" It's a basic, human, "Why are we here?" metaphor, one the writers obviously couldn't answer; instead, they showed us what questions we need to ask in order to lead us to that answer ourselves. As viewers watched the moral conundrums played out on the show, we saw an opportunity to ask, "How would I have reacted in that situation?" *Lost* made viewers question their notions of right and wrong, and perhaps made them re-evaluate things in their own lives or cherished opinions they may have held. In "Across the Sea," Mother says, "Every question I answer will simply lead to another question," and if the writers had begun offering up answers to every question, the same thing would have happened.

Consider the reactions to some of the big answers viewers *did* get this season. When Michael revealed that the whispers were coming from the people who had died on the island and remained in a kind of purgatory, many viewers thought that was a pat answer, too easy. Smokey's throwaway line "Jacob had a thing for numbers," explaining away the prevalence of Hurley's cursed numerals was similarly scoffed at by some viewers, especially those who thought the purpose of the numbers divulged in *The Lost Experience* ARG (see *Finding Lost — Seasons 1 & 2*, pp. 22–26) was a far more interesting reveal than the one on the show. So if the writers had simply come out and said in plain English what the island is, what the light represented, why Jacob and his brother were there, and what really happened to Ben Linus, the audience would now simply be debating whether or not those answers were satisfactory. Instead, in the months following the finale, fans have continued to speculate and discuss all of the many mysteries of the show as if it were still airing, and the discussion is as lively as it's ever been. Here's hoping that discussion continues for many years to come.

Luckily, I was among the fans who loved the finale and thought it was as close to perfect as a finale could be. So the following analysis will be my interpretation of what really happened in that final two hours, and how it was intended to conclude such a complex and deeply personal show. Again, as with the rest of this episode guide, this is my interpretation, and I will offer up some tools for you to interpret the finale in your own way, just as the writers have done with the show.

First, despite what some fans thought happened on the island, NO, they didn't all die in the plane crash, and YES, the island does exist. There was a lot of controversy immediately following the airing of this finale, especially when ABC showed footage of the plane wreckage on the beach during the end credits (something the network immediately admitted they'd added in on their own without Darlton's input). The rusted-out fuselage led many fans to declare that everyone had died in Oceanic Flight 815 and that everything that had happened for the entire series was actually some sort of life flashing before their eyes before they crossed over in the sideways world.

That's not the case.

In the pilot episode, the plane really did crash onto the island, and everything that has happened since in the original timeline has been real. Christian reassures Jack of this in the final minutes of the finale, telling him that everything that had ever happened to him was real. Many people died, some people lived, Jacob and the Man in Black have been engaged in this feud for centuries, the Dharma Initiative occupied the island for a couple of decades, the Others really lived on the island, the Oceanic 6 left and came back, and Jack died on the island after completing his mission. At the show's close, we can assume the people who left on the Ajira plane — Lapidus, Miles, Kate, Claire, Richard, and Sawyer — flew back to civilization where they continued to live their lives and were either able to move on from the island's events or had to deal with the psychological trauma of what had happened to them. Ben and Hurley probably rounded up Desmond, as well as Cindy and the two children, Zach and Emma, and everyone else, and put them on Desmond's boat so Des could take them back home. Perhaps some of them stayed on the island after all. Rose and Bernard continued to live in a hut on the island with Vincent, happy to be on an island that was protected by the benevolent Hurley and not the questionable Jacob, and Hurley possibly lived for many centuries, saw many people come and go, helped them through their problems rather than turning those problems into a game the way Jacob and Smokey had, and Ben was his loyal Number Two, working together with him and teaching him all of the island secrets, happy to have finally been acknowledged as being important. They will eventually die, and Hurley will pass the guardianship of the island over to someone new. Or maybe, because Jack didn't actually say the incantation over Hurley's water, Hurley didn't become immortal, and he and Ben will simply live a few more decades on the island and protect it for as long as they can before passing it on to someone else. So yes, all of this *really did* happen, and those flashbacks you saw for the first three seasons, and the storylines we were so invested in all this time, were real.

The opening act of "The End" is one of the best we've seen all season. From the slow majesty with which the coffin is removed from the Oceanic aircraft to the cuts between the sideways-world characters and their island counterparts, we have the tension of the season laid out at the very beginning, which establishes the main focus of this final episode. Sawyer is at his sarcasm-wielding best, comparing Jack to Moses, referring to the ceremony with Jacob as his "inauguration," and then heading off to find Desmond. Hurley makes *Star Wars* references, Kate makes a crack about having to wait for Sawyer to be far away before she can follow him, and Jack remains stoic, trying to figure out what to do next. It was like a momentary return to the characters of the first season. In the sideways world, the key moment belongs to Desmond, who tells Kate that he's finally going to show her what *that* world is all about.

At the end of "What They Died For," Smokey revealed that the reason Desmond was important was because he was a failsafe — someone who could become the new Jacob should all the other Candidates perish. Desmond is impervious to electromagnetism, which is important because it meant he could get close to the Source without dying — something no one else was capable of doing, as evidenced by the many skeletons he passes along the way — and therefore he could protect it in a way no one else could. What makes him important to Smokey is the same thing: he could get close enough to the Source to turn it off and thus destroy the island, and — if Jacob is to be believed — the rest of the world with it.

Desmond has seen the sideways world, but he didn't quite understand its purpose. We now know that the serenity he felt after being zapped by Widmore's team stemmed from the fact that he'd seen a happy world where everyone was okay, where they were together with their loved ones, and where they were preparing to move on (more on that below). In "Flashes Before Your Eyes," Desmond was sent to another world where he saw a glimpse of what could have been. Even though he didn't make any different choices, when he opened his eyes and was lying in the jungle, he just wanted to go back there. While he encountered many difficulties in that world — Widmore was dismissive of him, Eloise told him he couldn't marry Penny, he was reminded once again of his dishonor — Desmond wanted to go back the moment he realized he was on the island. Any place was better than the island. In "Happily Ever After," he saw a world that was calm and beautiful, and again he wants to return, but this time, rather than railing against a world that is keeping him on the island, he's going to calmly do what he needs to in order to return. He believes that if he gets close enough to the Source to get zapped again, he'll return to that place for good, where he'll be with Penny and everyone will be okay. He believes that nothing on the island matters.

But he's wrong. What happens on the island matters immensely, and whatever Jack does or doesn't do on the island will inform what happens in the sideways world, and it will decide whether or not he'll be able to move on. When Desmond goes into the cave, removes the "cork" from the Source (who'd have thought Jacob's explanation of the island in "Ab Aeterno" would be so literal?), and all hell breaks loose, it would seem he was ultimately rather useless. Jack recorks it, and everything goes back to the way it was. So . . . why bother having Desmond uncork it in the first place?

First, the light going out made Smokey human again. Perhaps Smokey knew this, and thought he could take away the curse of being the smoke monster so he could once again feel the ground beneath his feet and live the rest of his mortal days off the island. From Jack's point of view, however, Smokey needed to become mortal so he could die. And that would only happen if they momentarily turned off the Source. Desmond was the only one who could do it without experiencing fatal damage.

On another level it was important for everyone to see what would happen if the light went out. Mother suggested that if the light went out here, it would go out everywhere. And truly, we saw the sky turn black, the magic of the island disappear, and piece by piece, the island began to fall into the ocean. If the island can crumble away, then presumably the effects might slowly extend outward to affect the rest of the world, which is what Jacob meant when he kept insisting that everyone in the world would die. The rest of the people on the island — Jack, Kate, Sawyer, Hurley, and Ben in particular — needed to see this if they were to believe that they were fighting for something real. Sawyer was constantly waffling on whether Smokey was right or wrong, lying or telling the truth. They all needed to see just how dark the world could be, and they needed to make things right.

Desmond was destined to move that stone so that Jack and Kate could kill Smokey and rid the Source of its threat. Then Jack had to go back to the cave and turn the guardianship of the island over to Hurley, because Hurley was always meant to be the island's protector. Jack needed to then go down into the cave, save Desmond, and turn the light back on. Only then would he know that he really had been right about everything. He would know then that John Locke had been telling the truth, that Jack needed to believe in it all, believe that his life had purpose and meaning, that he *could* fix things, and that he could delegate responsibility to someone like Hurley and finally let go of the hold he had on leadership. Just before Sayid died, he said, "It's going to be you, Jack." In "What They Died For," it seemed Sayid meant that Jack would be the new Jacob. But in fact what it looks like he meant was that it would be Jack who would enable the light to keep shining and rid the island of its darkness. If Desmond hadn't removed the stone, Jack wouldn't have been able to fulfill his life's purpose and "fix it," something that the writers have spent six seasons leading up to.

In "Across the Sea," when Jacob asks Mother what the light represents, she says, "life, death, rebirth. . . ." The same could be said for what *Lost* is about. *Lost* is a show about life, death, rebirth, hope, redemption, power, anger, sadness, isolation, greed, vengeance, understanding, community, love, and the importance of memory. It's about the tension between self-preservation and self-sacrifice. By grounding many of its themes in opposites — black/white, good/evil, wrong/right, fate/free will — it presented cases for both sides, only to show us that the truth was somewhere in between. At the end of the series, the writers tended to show that there was no such thing as good people or evil people; instead there were people who made mistakes, or had a selfish purpose in mind, but weren't all good or bad. Black and white always blended to create a gray area: the Man in Black had been wronged and he fought back, but he wasn't all evil; Jacob had made mistakes in his past and was trying to correct them, but he wasn't all good. Many concepts and people blended together with their opposites by the end of the series.

Nowhere is this mixing of opposites more apparent than in the characters of Jack and Locke. Jack Shephard was the man of science who didn't believe in destiny and John Locke was the island's disciple whose blind faith was unwavering . . . until Jack began to believe in miracles and Locke died confused and despairing.

The evolution of Jack from a man of science to a man of faith can be traced through a few key moments with John Locke. The first important scene between Jack and Locke was in season 1's "White Rabbit," where Jack was following a man he thought was his dead father through the jungle and he came upon John Locke. Locke told Jack that the survivors needed Jack to be their leader. Jack said he couldn't comply: "I don't know how to help them. I'll fail. I don't have what it takes." Locke encouraged Jack to look within himself and ask why he was really walking through a jungle chasing the specter of a dead man.

The crew sets up the cars in the parking lot at the church for the upcoming nighttime shoot. The church in the finale is the Sacred Hearts Academy in Honolulu, the same one used in "316" as the Lamp Post Station. (Courtesy Ryan Ozawa)

He told Jack to consider for a moment that Christian might be real. Jack refused to believe that, and Locke asked, "But what if everything that happened here happened for a reason?" He told him he'd seen into the eye of the island, and believed the island was a special place where miracles happened. As he began to walk away, Jack offered to accompany him, and Locke responded, "No. You need to finish what you've started. . . . Because a leader can't lead until he knows where he's going." This first conversation set Jack and Locke up in the roles of student and mentor, but Jack, despite taking the leadership that was offered to him, refused to go any further than simple, mechanical leadership, and couldn't believe in something that didn't make scientific sense.

By the end of the season, when the relationship between the two men had changed drastically due to Boone's death and Jack's discovery that Locke had been hiding the hatch from everyone, Jack wanted to know why Locke still believed the island was special. John tried reiterating the words he'd said to Jack earlier, suggesting that no one is wrong or right, it's that they simply aren't seeing eye-to-eye on things because of their different backgrounds. And then he says, "I'm a man of faith. Do you really think all this is an accident — that we, a group of strangers survived, many of us with just superficial injuries? Do you think we crashed on this place by coincidence — especially *this* place? We were brought here for a purpose, for a reason, all of us." Jack, annoyed at someone who he already thought had clearly lost his mind, wanted to know *who* had brought them there (we now know the answer to that question). Locke insisted the island had done it, and added, "[T]he island chose you, too, Jack. It's destiny." He said that everything that had happened on the island was part of a series of events that had been put in place for a purpose. At the time, Locke believed that this series of events would culminate in opening the hatch; in fact, it would only be the beginning of the real journey they'd all been sent on. But all Jack could see before him now was a man whose maniacal beliefs had led to the death of a young man on the island. "I don't believe in destiny," he replied. To which Locke retorted, "Yes, you do. You just don't know it yet."

When the hatch was opened, and what was found underneath was a computer with a button that had to be pushed every 108 minutes, we were in the realm of the absurd, and Jack thought he'd been proven right, and that Locke was nothing but a delusional old man. For a moment, Locke's belief wavered, until he saw the orientation film and realized the importance of the button. In "Orientation" we saw the next vital scene between Jack and John. Locke began to enter the numbers, then stood up as the timer counted down, and told Jack to push the "Execute" button. "This is a two-person job, at least," he argued. He wanted Jack to share in the responsibility — the faith — believing that maybe they'd both been brought to the island for this purpose. But Jack would have none of it. "Why do you find it so hard to believe?" he pleaded with Jack. Jack shot back, "Why do you find it so easy?" Locke, frustrated by this point, shouted, "It's never *been* easy!"

Locke had told Jack back in "White Rabbit" that before the crash, he was a normal guy who hadn't believed in miracles. We've since seen in various flashbacks that while Locke may not have believed in miracles, he always hoped things could be better. And when they weren't better — when Richard Alpert, who may have taken a Young John to a better life in "Cabin Fever," stormed out of his house, or when his long-lost mother turned out to be crazy, or when his long-lost father was a con man who stole one of his bodily organs, or when the woman he loved left him because she couldn't trust him, or when he couldn't go on the walkabout — John Locke railed against a world that seemed dead set against him. Locke has wanted to believe, but life has made it impossible for him to do so. On the island, however, he's experienced a miracle, and after a lifetime of fate dealing him one terrible hand after another, he's finally been given a royal flush. But since the crash, he's considered the idea that he wasn't the only one chosen by the island — Jack, too, has been chosen for a reason, and while Locke doesn't quite know what that reason is, he feels destiny has brought them together for the sole reason that John can convince Jack of his life's purpose. He says quietly, "I can't do this alone, Jack. I don't want to. It's a leap of faith, Jack." And as the clock counts down, a very surly Jack pushes the button.

Jack's reluctant gesture is essentially hollow, however, and throughout the rest of the season he argues with John Locke until he actually wears Locke down, causing Locke's faith to waver. John allows himself to be swayed by Jack, and the results are catastrophic. Throughout the next two seasons, Locke's efforts to keep everyone on the island — including blowing up the sub and the Flame station, which is filled with important information — causes the strain between the two to become so great that Jack points a gun at Locke's head and pulls the trigger, unaware that the gun isn't loaded. (He does so mere hours after Locke had pointed a gun at Jack but couldn't bring himself to shoot him, again believing that if Jack had a purpose on the island he couldn't kill him.) The two become enemies, dividing the people into two and taking their groups to opposite ends of the island.

By the end of the season, Jack finds a way off the island and Locke again tries to get him to reconsider. Perhaps sensing that the events we've seen in season 6 would be coming, he tells Jack that he's "not supposed to go home." Jack mocks his destiny talk, and John replies, "You know that you're here for a reason. You *know* it. And if you leave this place, that knowledge is going to eat you alive from the inside out . . . until you decide to come back." Jack decides he's had enough of John, and walks away, but John tells him if he insists on leaving, he'll have to lie to protect the island. "It's an *island*, John. No one needs to protect it," Jack says. Locke disagrees, and says when Jack sees him move the island he'll realize that he was wrong. Jack scoffs at him again, and Locke replies, "Well . . . we'll just have to see which one of us is right."

And after Jack leaves the island and begins feeling its pull, he starts to believe that Locke was right. He can't yet admit it to himself, though, and when, shockingly, Locke ends up at his hospital after a car accident, they have their final argument. In pure Locke fashion, John says that it must be fate that brought him to Jack's hospital. Jack counters that it's not fate, it's coincidence. John argues that someone is trying to kill him, "because they don't want me to succeed. They want to stop me. They don't want me to get back because I'm important." Jack loses his cool and tells Locke that he's nothing but a lonely old man and will never be important or special, and makes an attempt to leave the room until John tells him that Christian talked to him. Jack pauses, and John makes one final plea: "Jack, please, you have to come back. You're the only one who can convince the rest of them. You have to help me. You're supposed to help me!" Jack yells back, "John, it's *over*! It's done. We left, and we were never important." And he walks away from his last-ever argument with John Locke. After that, John was dead.

But the impact of John's plea sticks with Jack, and he can't shake the feeling that John was right. Jack is already starting to fall apart when Locke showed up at the hospital. He is addicted to painkillers and doubting his decision to leave the island, and his hostility to Locke stems from the fact that Locke in this scene is simply saying the things that Jack is worried are true, and Jack didn't want to hear it. He begins testing fate, taking flights that might crash on the island, in a weird and yearning kind of death wish. In these episodes, Jack is a raw nerve, the perfect image of the guy who is angry at himself for being wrong. When he does manage to return to the island, he thinks the answers will be there waiting for him, but again, he takes another journey throughout season 6 to discover more about what John Locke meant, and in turn, to understand his own destiny even more.

Fundamentally, John was right about everything. He and Jack were both important, and had both been chosen for a reason. Jack was the one who was meant to save everyone, and John's purpose was to make Jack accept his own role. John becomes Jack's savior, and Jack in turn becomes the savior for everyone else. In "White Rabbit," Locke made Jack realize he was a leader. In "Exodus, Part 2," he put the kernel of the idea in Jack's head that they might have been brought to the island for a reason. In "Orientation," he showed Jack the importance of working together on something, and not trying to shoulder the responsibility alone, the way Jack usually did. In "There's No Place Like Home, Part 1," he predicted that Jack would want to come back to the island, and that the island needed protecting, foreshadowing not only the fact that Jack would willingly, deliberately return to the island three years later, but also that Jack would ultimately become the guardian of the Source. And in "The Life and Death of Jeremy Bentham," John felt like he had failed to convince Jack, but it was his words that made Jack start taking those flights. And when Locke mentioned Christian, he not only brought up the person who first led Jack down the rabbit hole of the island, but who would ultimately, in the final 10 minutes of the series, help Jack see what his true purpose had always been.

When John Locke was strangled by Ben Linus and we discovered at the end of "The Incident" that he was, in fact, dead, it was a shock for the fans. How could this character who seemed so immensely important in the first five seasons, be dead before the series even entered its final year? Could it be that he wasn't as important as we thought he was? Could his entire life have been for nothing? Was Jack right, and he wasn't special at all, but just a delusional old man?

No. Because in season 6, his importance is made clear: without John Locke, Jack never would have realized his own true purpose, would never have come back to the island, would not have decided to stay there. He wouldn't have dropped a bomb down a shaft in the hopes of a miracle happening. He wouldn't have followed Hurley's leadership and listened to the instructions of a man he couldn't even see. He wouldn't have had the faith to sit in *The Black Rock* next to a stick of lit dynamite and have a chat with Richard Alpert. He wouldn't have begged Sawyer to just let the timer on the bomb run down. He wouldn't have drunk Jacob's water and vowed to spend eternity protecting a light. He wouldn't have given his life to the island.

He wouldn't have been able to let go.

Much of *Lost*, then, has been about Jack's journey from reason to faith. In "316," as Jack was sitting in the church after Eloise's long sermon about the Dharma Initiative, Ben tells Jack about the Caravaggio painting on the wall, *The Incredulity of Saint Thomas* (see *Finding Lost — Season Five*, p. 69). In that moment, Jack has just been told that he needs to take John Locke's body back to the island as a proxy for his own father, and while he believes that they need to go back, he doubts a lot of what Eloise has said. Jack has been a Doubting Thomas when it comes to John Locke from the moment John first started talking to him, but just as Thomas the Apostle became a believer once he saw Jesus's wounds and inserted his finger into them, so does Jack believe that Locke was right when he feels his own emotional wounds begin to heal upon his return to the island. He feels the island pulling him to it, and knows that Locke was right. It's not a coincidence that Smokey stabs Jack in the ribs on his right side — it's exactly the same wound Christ is showing Thomas in the painting.

Throughout season 6, Jack has acknowledged that John was right. In this episode, Smokey crouches beside him and looks down into the cave in exactly the same way Locke and Jack sat at the top of the hatch, peering down together. Smokey, who clearly has Locke's memories, comments on the similarity of the moment, asking Jack if this reminds him of anything. He says, "If there was a button down there to push we could fight about whether or not to push it. It would be just like old times." And Jack's response shows us exactly how much his opinion of Locke has changed. He says, "You're not John Locke. You disrespect his memory by wearing his face but you're nothing like him. Turns out he was right about most everything. I just wish I could have told him that when he was still alive." It's a glorious moment of posthumous vindication for John Locke. At the end of season 4, Locke told Jack that they'd have to see which one of them is right, and Smokey offers the same response here. At the end of season 2, Locke stood amidst the Swan station as it was shaking and falling apart, threatening to destroy the world with it, and he mouthed those sad three words that defined him throughout the series: "I was wrong." Here, the man who looks like John Locke stares at Jack and says, "I guess you were wrong" before striding confidently away, bringing that season 2 incident full circle — Jack *had* been wrong back then, and it was his powerful, unwavering disbelief that caused Locke to waver in his own faith. But unlike Locke, Jack doesn't waver in his convictions in this episode. He races after Smokey, punches him and declares that they were both wrong. It is essential that Smokey looks like John Locke; this wasn't just a ploy to keep Terry O'Quinn in the cast. The reason that Jack beats Smokey on the flats above the ocean with such hatred isn't because he reminds him of John Locke; it's because he doesn't believe Smokey has the right to appear as the one person who had been so devoted to the island that he was willing to die to save it.

In the sideways world, Helen thanked Jack in "The Candidate" for saving John's life, but later in that episode, when she realized Jack was pushing John to have the surgery, she said, "You saved John's life; why can't that be enough?" Jack replied, "Because it isn't." The reason Jack can't let go of his need to help John Locke is because he has a sense that he owes John this miracle. In "The End," when John gets his realization flash and remembers his life, he says to Jack, "I hope somebody does for you what you just did for me." But John already has: it took five seasons, but John had freed Jack from his doubts and allowed him to open his mind to a new perspective, finally seeing his true purpose. As Jack says those key words to John pre-surgery — "See you on the other side" — John tells him that he hopes he can find peace. Jack responds, "If I can fix you, Mr. Locke, that's all the peace I'll need." John and Jack are now even, and it's when that happens that sideways-world Jack starts to see glimpses of his real life.

If nothing else was answered in this episode, fans wanted an explanation of what the sideways world was. And at the end of the episode, we got it. Some fans loved it, some hated it. The revelation of what the sideways world represented was consistent with where the show had been going for six years.

In season 1, we learned who everyone was and saw important moments in their lives through their flashback memories. On other shows we might get to know characters in the present, and perhaps in future seasons we'd understand the characters more as details of their past would be revealed, but on *Lost*, we got to know them *through* their pasts, which gave us sympathy for them and allowed us to see their stories on the island through their perspectives. We could understand why Jin was telling Sun to button up her sweater, why Jack wore a key around his neck and refused to let anyone touch it, why Kate insisted on sneaking off to follow every expedition through the jungle, simply because we knew their secrets. The survivors were focused on rescue, and season 1 was all about trying to get off the island. The literature that was referenced in that season — *Watership Down, Lord of the Flies, Heart of Darkness, Alice's Adventures in Wonderland* — was all about surviving in a new place, and wanting to return home. The philosophers alluded to — John Locke, Jean-Jacques Rousseau — had a lot to say about the behavior of man in a state of nature removed from society, which was exactly the state the survivors found themselves in.

Season 2 was about taking what we knew to be true about the survivors' backgrounds and enriching it or twisting it. Now that we sympathized with the characters, the writers could shake things up and show us some troubling things about them — Kate killed her father; Charlie conned a girl in order to steal something from her; Sun had an affair. It was a test of the audience, to see if we would continue to see things through the characters' eyes knowing these new things about them; but because we had seen things from their perspectives already, we understood the catalysts for the wrongs they committed, even if we didn't approve of them. On the island the characters had been thwarted in their efforts to escape, and were now focused on trying to learn how to live on it. They joined with the Tailies and reluctantly learned to trust them, and now knew of a group of natives on the island, who they called the Others (setting up the Self/Other dichotomy that would become central to the show). The Swan station opened up a new world to them and caused them to ask questions about faith, and the literature referenced in this season — *The Third Policeman, The Turn of the Screw*, and the short story "An Occurrence at Owl Creek Bridge" — moved to more esoteric themes about life, death, and belief. The mystery of the Dharma Initiative was one of the pervading questions of the season: who were the members of the DI?

Why had they come to the island? What were they trying to discover or prove? The unveiling of the Pearl station brought a psychological angle to the series, with the survivors feeling like they were being watched and judged all the time. Desmond Hume's backstory ended the season with the idea of self-sacrifice and acting out of love for another person.

If season 1 was about trying to escape and season 2 was learning to live with the people on the island, season 3 was about dealing with the island's inhabitants. The Others moved front and center in this season when Jack, Kate, and Sawyer traveled to the other side of the island. Splitting up the survivors for the first time caused disorientation in the group (and, with many viewers, a disillusionment that led them to change the channel) and the cracks in the relationships on the island started to grow wider. The dark revelations of some of the characters in season 2 were elaborated on in season 3: Jin's mother was a prostitute and Sun had threatened to kill her if she ever revealed that to Jin; Hurley's father had abandoned him as a child; Locke's paralysis was caused when his father pushed him through a window; Jack's distant nature was caused by a . . . tattoo. We learned more about the Others, seeing the very unsympathetic Ben Linus's backstory and, incredibly, gaining sympathy for him the same way we did for the survivors in season 1. Juliet Burke had been brought to the island under false pretenses and wanted to go home as badly as anyone else. Suddenly the story was turning from a polarized us-versus-them scenario into a delicate argument for the notion that the Losties and the Others weren't that different after all. The writers' focus began to shift from philosophy and psychology to our first suggestion of physics, through allusions to Stephen Hawking's *A Brief History of Time*, a book that would take on more significance in the next two seasons. The literary references included children's books *The Wonderful Wizard of Oz* and *Through the Looking Glass*, both about being trapped in a world that isn't one's own, engaging in conflict, and finding a way back home.

In season 4, the outside world invaded the island of the form of the freighter. The survivors divided themselves into two groups — those following John Locke, the man of faith, and those who chose Jack, the man of science. The time travel hinted at in season 3 became a reality in season 4 with the Desmond-centric episode, "The Constant," which is one of the most important (and best) episodes of the series. We saw Ben travel off the island through space and time, and realized that six of the survivors were going to make it back to the outside world. With the arrival of quantum physicist Daniel Faraday, viewers had to try to understand more about wormholes and the science behind time travel. Books referenced in the season like *VALIS* and *Slaughterhouse-Five* explored the idea of a character's consciousness bouncing around through time and space, much like Desmond's did in "The Constant." The flashbacks became flashforwards, and we saw where our Losties would go in the future, since we'd seen where they'd already been. This intriguing plot device allowed viewers to know even more about the characters, and we were curious to know how they were going to end up in those future situations. Ben Linus moved to the foreground as a key character as his rivalry with John Locke grew, while we became privy to the fact that Widmore was Ben's mortal enemy. Again, despite all of the physics lessons and plot devices and heady literature, we were concerned about the Oceanic 6, the people left behind on the island, and even Ben.

Season 5 was about returning to the island, and learning that the island itself was an important "being," one that had so much power it could draw people back to it. Everyone who had left (with the exception of Aaron) returned to the island to finish what they'd started. Jack hoped to fix whatever was wrong with himself. Hurley didn't want to go back, but he had a sense that he should and that by doing so he might be able to help people. Kate wanted to find Claire and bring her back to her son, Aaron. Sayid returned against his will, in handcuffs. And Sun came back to find the husband she hoped had not perished. On the island, the characters blooped through various time periods as the island had become unmoored in time, and viewers were privy to flashbacks of previously unknown events on the island — the Others in 1954 (featuring an ageless Richard Alpert and a snotty young Charles Widmore), Rousseau's team in 1988, the island pre-nineteenth century. The characters ended up in 1974 and were part of the Dharma Initiative, which allowed us to see what the organization was all about.

The time travel that had been raised in season 3 and explored in season 4 was now integral to the series, but with it came an important question: could you change things? Was anything truly reversible? Could you go back in time and prevent something from happening by changing history? The show had been so steeped in the past through the characters' flashbacks — this of course illustrated that their minds were still deeply rooted in the past, often haunted by the things they'd done or seen. But now they were *in* the past, and had a chance to change things. While characters debated the particulars of time travel, Sayid finally stepped up and shot young Ben Linus in an attempt to eradicate him from the future. Meanwhile Jack was turning into a much different person than he had

Through the Looking Glass: The Mirrors

In almost every sideways-world story in season 6, we see one of the key characters look into a mirror, pause, and frown for a moment as if they're seeing something more than their usual reflection looking back at them. The imagery is meant to invoke Lewis Carroll's *Through the Looking-Glass*, where a young girl named Alice steps through the looking glass into a world that is very different from her own and comes to a different understanding of herself through the experience. It's also alluding to psychoanalytic critic Jacques Lacan's groundbreaking theory of the infant mirror stage. In his theory, which has become hugely influential in literature and literary criticism, he stated that somewhere between six and 18 months an infant first sees his reflection in a mirror and realizes it's him. The infant subconsciously realizes he is a being in the world, and the ego is formed because he sees himself as an object outside of himself and judges what he sees. This is a moment of joy, but after the mirror stage everything changes, and the child lacks the wholeness he had before he realized this separation. The characters who look in the mirrors throughout the season are experiencing a lack — they don't remember their actual lives, but there's a sense they are experiencing a nagging feeling that they should be remembering something — and the way they look into each mirror says a lot about who they are.

"LA X": Jack sees himself in the airplane bathroom; he pauses and looks more intensely at himself before noticing a cut on his neck that baffles him. (The marshal also looks into a mirror but he's a peripheral character and not important to the finale.)

"What Kate Does": As Kate opens Claire's bag and realizes she's robbed and terrified a pregnant woman, she looks into the mirror and sees herself for what she is. Like Jack, she pauses and leans in to look at herself longer.

"The Substitute": John sits before a cosmetic mirror and then pushes it away before he dials Jack's number (a call he doesn't complete). Interestingly, he doesn't actually look into the mirror, but if he did, his image would have been magnified. Just as Locke was always larger than life, this mirror is a reflection of that.

"Lighthouse": Jack looks into a mirror at his appendix scar, and suddenly can't remember when it was removed, as if the reality of having it removed as an adult was shoving aside his memory of having it out as a child.

"Sundown": Sayid sees his reflection in the glass of Nadia's front door, but he only sees half his face. Just as Sayid has always been split into two halves, in the sideways world he denies the lover side of himself and only allows himself to see the bad.

"Recon": James looks into the mirror and smashes it. He doesn't like the person looking back at him, and his action causes his image to be fragmented, the way James was always a shattered person on the island.

"The Package": Sun looks into a mirror as she makes her way to the door, and stops and looks more intently than anyone else does in the sideways world, as if she almost sees the other Sun. As Omar is pushing Jin into the refrigerator, Jin sees his reflection very quickly in the window of the fridge. Unlike Sun, he doesn't take a good look at who he is. In real life, Sun was a much different person than she appeared to be on the surface, and perhaps that's why she takes such a long, studied look at herself.

"Happily Ever After": As Desmond walks up to the police station, we see his reflection in the glass door, but it's not clear if Desmond sees it (he takes off his sunglasses as if he's looking at himself). Later, the dark silhouette of Daniel is seen in Desmond's limo window, but there are no details and you can't see Daniel's face. Perhaps that is an indication that he won't be crossing over with everyone else in the church.

"Everybody Loves Hugo": Hugo is the only one of the Candidates and key characters who does not look at himself in a mirror in the sideways world. However, because he doesn't really have to come to terms with much in that world because he was a good person in his own life, I'd argue that he sees himself reflected in Libby instead. When she looks at him, he sees the amazing person he is because that's what she sees.

"The Last Recruit": As Jack is scrubbing in to do the surgery on John Locke, he sees John's face in a mirror, and immediately recognizes him. John is anaesthetized, so he doesn't see his own reflection. Again, Jack looks but doesn't realize what he's looking at.

"The Candidate": When Claire shows Jack her music box, they both look in the mirror together. Jack turns it toward himself, and she moves out of the image, perhaps alluding to the fact they'd be separated from each other in their real lives.

"What They Died For": Ben looks into a mirror when he's being cleaned up after Desmond punches him. He's just had his flash, and it's like he's seeing who he really is for the first time. He makes a strange face, as if he's unable to reconcile the person he sees in the mirror with the person he's always been.

"The End": Charlotte looks at herself in a mirror and sees Daniel for the first time as a reflection behind her, and she turns to talk to him. When they shake hands, they don't have their revelation moment, as if neither one is ready to move on quite yet.

been, and we watched and worried about the fates of everyone on the show, noticing how much they'd changed from the beginning of season 1.

The books referenced in this season included *Ulysses*, *The Little Prince*, and *Everything That Rises Must Converge*, books that seemed to have only one thing in common. Each of these books is remembered for its ending (or, in the case of the latter, the endings of each of its short stories), showing the power of an ending and how it can alter one's assessment of the story as a whole. As we neared the end of the series, viewers and critics began focusing on how the show might conclude. Season 5 ended with a reveal of the mysterious Jacob, and an even more mysterious man sitting beside him, promising that season 6 would bring on the war that we all knew had been coming since the show began.

Season 6 brought together everything we knew from the first five seasons — the backstories of each of the characters; the knowledge of time travel, philosophy, physics, history, and literature that had been explored; the stories and themes of opposites on the island; the us-versus-them tensions that had informed so much of the show's drama — and pulled it into the mythology of the island.

Everything that had happened in the past mattered now. Every piece of literature referenced seemed to have some bearing on the ending. New literature referenced this season included works by Kierkegaard and Dostoevsky, putting the focus on existentialism and the idea of taking responsibility for one's actions and the angst that accompanies that task. All of the flashbacks we saw in the early seasons were integral to understanding how and why the characters would do what they did in the final episodes. We saw the history of the island through the perspectives of Alpert, the Man in Black, and Jacob. The characters who had dismissed John Locke's wackiness now realized he had been right all along, and the wisdom he had conveyed to them — even if at the time they saw it as nothing more than maniacal ranting — informed how the characters would go about doing what they did. The war ended, people died, and it's hard to say if the good guys or bad guys triumphed, simply because there were no clear-cut good or bad guys by the end of it.

Despite everything that has been explored on the show for six seasons, however, what always remained important were the characters. When we lost Boone, we knew that any character could be taken from us, no matter how important to the show. Despite being drawn in by the season 2 debate about science versus faith, we were more concerned about how Shannon's death would affect Sayid or whether Henry Gale's trickery was going to cause untold damage to the others. We were moved by Rose's reunion with Bernard, and saddened by Charlie's growing isolation from the group. We watched Claire become a doting mom, and Kate become attached to both Jack and Sawyer. We cried along with Hurley when he lost Libby, and struggled with our feelings about Michael: was he a parent acting in savage protection of his kidnapped child, or did he truly do something unforgiveable? We worried about the implications of Locke's mistake at the end of the season and wondered what it would do to this most earnest of people personally, and we swooned at the love story between Desmond and Penny.

In later seasons we grieved along with the other survivors over the deaths of Charlie, Eko, Charlotte, and Daniel. While "The Constant" introduced new heady concepts about consciousness and time travel, we were swept up in the elation of that wonderful phone call between Desmond and Penny at the end of the episode. We cheered as Hurley drove the Dharma van around in joyous circles with Sawyer, Jin, and Charlie laughing with him. We worried about the dark futures we could see in the flashforwards. And we were confused and devastated by John Locke's death.

Season 6 brought things to a close by focusing on the dichotomies of good versus evil and showing that opposites don't exist in black and white in the real world. But the exploration of existentialism took a back seat to the transformative deaths of Sayid, Sun, and Jin, who we lost in one profound moment. The speculation of who Jacob and the Man in Black were gave way to the emotion that rose up in us as we saw them as little boys, forced to live out a destiny that was out of their control. The episode that stands out as this season's masterpiece — "Ab Aeterno" — wasn't so much about physics or psychology as it was about a man's love for his wife and the lengths to which he would go just to see her again. This season gave us the best acting from the cast we'd seen all series, with Michael Emerson giving a powerful performance in his scene with Ilana in the jungle; Terry O'Quinn convincing us that the Man in Black was not John Locke, yet had subtle hints of him within; Josh Holloway showing us Sawyer's agony as a result of Juliet's death; Jorge Garcia showing us the more serious side of Hurley; Matthew Fox putting in an extraordinary season-long performance that showed us a world where Jack was actually happy, followed by a beautiful death scene. Every actor who appeared in the sideways world played the sideways version of their character as someone similar, but with subtle differences. At the end of the series we wanted everyone to be okay. No matter what concepts were explored over six years of the series, *Lost* was a show about people.

And that's where the sideways world comes in. In the final 10 minutes of the series, we discover that the sideways world was a place where everyone was actually dead, where they couldn't "move on" until they remembered their lives and could finally rid themselves of the burdens they had carried during their lives. They needed to remember their connections to other people, and they needed to realize they couldn't move on unless they did it *together*. We realize that it wasn't the Jughead bomb that created the sideways world, nor did it put the island at the bottom of the ocean; the characters each created their own scenario for themselves to work through the baggage they hadn't resolved in their lives, and the island simply didn't play a part in that, so it was at the bottom of the ocean, metaphorically, because it wasn't in their minds.

Some viewers have referred to the sideways world as a purgatory, but from a Catholic perspective, a place of purgatory is usually a place of punishment; Michael is trapped on the island and for him it is more of a purgatory; he's not quite in Hell, but rather imprisoned in a state where he is aware of the error of his ways. Other critics have referred to it as limbo. This term is perhaps a more apt one, because limbo is less a place of punishment than it is a space that exists between life and the afterlife, where people go after they die but stay if they cannot enter Heaven. Again, in the Catholic belief, limbo is a place where people had to remain until Christ would redeem them and give them entrance into Heaven (and where infants who haven't yet been baptized spend eternity). If Jack is seen as the Christ figure in this scenario, then we could draw the parallel of everyone waiting for Jack's arrival before they could all move on.

But the sideways world isn't exactly either one of these places. A more fitting interpretation of it would be to call it bardo, which is a term from the *Tibetan Book of the Dead*. According to scholar Francesca Fremantle, "*bar* means in between, and *do* means island or mark; a sort of landmark which stands between two things." The term refers to the world between birth and rebirth. According to the book, also called *Bardo Thodol* or *The Liberation Through Hearing During the Intermediate State*, there are three stages, or bardos, of death. The first occurs at death, when the body moves from a living consciousness to a non-living one and loses contact with the physical world. Now the physical body no longer exists, only the consciousness of that body. Then the mind enters the second bardo, which is a state of consciousness after death, where the deceased encounters several hallucinatory experiences, many of them brought on karmically by their former life. After the deceased goes through the visions, which range from gentle to terrifying, they enter a state of awareness and understanding. In some cases, a savior enters to help the person through this stage and lead them to the moment of awareness; this savior is "usually one that individuals formed a bond with in their former life." In the final bardo, the deceased's consciousness karmically travels to a new place where it is reborn, either in the physical world or in a heavenly one. Similarly, the sideways world is revealed in the finale to be a place where the characters are in a bardo state of in-betweenness, going through experiences that lead them to an ultimate understanding of who they were before they can move on. Poet Heathcote Williams once said that "death develops life's photographs," and that's what we see happen in the sideways world with these characters.

The key moment in the episode — and now one of the central moments of the series — is the discussion between Jack and Christian Shephard. Christian waits for Jack to realize that he's actually dead before he explains to him what the sideways world really is: "This is the place that you all made together, so that you could find one another. The most important part of your life was the time that you spent with these people. That's why all of you are here. Nobody does it alone, Jack.

You needed all of them, and they needed you." In other words, everything that happened to these people on the island really did happen, and when they were there, they made connections with other people, they shared intimate moments, and they realized things about themselves that they could only have done on the island. The pull back to the island for the Oceanic 6 was partly due to their sense of responsibility to do the right thing, but it was also because it just felt right. Jack said in "The Last Recruit" that it felt wrong to leave the island, because it was on the island where the most important things in his life had happened. At the end of season 5, he wanted to erase everything that had happened in his memory since September 22, 2004. What he didn't realize was that those experiences were vital to who he was. Like George Bailey in *It's a Wonderful Life*, Jack had to discover for himself that the impact he had made on the lives of everyone on the island — and the impact they, in turn, had made on him — was essential to who he was, who they were, and how the world had changed as a result. In his flash of recognition, Jack finally sees all of those moments where he really did fix things.

In the sideways world, time as we know it doesn't exist. That's why the timelines of the various characters in the sideways world don't actually match up (see p. 256). Each person was experiencing their own journey of self-realization at their own pace, and while their paths crossed, each was doing it on their own timeline. Christian says, "There is no *now*, here." The reason the writers exposed us to fiction like *Slaughterhouse-Five*, in which a character can visit various points of his life when his consciousness bounces through time, was so we could get our heads around this difficult concept. Time is fluid in the sideways world. They all arrived at the church at the same time, even though Charlie had died three years before Jack did, and Hurley may have died hundreds of years later. Kate and Sawyer may have lived to be senior citizens or they could have died earlier, but now they're all back at the church, and they look the same as they did when they were on the island, because that's the last place where they were all together. Aaron left the island as an infant, and that's why he looks like one in the church. Ji Yeon is still an unborn fetus, just as she was on the island. These people experienced their greatest joys and deepest sorrows on the island, and now they're back to commemorate the fact that they experienced those things together; and only together can they move on. But first, as we've seen all season, they have to remember their lives.

Memory has always played an immensely important role on *Lost*. In the first three seasons, we saw flashbacks of each of the major characters, showing us the moments in their lives that shaped who they were. In "The Incident, Part 2," Jack wanted to drop a bomb to destroy the island, thereby removing the experiences and all the memories of their time on the island. But in doing so, they would also erase the personal journeys they had taken, and change who they were.

The bomb doesn't work the way Jack expected it to, but the sideways world shows the viewers what would have happened to the characters if they didn't have the memories of the island with them. For the characters, losing those memories helps them to work through their emotional baggage, but the flashes of realization remind them of what they did have, and only then do they truly appreciate what really happened on the island. The memories of their real lives were not something to be forgotten, rather, these were events they should cling to and honor in their final moments. If we lose our memories, we lose much of who we are. The island showed them who they were. Jack begins to see the truth as he lowers Desmond into the cave, saying, "No more shortcuts, no do-overs, whatever happened happened. All of this matters."

Existentialist thinker Jean-Paul Sartre argued that our memories are interpretations of what actually happened, each memory filtered through the personality of the person having it. Even the act of remembering involves choice, because we choose what it is we want to remember. J.D. Rabb and J.M. Richardson, in a paper on the subject of memory in the television show *Dollhouse*, argue that it is through Sartre's idea of interpretive memory that the past, present, and future are all tied in together: "How we remember the past and thus how the past influences us in the present can be determined by our future goals," they write. "We not only choose our goals, we thereby also choose our memories, or at least *how* we remember the past." In other words, as our goals in life change, how we remember our past is also affected. As Jack begins to move toward a new goal that involves saving the island, he begins to reassess his interactions with John Locke — no longer is Locke remembered as the stubborn curmudgeon who selfishly clung to his delusions, instead he's the guy who had the necessary faith, something that no one else on the island did. Rabb and Richardson conclude that how we choose our future alters our memories of the past, which changes who we are in the present, or, as they put it, "the future (in terms of our sometimes newly chosen goals) reaches into that past to produce the present," thus proving we enact free will. In this situation, even the act of remembering seems to involve time travel.

Throughout the season, the sideways world felt like a place driven by karma, where things the characters had done in the island timeline affected things in this one. The concept of karma was introduced as far back as season 1's "Outlaws," where Sawyer could hear the whispers on the island saying, "It'll come back around." Now we know that the sideways world isn't a timeline at all, but it is true that what they did in their lives affected how they saw themselves in the sideways world. Once their sideways lives brought them to a place where they could connect with their real lives, they were able to "see" who they had really been, and when they put together the reality with the issues they'd been working through in the sideways world, each was able to see what truly mattered to them, dump their baggage, and be ready to move on.

We saw many of the characters have their flashes of realization, and it happened when they made a connection with something that they had in both worlds. In "The Constant," Desmond almost dies when he can't ground his consciousness in one place, and it's only when he realizes Penny is his constant that he stops bouncing. His connection to her is his anchor. And that is exactly what happens in the sideways world. Desmond has a momentary flash — he saw Charlie hold up his hand with the "Not Penny's Boat" message on it — because that represented one of the most important moments of Desmond's life. He saw something again when he was in the MRI machine, and he felt something pulling him to Penny. But it was only when he first took Penny's hand that the overwhelming nature of his love for her, his understanding of what she meant to him, and the connection that he felt for her hit him so hard he lost consciousness completely.

On the island, Desmond caught a glimpse of the sideways world, something no one else was able to do (unless, like Juliet, they were about to die). In the sideways world, he flashes not only to his life with Penny, but sees what else he did on the island, and realizes that he has to help everyone else see what he's seen in order for him to be able to move on (in Buddhism, this is called the bodhisattva vow, putting off one's departure until all the others have gone first). And so, he becomes a shepherd in the sideways world, guiding everyone else to see. Desmond's role shouldn't come as a surprise. His oft-repeated farewell line — "See you in another life, bruthah" — has always given us a hint that we'll see him in *another world*, and that Desmond will play a major role in that world. Jack has said the same line back to Desmond on a couple of occasions, which is fitting; Desmond is the first person to fully see the other world, and Jack is the last.

In his own life, Desmond had given up Penny to get his "honor back," and sacrificed his own happiness to pursue acceptance from Widmore. He spent three years pushing a button thinking he was saving the world, and ultimately turned a key assuming he would die in the process. After that he tried to become Charlie's savior, he led the Oceanic 6 to rescue, he risked everything to give a message to Eloise to save the people still left on the island, and he was torn away from his family in order to fulfill the mission he needed to finish on the island. Desmond has always put Penny and everyone else before himself. He's rewarded for it in the sideways world. Widmore gives him the acceptance that he always longed for and he's a successful man. But the one thing that made Desmond who he was — his connection with and generosity to everyone around him — was missing, and he found his way back to that by becoming the guardian, helping lead everyone else to their own moments of understanding. It's fitting that it would be Desmond who would do this, simply because "The Constant" was foreshadowing the sideways world three years before it happened: Desmond figured out that he needed to find a constant in order to find peace, and it was Daniel who helped him come to that conclusion. Similarly, in the sideways world, it is Desmond who achieves understanding first, and again it's with Daniel's help that he does so.

Sideways-world James Ford was still dogged by his past with Sawyer, but he wasn't destroyed by it. On the island, he'd dealt with the problem by throttling Cooper, but immediately realized that it didn't bring him the satisfaction he'd thought it would. Throughout Sawyer's life he probably thought a lot about what he had turned himself into because of his hate, and even though his feelings toward Cooper didn't change, he probably realized he had unneccessarily sacrificed a large part of himself in the process. So in this world, he chooses a different path, one that might give him some resolution but that won't destroy his life in the process.

Juliet had difficulties with relationships her entire life. As a child she watched her parents' divorce, and as an adult she married a tyrant who left her for his younger assistant. When she came to the island she became the other woman — first having an affair with Goodwin, then being with Jack, who seemed more devoted to Kate. She finally found Sawyer and when everyone else went away it looked like the two of them would have a happy life together . . . until Kate returned and Juliet saw the fondness Sawyer still had for her. Sawyer loved Juliet, but he felt deeply connected to Kate, and it was when he saw her that he realized he hadn't been able to let Kate go. However, when Juliet died, things changed, and it was only in losing her that Sawyer could feel clearly how much he had loved her. In the sideways world she's a successful fertility doctor, no longer losing women

Juliet and Sawyer's realization moment is where most *Lost* fans say they started crying, and for many, the tears didn't stop until the end. (Mario Perez/ABC via Getty Images)

and babies to the terrible, mysterious effects of the island, but bringing happy news to couples. She was married to Jack, and while it didn't work out, they had a son they both adore, and they seem to have a friendly relationship.

Juliet caught a glimpse of the sideways world in her final moments before dying, and her face was suddenly filled with peace as she lay in Sawyer's arms ("LA X"). And in the sideways world, her moment of realization happens when she touches his hand. While Sawyer had crossed paths with Kate in the sideways world and had a moment's pause as he walked by Jack in the hospital, it's Juliet who brings his memories flooding back. Juliet and Sawyer are each other's constants in this world, each pulling the other closer and facing eternity. As Juliet died in "LA X," Sawyer kept repeating, "I got you," but her final words to him seemed feverish and crazy, asking him if he'd like to go for coffee, offering to go Dutch. Now we realize she was bridging those worlds, seeing the conversation in hospital waiting room. As James comes to the same understanding, he holds her, repeating, "I got you" over and over, and meaning it.

Miles told Sawyer that Juliet's last thought was, "It worked," and we took that to mean that the bomb's detonation had caused the sideways world. Now we realize it didn't, so does that mean her words were a cheat? You can interpret her meaning in one of two ways — like Desmond, she caught a glimpse of the sideways world and believed it to be another place where they were actually living and happy. She can't be blamed for assuming they were alive in that world, the same way Desmond believed it when he caught a much longer glimpse of it. But perhaps the explanation is simpler than that: not only does she see the conversation they have about going for a coffee and begins repeating it, but when James unplugs the vending machine and plugs it back in, Juliet says, "It worked." Maybe Juliet was simply continuing to repeat the lines from their reunion. In "LA X," the last words Sawyer said to Juliet were "We're all gonna go home together." And after they come together in this scene, they move to the church where they will go home with everyone else, together.

Jin and Sun both have a constant in Ji Yeon. Sun sees her daughter on the ultrasound monitor and remembers the happiest moment she experienced on the island — seeing her baby move for the first time and realizing that it belonged to Jin, which connected her to Jin forever. During their lives together, Sun and Jin were frequently separated, but always found a way back to each other. They both blamed Daddy Paik for their problems, but in the sideways world, while Paik is still a force to be reckoned with, his plans to keep them apart once again fail. When Jin has his flash of recognition, it's also provoked by seeing the baby, which connects him to Sun, and the two of them see all of the key moments between them on the island — their quiet moment of understanding and love after Sun told him Ji Yeon was his, the explosion of the freighter, their reunions after so many separations. They look at each other and know what their lives had been like, and also know that they died together, their bond unbroken even in death.

Just as Ji Yeon was the constant that made Sun and Jin see the reality of the sideways world, Aaron is the constant for Kate and Claire. The moment that connected Kate and Claire for the rest of their lives was when Kate helped deliver Aaron. The woman who ran away from everything her entire life stuck around to help a baby be born, no matter how terrified she was. In the sideways world, she's put right back into the role of midwife, once again the first person to see him and to hand him to his mother. In this world, Kate is on the run from the police, but insists she didn't do it, and I believe her. In her life, Kate couldn't stop running, but in the sideways world, Claire and Aaron force her to stop, and her life slows right down the same way it did on the island. At the beginning of the episode, Kate is with Desmond and asks, "Why am I here?" Desmond replies, "No one can tell you why you're here, Kate." Only she can come to that understanding. Desmond can help lead her to that place, but she needs to find her constant to see for herself what happened. The moment she sees the top of Aaron's head, she has an instant flash of recognition, and similarly it's when she holds him up and hands him to Claire that Claire remembers everything.

In her real life, Claire was ready to give up Aaron, but the crash gave her no choice but to raise him herself. In doing so, she realized she never wanted to be apart from him, and then he was taken from her. In this world she once again is stopped from giving him up, and Kate — the woman who delivered Aaron to Claire on the island and then delivered Claire back to Aaron off the island — is the one who helps her do it. We don't see what happens to Claire and Kate after they leave the island on the plane, but Claire's happiness at seeing Aaron and remembering everything that had happened lets us know that when Kate and Claire returned to the outside world at the end of the episode, they were both able to remain an important part of Aaron's life and work together to raise him. They look at each other with the memories of what happened after they left the island, and there's a solidarity and deep friendship in their eyes.

Charlie had had a flash of something when he had a near-death experience in the bathroom in "LA X," and he tells Desmond in "Happily Ever After" that "this doesn't matter. None of it matters. All that matters is that we felt it." Like Desmond when he sees the sideways world on the island, Charlie doesn't quite understand the meaning of the flash, but he has a sense that the only important thing was that people see and feel what really mattered, and that the events in the sideways world were simply a means to that end. In his life, Charlie always wanted to help people, but people wouldn't let him. His father was a hard man; his weak brother Liam helped destroy him, and then abandoned him when Charlie needed his help. Before he died, we got a sense in "Greatest Hits" that Charlie was able to focus on the good parts of his life and realize it wasn't all bad, that he had had happy moments with both Liam and his father. In the sideways world, Liam appears at the police station looking concerned for his baby brother, so we know that Charlie has a more caring family in this world. But just as the #1 greatest hit on Charlie's list was the first time he met Claire, it's an image of Claire that first opens his eyes and tells him that the sideways world isn't what it seems; and it's when he grasps her hand that the memories of his life come flooding back to him. He knows exactly who Claire is and why she'd been so important to him — she and Aaron had given him the opportunity to take care

Charlie cherishes the "Living is easy with eyes closed" tattoo on his arm, but he realizes in this moment that life is happier with eyes wide open. (Mario Perez/ABC via Getty Images)

of someone else, and to save them, which is exactly what he'd yearned to do his whole life.

Hugo was one of the first to see the sideways world for what it was, possibly because he was the most open to looking closely at his life. Unlike the others, Hurley got rid of his baggage during his lifetime, and didn't have to work through it after death. He'd gotten past the curse of the numbers, he was no longer sensitive about people thinking he was crazy, and he'd become a leader, guiding his friends to Jacob and to their true purpose. He became the guardian of the island, and even helped make Ben Linus a good person, a feat in itself that cannot be overstated. Where everyone else's life in the sideways world was wrought with difficulties, Hugo is the self-proclaimed "luckiest guy in the world." He's uncorrupted by his lottery win, instead using it to spread goodwill throughout the world, just like the real Hurley could have done. He's lavished with awards, honors, and praise. He's filled with confidence. And the difficult moments of his past — including his father leaving the family, the accident that happened on the deck, his stay at a mental hospital, the death of his Grandpa Tito — never happened. The only thing missing from his life is a companion to share it with, and when Libby talks her way into his life and kisses him, Hugo gets his flash of recognition. No surprise it's Hurley who joins with Desmond to help him lead the others to their own self-discoveries.

One of those people was Sayid. His story is the saddest in the sideways world. If this is a place they created to work through their issues, he has created an unhappy place for himself. In his life, he kept trying to find Nadia; but here he denies himself the pleasure of having her. He will still kill when the situation calls for it, but he punishes himself perpetually for it. In "He's Our You," Ben tells Sayid, "[Y]ou're capable of things that most other men aren't. Every choice you've made in your life, whether it was to murder or to torture, it hasn't really been a choice at all, has it? It's in your nature. It's what you are. You're a killer, Sayid." Sayid denies it, but Ben's words go right to his core. Eventually, he embraces that darkness, and yet his final act is one of self-sacrifice. His entire life, Sayid told himself he was killing or torturing in order to protect those he loved. And in the end, he killed himself to save them. But now, sitting in Hugo's car, Hugo tells him that maybe he believes he's a bad person only because people have been telling him that his entire life. In the wise words of Hurley, "You can't let other people tell you what you are, dude. You have to decide that for yourself." And just then, Sayid sees a girl being pushed around in an alley. As he rushes over, takes care of the guy, and helps the girl up, it turns out to be Shannon, and he has his flash.

At the time of the finale, the fact that Shannon and Sayid were each other's constants was unsatisfying to me and to many other viewers. Are we really to believe that Shannon is the person who was so connected to Sayid that she would make him see the other reality? Why not Nadia? He spent a lifetime looking for her, pining for her, and the only time we saw him truly happy was when he was married to her for nine months. On the island, Sayid and Shannon began to feel an attraction, but the very same day they had their first date (a picnic on the beach), Boone was killed, sending Shannon into a depression. She spends about a week coming out of her funk, along the way asking Sayid to murder Locke, and when he refuses, she tries to do it herself. Their relationship lasted about two weeks in total, and more than half of that was steeped in misery. When Sayid shows her the shelter he'd built for her, they sleep together; she's dead less than a day later. How does this possibly compare to his life with Nadia? It just seemed like a ploy to work Maggie Grace into the script.

Now, for the viewers who liked seeing Shannon and Sayid together, there is something to be said for the two of them being each other's constants. Nadia was a regular reminder to Sayid of what he was and always would be. Nadia was not only a woman he loved, she was also a woman he had tortured. Just as he said he'd never get the look in Amira's eyes out of his memory in "Enter 77," he will never forget what he once did to Nadia. He might have found happiness with her, but after she was killed he turned into a cold-blooded murderer in her name. As Sayid sat by the well in "The Last Recruit," preparing to shoot Desmond, Desmond asked him what he would tell the woman he loved when she asked what he did to bring her back. It's another reminder that if he were ever to be reunited with Nadia again, she would only remind him of the terrible person he'd been. For Sayid, Nadia was ultimately unattainable, and to spare himself the pain of being with her, he has created a sideways world where she is married to his brother — close but off-limits. Shannon, on the other hand, only reminds him of how happy he was when he was with her. He was a shoulder for her to cry on when Boone died, and he made her feel loved and wanted, something he'd always wanted to do for another person. Nadia's constant question, "What did you do, Sayid?" always made him feel guilty, because she knew about the killer inside him.

Shannon had had a difficult life, even if her prima donna posturing on the island made us largely unsympathetic to her. She'd been very close to her father (one of the few father/child relationships that was actually positive on the show) and when he died, she was left with an uncaring stepmother who took everything from her without remorse. Shannon's future dreams of being a ballerina were dashed, and she was forced to keep turning to her stepbrother for assistance. Everyone told her she wasn't a good person, that she was selfish and demanding, and so she began to play the part. She felt unimportant and unloved, until Sayid came along and told her that her French-speaking skills were essential to helping him decipher some maps. It may have been the first time in her life when she felt useful, and as they began working together, she fell in love with him. When she was shot by Ana Lucia, Sayid had just reassured her that he believed her when she was saying she could see Walt, and having someone believe her — and believe *in* her — was something she'd longed to have her entire life. And so, as Sayid helps Shannon up from the alleyway in the sideways world, once again helping pull her out of a tough situation and being there for her, they remember each other, and Sayid sees in her eyes that, to her, he's not a torturer and a killer, but a lover; she in turn sees the man who made her feel good about herself. Sayid tortured Nadia; he nurtured Shannon.

And then there's John Locke. The island gave John a miracle. In the sideways world, however, he's still paralyzed and trying to work through his difficult feelings about his life and his future in a wheelchair. The island John Locke was a believer, made so because the island had shown him that destiny can make things happen that don't make empirical sense. In the sideways world, he's not given a whopping miracle, he can't walk, but he surely gets more subtle hints that there are larger forces at work: he runs into a spinal surgeon at the baggage claim department at the airport; he's hit by a car driven by a man who says he's trying to help him "let go"; he ends up back in Jack's hospital; Jack says words to him that feel like déjà vu, but he doesn't know where he's heard them before. The island gave John something undeniable that made him a believer on the spot; but the sideways world keeps him in the wheelchair and forces him to work harder to find faith. John has to put all of these moments together in order to come back to Jack and see if he'll give him a miracle . . . and Jack does. John's flash of understanding happens when he looks down and wiggles his toe (on the opposite foot that he wiggled in "Pilot," showing once again that things happening in the sideways world are mirror images of what happened in their lives) and he finds his constant. It could be argued that Jack was his constant, but we've seen him shake Jack's hand or talk to him with no recognition whatsoever: it would seem that it's the miracle of wholeness that is John Locke's constant. The island gave him that miracle in his life, and he was devoted to the island for the rest of his days. In the sideways world, it's Jack who gives him this miracle, and he shows his devotion and gratitude by trying to lead Jack to his own realization in turn.

Of all of the people in the sideways world, Jack resists seeing his life more than anyone else. Not only was he agnostic for most of his real life, but his constant is one that is more elusive than anyone else's. Before the other full-on realization flashes, many characters had a sense of déjà vu — Charlie saw a blonde woman in a vision, Desmond saw Charlie with the writing on his hand, Hurley had a peculiar look on his face when he saw the Santa Rosa van, James paused as he passed Jack in the hall. But the sideways world itself seemed to be trying in vain to prod Jack into seeing reality. The left side of his neck had a cut that got bigger as the season progressed, as if the island world was bleeding into the sideways one — now we realize it's the very gash that the smoke monster made as he pressed the knife into Jack's neck on the flats and told him, "I want you to know that you died for nothing." (The moment Jack realizes how important his life has been, the gash completely disappears.) On the sideways-world plane,

Rose told him to "let it go" after the turbulence, as if she'd already had her realization flash and was, like Desmond, trying to help Jack see the other side. Bernard, similarly, seemed calm and happy, and as he handed Jack the piece of paper with Cooper's name on it, he said, "I hope you find what you're looking for." Like Desmond, Bernard wasn't going to give Jack answers, but would give him the tools to find them on his own. Whenever Jack looked in a mirror in the sideways world, there was a look on his face like he was on the cusp of remembering something. He knew Desmond from somewhere, and thought Kate was familiar to him. He felt a connection to John Locke, and was driven to do more for him, like he knew he owed him something. And that connection to John is what causes Jack's first flash — the image of the two of them peering down the hatch at the end of season 2. The flash isn't enough to make Jack remember his life, so John Locke isn't his constant.

At the concert, Jack runs into Kate, and she looks at him, this time knowing him as the Jack Shephard she'd fallen in love with on the island. She sees him and says, "I've missed you so much." Again, we see in the final shot of the series that Jack died minutes after Kate left the island, and she probably went on to live many more years, remembering Jack and loving him for the rest of her life. Before she parted ways with him on the island, she asked him to promise her that they'd see each other again, but after making so many promises that he couldn't keep — the most recent one being the promise to Sun that he would get her and Jin safely off the island — he remains silent, knowing that he couldn't do that. In "Recon," Sawyer is watching *Little House on the Prairie*, and we hear Pa Ingalls say, "Life is about laughing and loving each other, and knowing that people aren't really gone when they die." The writers could have chosen any line from any episode of that show — they chose that one. Kate and Jack can be together again in this world, this place between death and the afterlife. She touches his face, and he sees a series of flashes of the two of them being together, of the immense joy and pain that their relationship brought to him. But again, the flash doesn't bring with it any recognition of where he is.

It's only when Jack gets to the church that he finally understands. Of all the people, he's the one who has the hardest time letting go. He spent his life trying to relieve people of their burdens while continually letting his own weigh him down. Throughout the series, the idea of being unable to let go has always been associated with Jack. When Jack was desperately trying to save Boone's life, it was Boone who finally told Jack to let him go. In a flashback, we saw Christian

Shephard tell Jack, "The problem is you're just not good at letting go." As the black smoke was about to pull Locke down into the hole, Jack held on as Locke shouted at him to let him go. In "A Tale of Two Cities," when Jack was imprisoned in the aquarium at the Hydra station, he could hear Christian's voice crackling over the intercom, saying, "Let it go, Jack." In the flashback of that same episode, we see Jack obsessively trying to find out the name of Sarah's new boyfriend, and Christian tells Jack to let it go, seeing how Jack's obsession is destroying him. In "Something Nice Back Home," just as Kate and Jack have begun their happy life together and he's asked her to marry him, he becomes caught up in needing to know where she's been going and who she's calling. His compulsion to know is tearing them apart, so Kate begs him to "just let it go," but he doesn't. In the sideways world, Rose tells Jack he can let go now when he's clutching the seat of the airplane. Jack tells Hurley on the island that maybe he's supposed to just let go, and it's only when he starts to do that on the island that he clears his mind and sees his purpose. And, as if that realization had somehow bled through to the sideways world along with the gash on his neck, Jack begins telling John that *he* needs to let go of *his* doubts and allow Jack to help fix him.

So in the church, when he places his hand on the coffin and suddenly sees his life on the island, Jack is taken aback for a moment, and then puts his hand back, letting the memories wash over him. In his flash we see all of the people that he helped on the island. He finally remembers his life, and opens the coffin to find it empty. He turns to his father and utters the words that prove he finally understands: "I died, too." Jack needed to let go of everything — his resistance to letting people help him, his compulsion to fix things, his doubts that his father actually loved him. His constant wasn't John, or Kate, or the coffin, or his father. It was all of them, and all of the other people waiting for him in the church. In life, Jack touched all of their lives and sacrificed himself to save most of them. He was, in turn, touched by all of them and they helped carry him through his Zen-like journey of self-discovery. The moment he touches the coffin he understands that he has helped many people, he has fixed things, and he was loved by his father. He can finally let go of the burdens, because the burdens have been turned into gifts.

In "Stranger in a Strange Land," Achara told Jack, "You are a leader, a great man. But this makes you lonely, and frightened, and angry." She marked him with a message saying that he may walk among people, but he is not one of them. That tattoo was yet another piece of baggage that Jack carried with him, and just as

Hurley tells Sayid that he allowed himself to be defined by the descriptions other people bestowed on him, Jack believes what Achara has written on him, even though it didn't occur to him that he actually *didn't* separate himself from other people. Dogen told Jack that he had to remain separate from his people so he could more easily make the decisions they didn't like. But Jack could never do that. He was always one of them, making the decisions and living with the consequences. From the first moments of the show, Jack involved himself in people's lives, talking to Rose the first day on the beach, getting to know Hurley, saving Claire's life, helping calm Boone by giving him a task to keep him occupied. He stepped up and took the leadership position when everyone around him was too worried and frightened to help themselves. Three years later, he stepped forward and drank Jacob's sacred water because he felt it was his destiny, and in doing so he saved everyone else from having to make their sacrifice. Jacob had passed an important message to him — "You have what it takes" — and in this episode, when Hurley tells Jack that he believes in him, it's the most important thing he could say to him.

Jack has always struggled with his feelings about his father, thinking his dad didn't love him, and the sideways world that he created was one where he could finally work through those doubts by understanding his father in a way he never could in his real life . . . by becoming one himself. As hard as this is for some viewers to accept, David didn't actually exist. He was a creation in the sideways world, one of the gentler hallucinations of the bardo that allowed Jack to put himself in his father's shoes and know that his father was as proud of him as he was of his own son. He represented Jack himself — John mentions how much David looks like him, and Jack's speech to David was the one he'd always longed to hear from his own father. But David also allowed Jack to become Christian. Jack had always been so caught up in thinking his father was working against him that he never realized that perhaps Christian was trying so hard to provide for his son and fumbling through this whole father thing because, quite simply, he'd never done it before. He was going to make mistakes. He was going to screw his kid up, even if he was going to try his damnedest not to. Christian probably believed he would be a better parent than his parents, and his father before him thought the same.

And when Jack fell into the same routine — not being there for David, working his fingers to the bone, all the while wondering why his kid was so morose and resentful — he suddenly saw Christian in himself. He talked to David, told him how he felt, and David for the first time realized his dad was a kid once, too. Jack finally understood that his dad probably felt exactly this way,

With the help of his father, Christian Shephard, Jack finally understands what the sideways world had been all along. (Mario Perez/ABC via Getty Images)

but unlike Jack himself, didn't know how to show it.

In the real world, Jack doesn't have a son. But it's only through creating that child in the bardo that he finds redemption, for himself and for his father. And he decides to break that cycle of "man hand[ing] on misery to man," as Philip Larkin once wrote, and he changes his life to be there for his son. He knows it will not only strengthen his relationship with David, but that it's probably the sort of relationship Christian always wanted with him, if he'd just known how to say the right words.

So when sideways Locke, fresh from his flash, tells Jack, "You don't have a son," it's the first step toward Jack's realization. David wasn't his son, but in fact, *he* was David. In "316" Jack put Christian's shoes on John Locke when Locke was in the coffin, but it was Jack, not John, who ultimately had to metaphorically walk in his father's shoes to find redemption.

Because Jack took the longest to let go, everyone else was already waiting for him in the church. They'd worked through their baggage earlier, and had come to terms with their lives, and when Jack finally did, they were all standing there waiting for him.

Not every character is in the church. Waiting for Jack is Kate, Locke, Libby and Hurley, Desmond and Penny, Boone (it's never clarified what or who his constant was), Shannon and Sayid, Bernard and Rose, Charlie and Claire (holding Aaron), Sawyer and Juliet, and Jin and Sun. Almost all of these people were on the beach when Jack first opened his eyes, and the reason Libby and Bernard are there is because they are the constants for Hurley and Rose. Desmond is essentially different. It was he who shepherded them all to the church in the first place, and his constant, Penny, is the only person who was not physically on the island when Jack opened his eyes. As mentioned earlier in the episode guide, it seems like Rose and Bernard had already had their recognition moment before sideways Flight 815, and therefore were acting like Desmond was, as shepherds who were helping Jack and John along the way, each one providing them with some much-needed advice to help speed up their recognition process.

But what of the missing? Michael is trapped in a purgatory on the island, and he is unable to come to the church. Walt is missing, and unfortunately his absence is due to nothing more than a technicality: the actor has grown up and at the time of filming the final scene was a couple of weeks shy of his 18th birthday, or, as Damon Lindelof joked in an interview a few days before the finale, "Malcolm David Kelley is now thirty-nine years old and six-foot-five!" As for Mr. Eko, according to reports after the finale, the actor, Adewale Akinnuoye-Agbaje, was asked to appear in the finale, but asked for five times the amount they were able to pay him, so they couldn't make it happen. However, prima donna theatrics aside, I believe we already saw a glimpse of the sideways world through Mr. Eko: when he died in "The Cost of Living," the episode ended with a poignant image of a young Eko, throwing a soccer ball up in the air as he walked down a sandy road with his arm around his little brother, Yemi. We know that at the end of the soccer game in his youth, first shown in "The 23rd Psalm," Eko was forced to shoot a man and then was taken away by the guerrilla army. But in death, the last image Eko sees is a world where that didn't happen, and where he walked away from the game happily with his little brother, heading off to a life where he wasn't turned into a nasty drug lord. In other words, we caught a glimpse of Eko's sideways world already, and it actually makes sense that he wouldn't be a part of the church scene at the end, simply because he didn't play a major role in the lives of the other people sitting there, save for John Locke.

When Eloise realizes that Desmond isn't going to heed her advice and is instead intent on "moving on," she stops lecturing him and suddenly looks sad, saying, "Are you going to take my son?" Desmond simply says, "Not with me, no." Eloise has obviously had her recognition flash and knows what her life was. The fact that she's not yet ready to move on means she hasn't come to terms with what she did in her life, and wants to remain in a state of limbo for as long as she can, still holding onto the one person she wants to be with more than anything — Daniel — whose death was not only by her hand, but by her premeditation. It was revealed in "The Variable" that Eloise convinced Daniel to give up music lessons so he could devote his life to physics — leading him to his discoveries, which would lead to his forgetfulness, which would put him on a freighter to the island, which would help everyone survive the time jumping and ultimately give them the tools to bring them back to 1977 . . . which would lead him into her camp, where she would kill him. As has been shown in previous Eloise episodes, she believes strongly in destiny, and in much the same way Abraham was willing to sacrifice his son Isaac because God told him it was required (see page 197), Eloise sacrificed her son to save the island and all of humankind. If Daniel hadn't been able to tell Jack how to drop the bomb, he never would have been able to get back to 2007 and stop the smoke monster that was now inhabiting Locke's body and threatening to destroy the world. But in season 5, Eloise's intentions seemed malicious, and viewers were shocked that a woman could do what she did to her own son. Now we see that she, too, believes that what she did was wrong, and since she clearly understands the nature of the sideways world, she has probably tried to work through over and over what she could have done instead. Could she have found another way to convey the information to Jack in 1977? Was there a way to go back in time and warn her 1970s pregnant self that the man in the camp was her son and not to shoot him? Because there's nothing she can do about it now, she will live with the regret of what she's done for eternity, and it's not clear if Eloise will ever be able to cross over.

Similarly, in "What They Died For," Desmond punched Dr. Linus, and Ben finally caught a glimpse of his life before this, flashing to Desmond hitting him on the dock in one of the lowest points of Ben's life. While that moment in itself didn't clue Ben in to the fact that the sideways world wasn't real, it seems to have paved the way, either because he slowly started piecing it together for himself, or perhaps in another flash involving Alex. (Michael Emerson revealed in an interview that they filmed a scene in which Ben was flipping through a yearbook and when he saw a picture of Alex he suddenly flashed to everything, but they decided to remove that revelation to make it more mysterious.) Regardless, by the time

John Locke encounters him sitting outside the church, you can tell Ben understands what's going on but isn't ready to move on. Like Eloise, he has a lot to come to terms with, and again it involves his child. Not only did Alex die because he allowed her to be sacrificed in the name of the island, much like Eloise did to Daniel, but he actually stole Alex as an infant from someone else. Many of the survivors saw the happy moments of their lives flash before their eyes in the sideways world, but Ben didn't have very many happy moments. Presumably, his years on the island with Hurley after everyone left went a long way to him finding redemption for the terrible things he'd done. Hurley coming outside of the church to tell Ben he was a great Number Two is one of the best moments of the episode — but Benjamin Linus has more baggage than perhaps anyone else in the series, so he still has a long way to go.

In his flood of memories, he would have remembered killing his father, the entire Dharma Initiative, John Locke, Charles Widmore, Jacob, and being responsible for Alex's death. He would have remembered the pain and fear he inflicted on hundreds of people, and his Machiavellian reasons for doing so. He would have been reminded of the fact that he wasn't special, but had done everything he did in the pursuit of specialness. He would have remembered that where everyone else in the sideways world was able to forget the little things that no longer mattered and hold onto the people who did (notice how Kate wasn't caught up in the quest for her toy airplane anymore, and just cared about her connections to people, for example) Ben lost everyone who mattered to him — often by his own hand. Unlike Eloise, he actually makes it to the church, as if he originally did plan to try to move on, but by the time he gets there, he sits outside the gates, unable to move any further, paralyzed by the awareness of the atrocities he's committed. Dr. Linus — the man who wasn't treated like dirt by his father, who wasn't pulled into the Others by Richard Alpert, who wasn't manipulated by Jacob and the Man in Black, the man who'd never killed a soul and wasn't consumed by jealousy and greed — is the man he created in the sideways world, a man who, without the island ruling his life, was a good, generous, kind, and caring man. Ben's sideways story best demonstrates how different a person's life could turn out as a result of different choices. The little Ben Linus we saw in "The Man Behind the Curtain" had the potential to grow up to be a good man. But because of a couple of incidents that were out of his control — his father's abusiveness, being shot by Sayid and taken to the Temple by Richard — and through a series of bad decisions he made throughout his life, he became a monster. It's that monster that Ben must learn to let go of, but it's going to take a long time for him to be able to do that. Until then, he'll remain outside the church, trapped in the purgatory of his own mind.

The other characters on the island who weren't in the church may eventually cross over, but right now they're not part of the journey. These are the people who experienced the island together, and now, together, they will move on to what awaits them on the other side of those brightly lit doors.

Jack's first major speech that helped buoy everyone up and bring the group of survivors together was his famous "If we can't live together, we're going to die alone" speech from "White Rabbit" (see page 151). From that moment, he has stressed the importance of everyone sticking together. Even in those moments when Jack separates himself from the group, when he needs to be alone (exhibited as recently as the end of "The Candidate" when he walks away from the survivors of the sub explosion to cry on his own in the water), Jack believes that the only way they will survive is by being together. When the group was separated after the Oceanic 6 left the island, it was Jack who pushed hard to return and to bring everyone back together. Every time the group has been split it has spelled disaster — in almost every instance, people are threatened, endangered, kidnapped, or killed. Now, in the final speech of the series, Christian tells Jack that the sideways world was a place they all made "together," so they could find each other in order to move on.

Sawyer tried repeatedly to separate himself from the rest of the group and be the solitary man on the beach, but he only truly came alive when he was making an effort to be with others. In "What Kate Does," he tells Kate, "Some of us are meant to be alone," but once again, when Smokey visits him, he returns to the group and helps lead them to freedom, rather than trying to go it alone. John Locke, on the other hand, separated himself from the group, and that was his mistake. He was right in his beliefs about the island, but wrong in the way he went about executing them. He spent more time alone in the jungle than being a part of the group, and when it came time to convince everyone that he was doing the right thing, they didn't believe him because he wasn't one of them. When he tried to get the Oceanic 6 to return to the island, he failed again for the same reason. John had separated himself from the others, and he died alone in a hotel room. In the sideways world, when Miles is trying to convince Sawyer to go out on a blind date with Charlotte in "Recon," he jokes, "Do you want to die alone?" Even Miles sees the importance of sharing one's life with friends and family. On the island, Jack and Claire never opened up about their lives to one another and therefore never figured out they were related, but in the sideways world he immediately invites her to come and stay at his house, telling her they're no longer strangers, but family.

Perhaps the biggest mistake Mother made was when she took her two adoptive boys to the cave and told them she wouldn't be able to protect the light forever, and instead it would fall to one of them. As Jacob's brother gazes on the cave, his face is alight with wonder; Jacob looks sceptical. If she'd said, "It will have to be both of you," they might have worked together. They might not have fought and ultimately killed one another. When the Boy in Black realizes that his mother had deceived them, he leaves, but he first wakes up Jacob and begs him to come with him, saying "I don't want to go by myself." Two thousand years later, Smokey looks at Sawyer in the cave and offers to take him and everyone else off the island and never look back. "And how do we do that? Together." Of course, Smokey has ulterior motives, as we later saw in "The Candidate," but even then, he didn't kill them off one by one — he pulled them together to kill them together. What he didn't count on, surprisingly, was that their strength was in *being* together.

Hurley seems to have realized the importance of working together — on the island, he almost never did anything alone. He built a golf course so the group could come together and do something fun. He accompanied the groups on their treks. Even when he wanted to turn back, if no one would come with him he'd stick with the group instead. Hurley was always seen with Charlie, and then he was partnered with Miles. He saw the importance of keeping people together and treating everyone like his extended family. And that's why he is the perfect choice to be the guardian of the island. Hurley has always been the heart of the show, so it makes sense that he would be the guy to protect the heart of the island.

In a pivotal scene in "Everybody Loves Hugo," Richard Alpert calls Hurley's bluff when he yells at him that Jacob couldn't have told them what to do because "Jacob *never* tells us what to do!" And normally, Richard would be right. As we saw in "Ab Aeterno," Jacob prefers to let other people make their own decisions. But he's different with Hurley — Hurley alone gets direction. In "LA X" he told Hurley to take Sayid to the Temple; in "Lighthouse" he told Hurley to take Jack to the lighthouse and told him exactly how to do it. Hurley was the only person to whom Jacob gave instructions on how to return to the island, and he must have known that Hurley would do it because he entrusted to Hurley his letter to be delivered to Dogen (in the guitar case). In "What They Died For," Hurley was relieved when Jack drank Jacob's eternity water, muttering, "I'm just glad it wasn't me." He was still afraid to be leader, but Jack instills in him the confidence that he needed, because all along, Hurley was the best man for the job.

In my companion guide for the show's third season, I wrote, "the world could crumble around [Hurley] and he'd still be standing," and in this episode, it literally does, and he's still there. Of all the numbers to have assigned Hurley, it's fitting that Jacob paired him with the number 8. The numeral 8 is a sign of eternity, and if we can assume the water Jack had him drink made him immortal, Hurley would have outlasted all of them. But he didn't do it alone.

Scenes between Ben and Hurley have always been highlights (bickering in the jungle, sharing a chocolate bar), so the idea of them having a long, long future together is perfect. (Chris Pizzello/AP Photo)

Jacob protected the light for two millennia on his own. His mother did it alone for an untold number of years before that. Jack protected it on his own . . . for a couple of hours. But as soon as the torch was passed to Hurley, he looked immediately to Ben and asked if he would help him. He was the only person who didn't have the hubris to think he could do it alone. Now, he can make his own rules, and Ben will help him (and can I just say, I would love to see what Hurley's rules would be — infinite amounts of ranch dressing allowed without any weight gain? A full amusement park erected in the center of the island? A Mr. Cluck's Island Chicken Outlet on the beach?). Hurley knew he would need help, like John Locke knew he couldn't push the button alone, and just as all of the people in the sideways world couldn't have had their flashes of realization without a real connection to at least one other person. And now, they can't cross over until everyone is there. "Nobody does it alone, Jack," Christian says to his son, and he leads him out to where everyone is sitting.

The church scene almost doubles as a cast wrap party, as we see the characters (and actors) shaking hands, saying hello and goodbye to one another, and enjoying each other's presence. The setting of this scene has been the subject of most of the controversy surrounding *Lost*: people wondered why Darlton went for a spiritual ending rather than one more secular. Perhaps they could have chosen a setting that didn't have religious overtones, rather than placing it in a church. However, the final scene was very much intended to be spiritual; the characters don't have to believe in a god, they just believe in each other. Regardless of the setting, it's the togetherness of everyone that lends this scene its spirituality.

The final couple of minutes of *Lost* are glorious. We cut constantly between Jack being reunited in the church with the people who meant the most to him in his life and the real Jack, stumbling through the jungle after he'd fulfilled his life's purpose. Mortally wounded, he realizes he's fixed some things but can leave the rest of them for others to fix, and he's left the island in good hands. We see sideways-world Jack welcomed by the people who once questioned and resented his decisions, the same ones who now acknowledge they couldn't have had the lives they did without him. Island Jack looks up to see the plane flying overhead, and chuckles because his friends are getting off the island. And in a beautiful moment, Vincent comes bounding through the bamboo, just as he did three

The final shot of *Lost* – a mirror image of the opening shot from the first episode – has already become an iconic television moment. (Mario Perez/ABC via Getty Images)

years earlier, only this time he curls up at Jack's head. With the dog by his side, Jack Shephard doesn't die alone.

In the sideways world, with all of his friends at his side, Jack moves on to the next stage of his existence. The screen is filled with beautiful white light. On the island, Jack closes his eyes, and finally, beautifully, peacefully . . . lets go.

Highlight: There are so many it's hard to choose just one: Sawyer referring to Desmond as "the magic leprechaun"; the grin on Hurley's face when he sees Charlie at the motel; the look on Sayid's face when Hurley tosses an unconscious Charlie into the back of the Hummer; the note that Hurley sticks on Charlie at the concert that reads "Bass player, wake up for the show"; Charlie mumbling to Charlotte, "I was shot by a fat man"; Kate shooting Smokey (yeah!!); Frank screaming at Ben not to bother him and Ben saying to the others, "Sounds like they're making progress"; Miles saying, "I don't believe in a lot of things, but I believe in duct tape"; the ending.

Did You Notice?:
- The stickers on the cardboard box Christian's coffin was shipped in bore the following airport stickers: GUM (Guam, a reference to where the Ajira flight had originally been headed); BWN (Brunei); HKG (Hong Kong); and LAX.
- Kate touches Desmond's hand in the car and the camera zooms in on their contact, as if highlighting that she touches his hand and has no revelatory moment; Desmond was never important to her on the island.
- When Sawyer first comes upon Jack after his "inauguration," Jack is talking to himself. Some fans speculated that he was blessing the water in that instant by saying Jacob's incantation, because when he later gets Hurley to drink the water, he doesn't say the incantation first. If he'd already blessed it in advance, then whoever would drink it could take over as guardian from him.
- There are two *Star Wars* references in the opening act (see *Finding Lost — Season Five*, p. 195): Hurley says Jacob's elusiveness is worse than Yoda, and then he says, "I've got a bad feeling about this," which is a line said in every *Star Wars* film.
- During the credit sequence that runs during the second act, every actor who appears in this episode and was ever a cast member is now listed as one once again (Zuleikha Robinson is also listed, even though she doesn't appear). François Chau is credited for the first time: despite appearing in

many episodes, both live and in Dharma videos, he was never credited as Pierre Chang (or Martin Candle, Edgar Halliwax, or Mark Wickmund).
- Charlie is staying at the Flightline Motel. This is the motel where Kate was staying in the flashback in "Born to Run" where she dyes her hair and asks for a letter from the front desk, the motel where Anthony Cooper was staying when John brought him his money and was caught by Helen in "Lockdown," and the motel where Sayid took out the guys with the old "chef's knives in the dishwasher" trick in "Because You Left."
- Kate says to Jack, "Nothing is irreversible," which is what Jack said to John Locke in the baggage claim area in "LA X." On the island, Jack reverses the evil that the smoke monster has unleashed on the island, and in the sideways world, the characters are able to reverse some of their actions to get beyond them.
- As Sawyer walks away from the well, he says, "I'll be seein' ya," which is an oft-repeated line in the 1960s series, *The Prisoner*.
- Seeing Vincent's footprints around the well made the dog seem like Lassie; "Timmy" (who in this episode was played by Desmond) was stuck in a well, and the dog helped get him out.
- When Miles calls James, James is doing a crossword puzzle. On the back of his paper there's a column called, "Ask Me!" Perhaps that's an inside joke among the writers; after all, if they were the ones writing the column, they'd probably keep saying the answers to the questions would be in the next issue.
- Juliet goes by the name Juliet Carlson in this timeline; Carlson was her maiden name in her life.
- The way Juliet describes the fetus on the ultrasound is much the same way she described it in "D.O.C." when she did the ultrasound for Sun in the Caduceus station on the island, pointing out the baby's heartbeat as a "flutter" and telling her it looked very strong.
- As Miles and Richard get ready to go to the Hydra island, Richard tells Miles that he wants to live. His reaction is similar to the one in "Ab Aeterno," when he told Jacob he wanted to live just as Jacob was dunking his head under the water.
- James enters the hospital to protect the very people who, in his life, he believed he had killed accidentally.
- Listen to the musical motifs throughout the episode: when Richard discovers

his first gray hair, you can hear the Isabella theme playing. As Desmond talks to Jack about the other world he's seen, you hear the Penny and Desmond love theme. Sayid's motif plays when Hurley tells him he's a good guy. And at the end, as Ben sits outside the church, you can hear Ben's discordant theme playing, only it sounds like it almost finds a resolution in a slightly altered version of it.

The Flightline Motel sign — used in several episodes — was resurrected for use in the finale. (Courtesy Ryan Ozawa)

- The knife that Smokey stabs Jack with is the same one Ben used to kill Jacob.
- Smokey dies on his back, in the same position that we'd seen John Locke in so many times throughout his life.
- The sun comes back out the moment Smokey dies, as if the storm was pathetic fallacy that was supporting the wave of evil that Smokey represented.
- Jin looks like he's going to laugh when James walks in and introduces himself as Detective Ford.
- Juliet tells James that the best way to make the vending machine work was to unplug it and plug it back in; in a sense, Desmond unplugs the machine of the island, and Jack plugs it back in to make it work again.
- The Oceanic water bottle that Ben hands to Jack is the one that he pilfered from Sawyer's tent in "Dr. Linus."
- The ritual of assigning guardianship seems to devolve with each passing of the torch: when Mother gave it to Jacob, she gave him wine in a chalice; Jacob gave Jack stream water in a metal cup; Jack gives Hurley muddy rainwater from a puddle in an old water bottle. (Jack doesn't appear to say the

incantation, but perhaps his rules don't require it.)
- In the room in the back of the church, Jack passes various religious artifacts that show the church doesn't belong to one faith: there are crosses, menorahs, Buddha statues, beads, and a stained glass window with the symbols for Islam, Judaism, Hinduism, Christianity, Buddhism, and the yin/yang symbol of Taoism.
- As Jack stumbles through the bamboo forest, he passes an old, dirty tennis shoe. He'd passed this same tennis shoe on his way out of the forest in the pilot episode — it was white and brand new then — and many fans speculated that it was one of Christian's tennis shoes that he'd been wearing in the coffin.
- Christian is wearing the white tennis shoes in the church.
- Kate is wearing a different outfit when Jack walks into the church (she's ditched the little black dress and switched to a greenish-teal blouse and dark skirt). It is more appropriate to her character, and could represent how she perceives herself, or how Jack sees her.

Interesting Facts: Matthew Fox said that he knew from the beginning of the series that the final shot would be Jack's eye closing.

Only Matthew Fox and John Terry had the pages of the script containing the scene in the back of the church; the rest of the cast did the church scene without knowing the full explanation of what the sideways world was or where their characters were going after the church scene.

When interviewed a week before the finale, Nestor Carbonell talked about why he thought it would be successful: "[*Lost*] has people talking about Biblical themes, mythological themes and literature, science versus religion. The big questions in life — incredible questions. At the heart of the show are these characters that they created, these really complex characters layered with so much misbehavior. No one is completely good and no one is completely evil. They are just well drawn out characters and that's the heart of the show. I think the finale, without giving anything away, will bring some resolution to a lot of the dynamics between those characters and relationships."

When asked about whether or not the finale would answer all of the questions, Henry Ian Cusick offered, "There was a point in the show where I thought I don't care about the answers anymore . . . I knew what I wanted from the ending and what I wanted the message to be. I like this thing of it coming from a place of love and coming from a place of no fear. All of a sudden it just seemed a lot bigger. Small questions, I just thought, 'I don't care anymore.' I don't care why I can see the future. It didn't matter. It just seemed to be bigger than that." He added, "You know I get asked why Desmond wasn't on the plane at the beginning of season six . . . He disappeared and you didn't see him again. People were making a big deal out of that. I think he just went to the toilet. Sometimes the answers are as simple as that."

The finale pulled in 13.5 million viewers, which was its highest ratings in two years.

Nitpicks: I really wish Smokey hadn't kept talking about how there was a storm coming and it was "gonna be a bad one." It was such obvious foreshadowing (the writers used the same bad dialogue in "Across the Sea" when Jacob commented that a storm was coming just before his mother and brother were killed). How did Ben get free? One minute he's trapped under a tree and the next he's wandering onto the flats. For a moment it looked like he was permanently trapped, and then it turned out to be nothing. When Jin speaks to James in the hospital room, there's no trace of a Korean accent whatsoever. When Jin died, he was far from speaking perfect English, so why would he suddenly be speaking English with an American accent (i.e., Daniel Dae Kim's real one)?

Although Richard Alpert and Desmond Hume never appear together on-screen, they're both motivated by their deep love for another person. (ML Agency)

Oops: I understand that Smokey is impervious to bullets, but is he wearing a magic shirt as well? There isn't a single hole in it no matter how many bullets hit him. Yet back in "Sundown," when Sayid stabbed him, it left a huge hole in the shirt under the pocket (that magically disappeared a few episodes later).

4 8 15 16 23 42: In the sideways world, Locke is in room 218. Claire, Kate, and Desmond are sitting at table 23 at the concert. The number Sawyer punches in for the Apollo bar is G23.

It's Just a Flesh Wound: Desmond is blasted with a lot of electromagnetic energy when he moves the stone and loses consciousness. Jack jumps on Smokey's back and hits him in the mouth. Smokey knocks Jack unconscious by hitting his head on a rock. Jack and Smokey have their wicked Mortal Kombat fight on the flats, where they run at each other, strangle each other, Smokey stabs Jack between the ribs, and holds the knife to his neck. Kate shoots Smokey. Jack kicks Smokey off the ledge and he dies in his fall. Jack crashes to the ground when the rope slips as he's lowered into the cave. Jack is exposed to large amounts of electromagnetism and loses consciousness. Jack dies in the forest.

Any Questions?:
- Nope, that finale cleared them all up, thanks! Okay, fine. See page 289.

Ashes to Ashes: RIP Jack Shephard.

"There Is No *Now*, Here": The Sideways Timeline

When Christian says to Jack, "There is no *now*, here," he suggests that time is fluid in the sideways world. Everyone is having their own experiences, and eventually they'll all meet at the church, but they're definitely all doing things at their own pace. What appeared to be huge continuity errors throughout the season can now be explained by the fact that time moves differently for everyone in the sideways world. The timelines don't match up because time doesn't work the same way in the sideways world as it does in the real world.

The same day the flight arrives from Sydney, Desmond goes to see Charles Widmore, then picks up Charlie from the police station, is involved in the car accident, leaves the hospital, goes to see Eloise, talks to Daniel, meets Penny, has his flash of realization, and begins his quest. Everything seems fine . . . except for the fact that Eloise was setting up the cutlery, napkins, and tablecloths for the outdoor concert as if it was happening that night, but we know it won't happen for at least another week.

Desmond meets Hurley a week later at Mr. Cluck's, the day after Hurley had met Libby for the first time. He encourages Hurley to follow up with Libby, and Hurley goes to Santa Rosa either that afternoon or the next day. He sees Libby, and the day after that they decide to go on a picnic on a beach. Hurley has his flash of realization, Desmond watches, and then drives to the high school where he mows down John Locke. John is rushed to the hospital.

Jin and Sun leave the airport after Jin is detained, and that night at the hotel Jin says he's going to the restaurant, and Sun tells him the watch delivery can wait til the next morning. The next day Keamy shows up at the room and takes Jin down to the restaurant while Mikhail takes Sun to the bank. Mikhail returns to the restaurant, he and Sun are both shot, and Jin rushes her to the hospital. This is the day after they were on the flight, yet she's wheeled into the hospital alongside John, who was run down by Desmond over a week after the flight.

Sawyer pulls the con job on Ava the evening the flight arrives (Wednesday), then has his blind date with Charlotte on Thursday. On Friday he argues with Miles, who quits as his partner, and a day or so later he shows Miles the Sawyer file. Kate slams into him in her car and they hold her in a temporary cell.

Sayid goes to see Nadia and his brother, and on his first night there, his brother asks him to help him with a problem and he refuses. The next day his brother is attacked and taken to hospital. Sayid returns to the house to take care of the children while Nadia stays in the hospital. A couple of days later, he's taken to the restaurant, where he shoots Keamy and his men . . . except in the Jin/Sun timeline, they were shot about two or three days earlier. Sayid rushes back to Nadia's, where he's caught by Sawyer and Miles. Even that is a time discrepancy: Sayid leaves the restaurant and heads back to Nadia's to pack up and leave quickly. In the meantime, Jin has to slowly try to cut himself free at the back of the restaurant, then walk out to the main kitchen, confront Mikhail, shoot him, and call an ambulance for Sun. Miles and Sawyer would have gone down to the restaurant, checked out the scene, probably questioned Jin, then headed back to the station, watched the security tape to find Sayid, run his face through a database to find out where he was staying, checked his passport in the system, figured out he was at Nadia's, jumped into the car to get there . . . and arrived at Nadia's at the same time as Sayid. Unless Sayid stopped on his way home to visit a few old torturing buddies, it's not likely they would all have gotten there at the same time.

It's hard to say how long a period is covered in "Dr. Linus." Ben is told to cover detention for the week, starting the Monday after the flight. He complains in the lunchroom on Monday, where John chimes in, and then talks to his father that night. The next day he attempts to stage his coup d'état, and Reynolds turns the tables on him. Alex has her recommendation in hand by Wednesday, and Ben gets Reynolds to reinstate the history club. It could have happened over a week or so, but it's likely that it all happened on the Monday and Tuesday before Locke's accident on Wednesday.

Locke is run over by Desmond and has emergency surgery, and he recovers in the hospital for a few days before returning to the school. Desmond shows up at the school again, only this time, he beats up Ben Linus. He goes down to the police station and turns himself in, and it's supposed to be around the same time that Kate and Sayid were detained (since they were all in temporary custody), but Sayid and Kate were put in the cell on Monday or Tuesday, and Desmond would have been there later that week or early the following.

Claire gets out of the hospital probably a day or two after the flight, finds out about the adoption agency and makes an appointment. She meets Jack, but he's pulled out of his first meeting with her to rush off for Locke's surgery, which happened a week after the flight, so we know it's also a week later for Claire. She reappears at the hospital later that day as John's coming out of his anaesthetic, and Jack asks her to come and stay with him. The next morning when she wakes up, David talks about the concert as if it will be that night, but we know it won't happen until the night of John's second surgery.

John Locke had to have had some recovery time from spinal surgery, and from the "welcome back!" he gets from one of his students, it's clear he was away for a few days. But the concert happens, according to Miles, about a week after Flight 815. So the concert date simply doesn't line up with Locke's schedule at all. Sun only recovers for less than an afternoon before heading over to the church, which happens a few hours after the concert, and for her it's only about three days after the flight. For Jack it's about a week. For Desmond it's closer to three weeks. Eloise is acting like it's the same day as the flight. For Sayid it's about five days. For Claire it's on the eighth day. There's no continuity at all in the timeline of the sideways world, but that's because time doesn't exist there. There's no *now*, here, as Christian says. It makes sense that the events wouldn't be lining up, because each of the characters died at different points in the real world timeline, so it stands to reason that their journeys in the sideways world would be happening at whatever pace each of them needed.

The Stand by Stephen King (1978, 1990)

Since *Lost* began, Carlton Cuse and Damon Lindelof have been citing Stephen King's *The Stand* as the show's most significant influence. After season 2, Cuse said the writers are "never without a copy of *The Stand*" in the writers' room. They have admitted that Charlie Pace was an homage to a major character in King's book, and that early on they'd been drawing parallels between John Locke and Randall Flagg. They compared their method of telling a very long, epic story over several hours to King's epic saga that spans over a thousand pages. I can't even begin to do this incredible book justice here, so I urge you to read it for yourself to see *Lost* in an entirely new and much richer way.

Stephen King's apocalyptic novel was first published in 1978 and was set in 1980. After its immense success throughout the following decade, King reissued it in 1990, updating the story's timeline to 1990 and restoring all of the sections of the book that had been cut. The mass market edition now stands at nearly 1,200 pages, and is an exploration of good versus evil and free will versus destiny. (Sound familiar?)

The book opens with a man named Charlie anxiously shaking his wife awake, telling her they have to leave quickly, grabbing their three-year-old daughter, throwing a few belongings in a car, and racing off the government compound where they are living. Charlie has developed a mysterious cough, and knows a virus has been accidentally unleashed on the base, and he needs to get his family out of there. As they race to the gates, he swears that if they're closed he'll smash the car through them. But he doesn't need to worry; they're open. And if they hadn't been open, none of the chaos of the rest of the book would have happened. The inside of Charlie's car will ultimately become Ground Zero of the worst plague in human history.

In Book 1, entitled "Captain Trips" (the virus's nickname throughout the book), we watch as the virus spreads rapidly via human contact. We meet most of the main characters of the story who are immune to the virus, and watch them lose their loved ones and realize how alone they are in the world.

Stuart Redman is one of a group of men sitting at a gas station when Charlie's Chevy slowly rolls into the station and crashes into a pump. He's standing there when the car door is opened and everyone around him is infected, but once word gets out that the superflu is spreading and that it started at the gas station, he, along with everyone else who'd been exposed, is brought in by government authorities for observation. When he shows absolutely no symptoms of the flu while everyone around him drops dead, the authorities become suspicious that he's still a carrier and send government agents to kill him. He escapes and begins his journey to find others who are immune to the virus. Along the way he meets Glen Bateman, a university sociology professor who is incredibly insightful.

Frances Goldsmith has just discovered she's pregnant, a fact that leaves her boyfriend speechless and her parents angry, especially her mother. Both parents die of the superflu a few days later and she buries them in the backyard. The only other survivor in her entire town is Harold Lauder, an overweight nerd from school who is the younger brother of Frannie's best friend, and who has a crush on her. Knowing how obnoxious and intolerable he can be, Frannie has no choice but to join with him as they set off on their own journey. At the end of Book 1, Frannie and Harold meet up with Stuart and Glen Bateman.

Larry Underwood is a hitherto unsuccessful musician who has suddenly reached one-hit-wonder status with his hit single, "Baby Can You Dig Your Man?" He takes full advantage of the excesses of his fame, becoming an intolerable jerk and alienating his friends, and he eventually returns to his mother's apartment in New York City with his tail between his legs. She catches the superflu and he watches her die, and he meets an older woman named Rita on his way through the city. They become lovers, but separate when he has an argument with her. He decides he needs to leave the city, and the only way to do that is through the Lincoln Tunnel. His harrowing journey through the 1.5-mile tunnel in complete darkness, climbing over corpses as he goes, is the gory centerpiece of this section of the book. Rita rejoins him partway through, and they continue walking together. They make it to the other side, and Rita overdoses on sleep medication, leaving Larry alone and guilt-ridden that her death was somehow his fault.

Nick Andros is a deaf-mute who is first introduced to us when he's beaten up by thugs in a bar and hauled into jail for fighting back. He communicates by writing on pieces of paper and befriends the sheriff and his wife, helping the sheriff track down and arrest the men who beat him up. When the sheriff and his wife become sick, Nick is appointed deputy and watches the men die of the superflu. He eventually lets one of them out, which turns out to be a mistake, and he is almost killed as a result. When the other man dies, Nick hops on a bicycle and sets out to find others like himself.

Lloyd Henreid, along with his partner in crime, Poke Freeman, sets off on a killing spree across the southwest that ends with Poke's death and with Lloyd being thrown in prison. The other inmates begin dying of the superflu, and then the guards begin dropping, and suddenly Lloyd realizes he's alone in a prison cell and no one is going to come to get him. He begins to go mad, eventually reaching through his cell bars and pulling a body over, thinking he's going to have to eat it. But then a dark, eerie presence without a face, Randall Flagg, shows up. Randall taunts him, and eventually frees him on the condition that Lloyd will be his right-hand man — "Going to put you right up there with Saint Peter." (The scene is very similar to the one in "Ab Aeterno," when the smoke monster frees Richard Alpert from the bowels of the ship as long as Alpert agrees to help him.) He gives Lloyd a black stone with a red flaw in it to indicate he is now with Flagg.

"Trashcan Man" is a pyromaniac who celebrated his solitude by blowing things up before he broke and then burned his arm, which healed at a weird 90-degree angle. He's had a rough childhood because of his schizophrenia, and is haunted by the kids who mocked him for being different when he was a child. He hears voices in his head, which constantly make fun of him, and which cause him to set more fires and explosions. He heads out of town on a bicycle, searching for Randall Flagg, whom he knows of intuitively from his dreams.

Aside from introducing us to many of the main characters, Book I is an account of the plague and how it killed off 99.4 percent of the world's population. King breaks up the main narrative several times to simply list one death after another, showing how quickly the virus could spread, and forcing readers to realize how doomed we would be if something like this really did hit the human population. Once the flu has devastated humanity and the only survivors are the ones who were mysteriously immune to it, he includes a harrowing chapter that lists off how some of the survivors of the superflu die later thanks to accidents or extenuating circumstances. Each of the characters in the book is haunted by Randall Flagg (whom they refer to as the Dark Man or the "Walkin' Dude"), who appears to them in their dreams, causing either extreme fear or loyalty. When the Dark Man ultimately shows up in person to see Lloyd Henreid in his jail cell, it is clear that he represents evil. He has been around for all time, but he seems to keep being reincarnated, because other than brief snippets of memory, he doesn't remember exactly who he was before. His initials are always R.F.

Book II, "On the Border" (curiously misspelled as "Boarder" in the mass-market paperback edition), follows the various groups as they follow one side or the other. Stuart, the man from the gas station, and his group (Frannie, Glen, and Harold) meets up with Perion and Mark, who are lovers, and a group of women, Susan, Dayna, and Patty, who are being held as a sex harem by a few toughs (much blood is spilled as the women finally make their break). When Frannie and Stuart become lovers, Frannie is desperate to keep it secret from Harold, knowing how destructive he can be. As the group travels, Harold begins leaving giant painted signs on the sides of barns to let others know that their group is alive, and where they are headed.

Nick meets Tom Cullen, a mentally challenged young man whose catchphrase is to say the letters that spell "moon" and then say they spell something completely different, like, "M-O-O-N, that spells ruptures." Tom can't read, and Nick can't hear what Tom is saying, so the two of them have to communicate by Nick attempting to lip-read and act out for Tom what he's trying to tell him. After Nick and Tom begin traveling together, they meet Julie, a teenager who has sex with Nick before she ridicules and tricks Tom. Her cruelty causes Nick to leave her behind, and she vows her revenge. Nick and Tom meet up with Ralph Brentner, a kind farmer, who is traveling with a small group of others.

Larry Underwood wanders alone, wracked with guilt over Rita's death and haunted by the memories of the Lincoln Tunnel and everything he's been through, and he eventually collapses. When he awakes, he soon realizes he's being followed by Nadine Cross, a former teacher who is only 37 despite having completely gray hair, and her young companion, Joe, a strange child who doesn't speak and seems intent on killing Larry. Eventually Larry finds a guitar and plays it for Joe, which wins the boy over.

Trashcan encounters "The Kid," a tough-talking psycho driving a sports car, who constantly threatens and taunts Trashcan, even sexually abusing him at one point. Ultimately Randall Flagg steps in when The Kid threatens to kill Trashcan, and The Kid is trapped in a car surrounded by Flagg's wolves, which allows Trashcan to walk away to join Flagg.

In this section of the book, the people continue to have dreams of the Dark Man, but many of them also begin to dream of Abagail Freemantle, a 108-year-old black woman who lives on a farm in Nebraska. When we are introduced to her, she is having nightmares of the Dark Man coming to her, but she also has had a vision of many followers coming to find her, and she needs to stay focused in order to greet them. Stuart's, Larry's, and Nick's groups all begin heading in her direction. Larry finds Harold's signs and uses them to find his way.

We discover that Nadine is still a virgin because she has been having visions of Flagg for years (she first communicated with him through an Ouija board) and has been saving herself for him. Joe, whose real name is Leo Rockaway, as he reveals in this section, has some psychic abilities, and he begins to detect that Nadine is aligned with Flagg, so he starts to avoid her.

Eventually, everyone arrives at Mama Abagail's house, and she greets them (although Abagail gets a strange vibe from Nadine). She sends them in the direction of Boulder, Colorado, where they all go and set up the "Free Zone," putting out notices on a ham radio and posting signs for other followers. When the people begin to settle into this new community, they form a democratic government and hold town hall meetings, divvying up tasks based on who is best to perform them (because they don't have a doctor, the poor veterinarian finds himself being run ragged). In this section of the book we see them all sitting in political meetings, trying to figure out how to create order out of the chaos that has been thrust upon them.

Frannie and Stuart become closer, and she writes of her deep love for him in her diary, but when Harold finds the diary (which includes several nasty things about him), he becomes hell-bent on revenge. Frannie, meanwhile, discovers Harold's thumbprint on her diary and knows he's read it, but is scared to tell Stuart about her paranoia. The very pious Mama Abagail, worried that she has been too prideful in allowing herself to attract so many followers, exiles herself into the wilderness to try to find peace, and when she goes missing, the town becomes unsettled. During one of the search parties, Harold plans to corner Stuart and kill him, but his plans go awry at the last minute.

Nadine, realizing that Harold might not be one of the good guys, goes to his house and seduces him at the behest of Randall Flagg, performing sexual acts with him that don't compromise her virginity, despite, at times, wanting to because she is so afraid of the eventual consummation with Flagg.

Meanwhile, in Las Vegas, those people who were attracted to rather than repulsed by the visions of Flagg have gathered to form a different society. These people are the degenerates of society, and they were drawn to Flagg's world over Abagail's, and followed him there. Holed up in casinos with generators keeping everything running (many technically able people came to Vegas so they were able to get things running quicker than the people over in the Free Zone), they are working for Flagg, even though not many people have actually seen him. Lloyd is a leader of sorts, because he has the black stone with the red flaw that everyone knows came from Flagg, and he welcomes Trashcan into the group by giving him one of Flagg's stones. Another member who seems welcoming is "Heck" Drogan, but when it comes to Flagg's attention that Heck was doing drugs, a giant cross is erected in front of one of the casinos and Heck is crucified in front of everyone to show what happens to people who wander from Flagg's path. The people in Vegas are constantly working for Flagg's ends, even amassing

The scene in "Ab Aeterno," where the Man in Black frees Richard from his chains on the condition that he'll follow him, was an homage to a similar scene in *The Stand* between Randall Flagg and Lloyd Henreid. (Mario Perez/ABC via Getty Images)

a group of planes and helicopters, putting together an army intended to fight the other group in the Free Zone.

The Free Zone committee becomes aware of Flagg's people gathering in Vegas, and they decide to put together a spy network, recruiting three people (each knows nothing of the others, so if caught, they can't name names) to send over — Judge Farris, Dayna Jurgens, and Tom Cullen, the mentally challenged man. Judge Farris is a retired judge who is very smart, and who they assume will never be caught because no one would suspect they'd send an elderly man as their spy. Flagg, who is telepathic, sees him coming, and has his minions kill him before he gets to Vegas. Dayna successfully infiltrates the Vegas group by sleeping with Lloyd. When she sees Tom Cullen walk by her one day, she realizes he must be the third, and Flagg reads her thoughts about being a spy and calls her into his office. He has received a vision that she will attempt to assassinate him, but, knowing that he will extract the information about Tom from her, she commits suicide by running at the glass window of his office and putting the top half of her body through it, impaling herself on the shards of glass and dying before he can find out who the third spy is. Flagg is unnerved, because he didn't foresee her act of free will, and he begins to feel his tight reign over the dark empire begin to crumble. Tom Cullen is impenetrable to Flagg, because his mental disability makes his mind work differently than everyone else's; as well, he's been hypnotized by the Free Zone Committee to be unaware of the fact he's a spy, but to return to the Free Zone when he sees the first full M-O-O-N in the sky.

In the Free Zone, Harold becomes even darker and nastier than ever and is growing increasingly infuriated by Frannie's relationship with Stuart. Nadine has aligned with him through her allegiance to Flagg. The two of them wait for the Free Zone Committee (which consists of most of the main characters) to meet up, and they hide sticks of dynamite in the house that are rigged through a remote detonator. Harold and Nadine stand just outside the town limits on a hill, looking down. Just before Harold pushes the button, an exhausted and dehydrated Mother Abagail comes walking back into town, causing a few of the people in the house to race outside to see her. But when the dynamite explodes, seven people are killed, including Nick Andros. Frannie is badly wounded (but her unborn baby is unharmed), which lands her in hospital, and Nadine and Harold flee the town. At the hospital the remaining committee members — Frannie, Glen, Stuart, Larry, and Ralph — convene around Mother Abagail's bed, where she tells them that the men have to go to Las Vegas. Frannie objects, not wanting to lose Stuart, but Abagail insists that she's received a sign that the four men must go, that one won't make it to the destination, and that the remaining three must take a stand against Randall Flagg, "who is not a man at all but a supernatural being." She says she doesn't know if they will defeat evil or what God's will is for them in this moment, just that they must leave immediately. Abagail dies, and the men set off.

Book III is the climax of the novel. Harold and Nadine take off for Las Vegas on a motorcycle, but when they hit an oil slick and Harold loses control of the bike, he breaks his leg when he careens over the edge of the cliff. He knows that Flagg has arranged the accident because of the way Harold had been thinking, and he shoots at Nadine, narrowly missing her (and Nadine is surprised that she was almost killed, wondering if Flagg really *is* protecting her or not, and is also a little shocked to discover that she didn't move, as if she really preferred to die rather than meet Flagg). She leaves to go to Vegas on her own, and Harold writes a suicide note, telling people that he acted of his own free will right to the end. He puts the gun into his mouth and pulls the trigger.

The four men from the Free Zone find Harold's body as they journey to Vegas, and Stuart comments on what a waste his death was, and despite everything, vows to avenge Harold's death when he meets Flagg. Unfortunately, along the way as the men are climbing a steep cliff, Stuart slips, and the moment he feels his leg break in several places on the way down, he knows his journey has ended. The others are distraught, not wanting to leave him there, but Stuart encourages them to go on. Kojak, Glen's dog (one of the very few dogs who survived the superflu, and who had followed his master's scent several thousand miles to find him in the Free Zone), stays behind with Stuart and becomes a saving grace.

Meanwhile Nadine finally meets up with Flagg in the desert, and the scene of the consummation of her destiny is a graphic description of Flagg's animal lust and Nadine's horrific realization that she'd made a mistake. The incident puts her in a zombie-like state (her gray hair turns completely white); she is unable to communicate with anyone and is now simply the carrier of Flagg's baby.

Back in Vegas, things are starting to unravel. Despite being one of Flagg's best men, Trashcan has gone off the rails because he heard someone mocking him. The switch inside him flips, and he begins rigging all of the helicopters to explode. After the first one goes off, killing all of the best pilots, the others are able to dismantle the rest of his plan, but Trashcan heads off in an ATV to a nearby weapons base and decides he will prove himself to Flagg one final time. He enters the facility, exposing himself to high, lethal doses of radiation, and grabs an atomic bomb, securing it to a trailer for the drive back to Vegas.

Glen, Ralph, and Larry make it to Vegas and are immediately captured as spies for the Free Zone. Lloyd and Flagg enter Glen's cell and Flagg offers him mercy if he will get down on his knees and beg for it. Glen laughs in his face, and Flagg, infuriated at the insubordination, orders Lloyd to execute him. He shoots Glen, and Glen reels back, quietly saying, "It's all right, Mr. Henreid . . . you don't know any better." Infuriated and crying, Lloyd unloads the rest of the gun into Glen.

Larry and Ralph are marched out into the same square where Heck had been crucified, and the two men take a look at the cages, the chains they'll be attached to, and the cars that are idling nearby and realize they're about to be drawn and quartered. As they step into the cages, they begin yelling to the crowd that what they are doing is wrong. Eventually, Whitney, one of the security guards, steps forward and questions what Flagg is doing, shouting to everyone that they were all Americans once, and this is not how Americans act. He says that Flagg isn't a man at all, that he's the devil. Flagg holds up a finger and a glowing ball of light appears. It slowly moves over Whitney's face, sealing his mouth, eyes, and nose, before burning his head, and soon, Whitney falls face down, dead. Flagg makes a speech to everyone about what they are about to do to Larry and Ralph when suddenly Trashcan comes squealing back into town with his ATV and the bomb. He is in the final stages of severe radiation poisoning: his skin is peeling off and his muscles are hanging from his arms as he limps toward Flagg, vowing his undying allegiance and telling him he's brought him something. From inside the cage, Ralph looks up and sees that the ball of light that Flagg had created has become a huge glowing ball in the shape of a hand. He screams to Larry, "It's the Hand of God!" and they watch, elated, as the hand first obliterates Flagg (he completely disappears, leaving his clothes standing for a second before they fall) and then quickly finds the atomic bomb and comes crashing down on it, detonating it and destroying everyone with it. "Silent white light filled the world . . . And the righteous and unrighteous alike were consumed in that holy fire."

Meanwhile, Stu is about to give up hope when suddenly Tom Cullen stumbles upon him. The two of them make a long journey back to the Free Zone, eventually holing up in a small town in the dead of winter, unable to move and with Stuart's leg slowly healing in a strange way. When Stuart is delirious and unable to communicate with Tom, Tom sees the ghost of Nick Andros, which tells him what to do and how to do it (Tom doesn't realize it's a ghost and is thrilled to see Nick can now speak), and he gets to a pharmacy and finds penicillin for Stu. He can't wait to get to the Free Zone to thank Nick for what he did, but Stu has to break the news to him that Nick is dead. The two men eventually make it back to town, where Frannie has just given birth to a baby. Everyone is on pins and needles to see if the baby will come down with the superflu, and a day after it's born, it does. Frannie is devastated, until the baby suddenly takes a turn for the better and the doctor realizes that it has the antibodies within it to fight the flu. Frannie and Stuart eventually move to Maine to raise their family, and at the end of the book, the people in the Free Zone realize they can begin to spread out and start a new civilization again.

At the end of the book there is a brief coda (added to the 1990 uncut edition) where Flagg suddenly awakes on a beach, surrounded by a primitive-looking group of natives. He has no memory of what came before him, and quickly realizes these people have no language. He stands up, announces that his name is

Russell Faraday, and assures them that he is here to help them. The people shout in both fear and agreement.

The Stand is regarded as one of Stephen King's best works, if not his best. It is an epic story of good and evil, told through the eyes of a key group of characters. Its scope is huge, even though its focus is small (we never really hear about the rest of the globe, for instance). It is about whether people will lean toward good or evil in a time of hardship, and it's about how community ends up saving people in the end. Thus, it's the perfect book for any *Lost* fan. First let's look at some specific moments in the book that were reminiscent of the TV show.

At its very core, this is a look at good versus evil, but as with *Lost*, where the representatives of good (Jacob) and evil (Smokey) are complicated creatures who are neither all bad, or all good, Randall Flagg has moments of doubt, and Mother Abagail fears she is filled with pride and she punishes herself for it. Flagg doesn't remember his previous lives (Smokey does) and all he knows is that he was a man once . . . at least he thinks he was. The two sides are more obvious and divided in *The Stand* than they are on *Lost*, but there is a sense of grayness in King's world that extends to *Lost*. At one point the inimitable Glen says that the reason the Free Zone has so many more people than Vegas is because, when given a choice, more people will choose good over evil.

Tom Cullen is a character considered mentally deficient by other characters, and yet he has moments of clarity when he puts himself into a trance-like state that breaks through the mire and helps him see what everyone is thinking. Nick says at one point that often the insane or the "retarded" are closer to the divine, which is something that's also been played out on *Lost*, with Hurley and Locke both being considered "special" even though in the past they'd been called crazy. In one scene in the book Stuart asks Tom Cullen to explain what the Dark Man looks like to him, and Tom replies (in a trance):

> He looks like anybody you see on the street. But when he grins, birds fall dead off telephone lines. When he looks at you a certain way, your prostate goes bad and your urine burns. The grass yellows up and dies where he spits. He's always outside. He came out of time. He doesn't know himself. He has the name of a thousand demons. Jesus knocked him into a herd of pigs once. His name is Legion. He's afraid of us. We're inside. He knows magic. He can call the wolves and live in the crows. He's the king of nowhere. But he's afraid of us. He's afraid of . . . inside.

Like Flagg, Smokey looks like anybody you'd see on the street, but once he speaks to you, you're doomed, as Jacob and Dogen have said. And like Flagg, he is always outside. He tries to recruit people one by one, by isolating them from the others to bring them to his side. As a child the Man in Black left his mother and brother to go live with other people, but as an adult he didn't feel like he was part of their tribe, either. He's had many names and faces, and he has supernatural tendencies as the smoke monster. (Interestingly, Flagg has had many names, but Smokey has none.) But ultimately, Flagg was afraid of being destroyed. But the key thing with Tom's speech is that Flagg is afraid of what is inside the people he faces — love, companionship, and their connection to others. Flagg didn't foresee that Dayna would commit suicide to save Tom's life, and when he saw free will in action, Flagg's world began unraveling. Similarly, when people on the island began changing their minds and using free will to avoid certain traps, they were undoing everything Smokey had set up for them. Echoing Eloise Hawking's line, Flagg's followers realize that if they screw up their jobs in any way, "God help them all."

Mama Abagail represents good. She is a noble and Christian woman who has accepted her post and tries to guide the others, but when they needed her the most she left them. Similarly, Jacob didn't choose the job he was given, but accepted it, and when his people needed him, or wanted to ask questions, Jacob was unreachable. When a dying Abagail tells them that the four men must go to Vegas, Frannie is very upset, and Abagail grabs her arm, healing her of her wounds in much the same way the island heals people quickly. The four men realize they have to go to Vegas whether they want to or not, because if they don't, they and everyone they know will die, much like Jacob's warning if Smokey were to get off the island, the world would be destroyed. When Abagail dies, chaos ensues and people are unsure of their futures. The island's uncorking causes Jacob's magic to disappear, both Richard and Smokey become mortal, and Smokey's chains to loosen.

Glen Bateman and Stuart Redman have a discussion at one point in which Glen talks about the statistical improbability of a baby being born and surviving the superflu. If the parents were immune, the baby will be safe in utero, but once out, it will be exposed to the fallout of the flu and will surely die. Their discussion brings to mind the fact that babies cannot be born on the island in the fallout of the Jughead bomb, and how that has devastated the population of the Others to the point where they brought Juliet to the island to help save them. In a later section in the book, Stuart is told of the first woman post-flu who does have twin babies, and they both die of the plague. The mother's name is Regina, and she goes insane (on *Lost*, Regina was the name of the woman on the freighter who wrapped herself in chains and stepped off the side of the ship).

When Stuart first asks Glen to come with him, Glen turns him down, arguing that sociability is actually the downfall of the human race, giving a speech that stands in polar opposition to Jack's "Live together, die alone" speech:

> Shall I tell you what sociology teaches us about the human race? I'll give it to you in a nutshell. Show me a man or woman alone and I'll show you a saint. Give me two and they'll fall in love. Give me three and they'll invent the charming thing we call "society." Give me four and they'll build a pyramid. Give me five and they'll make one an outcast. Give me six and they'll reinvent prejudice. Give me seven and in seven years they'll reinvent warfare. Man may have been made in the image of God, but human society was made in the image of His opposite number, and is always trying to get back home.

The society that Glen ultimately helps Stu build in the Free Zone proves him wrong, and this reversal reinforces the message of *Lost*'s series finale.

Another passage that reinforces a plotline in "The End," where Jack must come to terms with his father, is spoken by Judge Farris before he meets his fate in Vegas. Remembering his life, he says his father died when he was a teenager, and "I have missed him ever since. A boy does not need a father unless he is a good father, but a good father is indispensable." Considering the lack of good fathers on *Lost*, the judge's comment is a powerful one. And interestingly, Christian Shephard has been seen as one of the bad dads for several seasons, only for us to discover he was actually a very loving father the entire time; his son just perceived him differently.

Leadership is one of the key themes on *Lost*, whether it's who is the best person for the job, or whether the leader wants the position. In *The Stand*, Nick Andros ponders the fact that he is in a position of leadership, wondering why he, a deaf-mute, would be considered able to lead, and he's not sure he's up for the job and thinks of other people who would be better suited to it. Later, in the Free Zone, they look to the doctor in the group and immediately put him up for leadership, as if he's an obvious candidate, but the doctor argues that he's far too busy saving lives to become the leader, and so he turns them down.

Before getting to Mama Abagail, Perion tells everyone that Mark is in serious pain, and they realize it's his appendix. Unlike on *Lost*, they don't have two surgeons on hand to take out the appendix, and instead rush to find biology books to figure out how to remove it, but despite Stu promising Mark that he'll save him (much like Jack promised Boone he would save him), Mark dies when the appendix bursts and infects him.

In one of many fascinating Glen Bateman scenes (his monologues are some of the highlights of the book), he talks about how people have an innate psychic ability, and that if you look at the flight manifests of planes that crashed, you'll see in many cases they were flights that had a lot of no-shows, as if some of the travelers suddenly came down with ailments because their bodies knew the plane would crash. This long passage about a plane crash is obviously something that makes one think of *Lost*. But also, on *Lost* there's a sense at the end of the series that the people have an innate sense of what is really happening around them, and it's only when their conscious mind catches up to their subconscious that they can have their revelations in the sideways world. Glen goes on to say that some people dream of future events, commenting on their own dreams of "a protagonist . . . and an antagonist." ("Two players, two sides . . .") He says this is, in a sense, a "fourth-dimensional free will: the chance to choose in advance of events," and this touches on one of the most important themes on *Lost*.

The argument of free will versus destiny is one that, on *Lost*, is always tied in with the season 2 argument between Locke and Jack — that of faith versus reason. In *The Stand*, there's a scene where Stu and Glenn discuss the very idea, with much less antagonism than Jack and Locke ever had. Glen wonders aloud if after everything that's happened to them, the people might start to imagine a new kind of existence, one that's less rational than the one they knew, instead based more on a belief, or even irrationality. Stu laughs and says that he's definitely superstitious, but "to live with no science . . . worshipping the sun, maybe . . . thinking monsters are rolling bowling balls across the sky when it thunders . . . I can't say any of that turns me on very much, baldy. Why, it seems like a kind of slavery to me." Glen persists, and says that, in this new world where dreams of Mother Abagail and the Dark Man are coming true, maybe the world is changing and magic is real: "A universe of marvels where water flows uphill and trolls live in the deepest woods and dragons live under the mountains. Bright wonders, white power. 'Lazarus, come forth.' Water into wine. And . . . and just maybe . . . the casting out of devils." Like the brave new world they're all experiencing in *The Stand*, on the island the rules are different, and magic is real, and smoke monsters do exist, and dead people seem to be walking around with regular people.

Harold Lauder, interestingly, is a character that straddles both sides of the argument. Nadine believes that it is her destiny to have sex with Flagg and be the vessel that will bring his offspring into the world, and when she appears to Harold to seduce him, he at first resists, but ultimately, the narrator says, "Harold Lauder succumbed to his destiny." But when Harold commits suicide, he leaves a note saying quite the opposite: "*I apologize for the destructive things I have done, but do not deny that I did them of my own free will . . . I am going to die in my right mind.*" He accepts responsibility for all of his actions, as terrible as they may have been, and in a way it partially redeems what he's done. Unlike Flagg's other followers, who say they're living out their destiny, Harold refuses to go with that cop-out and owns up to his actions.

One of the key moments in season 6 was when Dogen said that Sayid was infected. In a scene where the ghost of Nick Andros appears to Tom Cullen to explain to him that Stuart's leg is infected and Tom needs to help him, he talks to him about what that word means, and in this we see a lot of parallels to what happened in *Lost*'s last season: "Infection means that the bad germs got into it. Infection's the most dangerous thing there is, Tom. Infection was what made the superflu germ kill all the people. And infection is what made people want to make the germ in the first place. An infection of the mind."

The black stones with the red flaws that Randall Flagg gives to his key followers are alluded to on *Lost* when we see the black rock on the scales in Jacob's cliff-side cave (and the name of the ship in the middle of the island). In Vegas, Flagg's followers sit around much like the Others do, just biding their time and waiting for their leader to tell them what to do next, but not actually choosing to do it themselves. Flagg thrives on their lack of free will, much the way Smokey believes that people will always choose to do the wrong thing, and the cycle ("they come, they fight, they destroy, they corrupt") will continue on endlessly because that's what they're destined to do.

In this same vein, King has a beautiful passage in the book where the narrator makes a comment that could very easily be applied to *Lost*:

> The beauty of religious mania is that it has the power to explain everything. Once God (or Satan) is accepted as the first cause of everything

which happens in the mortal world, nothing is left to chance . . . or change. Once such incantatory phrases as "we see now through a glass darkly" and "mysterious are the ways He chooses His wonders to perform" are mastered, logic can be happily tossed out the window. Religious mania is one of the few infallible ways of responding to the world's vagaries, because it totally eliminates pure accident. To the true religious maniac, it's *all* on purpose.

Just as King's narrator says, the characters on *Lost* blindly followed Jacob with religious mania, and the characters who are religious in some way — Eko, Desmond, Charlie, Locke — believe more firmly in destiny than those who are not. At one point in *The Stand*, Trashcan is thinking of his devotion to Flagg, and thinks that he should buy a big black book and write down his thoughts, which would eventually become the Bible for Flagg's followers. Lloyd Henreid becomes the Richard Alpert–like advisor to Flagg. At one point Flagg requests Trashcan's presence (much like John Locke going to the statue at the end of season 5) but Lloyd refuses to go in with him, just as Alpert refused to enter the statue with Locke.

One of the characters in Larry Underwood's group, Lucy Swann, becomes his lover, even though he has his eye on Nadine. Once they reach the Free Zone, Larry and Lucy become a couple, and much of that is due to an outburst she has when she tells him what she thinks of him: "I just happen to think love is very important, only love will get us through this, good connections; it's hate against us, worse, it's emptiness." Better words couldn't be found to describe the *Lost* finale.

Near the end of the book, Stuart gives the Greek omega symbol, shaped like an 8, to Tom Cullen and says it represents infinity, and that he has hope they will make it back to the Free Zone alive. Interestingly, on *Lost* the Candidate who ends up protecting the island at the end of the series is Hurley, the one who'd been assigned Jacob's number 8.

When the Free Zone Committee decides to send spies to Vegas, it echoes several spy missions on *Lost*. Henry Gale infiltrates the survivors' camp. Michael is acting like a spy of sorts for the Others when he returns. Juliet is Ben's spy when she first goes to the survivors with Jack. In a way, Jack, Kate, and Sawyer all become inadvertent spies when they're held hostage by the Others and see how some of them live.

Some of the parallels between *Lost* and King's novel are more specific and less thematic:

- Hurley's numbers appear throughout the book, but none as prominent as Mother Abagail, who is 108 years old.
- There's a scene where someone describes tortures — water torture, electric shocks, and splinters under the fingernails — all which have been shown on *Lost*.
- Mother Abagail writes down some biblical references, much like the ones Eko etches on his Jesus stick.
- In a scene between a particularly hostile Harold Lauder and the long-suffering Nadine Cross, they discuss setting up the dynamite to blow up the Free Zone Committee, and he tells her, in a very Arzt-like passage, about how unstable dynamite is: "It *perspires*, to be perfectly couth. And what it perspires is pure nitroglycerin, one of the world's great unstable substances. So if it's old, there's a very good chance that this little Science Fair project could blow us right over the top of Flagstaff Mountain and all the way to the Land of Oz."
- Larry and Stu talk about how they've each read *Watership Down* (a book Sawyer read in season 1, see *Finding Lost: Seasons 1 & 2*, pp. 55–57), and how the book resonates with their current situation.
- Charlie Pace was clearly based on Larry Underwood (from the one-hit-wonder status that turned him into a louse, to his redemption afterwards and becoming one of the most beloved characters of the group to his ultimate sacrifice at the end of the book). Larry considers himself a lucky bastard: bad things happen to those around him, but never happen to him. In this sense he's also like Hurley. But because Hurley is a nice guy, he considers his luck a curse.
- When Flagg's goons kill Judge Farris, they have been instructed never to hit him in the head. Martin Keamy, in the sideways world, was upset when Jin was accidentally hit in the head with the fridge door, as if he didn't want to hurt Jin's head before killing him for Mr. Paik.
- There are a few references in the book to the Red Sox or the Yankees, as there have been on *Lost*, and King uses several baseball metaphors throughout the book.
- At one point Harold thinks of the book *Flowers for Algernon*, which was

prominently displayed on Ben's bookshelf in season 4.
- As Tom Cullen is returning to the Free Zone after the completion of his spy mission in Vegas, he sits down in the desert and recites the 23rd Psalm (the psalm that Eko and Charlie recite over the burning Beechcraft plane in season 2). The Hand of God scene is reminiscent of the world going white at the end of season 5, when the bomb went off, detonated by the hand of Juliet.
- As Tom and Stuart make their way back to the Free Zone, they find a car to drive and it's on a hill. They jump in, letting it run down the hill faster and faster until Stuart finally pops the clutch and the car roars to life. He and Tom whoop and cheer, and it's a joyous moment, not unlike Hurley's VW scene in "Tricia Tanaka Is Dead."
- Flagg's name at the end of the book is Russell Faraday, which is, incidentally, the name the writers were going to originally give to Jeremy Davies' character. But because they didn't want to draw that comparison directly to Flagg, they changed his first name to Daniel.

At the very end of the book, when Flagg wakes up as a new entity, he awakes the same way Jack does in the pilot episode, looking around him and bewildered because he doesn't know where he is. He soon realizes he's on an island of some kind, and he can see outrigger canoes. He looks straight up into the trees, takes a moment to collect himself, and then walks out to his new people, immediately pulling them together. He's much the same as Jack, except he's not here to heal people — he wants ultimately to destroy them. He's awakened in a new body, with a new life, and just as the Man in Black says, he's going to start everything all over again.

Paradise Lost by John Milton (1667)

John Milton's epic poem that recounts the fall of humankind through its first act of disobedience is one of the greatest works of the English language. Written as a Christian response to the epic poems of Virgil and Homer, it invokes Greek muses throughout, but Milton maintains that his subject matter is far more important than that of the epics that preceded his, because it involves all of humankind, not just individual heroes. Where the writers on *Lost* have said that *The Stand* is the book they had on the writer's table at every meeting, *Lost* more closely resembles a modern-day version of *Paradise Lost*, from its themes to its message. Milton intended for readers to read *Paradise Lost* as a parable of why we must be devoted to God in our everyday life, but today the poem resonates more as a story of hope and togetherness, and a vision of how humankind holds the keys to its own salvation.

Paradise Lost opens with Milton's invocation of the muse, a common trope in epic poetry. He states that his poem will be about "Man's First Disobedience," and man's fall until Christ was able to redeem him.

The narrative of the poem begins in Hell, where Satan is bewildered, floating on a lake of fire next to Beelzebub, his second-in-command. Strangely, the fire in Hell burns dark, not light, so they are engulfed in total darkness. They have just been cast down into the fires of Hell by God after attempting to take over Heaven in a war. The catalyst for war was Satan's envy of God's Son being the Chosen One. Satan immediately starts making plans for a second battle against God, but after what's already happened, Beelzebub is doubtful and thinks God is unbeatable. Satan is more optimistic, arguing that they haven't lost everything because they acted of their own free will, and at least they still have that (otherwise, he argues, God could make them lie still on the lake of fire for eternity, but instead they chose to stand up), and while they have been cast from the glories of Heaven into Hell, he says, "Better to reign in Hell, than serve in Heav'n."

Beelzebub is worried that fate or destiny has stepped in and caused this to happen, and he's lost all hope. Satan is a convincing political speaker, and throughout the first book he offers up many powerful speeches about how they may have been cast into Hell, but they are still strong, intelligent beings and God is not impossible to defeat. Milton refers to Satan's size throughout the section, and he seems to get larger as it goes on. Milton explains that angels are shapeshifters that can change their appearance and size at will, and Satan is often described as absolutely massive, towering over Hell. Satan calls the other fallen angels over to him and talks to them, telling them they can't give up now or they will be forever fallen.

The fallen angels do stand up, and with their swords and shields and banners they march over to Satan, still an impressive-looking army despite everything that has happened, and one by one they speak up. Milton introduces us to many of them — Moloch, Belial, Astarte, Dagon, Osiris, and Orpheus among them — and says they came to be worshiped later in the religions of Ancient Egypt and Ancient Greece. They each step up and give their speeches, and Satan listens. Satan argues that they must think through what they are going to do, and that while God's army was able to defeat them, an enemy "who overcomes/ By force, hath overcome but half his foe." He tells the angels that their pleasure should be in doing evil, not good, and he doesn't regret anything he's done. He says the war is still ongoing, and "War then, War/ Open or understood, must be resolv'd." The angels begin digging in the ground and find gold and other minerals, and very quickly construct a temple they call Pandemonium (a name that means "all spirits" or "all demons" depending on the translation) where they can all gather and decide how to embattle God.

In this opening book, Satan is set up as the hero of the poem, even though he will ultimately become the antagonist. Milton takes the usual structure of the epic poem and reverses it, thwarting our expectations by building up Satan in the same style as, say, Odysseus and showing us the beginning of his quest. Satan's words are powerful and brilliant, and he is an attractive character to the reader, and Milton actually creates some sympathy for him early on.

Once Pandemonium is built, the devils shrink themselves to go inside and have their hellish council. Moloch stands up first and argues that nothing can be worse than Hell, and he urges them all to rise up and fight against Heaven again. Belial speaks next, saying God hasn't punished them to the full extent of His wrath; the very fact that they're walking around is proof that He could do worse — He could chain them to the lake of fire permanently. Belial tells them not to fight and to accept their lot. Mammon argues next that he will never bow to God again, and they should make Hell their new Heaven by building it up and making it a better place where they can live. He says not to bother fighting God again, but they should do something about where they are. The devils seem to agree with him until Beelzebub speaks up and says he's heard that God has created a new place called Earth, and they need to go and find Man, which God has created in His image, and corrupt this new creation. The devils agree with resounding support, and Satan then steps up and says he will make the ultimate sacrifice and go to Earth to corrupt these people (and it's clear at this point that he'd set up Beelzebub to say these things so he could make this grandiose gesture).

Satan leaves and comes to the nine gates of Hell, which are guarded by two creatures: one is a woman from the waist up, a serpent from the waist down, and around her middle are the hounds of Hell, which run around her barking and screaming and biting her before going into her womb at night, eating her bowels, and being reborn every morning, just to start again. Behind her is a dark, formless creature who threatens Satan, and just as they're about to fight, the woman cries out that she is Satan's daughter. She says she was born from his head and was called Sin, and that Satan had lusted after her and had had sex with her after she was born, and she gave birth to Death. Death instantly raped her and begat the hounds that torture her for eternity (and the survivors on *Lost* think *they* have parent issues!). She says the only reason Death hasn't killed her is that if she dies, he dies, too. Satan immediately softens his approach and bribes them to give him the keys to the gates by telling them what he has planned. He passes through the gates and immediately starts falling, but he's caught and faces Chaos, Night, Confusion, Rumor, Tumult, Discord, and others. He tells them what he plans to do, and that if he succeeds he will increase disorder in the universe, which is what they all want, so they guide him the rest of the way to Earth.

We see God speaking to his Son, and God has been watching everything that's been happening and knows what Satan is up to, knows what he will do, and knows that Man will fall. He can see the past, present, and future as one long line (much like Desmond does at times), and there is a long section where He talks about how it was important for Him to give Man free will in order for Man to show sincere love to God and to each other. Even though He already knows what will happen in the future, He says that Man still acts out of free will, and not destiny: "Foreknowledge had no influence on their fault." He says Man must be punished for the sins that are about to be committed, but He intends to show mercy, because where the rebel angels rose up against God of their own accord, Man will be deceived by Satan. Christ suggests that God cannot kill Man, because by doing so He would let Satan win. God says someone else must die for the sins of Man so that humankind can be saved, and Christ volunteers. God is proud of His Son for offering to sacrifice himself (even though He must have already known his Son was going to volunteer), and the angels sing a Heavenly chorus.

Satan arrives at the gates leading to a stairway down to Earth. He can see Earth and how beautiful it is, and he's immediately envious of everything Man has. He sees the Archangel Uriel and shape-shifts to a cherub so Uriel thinks he's just a low-ranking angel, and tells him how interested he is in God's new creation and how he'd love to see it. Uriel, who is pure and therefore doesn't realize he's being bamboozled, lets him through the gates and wishes him well.

As Satan perches above the Garden of Eden he looks upon Paradise and is filled with envy and regret. He begins to wish he hadn't waged a war against Heaven so he could be free to dwell in Paradise. But he realizes that he cannot bow down to God and ask His forgiveness, and if he can't be forgiven, then he must remain filled with despair: "So farewell Hope, and with Hope farewell Fear,/ Farewell Remorse: all Good to me is lost;/ Evil be thou my Good. . . ." He sees Adam and Eve walking in the garden and is again filled with conflicting thoughts, thinking he would have loved them if he'd still been an angel. He sees how beautiful they both are, noting that "in thir looks Divine/ The image of thir glorious Maker shine. . . ."

Adam and Eve have a pure, innocent love, and Eve talks about what it was like when she opened her eyes for the first time after she'd been created. She was in a shaded area and went to some water, where she saw her reflection and was confused by it. She stared at it, starting to fall in love with it when God pulled her away and led her to Adam. When she saw him she at first turned away from him because she didn't think he was as good-looking as her reflection but she was told that man was even more beautiful than woman, and she fell in love with him (and yes, feminist critics have rightfully gone to town on this section of the poem). Satan, listening, notes that they are not equal, and in Satan's comments to himself and the conversation between Adam and Eve, we get a misogynist look at men and women, with Milton upholding the idea that Adam was created to serve God, and Eve was created to serve God and Adam. The two of them talk about tending the garden and Adam says that it's all theirs, except the Tree of Knowledge, which they're not allowed to eat from. Satan hears this and realizes that is how he will enact the downfall of humankind. Adam and Eve make love, but it's pure and devoid of any lust.

Meanwhile, Uriel has been watching Satan and has noticed the conflicting looks on his face. He realizes Satan can't be a cherub, because cherubs only have a look of unadulterated joy on their faces. He alerts the Archangel Gabriel, who begins to hunt through the garden and finds Satan disguised as a toad. He threatens to drag him back to Hell where he belongs, and just as they are about to do battle, God sends a sign — a pair of golden scales in the sky — and Satan interprets the image to mean that things are not balanced in his favor and he flies away.

When Adam and Eve awake the next morning, Eve tells Adam she'd had a bad dream that she'd met an angel at the Tree of Knowledge who told her she could be like the gods if she tasted the fruit. Adam assures her they have free will and that the dream was not an inevitable prediction of the future. In Heaven, God sends Archangel Raphael down to talk to Adam and warn him of the danger of disobeying God. Raphael complies, has a meal with Adam and Eve, and then Eve departs to give them time alone. Raphael explains to Adam that God created each thing on Earth as part of a hierarchy, with Man at the top, because Man has spirit. He says that Man is the only one of the groups that possesses reason, and he must use it to be obedient.

Adam asks why anyone would disobey God, and Raphael says that while Man was made to be perfect, he was also given the ability to lose that perfection. He then explains how the rebel angels were disobedient in Heaven: when God told the angels he'd begotten a son, most of them were happy, but Satan, who'd been one of the chief archangels, thought he should be given the same powers as God, and he rebeled. (Milton's assertion that Jesus was born and didn't always exist was at odds with the traditional Christian belief at the time, which said He and God had always existed together in the Holy Trinity.) A third of the angels joined Satan as he erected a throne in Heaven and explained that they should not accept God as a sovereign just because He told them to. One of the angels who'd joined Satan disagreed with his new rule and left.

The angel returned to God and was forgiven because he'd chosen good over evil, despite his earlier choice. Meanwhile Satan built an army from his followers. God decided it would only be fair to put together an army composed of an equal number of soldiers, so He recruited as many angels as Satan had on his side. Gabriel and Michael are the two leaders of God's army. The war built in intensity until Michael took up a sword and practically sliced Satan in half. The first day of battle ended as Satan's angels dragged him off. He healed (because the bodies of angels can change shape, any wound was superficial and healed quickly), and on the second day, Satan's army returned with their new invention: a cannon. They fired at God's army and for a moment God's army was overcome, until they grabbed mountains and hurled them at Satan's army, burying them. God decided the battle had gone on long enough and he sent his Son out in a chariot. Christ went to the battlefield, collected Satan and his army, and banished them from Heaven, sending them out of the gates where they fell through Chaos for nine days until they reached Hell. Raphael ends the story he's telling Adam, and warns him that Satan is still recruiting, and to watch out for him and not to succumb to his temptations.

Adam begins asking several questions about the creation of the world, his curiosity foreshadowing that he will later eat the fruit that Eve gives him (Raphael takes it further by acknowledging that "Knowledge is as food"). Raphael complies and tells Adam that God replaced the rebel angels with Adam and Eve as a way of proving that despite what Satan may have thought, he didn't weaken God's realm; his departure actually strengthened it. Raphael's description of Creation is much like the one in Genesis, with one major difference: in his version of events, Christ comes down from Heaven and constructs Earth based on God's commands. He creates the world in six days, just like it says in the Bible, and on the seventh day He rests. When He's finished, He connects Earth to Heaven by a chain. God plans to join the two worlds together eventually when Man obeys His will. Christ returns to Heaven and the angels praise His work.

Eve, who had been sitting nearby, gets up and leaves, saying she'd rather hear about the conversation later from Adam. Perhaps Milton is suggesting that Eve doesn't have the mental capacity to comprehend their conversation (since Milton clearly believes women are intellectually inferior to men) or perhaps she's simply asserting her deference to Adam by letting him listen to Raphael so that he can pass on to her whatever he wants her to know. Adam then asks Raphael about the universe, stars, and planets, and begins to ask rather scientific questions about how the universe works. Raphael tells him to stop trying to understand things that are outside of the scope of the knowledge that God had already imbued him with. He suggests that trying to find answers through science could be dangerous, and that one should simply pursue knowledge through faith. God will take care of all of the larger questions. Adam recalls waking for the first time after he was created, remembering that he woke up in the sunlight and immediately looked to Heaven. God came to him and asked him to name the animals, which he did, and then he longed for a companion. God created Eve and the moment Adam saw her, he immediately fell in love (interestingly, Eve awoke in a shaded area, looked at herself instead of to God, and didn't like the sight of Adam when she first saw him). Raphael tells Adam that he must not lust after Eve, and that their relationship had to go beyond sexual attraction. Adam says that he worries about his sexual attraction to Eve, because she is not as pure as he is.

The poem now turns to the downfall of Man. Milton once again invokes the muses and comments that unlike the poems of Homer and Virgil, his story concerns what happened to all mankind, and not just particular Greek heroes, and therefore his is more important. He begs the muse to help him keep on topic and focus on the story at hand, which is the tragedy of humankind.

Satan returns to the Garden of Eden after Gabriel had banished him, and he sneaks in and decides to take the form of a snake. Once more he's jealous when he sees Earth, and says it is actually even more beautiful than Heaven was. But this time he speaks with resignation. He knows it would have been better to have been good, but he's accepted that he's evil, and admits that now, "only in destroying I find ease/ To my relentless thoughts." He will destroy God's new favorite, because "spite then with spite is best repaid." His language is very different from the powerful rhetoric he displayed in the opening books; now it's simple and almost garbled.

Adam and Eve prepare to tend the garden, and Eve suggests they split up to do the work. Adam is reluctant, thinking that in her dream she'd been alone, and remembering everything that Raphael had warned him against. But Eve persists, saying it'll make them stronger, and adds that they'll never be happy if they always live in fear. They part ways, and Satan finds Eve alone and begins talking to her, appealing to her vanity by flattering her. She's amazed that another animal in the garden has the power of speech, and he tells her that he got it by eating the fruit. When he shows her that the fruit came from the Tree of Knowledge, she explains that God had forbidden her to eat from that tree. Satan begins to reason with her about how God would want her to show her independence, and then she begins to follow the same line of reason, realizing that God had told them if they ate from that tree they would die, and Satan is clearly still alive. Eve doesn't feel like she has the strength to deny this knowledge that the fruit promises her (one can't help but remember the pious mother in Stephen King's *Carrie*, who constantly yelled, "Eve was weak!" at her daughter). In this scene Satan is pro-reason, whereas Milton is clearly pro-faith. Eve makes her decision, and the Earth immediately responds to it with pathetic fallacy:

> So saying, her rash hand in evil hour
> Forth reaching to the Fruit, she pluck'd, she eat:
> Earth felt the wound, and Nature from her seat
> Sighing through all her Works gave signs of woe,
> That all was lost.

As the world around Eve responds to the fall of mankind, she rushes off to find Adam and tells him to eat the fruit, too. She's immediately worried that if only she falls, he will find another woman and she'll be alone. When she finds him she appeals to his sympathy, and tells him she now knows far more than she did before, and he needs to eat the fruit to be with her. He's saddened (he was making a wreath of flowers for her and the moment he sees her running toward him he knows what has happened and drops the wreath) but he would rather fall with her than be without her. He eats the fruit with less enticement than it took Satan to make Eve eat it, and the Earth groans a second time.

Despite Milton's chauvinism in his depiction of Eve, we can see that her fall is caused by her desire for knowledge and understanding, while Adam's is caused by his physical need of Eve. As soon as he eats the fruit the two of them bask in the new feelings they have, and he immediately looks at her with lust, seizes her hand, and runs with her into the dark forest where they have sex. The depiction of their lovemaking is very different in this scene — dark, hidden, forbidden — than it was in the earlier one, where they were in the light and happy and playful. When they finish, they suddenly look upon their own nakedness with shame: "innocence, that as a veil/ Had shadow'd them from knowing ill, was gone. . . ." They cover themselves with leaves, and then begin to argue. He accuses her of ruining everything and causing them to lose Paradise. She turns it back on him, saying if she is to serve him, all he had to do was forbid her to go off alone, but he didn't, and that's why she was tempted. The two of them argue for hours in the garden without finding a middle ground.

God and the angels know that Adam and Eve have fallen the moment it happens, and God sends his Son to Earth to punish them. Christ calls them from their hiding places, and they ashamedly approach him. Adam tells the Son that he was tempted by Eve, and she in turn blames the serpent. Christ first punishes the serpent by condemning it to slither on its belly for eternity, always looking up into trees and desiring the fruit it sees but never able to reach it. Then he condemns Eve and all womankind to painful childbirth and a lifetime of submitting to their husbands. He punishes Adam and mankind by taking away the plentiful garden and leaving them with an eternity of having to work and hunt for food. Christ leaves.

At the gates of Hell, Sin and Death have been building a bridge linking Earth to Hell, and they wonder if Satan has succeeded in destroying God's new creation. They meet Satan at the edge of Paradise, where Satan confirms that he's been successful. Sin says she will enter the world to corrupt the thoughts of humankind, and Death will enter the world to condemn each living thing to die in its time. Satan thanks them and proceeds to Hell, where he announces to the devils that he's been triumphant, but instead of applause he hears hissing. He realizes that all of the devils have been turned into snakes, and various trees appear in Hell, where if the snakes try to eat the fruit, it turns to ash. Satan suddenly drops to his belly and realizes he is also a serpent for all eternity. Belial was right; there *were* worse punishments than being banished to Hell.

Sin and Death arrive on Earth and begin corrupting the creatures. God sees them and tells the other angels to just leave them alone, because one day his Son will come to Earth in corporeal form and rid the world of both of them. The angels tilt the Earth's access so humankind will now have to endure both hot and cold climates rather than the weather being perfect year round. Discord, who had been living in Chaos, follows Sin and Death into the world and begins setting the animals at war with one another and with humankind.

Adam sees the extent to which their disobedience has damned every creature, and he despairs. He thinks life is now nothing more than a miserable state of waiting for death, uncertain of when it will come. He begins entertaining suicidal thoughts, and Eve comes to him and begs his forgiveness. She takes responsibility for what happened, and says the only way to continue forward is to do so together:

> Between us two let there be peace, both joining,
> As join'd in injuries, on enmity
> Against a Foe by doom express assign'd us,
> That cruel Serpent.

She suggests they refrain from having children, and therefore they will be the only two human beings who ever lived, and thus the only two punished. Adam counters that if they don't have children, Satan will have triumphed and destroyed God's creation before it really began. He takes responsibility for his own actions, and the two of them go back to the place where Christ punished them and they bow their heads and pray for God's forgiveness. In repenting and taking the blame for the fall of mankind, they rise above Satan and begin to create a future where mankind will not suffer the eternal punishments of Hell like Satan does.

God is pleased to see Adam and Eve praying, and He sends Michael down to lead Adam and Eve out of Paradise. We learn that only through Adam and Eve's disobedience was God able to show His full grace, and Milton explains that now humankind can only live with God's guidance and love. Man is unfit for Paradise, but if he continues to show a deference and devotion to God, he will find his way back to Paradise. Only through Christ's sacrifice will humankind be worthy of Heaven once again. But for now, Adam and Eve are no longer worthy of living in Paradise. God asks Michael to take them out into the world, which is a darker place, and if they endure the punishments that have been given to them but remain devoted to God throughout their lives, they will still find a place in Heaven. In the garden, Eve is still sad, and Adam once again tells her that she has been given an important role, and will be the Mother of all mankind. She says she is not worthy of that role, but says she will live in devotion to God in Paradise. Michael appears and tells them they are being banished from Paradise, and they are both devastated. He reassures them that they will not die right away, and that the entire world has been given to them and they will be watched by God and can talk to him whenever they like. Michael puts Eve to sleep and takes Adam up on a mountain.

From the mountaintop, Adam is shown the future of humankind through various biblical stories. He sees Cain and Abel — his own sons — and watches one of them kill the other, and is horrified to see death for the first time. He sees people who are happy and playing games and flirting with one another, and Michael explains that those people are atheists who will die and not be united with God. He sees visions of war, and Michael explains that many war heroes and great conquerors will be praised by people, even though they kill mercilessly. He shows him Enoch (who appears briefly in the Bible as Noah's great-grandfather), who tried to prevent war and could see a great flood coming, but no one believed him. Then he shows him Noah, another man talking of a flood. Again no one listens, so he leaves and builds a giant boat and fills it with animals and with his family. He explains that despite Adam and Eve being repentant, mankind will forget to show devotion to God and will not be good to one another, so God will punish everyone by sending a great flood and sparing only Noah. He shows him the rainbow following the flood as proof that God will never do this again. Adam watches all of these things unfold before him and is filled with sadness, but also hope that God's grace will save them. Adam realizes that it's through devotion to God and through a relationship with Him that one can truly express one's worth.

Next Michael shows him how humankind developed through the descendents of Noah. He moves to the story of the construction of the Tower of Babel, explaining how Nimrod was a man who believed he could control other men, but because God recognized that man was meant to be free, he made it so everyone spoke a different language and Nimrod's tower couldn't be built. He moves to Abraham, Moses, and David, explaining each biblical story and showing how in each instance the generations survived because of God's grace. David is the ancestor of Jesus, and Michael describes Christ's birth into the world, followed by his death and resurrection, and explains that it is through that resurrection that he will defeat both Sin and Death. The followers of Jesus will be persecuted, but Michael reassures Adam that when the Messiah returns a second time on Judgment Day, those who had followed him will be saved and those who don't believe will be punished. On that day, Heaven and Earth will be united once again.

Michael's explanation fills Adam with hope, and he's surprised and comforted by the fact that so much good will come out of the Fall. He understands that to live as one with God, obeying him and looking to him for answers, is the only way that mankind will overcome the disobedience that Adam and Eve had committed. God has been able to see the future and present simultaneously, and so knew that Adam and Eve would fall, but he gave them the tools with which they might overcome the punishments of that fall, and he knows that humankind will redeem itself. Eve awakens from her sleep and says she had a dream in which God explained a lot to her. Michael guides Adam and Eve to the edge of Paradise, where he stands with the other angels. He brandishes a flaming sword and points their way to exit. Wiping away tears, Adam and Eve join hands and make their first steps outside of Paradise:

> The World was all before them, where to choose
> Thir place of rest, and Providence thir guide:
> They hand in hand with wand'ring steps and slow,
> Through *Eden* took thir solitary way.

Milton's epic masterpiece is the ultimate story of good triumphing over evil, and faith and devotion showing the way to salvation and out of despair. It begins by showing us Satan's point of view, almost making us sympathetic to him, only to overturn that sympathy later in the story by making him the purveyor of the downfall of mankind. God represents everything that is good and holy, loving His creation so much that He gives them the tools through which they might help themselves out of the terrible mess they've created. While God can see their future and knows that they will fall, it doesn't mean they were destined to, just that they would do so through their own free will. He warned them to avoid the downfall, but it happened anyway. The poem moves through Satan to the allegory of Sin and Death, to showing us God, then the humans, and then we flash back to see what happened during the war in Heaven, then we see Adam and Eve's disobedience, Satan's punishment, and hope for the future.

Lost explored a lot of the same territory, but did so with a secular setting rather than a religious one. One could almost see it as a reverse modern-day retelling of *Paradise Lost* — where *Paradise Lost* is the story of how humanity was given everything and threw it away, *Lost* is about how humanity can be on the edge of despair and find its way to redemption. The show thus also acts as a sequel to Milton's poem. What happened after Adam and Eve fell? Did their hope for the redemption of humankind ever come to fruition? Yes, it did, in the sacrifices that many of the survivors made for the island and for all of mankind.

In many ways, the Man in Black is *Lost*'s Satan figure: in "Ab Aeterno" we see how he tells Richard the very things he wants and needs to hear in order to get him on side, just as Satan uses rhetoric to win over the devils in Pandemonium and again uses his silver tongue to appeal to Eve's vanity in the Garden of Eden. Just as Satan was cast out of Heaven and turned from one of the highest archangels into a terrible devil, so was the Boy in Black his Mother's great hope before he was cast into the waters of the cave by his brother and turned into the smoke monster. Satan is turned into a serpent at the end of the poem, unable to eat fruit because it turns to ash in his mouth; the Man in Black is similarly turned into a serpent-like creature on the island, unable to fulfill his own desires, and is repelled by ash. Smokey is determined to ruin everything that Jacob has put into place by killing the Candidates and destroying his precious island, much like Satan causes the fall of humanity and destroys Paradise. There are moments in Milton's poem when Satan regrets what he's done and longs to be an angel again so he can enjoy Paradise, but he knows that he cannot repent and must now embrace evil as his way of finding pleasure. While Smokey is more sympathetic than Satan — he attempts to destroy the island so he can leave, and the Candidates are casualties rather than targets — he embraces his darkness and kills without mercy, never once attempting to repent for what he's done or trying to work alongside Jacob. Jacob has less power over Smokey than God had over Satan however; when Satan is initially chased from the Garden of Eden, he leaves when he sees a pair of golden scales in the sky, and assumes that the odds are stacked against him. Smokey, on the other hand, when faced with a pair of scales holding a white and black rock, simply grabs the white rock and tosses it into the ocean, tipping the scales in his favor.

Jacob is less godlike than the God in Milton's poem, because he is flawed. Therein lies the biggest departure in the show — Jacob is not purely good: he killed his brother, he's made mistakes, he's a reluctant deity. But like God in the poem, he believes that people have free will, and even if he knows ahead of time how they will exercise that free will, he will not interfere with their decision-making, leaving them free to make mistakes or to follow the right path. Unlike God, Satan, Christ, and the angels and devils, Jacob and his brother were once human, and therefore they will never be wholly good or evil.

All of the survivors represent the humanity that followed Adam and Eve; where the book ends with the mother and father of mankind completely lost and frightened about what their future holds, the television show *began* with the characters already lost and frightened of the unknown that lay before them. The island itself is a paradise, filled with food and water and beauty, and yet it already holds within it the Satan character, who slithers serpent-like through the jungle in the form of the smoke monster, willing to tempt or terrify them by shape-shifting as Satan does into various forms that will lead them to their salvation or destruction, depending on how they choose.

When Raphael tells Adam the story of the war in Heaven as a warning against falling into temptation, Adam begins barraging him with questions, which Raphael ultimately refuses to answer, telling him that instead of asking so many questions he should simply be content with the knowledge he's been given, for that's all he needs in order to understand the world he's in. Much to the chagrin of many viewers, the writers too didn't provide answers to many of the questions raised by the series, but rather insinuated that whatever wasn't clear simply wasn't important to the understanding of the show.

After the fall, Adam and Eve begin hurling blame at each other, neither one willing to accept any responsibility for what they've done. For much of *Lost*, the characters blame their upbringing, their parents, their spouses, their friends, or the island for things that have happened to them, they squabble and the group fractures, and only when they finally begin to look for answers within themselves do they begin to find redemption and each other. Eve despairs after the fall, and both she and Adam begin to think suicidal thoughts, as many of the characters on *Lost* have, but Eve appeals to Adam's sympathy by telling him that if they stick together, they can get through it. Just as every separation on the island seems to lead people to bad places, it was Eve's separation from Adam that allowed the serpent to tempt her. Her plea for Adam to remain at her side and tackle whatever is coming together is what lies at the heart of *Lost* — in the sideways world, it's only when they all come together and realize that the island was a place of salvation, not the Hell they thought it was, that they're able to find peace with their lives and move on to the next one.

When Adam sees the future of mankind, he knows that he and Eve must be strong and must use their faith and devotion to overcome any hardships along the way. Throughout Milton's poem, he dismisses scientific reason as nothing more than a distraction away from life. On *Lost* the writers actually encouraged viewers to explore areas of science, philosophy, and reason, but ultimately, it was Jack's faith that led to his own redemption and the salvation of those around him. Adam stands at the edge of the mountain and looks upon the future of his descendants with hope that his and Eve's act of disobedience will not lead to the destruction of mankind. Many of the characters on the show give their lives for others, and restore hope in humanity, fulfilling what Milton's angel Michael showed to Adam on that mountaintop. As Jack closes his eyes at the end of the series, he's smiling, hopeful that because of his actions, his friends will live long, happy lives, and that as his faith was restored by John Locke, perhaps their faith will be restored after seeing what happened to the island. Both *Lost* and *Paradise Lost* look at what humanity is capable of losing through the exercise of its own free will, but truly, they both focus on how that could be regained. Good can triumph over evil, as long as people stick together, have faith and hope, and are devoted to keeping goodness in the world.

That's It?!: The Unanswered Questions

The biggest complaint about the series finale of *Lost* was that it didn't answer enough questions. In the weeks and months leading up to it, Damon Lindelof and Carlton Cuse had been trying to take the focus off the questions, especially when asked about them in interviews, insisting this was always a character-driven show. Fans began to suspect that perhaps the final season *wasn't* going to answer everything, and as the episodes counted down and so few mysteries were solved, some viewers began focusing on the characters instead, no longer worrying about the details, while others grew increasingly upset that the writers had built up everything for six seasons only to leave much of it unanswered, putting the burden on the viewers to come up with the answers themselves.

However, in the months following the finale, fans started to realize that many of the questions *were* answered, and those that weren't didn't really matter in the greater scheme of things. Darlton, as I mentioned earlier, spent a lot of time giving us the tools to answer these questions, and the answers are in there — it's just up to each viewer to find them. Some mysteries are more easily solved. But in most cases, if you just use common sense you can probably come up with a reasonable explanation based on everything we know about the island and the people on it.

During the many discussions I've had with fans over the course of season 6 and post-finale, I began noticing that the same core questions were being raised, but I think there are some obvious explanations for some of them, and some not-so-obvious answers for the rest of them. In the extra on the season 6 DVD *Lost* set, "The New Man in Charge," the writers offered up some answers to several of the questions, some that felt like a solid conclusion that could be drawn from the series itself, and others that were unsatisfactory.

So here are some possible — by no means definitive — answers to some of the many unanswered questions on *Lost* gleaned only from watching the series itself (and if you're jumping right to this chapter and skipping the episode guide, please note that I've also offered several potential answers to other questions in appropriate spots in the guide).

What's up with the polar bears?

The polar bears were brought to the island as part of a biological/anthropological experiment by the Dharma Initiative to see what would happen to cold weather animals in a tropical climate. They kept them in the cages and while they were in there, they decided to also try out some B.F. Skinner–type of psychological experiments on them, seeing if they could figure out how to push the lever to avoid an electric shock and get a fish biscuit (according to Tom, it took them about three hours). At some point before or after the Purge (it's not clear when) they got out of the cages and were loose on the island. Since polar bears can swim, at least two of them seemed to swim from the Hydra Island over to the main island, and Sawyer shot one in the pilot episode and Walt was chased by another one later in season 1. We can assume that one of the many experiments done on these bears was to take one down into the Orchid station and test the frozen donkey wheel out, perhaps to see if it still worked without using a human subject, or to trace where the polar bear would end up if he turned it. In "Confirmed Dead," Charlotte finds a polar bear skeleton in the Tunisian desert, exactly the same place where both Ben and Locke ended up, and it's wearing a Dharma collar. Clearly it was ejected from the island through the same wormhole the men traveled through. The moment the bear disappeared, the DI probably brought in some poor schmuck and had him turn it so they could discover where exactly he ended up (let's hope they left some time between the two, or the polar bear might have had the guy for lunch on the other end).

Why was Walt special?
This is probably the #1 fan question (and it forms the crux of the wonderful second half of "The New Man in Charge"). Why was Walt built up as an incredibly special child, only to end up being insignificant after the second season? I would argue that he wasn't insignificant at all. Walt's purpose was simply to establish that people *could* be special, and to introduce the very theme to the series. Later we see both John Locke and Ben Linus being treated as special children, which is why it's important that Walt is a child. The Others take him for the same reason that Richard Alpert approached Young Ben in the jungle in "The Man Behind the Curtain" and Alpert visited Young John in "Cabin Fever"; they're always looking for their next leader. Perhaps there's a link between the special children and Jacob's Candidate list; after all, Jacob and his brother were both still children when Mother decided that one of them was going to be the guardian of the Source. It would stand to reason that Richard would not only be looking for the one to lead the others, but the one who could succeed Jacob should the need arise. Just like a holy Dalai Lama is chosen as a child, so, too, is the next guardian of the island chosen. Walt's kidnapping is what gives Michael the motivation to travel across the island and ultimately double-cross his friends. Because of Walt's kidnapping, Libby and Ana Lucia are dead, and Ben was able to infiltrate the survivors with an insurance that he'd get out again, because they'd use Walt as their get-out-of-jail card. As we saw in the season 4 mobisode "Room 23," Walt actually scared Juliet and the rest of the Others — when they tried to test him in the same room where Karl had been strapped in to brainwash him, he began picturing birds flying into the window the same way he did in "Special," and dozens of dead birds were lying

"The New Man in Charge"

When the screen faded to black for the last time after "The End," some *Lost* fans still demanded resolution of some of the show's biggest mysteries. A few days later, fans discovered that when the season 6 DVD set was released on August 2010, there would be an extra included called "The New Man in Charge," a 12-minute short that would give some details of what life was like with Hurley in charge of the island and Ben as his Number 2. Fans were told there would be a lot of answers included in this extra. And . . . there are.

Directed by Paul Edwards and written by Melinda Hsu Taylor, Graham Roland, and Jim Galasso, the short is split into two parts, with the first taking place in the Dharma Logistics Warehouse in Guam and the second in the familiar Santa Rosa Mental Hospital. At the beginning, as two Dharma Initiative workers load up the island food-drop pallet, trying to hurry up so they don't miss their window, a man walks in and introduces himself: "My name is Benjamin Linus. I'm from the home office." He tells the men they're free to go . . . but they won't go. Just as the *Lost* fans couldn't say goodbye, these men stand their ground, saying, "We deserve answers!" And with an eyeroll, Ben decides to give them some.

The answers in this short come fast and furious. We find out why and how the food-drop pallets continued to fall to the island; why Pierre Chang used pseudonyms in the orientation videos; the true purpose of the Hydra station; why the Hurley bird said Hurley's name (surprisingly, this was a *really* popular question among fans when the show ended); why the polar bears were brought to the island; why females couldn't have babies on the island; what the original purpose of Room 23 was; and why the Hostiles hated the Dharma Initiative as a result. And, perhaps most importantly . . . why Walt was special.

If you were unhappy with the way *Lost* ended, "The New Man in Charge" might help you make peace with the show. The second half of the short is beautiful and suggests that, perhaps, the title of the short doesn't refer to Hurley at all. However, part of the beauty of the finale was the fact that many of the answers *did* remain a mystery. Most of the answers revealed in "The New Man in Charge" were ones that many fans had long ago figured out, while others seemed to put an entirely new spin on things — a spin that wasn't necessarily satisfactory. However, the short is a fun way for us to get just a few more minutes with some of our favorite characters, and for that reason it's worth watching.

outside the window. They knew they had to get rid of him, and they did. When he left the island, his arc was pretty much finished — his specialness simply paved the way for the childhood flashbacks of Locke and Ben, so we'd have a context with which to understand why the Others would be so interested in special children.

Who were the Others? Why did they steal children?

Since we saw Cindy, Zach, and Emma all become integrated into the Others as willing members, it's probably safe to say that the Others are the cast-offs of all of the planes and ships that Jacob brings to the island. Certain people are targeted by him and the Man in Black as they play their cosmic game of tug-of-war, but the rest of the passengers aren't important enough to be involved, so the Others begin snatching those people to become part of their group. The Others have embraced the psychological experiments that the Dharma Initiative had run on the island, and now use the stations to continue enacting those psychological experiments to test and play their own game with the people coming to the island. We can assume that between 1977 and 2004 there were other planes full of people Jacob brought to the island (aside from Yemi's Beechcraft); we just didn't see them. The Others steal children because they're always looking for their next leader, as mentioned above in the Walt question, but also because babies cannot be born on the island, so kidnapping children is a way to keep their own population numbers up.

Why did Richard Alpert tell Sun, Locke, and Ben in "Follow the Leader" that he saw Jin and everyone die?

The Others seem to be organically connected to the island, and no longer separate from it; notice in season 5 when Locke and the others began blooping through time, Richard and the Others disappeared. They didn't experience the time jumping that everyone else did, and instead they continued to live linearly while everyone else had become unstuck. So perhaps Alpert was there when the bomb went off and the electromagnetic energy sucked it into the earth, and when everyone blooped away he thought they'd all been obliterated, because he would have been left behind. Or, perhaps he saw the picture and didn't take a close look at everyone in it, and just saw the Dharma jumpsuits and was referring to the Purge. In that case, he did watch them all die.

What happened to Ben when he was taken to the Temple in "Whatever Happened, Happened"?

This was probably the question that I wanted answered the most. When Dogen walks into the Temple in "LA X" and sees the brown water, he instantly knows something is wrong. We can assume the water turned brown when Jacob died, so by that same rationale, it must have run clear and instantly healed people when Jacob was still alive. Richard, again hoping he'd found a special child, probably put Ben in the water much like people are baptized, and healed his bullet wound without having to drown him the same way they did Sayid. Then again, maybe drowning or some other crossing over is required for full healing: as Richard took Ben from Kate and Sawyer, he said, "If I take him, he's not ever going to be the same again." He explains that his innocence will be lost, and he'll always be one of the Others. What did he mean? If we can suspend our disbelief long enough to accept that the waters can instantly heal a person, it's not a stretch to believe that the waters are connected to the island, and therefore to the Others (as mentioned above). So once he's healed by those waters, he becomes like one of the Others, and connected to the island in the same way. Richard said that Ben would forget everything that had happened, so we can probably assume he didn't know Sayid was the man who had shot him when Sayid walked into the Armory the first time . . . although I'd still like to think Ben knew *exactly* who Sayid was, and that's why he targeted Sayid and turned him into his hit man.

Who were the Dharma Initiative and how did they find the island?

The DI was a scientific organization that was conducting several experiments on the island, mostly in the areas of psychology and quantum physics. They were interested in the island in particular because of its electromagnetic energy, which they knew they could use in all areas of science to alter the outcome of experiments that had already been conducted elsewhere with different results. In "316," Eloise Hawking explained the complicated process by which the Dharma Initiative found the island, and they built that station under a church to keep it hidden; they knew the pastor would be a man of his word and wouldn't tell anyone about it. The writers introduced the Dharma Initiative to give us a means by which the stations would all exist, and to show us that the outside world had invaded the island at one time and had been trying to harness its energy. Through the DI, the writers were able to explore religions and various scientific hypotheses that they'd later use on other storylines. In season 5, we saw the Dharma Initiative in action, and it was pretty clear how they operated, who they were, and that they had a particular interest in the electromagnetism on the island. The only thing that is harder to answer is how did they find out about the island in the first place? We can probably assume at some point there was another person like Widmore who went off the island and was talking about it, and the information made its way through channels and got to the DeGroots. After all, do we really believe that if people had figured out a way to come and go from the island that they'd always kept their mouths shut about it?

Why did the food pallet air-drops continue after the Dharma Initiative were purged?
After purging the DI, Ben Linus probably continued operating certain stations the same way, letting the head office in Ann Arbor think that the Dharma Initiative was just fine. We can probably assume the DI had several locations where they were conducting experiments, and the island was just one of them. If Ben could continue to send reports from the island to them, and Richard Alpert could go off the island and probably make some personal visits to the head office and maintain the ruse that the DI was alive and well, then the Dharma pallet drops would continue.

Why can't babies be born on the island?
Ah, another one of the big questions. The last baby that was brought to term on the island was Ethan, when Amy had him in 1977. We saw Alex and Aaron both born on the island as well. And yet every child in between died. Why? Simple: the Incident in 1977 caused the island to have so much electromagnetic energy on it that it made it impossible for women to carry babies to term, and the construction of the Orchid station so close to the Frozen Donkey Wheel probably released some of that energy into the island's atmosphere. In "Not in Portland," Richard Alpert showed Juliet an ultrasound of a woman she guesses to be in her 70s. When Richard tells her the woman is actually 26, Juliet is shocked. If we can believe the electromagnetic energy can heal John's paralysis, Rose's cancer, and Jin's impotence, then it's clearly speeding up the biological process, causing healing cells to enter the body and miraculously making everyone better. But there has to be a side effect to something that powerful, and it would appear that same energy is rapidly aging the wombs of women on the island. So these women are conceiving, but the uterus is unable to carry a baby to term, and the women die along with their unborn babies. The reason that Aaron and Alex were able to be born on the island is because their fetal development was too far along to be affected by the electromagnetism, and Ji Yeon was fine because Sun left the island before her uterus was damaged and before the embryo was big enough for the ambient energy to have any lasting effects.

Who made the Egyptian carvings on the island? Are they the same people who built the statues and ancient buildings?
In "Across the Sea," we saw the Romans on the island, and Mother had clearly been there even longer. If boats were crashing onto the island 2,000 years ago, we

can assume they were crashing there long before that. Not to mention, there's a chance the island was already moving at that time, and so it could have been situated much closer to Egypt than it is now. (And Egypt was a much bigger territory at one time than it is now.) The ruins on the island and the hieroglyphs are proof that other cultures had been coming to the island for a long time, and the Egyptians were clearly one of those groups of people.

What did Ben mean when he said Widmore changed the rules? Why couldn't Ben kill Widmore, but then he ultimately did?

This is a big question, and one that seemed to hang over the final season begging to be answered. It would seem that, originally, an Other couldn't kill another Other. (Say *that* three times fast!) Ben wanted revenge on Goodwin, so he sent him over to the Tailies where Ana Lucia killed him. Ethan was killed by Charlie. Several Others were killed in the island ambush in the season 3 finale. Colleen was killed by Sun. The only time we've seen one Other kill another is in "Not in Portland," when Juliet kills Danny Pickett. However, one could argue that Juliet was never willingly an Other. She was never organically connected to the island like the others were, she wasn't loyal to the group the way Cindy was, and she wasn't a cast-off from one of Jacob's shipwrecks. Perhaps she was able to skirt the rules because of that. When Alex was killed, Ben saw the shot as coming directly from Widmore, and his shocked "He changed the rules" could have referred to the fact that Widmore was responsible for the death of Alex in a way he shouldn't have been. When Ben goes to see Widmore in "The Shape of Things to Come," Widmore asks Ben if he's here to kill him, and he says no, again suggesting that because they were both part of the island at one time, they can't kill each other. That rule is lifted when Jacob dies. Or, more simply, there might have been an agreement between Widmore and Ben that we don't see, where when Widmore was banished he promised to not hurt Alex as long as Ben left Widmore's family alone. Ben kept his half of the bargain, but Widmore sent the mercenaries to the island and they killed Alex. Only then does Ben vow his revenge against Widmore's family.

In "Stranger in a Strange Land," Juliet is branded with a mark. What did it mean?

Like Jack's tattoo, Juliet's mark simply indicated that she was separate from the Others and would never be one of them. Juliet was therefore always stuck between the two worlds: never really an Other, but never quite accepted into the survivors' camp, either. It was only when she was in the DI with Sawyer that she stopped being an outsider . . . until the others returned.

Why did Claire abandon Aaron?

Claire seems to have been brainwashed by Smokey. He appeared to her as Christian Shephard (we know that wasn't the ghost of Christian because he was corporeal and was holding Aaron) and presumably he took her away and brainwashed her. She was in some sort of trance when Locke saw her in the cabin, which is why she was content and happy that Aaron had been taken away. When she snapped out of it, she probably had no memory of having been brainwashed or how she'd felt, and instead just saw that most of her friends had abandoned her, and her son was gone. She went mad as a result. She was referred to as "infected" in the same way Rousseau and Sayid had been because she was in cahoots with Smokey, but it would appear that she wasn't infected; she was tricked.

Were Hurley's numbers really cursed? Why did those numbers infiltrate the lives of all of the survivors?

Have you noticed how many times you've spotted one of Hurley's numbers in your life since the show began? Exactly. They probably no more infiltrated the characters' lives than they've infiltrated ours — they're numbers, and they seemed to show up a lot, but they probably show up just as much in your life as they did in Kate's. Jacob (or someone) created the transmission off the island that would repeat those numbers, knowing that Sam Toomey and Leonard Simms would be offshore and would pick up the transmission. Just as Jacob seemed to be omniscient about so many other things, this was a way of doing what he'd always done — draw people to him; rather than pull Leonard and Sam to him, he sent a message to them and let them go home with it. Leonard ended up in the mental hospital repeating the numbers, and Hurley picked up on them. His life became one big Murphy's Law, and it was just easier to blame the numbers than to assume it was just coincidence. The numbers appear on the hatch because it's a small island, and Jacob could have manipulated things to make sure they'd be stamped on that hatch door.

Why did the smoke monster kill Mr. Eko?

Other than the technical fact that Adewale Akinnuoye-Agbaje wanted off the show to pursue other endeavors, the smoke monster killed Eko because he could see that he was too righteous to brainwash and might be a potent opponent. John Locke was a believer and could be easily coerced or convinced. Eko, on the other hand, refused to repent regardless of how much the island tortured him to do it. When Smokey first looked at Eko in "The 23rd Psalm" and then retreated, he was perhaps intrigued by this person, and knew he would be a strong body to inhabit. But when he revisited the possibility in "The Cost of Living," he knew that Eko would not be the one whose body would help him. He wasn't as connected to the other survivors as John Locke was and he lacked John's blind devotion, and if Smokey's chief purpose was to find the person whose body he could inhabit and use it to convince Ben to kill Jacob, Eko wouldn't be that guy.

How did Mikhail keep overcoming death? Why was Ben able to withstand all that torture?

Again, we can probably chalk up the superhuman strength of these people to the electromagnetism on the island. The island had healing properties long before the Incident, and if Mikhail is to be believed (again, that's not clear), then he was in the Dharma Initiative first, and then remained with the Others after that. He's been on the island a very long time, and his body can probably withstand a lot of pain and several wounds, and then heals very rapidly. However, letting a grenade go in his hand in "Through the Looking Glass" clearly did him in. We see Ben exhibit superhuman strength in several instances, and his many, many, many, *many* facial lacerations from being punched many, many, many, *many* times are again a sign that the island is healing him. He, Juliet, and Ethan in particular also showed incredible fighting skills; their strength could have come from the island, but it's not clear how they got that amazing martial arts ability. Perhaps that was also something they picked up in Others 101.

Why did Radzinsky paint the blast door map? Why did he hide it from everyone?

By the time Radzinsky had begun painting that map, he'd clearly lost his mind. Everything he'd hoped for was gone, he'd messed up with the Swan hatch quite considerably, and now he was stuck pushing a button every 108 minutes because of his own greed and stupidity. He began painting the map as a way of remembering all of the important spots on the island, because he probably thought he'd be the last guy on the island and would have to leave it for posterity. Another possibility is that Kelvin Inman — who really did seem to just enjoy screwing with Desmond — was the one who drew it to baffle his successor, and he just *said* Radzinsky did it.

Why couldn't the smoke monster cross the line of ash?
This one still remains mostly a mystery, and I think we need to accept that the smoke monster isn't omnipotent and has weaknesses. It couldn't cross the sonic fence or any electromagnetic barrier (possibly because it was born of the electromagnetism in the Source). In many mythologies, evil cannot cross a circle of ash; there's usually no reason given, it's just a fact. (On *Angel*, for example, there was an episode where a boy was being possessed by a demon, and they poured a circle of ash around his bed to keep him there; they didn't explain the reason for doing so, they just did it and we accepted it.) Also, smoke and ash are associated by being borne of fire — ash is one result of fire, and smoke is another.

Why did Jacob say, "Help me" to Locke in "The Man Behind the Curtain"?
That wasn't Jacob; it's pretty clear it was the Man in Black manipulating Locke in that scene. In beginning his "long con" in that moment, he let Locke know there was someone in the cabin, and since Ben had told him that person was Jacob, Locke believed from that moment on that he was working for Jacob, the same way Ben thought he was. When he returned to the cabin in "Cabin Fever," the Man in Black had taken on the appearance of Christian Shephard to further manipulate Locke, so he would do everything that was to follow, which would eventually lead to his death and give the Man in Black the body he needed to try to complete his task.

How was Jacob able to cure Juliet's sister's cancer and save Dogen's son?
It's possible that once again, this was simply a con. Perhaps Jacob possessed supernatural powers and was capable of doing such things, but there's just as strong a chance that Ben handed Juliet a phony medical file telling her that Rachel's cancer had come back, when it hadn't actually returned at all. Similarly, Dogen came to the island on faith that they would make his son better, but since he was never allowed to see his son again, it's unclear if his son actually lived. He has no way of knowing if Jacob told him the truth.

Was Kate's black horse really on the island?

The Man in Black was probably appearing as the horse (he's appeared as other creatures, such as the spider that bit Nikki, so it's possible). We know that he can only take on the appearance of anything that is a corpse on the island, so there would have had to have been a horse somewhere on there. We saw in "Follow the Leader" that Charles Widmore rode a horse on the island, so it's clear horses have been brought to the island in the past (and with the number of ships that have wrecked on the island, it's inevitable that several of them would have contained horses). If one of those ships had a black horse on it, the Man in Black could have appeared as that horse.

How was Jacob able to leave the island?

Jacob could do whatever he wanted. In "Across the Sea" when Jacob complains that his brother is making up the rules of the board game as he goes along, his brother tells him that some day he'll be able to make the rules. Among Jacob's rules are that he can leave the island whenever (and probably however) he wants, and thanks to Mother's preference for him, Smokey can't. Everything else that happens on the island could be chalked up to whether or not Jacob allows it as part of his set of rules.

How was Eloise so omniscient and why was she so destiny-driven?

We've accepted that Desmond was special and could see the future after a certain electromagnetic incident, so it's safe to say Eloise possibly experienced something along the same lines (she *was* on the island for a few decades, after all). The key to understanding Eloise probably lies, quite simply, in Daniel's journal. She gave him that journal when he graduated and he wrote all of his physics notes in it. However, after he began to lose his memory he started to rely on that journal to tell him what to do. Eloise would have figured this out, and probably began writing things in the journal as notes to her past self. When Daniel walked into the Others' camp in 1977 and was shot by a younger Eloise, the first thing she did was pull the journal off his person and begin to flip through it. If she had the journal with her, she would have read about everything her son was going to discover and do, and she realized that he had to be a physicist because he had to achieve that level of greatness he was destined for, despite knowing what her own role would be in his future. Perhaps over the years she tried to change the course of history a few times, and it always course-corrected in a terrible way. That's why, in "Flashes Before Your Eyes," she talks to Desmond and convinces him not to ask Penny to marry him but rather to go to the island. She knows that Desmond has to go to that island so her son will meet him and give him the important message that Desmond ultimately relays back to Eloise. She is as obsessed with the island as Widmore and Ben are, but for different reasons, and rather than seeking reasons to go back, she's more interested in continuing the island's destiny. That's why she's the one in the Lamp Post Station who explains to all of them how they are destined to go back to the island so Jack can fulfill what he was meant to do. She comes off as omniscient because she knows what will happen in the future of Daniel's diary (in "The Incident" she tells Penny that for the first time in a long time, she doesn't know what will happen next; that's because her son's journal ended three years after he arrived on the island, and when she talks to Penny it's three years after Daniel left). She doesn't change things (and warns Desmond not to) because she's worried of the consequences of a more dire course correction. And despite trying to thwart fate and knowing it can't be done, she still must live with the guilt of knowing that she will one day kill her own son. That's why she's so emotionally paralyzed in the sideways world.

How did Anthony Cooper get to the island?
Cooper said that he was rear-ended and the next thing he knew he was on the island. It's pretty clear it was simply one of Ben's people who'd gone off the island and brought him back. They had looked through the files that Mikhail had been keeping on Locke and Sawyer and found that they had Cooper in common, and they brought him to the island.

What was the island?
As Jacob explained in "Ab Aeterno," (and we saw literally played out in the finale), the island acted like a cork of a wine bottle, a hellmouth keeping all of the evil trapped inside it so it couldn't get out into the world. But on a larger level, the island was a place separated from the rest of the world where people went to work through their problems. It seemed to have a mind of its own, guiding people around like pieces on a giant chessboard, and the island could help the people along their way — during the time-blooping sequence at the beginning of season 5 it was clear the jumps weren't random and that the island wanted them to see certain things. The island was a special place with special properties, with

pockets of electromagnetism that became the writers' handy-dandy explanation for any strange anomaly on the island, from people's wounds healing quickly to no one ever really getting so much as a cold (it was a brilliant device for the writers to have constructed back in the first season, because they were able to use it throughout the series). The electromagnetism became the thing that attracted the DI, that tested John Locke's faith, became a conduit for Ben moving the island, and was ultimately the thing that helped contain the light of the island. What the island *was* is probably the biggest and most important question coming out of the finale, but, without trying to sound like an apologist for the writers, I think the island is what you want it to be. It's bigger than a single explanation could handle — we can look at the island as a place that simply existed where the people could work out their own personal issues before moving to the larger issue of self-sacrifice for the greater good. The island was a microcosm of the universe and the world; it was a Garden of Eden and a Hell. It was a mystery at the beginning of the show, and it's fitting that it remains in some ways a mystery at the end of the show. Answering what the island really is would be akin to explaining to you what the meaning of life is: this is one thing that's rightfully open to wide interpretation by the fans.

What was the Source on the island? Why did it turn Jacob's brother into the smoke monster?
Similar to the previous question, the Source is once again what we want it to be. Mother said it was life, death, and rebirth. She said there's a little bit of it in every person — the light represented all that was good and bad in people. The Source seems to be the life energy that runs through the world, through all living things. It's what ties us to people and what tears us from them. It can be good, it can be evil. Desmond was pure of heart, and when he went down into the cave it didn't kill him or turn him into anything nonhuman. When the Man in Black went down into it, however, he'd just killed his mother figure, and his heart had been corrupted before he went down. He manifested into the smoke monster as a representation of the evil in his heart. At the end of John Milton's *Paradise Lost*, all of Satan's minions are turned into serpents, so it's fitting that the Man in Black would be turned into one, too.

When it comes to the questions on *Lost* that are still outstanding, we need to stop for a minute and ask ourselves, "Is the answer to this question really going to determine whether or not I liked the series?" If you liked the ending, but are upset that you don't know who carved the Egyptian hieroglyphics on the inside of the Temple walls, it's worth asking just how important the answer to that question really is. And then, as I've demonstrated above, find out if you actually *can* answer the question by looking at the clues the writers gave us in previous episodes (of course, as mentioned fans who rewatched the series after season 5 could do this more easily than fans who hadn't). Did you really need another season to show you a bunch of stuff you could have figured out anyway? *Lost* was meant to be an interactive show. It engaged us for six seasons, asked us to put pieces together and begin speculating on what the end result could be. Many fans had already come up with excellent hypotheses for what the answers to these questions would be long before the finale, and that was simply a testament to the excellence of the writing on the show. They gave us the tools. It's up to us to use what we have at hand and answer these questions in a way that will make us happy.

And now for the question that many people will be asking Damon and Carlton for the rest of their lives: did they really know where the show was going or were they simply making it up as they went along? A rewatch of the series will answer that one pretty succinctly. In season 1 you can see the faith versus reason theme already starting to bloom, and by season 2 you can begin to see the threads that will stretch all the way to the end of season 6. They didn't know exactly how it was going to end — they probably hadn't worked through all of the issues of the sideways world, and perhaps didn't fully flesh out the sideways world itself until a couple of years before the end. They didn't know the exact details of how people would leave the island and how or why they'd come back, they just knew they would.

But this is what storytelling is all about. No fiction writer sits down at a computer with the entirety of his or her book already worked out to the last detail, assuming it will remain unchanged throughout the process of writing the book. As the characters begin to take shape, the story evolves. That's the nature of fiction, whether it's writing for television, movies, books, or comic books. With television, there are even more outside factors at work — certain actors leave the show, suddenly abandoning a character; critics and fans come down hard on a storyline that seemed like a good one at the time (*cough*, Nikki and Paulo, *cough*) forcing the writers to drop it; networks begin to impose restrictions on the storytelling, causing writers to have to alter their story arcs; shows are canceled outright.

But if you look at how beautifully this particular story played out, how tightly the Jack-and-John story was woven, how neatly all of the other parts fit into the bigger picture, you can see a much more carefully constructed show than most other series on television in recent memory. The writers on *Lost* created something extraordinary and stayed true to it until the end. Here's hoping that as the years go by and new people come to the story on DVD, watching it the way it was meant to be watched (i.e., over a much shorter period of time than six years), the timelessness of the story of *Lost* will ensure its rightful place in history as one of the greatest television series of all time.

Lost Episodes

Ep #	Title	Writer(s)	Director
1.1, 1.2	Pilot, Parts 1 & 2	J.J. Abrams, Damon Lindelof (teleplay); Jeffrey Lieber, J.J. Abrams, Damon Lindelof (story)	J.J. Abrams
1.3	Tabula Rasa	Damon Lindelof	Jack Bender
1.4	Walkabout	David Fury	Jack Bender
1.5	White Rabbit	Christian Taylor	Kevin Hooks
1.6	House of the Rising Sun	Javier Grillo-Marxuach	Michael Zinberg
1.7	The Moth	Jennifer Johnson, Paul Dini	Jack Bender
1.8	Confidence Man	Damon Lindelof	Tucker Gates
1.9	Solitary	David Fury	Greg Yaitanes
1.10	Raised by Another	Lynne E. Litt	Marita Grabiak
1.11	All the Best Cowboys Have Daddy Issues	Javier Grillo-Marxuach	Stephen Williams

Ep #	Title	Writer(s)	Director
1.12	Whatever the Case May Be	Damon Lindelof, Jennifer Johnson	Jack Bender
1.13	Hearts and Minds	Carlton Cuse, Javier Grillo-Marxuach	Rod Holcomb
1.14	Special	David Fury	Greg Yaitanes
1.15	Homecoming	David Lindelof	Kevin Hooks
1.16	Outlaws	Drew Goddard	Jack Bender
1.17	. . . In Translation	Javier Grillo-Marxuach, Leonard Dick	Tucker Gates
1.18	Numbers	David Fury, Brent Fletcher	Daniel Attias
1.19	Deus Ex Machina	Carlton Cuse, Damon Lindelof	Robert Mandel
1.20	Do No Harm	Janet Tamaro	Stephen Williams
1.21	The Greater Good	Leonard Dick	David Grossman
1.22	Born to Run	Edward Kitsis, Adam Horowitz (teleplay), Javier Grillo-Marxuach (story)	Tucker Gates
1.23, 1.24	Exodus, Parts 1 & 2	Damon Lindelof, Carlton Cuse	Jack Bender
2.1	Man of Science, Man of Faith	Damon Lindelof	Jack Bender
2.2	Adrift	Steven Maeda, Leonard Dick	Stephen Williams
2.3	Orientation	Javier Grillo-Marxuach, Craig Wright	Jack Bender

Ep #	Title	Writer(s)	Director
2.4	Everybody Hates Hugo	Edward Kitsis, Adam Horowitz	Alan Taylor
2.5	. . . And Found	Carlton Cuse, Damon Lindelof	Stephen Williams
2.6	Abandoned	Elizabeth Sarnoff	Adam Davidson
2.7	The Other 48 Days	Damon Lindelof, Carlton Cuse	Eric Laneuville
2.8	Collision	Javier Grillo-Marxuach, Leonard Dick	Stephen Williams
2.9	What Kate Did	Steven Maeda, Craig Wright	Paul Edwards
2.10	The 23rd Psalm	Carlton Cuse, Damon Lindelof	Matt Earl Beasley
2.11	The Hunting Party	Elizabeth Sarnoff, Christina M. Kim	Stephen Williams
2.12	Fire + Water	Edward Kitsis, Adam Horowitz	Jack Bender
2.13	The Long Con	Leonard Dick, Steven Maeda	Roxann Dawson
2.14	One of Them	Damon Lindelof, Carlton Cuse	Stephen Williams
2.15	Maternity Leave	Dawn Lambertsen Kelly, Matt Ragghianti	Jack Bender
2.16	The Whole Truth	Elizabeth Sarnoff, Christina M. Kim	Karen Gaviola
2.17	Lockdown	Carlton Cuse, Damon Lindelof	Stephen Williams
2.18	Dave	Edward Kitsis, Adam Horowitz	Jack Bender

Ep #	Title	Writer(s)	Director
2.19	S.O.S.	Steven Maeda, Leonard Dick	Eric Laneuville
2.20	Two for the Road	Elizabeth Sarnoff, Christina M. Kim	Paul Edwards
2.21	?	Damon Lindelof, Carlton Cuse	Deran Serafian
2.22	Three Minutes	Edward Kitsis, Adam Horowitz	Stephen Williams
2.23, 2.24	Live Together, Die Alone, Parts 1 & 2	Carlton Cuse, Damon Lindelof	Jack Bender
3.1	A Tale of Two Cities	J.J. Abrams, Damon Lindelof (teleplay), Damon Lindelof (story)	Jack Bender
3.2	The Glass Ballerina	Jeff Pinkner, Drew Goddard	Paul Edwards
3.3	Further Instructions	Carlton Cuse, Elizabeth Sarnoff	Stephen Williams
3.4	Every Man for Himself	Edward Kitsis, Adam Horowitz	Stephen Williams
3.5	The Cost of Living	Alison Schapker, Monica Owusu-Breen	Jack Bender
3.6	I Do	Damon Lindelof, Carlton Cuse	Tucker Gates
3.7	Not in Portland	Carlton Cuse, Jeff Pinkner	Stephen Williams
3.8	Flashes Before Your Eyes	Damon Lindelof, Drew Goddard	Jack Bender
3.9	Stranger in a Strange Land	Elizabeth Sarnoff, Christina M. Kim	Paris Barclay
3.10	Tricia Tanaka Is Dead	Edward Kitsis, Adam Horowitz	Eric Laneuville

Ep #	Title	Writer(s)	Director
3.11	Enter 77	Damon Lindelof, Carlton Cuse	Stephen Williams
3.12	Par Avion	Christina M. Kim, Jordan Rosenberg	Paul Edwards
3.13	The Man from Tallahassee	Drew Goddard, Jeff Pinkner	Jack Bender
3.14	Exposé	Edward Kitsis, Adam Horowitz	Stephen Williams
3.15	Left Behind	Damon Lindelof, Elizabeth Sarnoff	Karen Gaviola
3.16	One of Us	Carlton Cuse, Drew Goddard	Jack Bender
3.17	Catch-22	Jeff Pinkner, Brian K. Vaughan	Stephen Williams
3.18	D.O.C.	Edward Kitsis, Adam Horowitz	Frederick E.O. Toye
3.19	The Brig	Damon Lindelof, Carlton Cuse	Eric Laneuville
3.20	The Man Behind the Curtain	Elizabeth Sarnoff, Drew Goddard	Bobby Roth
3.21	Greatest Hits	Edward Kitsis, Adam Horowitz	Stephen Williams
3.22, 3.23	Through the Looking Glass, Parts 1 & 2	Damon Lindelof, Carlton Cuse	Jack Bender
4.1	The Beginning of the End	Damon Lindelof, Carlton Cuse	Jack Bender
4.2	Confirmed Dead	Drew Goddard, Brian K. Vaughan	Stephen Williams
4.3	The Economist	Edward Kitsis, Adam Horowitz	Jack Bender

Ep #	Title	Writer(s)	Director
4.4	Eggtown	Elizabeth Sarnoff, Greggory Nations	Stephen Williams
4.5	The Constant	Carlton Cuse, Damon Lindelof	Jack Bender
4.6	The Other Woman	Drew Goddard, Christina M. Kim	Eric Laneuville
4.7	Ji Yeon	Edward Kitsis, Adam Horowitz	Stephen Semel
4.8	Meet Kevin Johnson	Elizabeth Sarnoff, Brian K. Vaughan	Stephen Williams
4.9	The Shape of Things to Come	Brian K. Vaughan, Drew Goddard	Jack Bender
4.10	Something Nice Back Home	Edward Kitsis, Adam Horowitz	Stephen Williams
4.11	Cabin Fever	Elizabeth Sarnoff, Kyle Pennington	Paul Edwards
4.12	There's No Place Like Home, Part 1	Damon Lindelof, Carlton Cuse	Stephen Williams
4.13, 4.14	There's No Place Like Home, Parts 2 & 3	Damon Lindelof, Carlton Cuse	Jack Bender
5.1	Because You Left	Damon Lindelof, Carlton Cuse	Stephen Williams
5.2	The Lie	Edward Kitsis, Adam Horowitz	Jack Bender
5.3	Jughead	Elizabeth Sarnoff, Paul Zbyszewski	Rod Holcomb
5.4	The Little Prince	Brian K. Vaughan, Melinda Hsu Taylor	Stephen Williams
5.5	This Place Is Death	Edward Kitsis, Adam Horowitz	Paul Edwards

Ep #	Title	Writer(s)	Director
5.6	316	Damon Lindelof, Carlton Cuse	Stephen Williams
5.7	The Life and Death of Jeremy Bentham	Carlton Cuse, Damon Lindelof	Jack Bender
5.8	Lafleur	Elizabeth Sarnoff, Kyle Pennington	Mark Goldman
5.9	Namaste	Paul Zbyszewski, Brian K. Vaughan	Jack Bender
5.10	He's Our You	Edward Kitsis, Adam Horowitz	Greg Yaitanes
5.11	Whatever Happened, Happened	Carlton Cuse, Damon Lindelof	Bobby Roth
5.12	Dead Is Dead	Brian K. Vaughan, Elizabeth Sarnoff	Stephen Williams
5.13	Some Like It Hoth	Melinda Hsu Taylor, Greggory Nations	Jack Bender
5.14	The Variable	Edward Kitsis, Adam Horowitz	Paul Edwards
5.15	Follow the Leader	Paul Zbyszewski, Elizabeth Sarnoff	Stephen Williams
5.16, 5.17	The Incident, Parts 1 & 2	Damon Lindelof, Carlton Cuse	Jack Bender
6.1, 6.2	LA X	Damon Lindelof, Carlton Cuse	Jack Bender
6.3	What Kate Does	Edward Kitsis, Adam Horowitz	Paul Edwards
6.4	The Substitute	Elizabeth Sarnoff, Melinda Hsu Taylor	Tucker Gates
6.5	Lighthouse	Carlton Cuse, Damon Lindelof	Jack Bender

Ep #	Title	Writer(s)	Director
6.6	Sundown	Paul Zbyszewski, Graham Roland	Bobby Roth
6.7	Dr. Linus	Edward Kitsis, Adam Horowitz	Melvin Van Peebles
6.8	Recon	Elizabeth Sarnoff, Jim Galasso	Jack Bender
6.9	Ab Aeterno	Melinda Hsu Taylor, Greggory Nations	Tucker Gates
6.10	The Package	Paul Zbyszewski, Graham Roland	Paul Edwards
6.11	Happily Ever After	Damon Lindelof, Carlton Cuse	Jack Bender
6.12	Everybody Loves Hugo	Edward Kitsis, Adam Horowitz	Daniel Attias
6.13	The Last Recruit	Paul Zbyszewski, Graham Rolan	Stephen Semel
6.14	The Candidate	Elizabeth Sarnoff, Jim Galasso	Jack Bender
6.15	Across the Sea	Carlton Cuse, Damon Lindelof	Tucker Gates
6.16	What They Died For	Edward Kitsis, Adam Horowitz, Elizabeth Sarnoff	Paul Edwards
6.17	The End	Damon Lindelof, Carlton Cuse	Jack Bender

Sources

Abrams, Natalie. "13 Questions with the Producers of *Lost*: Polar Bears, the Smoke Monster, and the Man in Black." TVGuide.com. Online. January 31, 2010.

"After-Death States: The Tibetan Buddhist and Spiritualist Views of After-Death States." Spiritual-travel.org. Online. Accessed July 10, 2010.

Alvarado, Virginia. "Meet Gotham City Mayor Nestor Carbonell." NYDaily News.com. Online. July 23, 2008.

"The British East India Trading Company — The Company that Owned a Nation." The Victorian Web. www.victorianweb.org/history/empire/india/eic.html. Online. Accessed June 23, 2010.

Brown, Mick. "How the Dead Live." *Telegraph*. November 13, 2005.

Buchanan, Kyle. "*Lost*'s Nestor Carbonell on his Famous Eyelashes and Soon-To-Be Famous Pecs." Movieline. Online. February 2, 2010.

Carroll, Lewis. *The Annotated Alice*. Ed. Martin Gardner. New York: Penguin, 1970.

Cuddon, J.A. *The Penguin Dictionary of Literary Terms and Literary Theory*. New York: Penguin, 1991.

Damon Lindelof's Twitter Feed. Twitter.com. @DamonLindelof.

Dos Santos, Kristin. "*Lost*'s Mr. Eko Turned Down Finale Guest Spot!" E! Online. May 24, 2010.

—. "Matthew Fox and Evangeline Lilly Say They're Done with Television After *Lost*." E! Online. February 1, 2010.

Dostoevsky, Fyodor. *Notes From Underground, The Double and Other Stories*. Trans. Constance Garnett. New York: Barnes & Noble Classics, 2003. 1864.

Endo, Shusaku. *Deep River*. Trans. Van C. Gessel. New York: New Directions, 1994.

Fernandez, Maria Elena. "*Lost*: Nestor Carbonell talks about the ageless wonder he plays." *L.A. Times*. March 24, 2010.

Fienberg, Daniel. "Nestor Carbonell and Henry Ian Cusick tease the end of *Lost*." Hitfix. Online. May 16, 2010.

Fremantle, Francesca, and Chogyam Trungpa trans. *The Tibetan Book of the Dead: The Great Liberation Through Hearing in the Bardo*. Boston: Shambhala Books, 2003.

Frye, Northrop, Sheridan Baker, and George Perkins. *The Harper Handbook to Literature*. New York: Harper & Row, 1985.

Gaiman, Neil. *The Sandman, Vol. IX: The Kindly Ones*. New York: DC Comics, 1993, 1994, 1995.

Garcia, Jorge. "Nunu, The Greatest." Dispatches from the Island. Jorge Garcia's Weblog. (http://dispatchesfromtheisland.blogspot.com/2010/05/nunu-greatest.html). May 31, 2010.

Garcia, Jorge and Bethany James Leigh Shady. "GJB 616 What They Died For." Audio Podcast. Geronimo Jack's Beard. (http://media.libsyn.com/media/horhay/GJB_616_What_They_Died_For.mp3). May 19, 2010.

Good News Bible: Today's English Version. Toronto: Canadian Bible Society, 1976.

Grimal, Pierre. *The Dictionary of Classical Mythology*. Oxford: Blackwell Publishers, 1996.

Hinman, Michael. "Could this be a forerunner of what we see for the Emmys?" *Variety*. June 4, 2009.

IMDb.com

Kalu, Kyabje, Rinpoche. *Luminous Mind: The Way of the Buddha*. Somerville, MA: Wisdom Publications, 2003.

Kierkegaard, Søren. *Fear and Trembling*. Trans. Walter Lowrie. Kindle book. Classics-Unbound, 2009. 1843.

King, Stephen. *The Stand: The Complete & Uncut Edition*. New York: Signet, 1991. 1978.

Larkin, Philip. "This Be the Verse." *Collected Poems*. New York: Farrar, Straus and Giroux, 2001.

Lostpedia.com

Makaryk, Irena R., Ed. *Encyclopedia of Contemporary Literary Theory*. Toronto: U of T Press, 1993.

Malcolm, Shawna. "Five Things to Know about *Lost*'s Nestor Carbonell." People TV Watch. Online. March 23, 2010.

Malkin, Mark. "*Lost*'s Michael Emerson Injured During Filming." E! Online. March 23, 2010.

Milton, John. *Paradise Lost*. Ed. Merritt Y. Hughes. New York: Macmillan Publishing Company, 1962. 1674.

Moore, Alan and Dave Gibbons. *Watchmen*. New York: DC Comics, 1987.

Nik at Nite. Nikki Stafford's Weblog (http://nikkistafford.blogspot.com).

"Q&A: *Lost* producers discuss emotional final season." *Hollywood Reporter*. January 5, 2010.

"Paradise Lost: An Interview with Josh Holloway." *TV Guide*. December 28, 2009.

Péréz-Lanzac, Carmen. "No puedo esperar a poner las manos en el guión de último episodio de *Perdidos*." El Pais. Online. April 4, 2010.

Piccione, Peter. "In Search of the Meaning of Senet." *Archaeology*. July/August 1980.

Porter, Rick. "John Hawkes joins for season six." Zap2it.com. Online. August 19, 2009.

—. "*Lost* finale ratings strong, not overwhelming." Zap2it.com. Online. May 24, 2010.

—. "*Lost* gets a letter from George Lucas." Zap2it.com. May 14, 2010.

—. "*Lost*: Meet Hiroyuki Sanada." Zap2it. Online. February 16, 2010.

Potok, Chaim. *The Chosen*. New York: Ballantine, 1996. 1967.

Rabb, J.D. and J.M. Richardson. "Memory and Identity in Whedon's Narrative Ethics: Reading the Whedonverses Through *Dollhouse* and *Dr. Horrible*." 4th Slayage Conference, St. Augustine, Florida. June 5, 2010. Unpublished. Used with permission of the authors.

Rushdie, Salman. *Haroun and the Sea of Stories*. London: Granta Books, 1990.

Ryan, Maureen. "The *Lost* Lowdown: Part 1 of a long interview with Cuse and Lindelof." The Watcher Blog. ChicagoTribune.com. Online. January 19, 2010.

—. "The Long *Lost* Interview with Lindelof and Cuse, Part 2: The Squeakquel." The Watcher Blog. ChicagoTribune.com. Online. January 24, 2010.

Ryan, Mike. "*Lost*'s Terry O'Quinn on the Secret to Playing Smokey-Locke." *New York Magazine*. Online. February 16, 2010.

SparkNotes Editors. "SparkNote on Napoleon Bonaparte." SparkNotes.com. SparkNotes LLC. 2005. Online. Accessed June 21, 2010.

Thompson, Andrew, exec. prod. Dir. Louise Lockwood. *Parallel Worlds, Parallel Lives*. BBC Four. 2007.

"Times Talks Live: Damon Lindelof and Carlton Cuse." Live Broadcast. *New

York Times. May 20, 2010.

"Transcript: Darlton and Bender Talk *Lost* Season 6 at Curzon Cinema." DocArzt.com. Online. July 4, 2009.

Wikipedia.org

Yang, Jennifer. "Obama's State of the Union Address won't conflict with *Lost* premiere." *Toronto Star.* January 8, 2010.

Acknowledgments

Thank you to ECW Press for carrying this series to the end, especially my editor Crissy Boylan, who resisted inserting photos of Ian Somerhalder throughout the book, despite her immense love of *The Vampire Diaries*. Thanks to Gail Nina once again for her excellent typesetting. And a huge thank-you to my amazing, funny, and brilliant copy editor, Gil Adamson, who had to take this massive tome and smooth out all those rough edges. You were the first person to read my guide for the series finale immediately after watching it, and there's no one I would have rather had do that.

To the ever-patient Barry Johnson, I cannot thank you enough for creating the gorgeous cover that graces the front of this book. We went through so many versions of it that I lost count, but you were gracious, funny, and gave me a beautiful cover to end the series with. Thanks again to the always accommodating Ryan Ozawa, whose photos make the entire *Finding Lost* series more interesting. Thank you to Ed Kos and Matthew Morici from KOS Tours, who sent me a ton of photos at the eleventh hour and who were immensely lovely to talk to.

Big, big thanks to Jeff Jensen at *Entertainment Weekly* and David Lavery for giving me the wonderful blurbs on the back cover. I admire the work that both of you have done in the *Lost*verse, and was thrilled and honored to receive your endorsements.

I want to give big thanks, hugs, and Vulcan salutes to Mark Askwith, Teddy, Ajay, and the whole crew at Space in Toronto. You guys have been such big supporters of my writing since the Buffy days, and it was a blast to come down and help host the shows with you when Lost ended. Another big thank-you to Andrew Ryan, Christina Vardanis, and the *Globe and Mail* for asking me to host the *Globe* online live chats every Wednesday afternoon following the season 6 episodes. I had so much fun doing it.

And a special thank-you to my tirelessly supportive publicist at ECW, Simon Ware, who managed to turn me into a Canadian *Lost* pundit when the series finished.

Thank you to Michael Richardson and J. Douglas Rabb for granting me permission to quote from your *Dollhouse* paper at Slayage for my analysis of "The End."

A big thank-you to Jon "DocArzt" Lachonis, who invited me once again to come and blog on his incredible Lost site, even if I didn't find time to do it very often this season. It's always great bouncing ideas off you.

The biggest thanks I reserve for the readers of my blog, Nik at Nite (many of whom are also on my Facebook page). In the past I've named every single person who has commented on one of my posts throughout the season, but this year the number of commenters simply got too big, and I'm so worried I'll leave someone off. So I just want to thank you all for being there. We learned to discuss together, so no one would be baffled alone. The blog was a place we made where we could be together, and we helped each other move on and let go at the end. (Okay, I lie . . . none of us has managed to let go.) I hope you continue to stick around as we discover new shows and find new topics to discuss, but we'll always be mentioning *Lost* for years to come. Thank you to the Nik at Niters who met up with me in New York and Toronto — it was great to finally put faces to screen names. I am blessed to have found such a diverse, hilarious, insightful, intelligent, and friendly group of people with whom to discuss such a complex show.

And among those readers, a few special shout-outs to: my front-cover focus group of Blam, Teebore, Josh, Batcabbage, Sonshine Music, and humanebean; Joshua Winstead for providing the amazing soundtrack by which I wrote the book; Sonshine for crocheting the little Desmond who sat on my desk and oversaw the writing of the book; and humanebean for reading through the very long first draft of my finale analysis and making sure it was fair and balanced.

I really feel like I've gotten to know so many of you personally, even though we're just a bunch of people pushing buttons on a blog. But I've always felt like that blog was our own personal island, where we all enjoy being together.

Thank you to Matthew Pateman for reading my section on existentialism and not telling me it was crap, and for the laughs and support along the way. A huge thank-you to my best friend Sue Kingshott, who had to listen to me gripe and moan about how much more work I had to do, and always pulled me up by my bootstraps (does anyone actually wear bootstraps?) and kept me going.

A loving thank-you to my husband, Robert, who took my beautiful children, Sydney and Liam, away for many, many weekends in the summer while I was trying to finish the book. I missed you all terribly, and look forward to next year, when we'll finally have a book-free summer.

And as always, my final heartfelt thank-you to Jennifer Hale. I hope somebody does for you what you just did for me.

"We Have to Go Back!!"

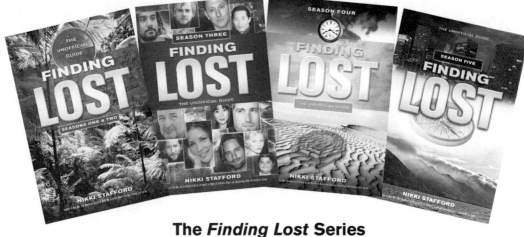

The *Finding Lost* Series
By Nikki Stafford

"Nikki Stafford [is] . . . one of the show's leading scholars."
– *Newsday*

"Nikki Stafford is a godsend to *Lost* enthusiasts in particular and TV lovers in general. I've written about TV for several years, and have always valued her opinion and insights on all things television."
– Amanda Cuda, *Connecticut Post*

"The *Finding Lost* series is quite simply the best resource for fans."
– Jon "DocArzt" Lachonis

"[A] top-notch *Lost* blogger."
– EW.com

The only books that offer an in-depth guide to every episode of each season of *Lost*, Nikki Stafford's *Finding Lost* series goes beyond the show itself to explore all of the references and allusions the writers work into the scripts. Each book explores the season's literary references (including *Watership Down*, *A Wrinkle in Time*, *The Third Policeman*, *Of Mice and Men*, *Slaughterhouse-Five*, *Ulysses*, and many more); historical and philosophical facts within the framework of the episodes; behind-the-scenes information; fan and critical reactions to each season; sidebars with fun trivia; exclusive behind-the-scenes photos of filming in Hawaii; bios of the actors on the show; and much, much more.

Find more from Nikki Stafford at her blog, Nik at Nite:
nikkistafford.blogspot.com